CW01290960

ༀ།

The Hundred Tertöns

A Garland of Beryl
Brief Accounts of Profound Terma and the
Siddhas Who Have Revealed It

by Jamgön Kongtrül Lodrö Taye

translated by Yeshe Gyamtso

KTD Publications
Woodstock, New York, U.S.A.

Published by:
KTD Publications
335 Meads Mountain Road
Woodstock, NY 12498, USA
www.KTDPublications.org

© 2011 Karma Triyana Dharmachakra
& Peter O'Hearn
All rights reserved.

Library of Congress Control Number: 2011944491

ISBN 978-1-934608-26-5
eISBN 978-1-934608-30-2
Printed in the United States on acid-free paper.

Contents

Foreword by Khenchen Thrangu Rinpoche xiii

Translator's Introduction xv

The Hundred Tertöns 1

Part One: Supporting Quotations and Arguments 9

Part Two: An Account of the Deeds of the Teacher of this Dharma and his Disciples 17

King Trisong Detsen 31
Nupchen Sangye Yeshe 36
Gyalwa Chokyang 38
The Bhikshu Namkhay Nyingpo 40
The Translator Nyak Jnanakumara 42
Yeshe Tsogyal, the Emanation of Sarasvati 44
Drokmi Palgyi Yeshe 46
Lang Palgyi Senge 47
The Great Translator Vairochana 48
Gyalmo Yudra Nyingpo 51
Nanam Dorje Düdjom 51
The Acharya Yeshe Yang 52
The Mahasiddha Sokpo Lhapal 53
Nanam Yeshe De 53
Kharchen Palgyi Wangchuk 53
Denma Tsemang 54
The Great Translator Kawa Paltsek 54

Shubu Palgyi Senge 55
Bay Gyalway Lodrö 56
The Mahasiddha Kyeuchung Lotsa 56
Drenpa Namkha 57
Odren Palgyi Wangchuk 57
Ma Rinchen Chok 58
Lhalung Palgyi Dorje 59
Langdro Könchok Jungne 59
Lasum Gyalwa Jangchub 60
Dhatishvari Mandarava 62
Mamaki Shakyadevi of Nepal 64
Pandaravasini Kalasiddhi 64
Samayatara Tashi Khyidren of Bhutan 65

Part Three Biographies of Those Who Have Revealed These Teachings 69

Section One: Earth Terma 71

Sangye Lama 73
Gya the Translator 75
Nanampa 76
Gya Shangtrom Dorje Öbar 77
Nyima Senge 78
Shakya Ö the Teacher from Uru 79
Bönpo Draktsal 80
Nyemo Shuyay 81
Ngödrup the Siddha 82
Tsuklak Palge 83
Kusa the Physician 84
Lhabum the Bönpo 86
Khyungpo Palge 87
Shami Dorgyal 88
Dangma Lhungyal 89
Drapa Ngönshe 91
Rashak the Great 92
Nyangral Nyima Özer 93
Wönsay Khyungtok 98
Ramo Shelmen 99

Guru Chökyi Wangchuk 101
Guru Jotsay 106
Padma Wangchuk 107
Doben Gyamtso 108
Rakshi the Teacher 109
The Physician from E in Jarong 110
Dragom Chödor 111
Yakchar Ngönmo 112
Drum and Karnak 113
Lhatsün Ngönmo 114
Nyima Drakpa 115
Padma Ledrel Tsal 116
Tseten Gyaltsen 118
Meben Rinchen Lingpa 120
The Nirmanakaya Ugyen Lingpa 122
The Omniscient Longchenpa 127
Rokje Lingpa 132
The Great Tertön of Mindröling 136
Padma Kunkyong Lingpa 140
Chokden Gönpo 144
Ugyen Tenyi Lingpa 147
Dorje Lingpa 149
Sangye Lingpa 153
Padma Lingpa 158
Jatsön Nyingpo 162
Samten Dechen Lingpa 166
Shikpo Lingpa 167
Dechen Lingpa 169
Gyaben Dorje Ö 173
Guru Humbar 173
Lhatsün Jangchup Ö 174
Atisha 174
Shangtsün Tarma Rinchen 175
Rongzom Chökyi Zangpo 176
Dorbum Chökyi Drakpa 176
Sangye Bar 177

Setön Ringmo 177
Gya Purbu 178
Geshe Dranga Dorje Kundrak 178
Lharjey Nupchung 179
Gyatön Tsöndru Senge 179
Chetsün Senge Wangchuk 179
Sarben Chokme 181
Nyen the Translator 182
Shakya Zangpo 182
Zangri Repa 183
Nyalpo Josay 183
Sangye Wangchen 184
Chupa Tokden 184
Bakhal Mukpo 185
Prince Mekhyil 185
Drugu Yangwang 186
Sumpa Jangchup Lodrö 187
Taklungpa Sangye Wönpo 188
Nyalpa Nyima Sherap 189
Trophu the Translator 189
Yeben Yabön 190
Balpo Ah Hum Bar 190
Ajo Palpo 191
The Three Tertöns 191
Dugu Rinchen Senge 192
Tsangring Sherap 193
Latö Marpo 194
Jomo Menmo 194
Melong Dorje 198
The Fortunate Child 199
Drangti Gyalnye Kharbu 200
The Four Assistants 200
The Earlier Dungtso Repa 201
Kunga Bum 202
The Later Dungtso Repa 203
Vajramati 204

Gyalsay Lekpa 204
Ugyen Zangpo 206
Sherab Mebar 207
Nyida Sangye 208
The Mantradharin Letro Lingpa 209
Zangpo Drakpa 209
Drime Lhunpo 210
Drime Kunga 212
Ngödrup Gyaltsen, the Vidyadhara Vulture Feathers 214
Palgyi Gyaltsen of Langlo 216
Karma Lingpa 217
Palden Jamyang Lama 218
Thangtong Gyalpo 219
Gönpo Rinchen 221
Ratna Lingpa 222
Kalden Dorje 224
Chokden Dorje 224
Chak Jangchup Lingpa 225
The Mantradharin Shakya Zangpo 225
Drodül Letro Lingpa 227
Jampal Dorje 229
Padma Wangyal Dorje 229
Mingyur Letro Lingpa 232
Namchak Mebar 233
Sherap Özer 235
The Great Vidyadhara of Ngari 238
Matiratna 240
Tsering Dorje 240
Khyentse Wangchuk Dongak Lingpa 241
Karma Guru 243
Ngaki Wangpo 244
Garwang Letro Lingpa 246
Yongdzin Ngawang Drakpa 247
Tashi Tseten 248
Padma Rikdzin 248
Düdül Lingpa 249

Düdül Dorje 250
Longsal Nyingpo 254
Tendzin Norbu 258
Zangpo Dorje 259
Garwang Dawa Gyaltsen 261
Yongey Mingyur Dorje 263
Kuchok the Actionless 267
Pönsey Khyungtok 268
Samten Lingpa 269
Ratön Topden Dorje 273
Khampa Rinpoche 274
Rölpe Dorje 276
Padma Dechen Lingpa 280
Padma Chögyal 283
Padma Wangchuk 283
Khyungdrak Dorje 284
Tsewang Norbu 285
Tsasum Terdak Lingpa 287
Tukchok Dorje 290
Drime Lingpa 291
Kunzang Dechen Gyalpo 292
Rokje Lingpa 294
Garwang Chime Dorje 295
Dorje Tokme 296
Rangdröl Tingdzin Gyalpo 297
Chokgyur Lingpa 300
Chögyal Dorje 311
Padma Ösal Dongak Lingpa 313
Other Revealers of Earth Terma 327

Section Two: Mind Terma 331
Dawa Gyaltsen 333
Rechungpa 333
Shakyashri 334
Yutok Yönten Gönpo 334
Kyergangpa 335
Rangjung Dorje 336

Longchenpa 337
Lekyi Dorje 337
Palden Dorje 339
Shrivanaratna 340
Kunga Paljor 342
Samten Lingpa 342
Tongwa Dönden 343
Rechen Paljor Zangpo 343
Bodong Sangye Gönpo 344
The Drukpa Kagyu Wrathful Kilaya 344
Jatsön Mebar 345
Tashi Gyamtso 345
Drikung Shapdrung Könchok Rinchen 345
Drikungpa Chökyi Drakpa 346
Lhatsün Namkha Jikme 346
Sangdak Trinley Lhundrup 348
The Fifth Dalai Lama 348
Bhuprana 351
Namchö Mingyur Dorje 354
Karma Chakme 356
Dorje Drakpo 358
Padma Nyinje Wangpo 360
The Eighth Pawo Rinpoche 364
The Fourth Chakme Rinpoche 364
Padma Gyepa 365
Tsewang Mingyur Dorje 365
The Omniscient Jikme Lingpa 366
Padma Chöjor Gyamtso 372
Jikme Trinley Özer 372
Ngawang Dorje 375
Kunzang Ngedön Wangpo 376
Mingyur Namkhay Dorje 376

Conclusion 378

Alphabetical list of the tertöns 389
Illustrations 397

Thrangu Tashi Choling,
G.P.O. Box # 1287, Boudha
Kathmandu, Nepal
Tel.: 4470028, Fax: 00977-1-4470763
E-mail: thrangurinpoche2002@yahoo.com

Vajra Vidhya Institute
Sa. 13/70-4-G, Khajoohe
Sarnath-221007, Varanasi, U.P., India
Tel.: 0091-542-259-5744
Fax: 0091-542-259-5746
E-mail: vajravidya@yahoo.com

THE VERY VENERABLE KHENCHEN THRANGU RINPOCHE

༄༅། །སངས་རྒྱས་གཉིས་པ་གུ་རུ་མཚོ་སྐྱེས་རྡོ་རྗེ་གཙོས་གྲུབ་པའི་རིགས་འཛིན་ཆེན་པོ་རྣམས་ཀྱི་མཚོ་

དང་འབྲག་ལ་སོགས་པར་སྦས་པའི་གཏེར་ཁ་རྣམས། ཕྱིན་ལས་དུས་སུ་བབས་པའི་སྐབས་བསམ་

བཞིན་ཆེད་དུ་སྐྱེ་བ་བཞེས་ཏེ་གཏེར་ནས་འདོན་པར་མཛད་པ་པོ། གཏེར་སྟོན་བཀྲ་ཤིས་རྒྱལ་མཚན་

རྣམས་ཀྱི་རྣམ་ཐར། འཛམ་མགོན་བློ་གྲོས་མཐའ་ཡས་ཀྱིས་མཛད་པ་འདི་ཉིད། ཉུབ་ཕྱོགས་

པའི་སྐད་ཡིག་ཐོག་བསྒྱུར་ཐུབ་ན། ཆོས་བྱེད་པ་རྣམས་ལ་དད་པ་དང་མོས་གུས་འཕེལ་བའི་ཆ་རྐྱེན་

ཡང་དག་པ་ཞིག་འབྱུང་སྲུང་བའི་ཀུན་སློང་གིས། པོ་ཙཱ་བ་བླ་མ་ཡེ་ཤེས་རྒྱ་མཚོ་མཆོག་ལ་རེ་

བསྐུལ་ཞུས་པ་ལྟར། ཁོང་གིས་འབད་ཚོལ་དང་དགའ་སྤྲུད་ཆེན་པོས་ཕྱོག་ནས་རེ་བ་དོན་སྨིན་

གནང་འདུག་པས་ཕྱོགས་རྗེ་ཆེ་ཞུ་རྒྱུ་དང་། དེ་ལྟར་འབད་བཙོན་གནང་བ་ཀུན་ཆོས་སུ་མ་གཏང་

བར་ཆོས་བྱེད་རྣམས་ཀྱི་ཕྱག་དཔེ་འདི་ལ་བསླབ་སྦྱོང་ཐོག་གཏེར་གཏོན་ཁྱད་པར་ཅན་རྣམས་དང་

གཏེར་ཆོས་ཟབ་པོ་ལ་དད་པ་དང་མོས་གུས་སྤྲེ་ལ་ནས་ཉམས་ལེན་གནད་ལ་སྨིན་པ་གནད་རིག་ཞེས་

འབོད་བསྐུལ་ཞུ་བ་ལགས།

ཁྲ་འགུ་བས།

Foreword
Khenchen Thrangu Rinpoche

The termas concealed in lakes and rock by Guru Lake-Born Vajra—the second Buddha—and other great vidyadharas have been revealed by the hundred tertöns, each of whom has taken intentional birth in order to reveal them at the appropriate time. This book, written by Jamgön Lodrö Taye, gives their biographies. Thinking, "If it is translated into Western languages, it will genuinely inspire dharma practitioners," I expressed this hope to the translator Lama Yeshe Gyamtso.

He has gone to great effort in order to fulfill my hopes, for which I thank him. So that his effort not go to waste, I ask that you who practice dharma study this book, increase your faith in and devotion for these extraordinary tertöns and their profound terma, and bring your practice to its fruition.

Written by Thrangu

Translator's Introduction

To understand why Jamgön Kongtrül the First (1813-1899) wrote the *Hundred Tertöns*, it is helpful to know the larger context of his writings. The works of Jamgön Kongtrül are collectively known as the *Five Treasuries*. These are the *Treasury of Knowledge*, the *Treasury of Instructions*, the *Treasury of Kagyu Mantra*, the *Treasury of Terma*, and the *Treasury of Vast Compositions*. The *Hundred Tertöns* is part of the first of the sixty-three volumes (in its original publication) of the *Treasury of Terma*, usually called the *Treasury of Precious Terma*. *Terma* means "treasure," and includes both teachings that are physically discovered and those that are revealed to the mind of the tertön. A *tertön* is a "revealer of terma."

When Jamgön Rinpoche had completed his first draft of the *Treasury of Knowledge*, which he initially intended to be a treatise on the three vows of Buddhism, he gave it to his friend and guru Jamyang Khyentse Wangpo (1820-1892) to review. Khyentse Rinpoche told Jamgön Rinpoche that the treatise would benefit from an autocommentary, given the terseness of the versified root text.

At about the same time Khyentse Rinpoche had a vision of the wisdom dakini Yeshe Tsogyal in the form of the Queen of Great Bliss (the form in which she appears in the *Heart Essence of the Vast Expanse* tradition of Khyentse Rinpoche's predecessor Jikme Lingpa). Yeshe Tsogyal said to Khyentse

Rinpoche, "Tell Guna that his present composition is to be one of five treasuries that he shall write and compile. This present one should be expanded to include the ten sciences as well as all Buddhism." By *Guna* she meant Jamgön Rinpoche, whose monastic name was Yönten Gyamtso, Gunasagara in Sanskrit.

This vision inspired the two great masters to begin the massive project of receiving and compiling the diverse teachings that now make up the *Five Treasuries*, which had previously been prophesied by the Buddha himself. It is due to their work that many lineages that would otherwise have died out subsequent to the Communist invasion of Tibet have survived.

In a tantra of the Great Perfection the following is written:

If the history of the teachings is not taught
The authenticity of guhyamantra will be in doubt.

As indicated by the above, it was obvious to Jamgön Rinpoche that an account of the lives of the tertöns whose termas are presented in the *Treasury of Precious Terma* was needed. Accordingly, he wrote the *Hundred Tertöns*.

Yeshe Gyamtso

The Hundred Tertöns

Jamgön Kongtrul Lodrö Taye

Namo Guru Buddhadhi Padmakara Padaya![1]

All the three secrets, qualities, and activity of those with tenfold strength
And their children are united in you who are kinder than all Buddhas to decadent beings.[2]
The clouds of your incredible feats fill the expanse of time and space.
With complete devotion I prostrate at your feet, Padmakara, embodiment of all jewels.

Prajnaparamita dancing with great bliss, your wisdom equals the Guru's.
You hold his secret treasury.
Kind mother and protector of all Tibetans,
Dhatishvari Tsogyal, please dwell in my heart's lotus.

Lord Manjushri, Dharmaraja Trisong; your sons;
The world's single eye, translator Vairochana;
And all you wise and accomplished disciples of Padma:
With devotion I prostrate to all you peerless guardians of dharma.

Through infinite emanations powered by aspiration,
You prolong the dharma through terma.
Stalwart protectors of all Tibet, Nyangral, Chöwang,

1. This invocation means "I prostrate at the feet of the Guru, the primordial Buddha, the Lotus-Born."

2. The three secrets of those with tenfold strength are the secret or inconceivable bodies, speech, and minds of Buddhas. Buddhas' tenfold strength includes: 1) knowledge of the possible and impossible; 2) knowledge of karmic ripening; 3) knowledge of beings' diverse interests; 4) knowledge of beings' diverse dispositions; 5) knowledge of beings' diverse degrees of acumen; 6) knowledge of the path common to all; 7) knowledge of dhyana, samadhi, vimoksha, and absorption; 8) knowledge of the past; 9) knowledge of death and rebirth; 10) knowledge of the exhaustion of defilements.

And all emanated tertöns: I bow to you.³

All their wondrous, profound secrets have passed down
To you who hold, spread, and guard their dharma.
Achieving the two aims through diverse activity,
You protect dharma and beings. I praise you all.⁴

Describing the brilliant and vast feats of noble beings
By drawing them through the needle's eye of a
   childish mind
Is less than ideal. Yet, for the enjoyment of the faithful,
I will, with few words, point them out vaguely.

The great dance of wisdom is beyond words and thought.
It is secret, beyond one and many.
A childish mind cannot even guess at it.
Yet, spurred by devotion, I will write with honesty.

The first envoys of our teacher, Shakyamuni, to this Himalayan land were the abbot Shantarakshita, the master Padmakara, and the king Trisong Detsen. They, together with emanated translators and pandits, caused the sun of the Buddhadharma to rise here as the Nyingma Tradition of the Early Translations. This included the teachings of the causal vehicle, the three dharmachakras and their commentaries, which were translated, taught, and studied. The three outer tantras and their commentaries and instructions also appeared during the period of the early translations. However, what I am going to describe here is the tradition of the early translations of the vajrayana's inner tantras.

The inner tantras have come down to us through three great lineages: the long lineage of kama, the short lineage of terma, and the profound dharma of pure visions.⁵ The first of these includes the three yogas, each of which consists of countless tantras, agamas, and upadeshas.⁶ Only the most quintessential of these were brought to Tibet. They include the Great Perfection teachings of atiyoga, which is divided

---

Margin notes:

3. A tertön is a master who reveals terma, or treasure.

4. The two aims are one's own buddhahood and the buddhahood of all others.

5. *Kama* means the Buddha's words as found in the sutras and tantras. *Terma* means treasure, the main subject of this book. *Pure visions* are visions in which a master receives dharma from a guru or deity.

6. Tantras are the Buddha's tantric teaching. Agamas are often explained as what has been recorded by bodhisattvas. Upadeshas are special or secret instructions, often composed by vidyadharas, holders of tantric wisdom.

into three classes, among which the secret instruction class consists of seventeen tantras, the chiti and yangti tantras, and the common and uncommon Heart Essence instructions based on them. These instructions come down to us from the traditions of three masters: Padmakara, Vimalamitra, and Vairochana. Among them, Vimalamitra's secret cycle teachings have been passed down through a kama lineage, and most of them have also appeared as terma.

The instructions from the tantras of the inner expanse class of atiyoga, the experiential wisdom of the master Shri Singha, were transmitted by him to the great translator Vairochana, who bestowed them on Pang Mipam Gönpo. These are the kama instructions of the *Vajra Bridge*. The instructions from the eighteen tantras of the outer mind class of atiyoga were mainly passed down by Vairochana and Yudra Nyingpo, and have been continued by three traditions: the Nyang tradition, the Aro tradition, and the Kham tradition. Countless lineage holders of the three classes of atiyoga have dissolved their aggregates into bodies of light, and the instructions on the six liberations mainly come from this tradition.[7] These teachings are especially profound in that they employ direct experience. They are the essence of all dharma. The accomplishment lineage of these teachings has continuously flourished up to now, mainly through the compassion of the omniscient Drime Özer and his lineage.

The agamas of anuyoga are such as the *All-Inclusive Awareness Sutra*. These instructions are the source for the *Vast Assembly* and its accessories. The ripening empowerments and liberating instructions of this tradition were received by Nupchen Sangye Yeshe Rinpoche from four masters of India, Nepal, and Chinese Turkestan. He passed them on to his disciples, and they have come down to us through an unbroken succession.

The eighteen mahayoga tantras, including their root, the *Mayajala Guhyagarbha* and its accessories; the explanation of that root tantra; and the ripening empowerments and

7. The six liberations are liberation through seeing, hearing, recollection, touch, taste, or wearing.

liberating instructions from these tantras were passed down by Buddhaguhya, the mahapandita Vimalamitra, and the translators Ma Rinchen Chok and Nyak Jnanakumara. The explanation of the root tantra, the empowerments, the instructions, and their practice has flourished widely.

There are also countless kama lineages of the tantras and instructions from the accomplishment class of mahayoga, such as the teachings on Heruka given by the master Humkara to Nup Namkhay Nyingpo; the Kila teachings given by Guru Rinpoche to various disciples; and the Yamantaka cycles that have come down from Nupchen Sangye Yeshe. The lineage holders of these traditions have been an uninterrupted succession of siddhas.

There is a saying, "Vajrayana descended first to Ma, then to Nyak, and finally to Nup." Their lineages were held by the great Zurs, kings among mantradharins whose teachings continued as an uninterrupted stream for some time. Eventually, however, their lineage started to become scarcer and scarcer. When the succession of explanation and practice seemed about to dissolve into space, the great tertön Gyurme Dorje and his brother put great and resolute effort into receiving all the existing lineages. They composed many remarkable sadhanas and mandala rituals, and started the tradition of their continuous accomplishment and offering observances. For example, these two brothers caused the explanation of the *Guhyagarbha* to become widespread. They revived all the Nyingma teachings and especially those of the *Guhyagarbha* and the anuyoga sutras. It is due to their kindness that nowadays dharma colleges of the early translations can proclaim their kama lineage. I have carefully received their lineages of the ripening empowerments, liberating instructions, and explanations of the tantras. As the history of the kama lineage has been extensively presented elsewhere, I have only briefly summarized it here to complement what follows.

Our main topic is a brief account of the profound terma dharma. This will have three parts: Supporting quotations and arguments; an account of the deeds of the teacher of this dharma and his disciples; and biographies of those who have revealed these teachings.

Part One

Supporting Quotations and Arguments

From the *Sutra Requested by the Naga King:*

> There shall be four types of inexhaustible treasure: great, inexhaustible treasure that maintains the continuity of the three jewels' lineage; great, inexhaustible treasure of the immeasurable realization of dharma; great, inexhaustible treasure that pleases beings; and great, inexhaustible treasure as vast as space.

That describes the nature or character of terma.

From the *Sutra on the Samadhi of Buddhas' Manifest Presence*:

> For four thousand years after my parinirvana this samadhi will be practiced in Jambudvipa. It will be widespread. It will then disappear into the earth. During the final five hundred years, when holy dharma is being destroyed, when practitioners of virtue are being killed, when people are abandoning holy dharma, when beings are being killed, when kingdoms are being overthrown, when morality is despised, when immorality is widespread, when holy dharma is despised, when unholy dharma is widespread, and when holy dharma is about to disappear, a few beings with brilliant roots of virtue will appear. They

will be those who have served previous victors, generated roots of virtue, ripened roots of virtue, and planted seeds of virtue. They will find sutras like this one. For their and others' benefit, through the power of the Buddha, they will bring this samadhi out of the earth. It will be practiced again in Jambudvipa. It will be widespread once more.

And elsewhere:

After my parinirvana
All my relics will increase.
This awakening of Buddhahood will be maintained.
It will be written down and placed in containers.
They will be concealed in stupas, the earth, rocks, mountains,
And in the hands of devas and nagas.
These custodians of the sutras will adopt
The behavior of devas.
In the future they will discard their caste identities,
Take up this awakening of Buddhahood,
And fulfill beings' wishes.

"It will be written down and placed in containers" describes the terma dharma and terma coffers. "They will be concealed in stupas, the earth, rocks, and mountains" describes the places of concealment. "And in the hands of devas and nagas" describes the terma guardians. "In the future they will discard their caste identities and take up this awakening of Buddhahood" describes the tertöns. "And fulfill beings' wishes" clearly describes their benefit of beings.

From the *Sutra on the Samadhi that Collects All Merit*:

Stainless Dignity, for the sake of bodhisattvas who seek dharma, dharma treasure is concealed in mountains, in crags, and inside trees. They will reveal these dharanis and dharma gates, which have been written down in books.

This clearly describes terma dharma, the places of its concealment, and the individuals who reveal it. And:

Even if no Buddha remains, dharma will appear for those with perfect intentions from the midst of the sky, from within walls, and from the trees.

That describes the *Sky Dharma* and similar termas. In other sutras and tantras, some well-known and some less-known, there are repeated descriptions of the nature, definition, varieties, and function of terma. This has been universally acknowledged in both India and Tibet. It is not something made up by a few Tibetans. Ultimately, since all the Buddha's teachings have come down to us through the wisdom lineage, symbol lineage, and whispered lineage, they are all terma. Even the common teachings of the supreme nirmanakaya Shakyamuni have appeared in this way. After the successive codification councils, most of the tripitaka, especially the mahayana, was preserved in the abodes of devas and nagas and disappeared from human sight. The tantras were collected by Vajrapani and the dakinis. They were then sealed and kept in the dharma library in Uddiyana. Eventually, at the right time, many of the mahayana sutras were received by masters of the Mind Only school from bodhisattvas such as Sarvanivaranavishkambhin. Other sutras, such as the hundred-thousand-stanza *Prajnaparamitasutra*, were revealed by Arya Nagarjuna from the abode of the nagas. Successive mahasiddhas who had attained supreme siddhi such as Saraha, Tachok, Saroruhavajra, Luyipa, and Chilupa revealed tantras such as the *Guhyasamaja*, *Chakrasamvara*, *Hevajra*, and *Kalachakra*. As all of these teachings are therefore profound terma, the only differences between them and our termas are between the countries of India and Tibet and the earlier and later appearance of the tertöns. In all other ways, they are the same.

The need for the concealment of terma is explained in the *Sutra on the Perfect Collection of All Dharma*:

> Ananda, so that the dharma remain long, write these teachings down in books, conceal them as treasure, and venerate them. Those who discover them will acquire ten treasures. What are the ten? Because they will attain the Buddha eye, they will acquire the treasure of seeing the Buddha's words. Because they will attain the form of a human or deva, they will acquire the treasure of listening to dharma. Because they will find the irreversible sangha, they will acquire the treasure of seeing the sangha. Because they will find fine jewels, they will acquire the treasure of inexhaustible wealth. They will also acquire the treasure of a body with all the marks and signs, the treasure of others' assistance, the treasure of confident recollection, the treasure of fearless victory over others' attacks, and the treasure of merit with which they can support beings.

From the *Terma Prophecies of Dharmaraja Ratna Lingpa*:

> I have placed instructions on the most profound
>   quintessence
> Throughout all this land, filling it,
> Out of my great love for degenerate beings,
> And because Tibetans are very fond of novelty.
> I have prayed that disciples with karma find them.
> In the future there will appear sophists fond of jargon.
> They will cause dissension among meditators.
> They will praise themselves and dispute the termas.
> Nevertheless, most practitioners in degenerate times
>   will be guided

By these termas, which are profound, complete,
   uncorrupted,
And extensive. Each single instruction will definitely
   free beings.
Therefore, those with awakened karma, receptivity,
   and previous training
Who remember death: Practice these termas!
My followers, you will travel the path to freedom in
   one life.
All those in degenerate times who are receptive and
   devoted to terma
Will be those who have now seen Guru Rinpoche's face
   and made aspirations.
You all have karma. Rejoice!
This woman's words are more valuable than gold.[8]

[8] This was written by Yeshe Tsogyal.

There are countless similar statements in other termas. Answers to disputation regarding terma, reasons for its acceptability, and extensive explanations of its function and benefit are clearly set forth in such books as the great tertön Ratna Lingpa's *Grand History of Terma*.

Part Two

An Account of the Deeds of the Teacher of this Dharma and his Disciples

Guru Rinpoche

The second Buddha, Padmakara, has tamed countless disciples in Tibet through the vajrayana of guhyamantra—the essence of dharma—and especially through the activity of his profound termas. This great master is not someone who has gradually traversed the path, nor is he merely an arya on the bhumis. He is the Buddha Amitabha, the peerless Shakyamuni, and other Buddhas appearing as a nirmanakaya in order to tame by various means those human and nonhuman beings who are hard to tame. Therefore, even great aryas would be unable to so much as partially describe his feats.

Briefly put, in the dharmakaya realm of the luminous vajra essence he is the primordial lord known as Changeless Light who has been naturally awakened from the beginning on the ground of liberation, primordial purity. In the sambhogakaya realm of self-appearance called Brahma's Drumbeat he is Vast Glacial Lake of the five wisdom families, the array of whose five certainties is boundless. Their self-arisen display appears in natural nirmanakaya realms of semi-external appearance as the measureless realms and bodies of the Buddhas of the five families that appear to lords of the tenth bhumi, all of it included in the realm called Mahabrahma. As all those realms and bodies are the array of Guru Rinpoche's inexhaustible ornamental wheels of wisdom, he is known as

Padma Holder of All. His display as nirmanakayas who tame beings in every realm in the ten directions is immeasurable. In this realm of Saha alone he has illuminated fifty worlds as the hundred predicted teachers of sutra and tantra. It is also said that he has emanated the Eight Supreme Names of the Guru in each of the worlds surrounding those fifty and tamed beings in them all.

His extraordinary array was seen by the dakini Yeshe Tsogyal. In the east she saw the Guru Vajra Vast Glacial Lake. In each of his pores she saw a billion realms. In each of those realms she saw a billion worlds. In each of those worlds she saw a billion Guru Rinpoches. Each of them had a billion emanations, each of which was engaged in taming a billion beings. She saw similar arrays of the other four families in the center and in the other three directions.

In particular, his display as a nirmanakaya who tames beings in this Jambudvipa alone has been seen in different ways by different disciples because of their individual fortune and acumen. In the *History of the Kama Lineage of Vajrakilaya* and in most Indian sources he is said to have been born as the son of a king or minister of Uddiyana. In most termas he is said to have been born miraculously. In some termas it is also said that he appeared from a stroke of lightning that hit the meteoric iron peak of Mount Malaya. Each of these three versions of his origin appears in infinite variations, all of them wondrous. As he wrote:

> I have concealed one thousand nine hundred autobiographies
> For the benefit of future beings with samaya.

Although his feats are utterly beyond the intellects of ordinary beings, I will relate merely a seed of his life as it has appeared to some of his disciples, following the well-known terma accounts of his miraculous birth.

To the east, south, and north of the western land of

Uddiyana are great oceans. On an island in the western part of the southern ocean, near the land of the rakshasas, there appeared through the Buddhas' blessings a lotus flower of many colors. From the heart of Amitabha, the lord of Sukhavati, emerged a golden vajra marked by a HRIH. Within the lotus, the vajra became an emanated boy with the appearance of an eight-year old, adorned by the marks and signs and holding a vajra and a lotus. He taught profound dharma to devas and to the dakinis of that island.

At that time the king of that land was Indrabhuti. As he had no heirs, the king had exhausted his treasury by making offerings to the three jewels and giving to the poor. He went to the islands in search of a wish-fulfilling jewel. While returning from this quest, a Buddhist minister named Krishnadharin who was in the king's party was the first to see the boy. Then the king met him, adopted him as his heir, and brought him to his palace. The prince was given the names Padmakara and Saroruhavajra, and was placed on a precious throne arisen from the jewel brought back by the king. Everyone in the land was satisfied by the rain of food, clothing, and wealth provided by the jewel. The prince ripened countless disciples while he engaged in youthful play. He eventually married the dakini Bearer of Light and ruled the kingdom of Uddiyana as crown prince in accord with dharma. He became known as Prince with a Topknot.

Realizing that he would not accomplish great benefit for others by becoming king, the prince requested his adoptive father's permission to abdicate the throne. The king refused, so the prince, while dancing playfully, pretended to accidentally drop a trident on the head of the son of an evil minister, and sent the boy's consciousness into the expanse. The prince was sentenced to exile for killing the boy and was brought to a charnel ground. He subsequently lived in charnel grounds such as Sitavana, Grove of Delight, and Sosadvipa. Engaged in yogic discipline, he received empowerment and blessings from the dakinis Mara-Tamer and Guardian of Peace. He charmed the dakinis of the charnel grounds and became known as Shantarakshita.

He then went to an island in Lake Dhanakosha and practiced guhyamantra using the symbolic language of the dakinis, charming the dakinis of that island as well. He engaged in yogic conduct in the charnel ground called Grove of Upheaval, where Vajravarahi revealed her face to him and blessed him. He bound all the nagas in the ocean and all the planets and stars in the sky to samaya. The viras and dakinis of the three places presented him with siddhi, and he became known as Mighty Vajra Ferocity.

He then went to Vajrasana, where he displayed a variety of miracles. When people asked him who he was, he declared himself to be a self-arisen Buddha. They disbelieved him and scorned him. Seeing that there were many reasons to do so, he went to the land of Sahor and undertook renunciation in the presence of the master Prabhahasti, receiving the name Shakyasingha. He listened eighteen times to the yogatantras and immediately saw the faces of their deities.

The wisdom dakini Guhyajnana appeared to him as the bhikshuni Ananda. When he requested empowerment from her, she transformed him into the syllable HUM and swallowed him. She performed the complete outer, inner, and secret empowerments within her body and then expelled him into her lotus, purifying his three obscurations.

From the eight great vidyadharas he heard the eight dispensations. From Buddhaguhya he heard the *Mayajala*. From Shri Singha he heard the Great Perfection. From many other scholars and siddhas of India he heard all the sutras, tantras, and sciences. Adopting the appearance of a student, he mastered every aspect of dharma simply by hearing it once. Without practice, he saw all the deities' faces. He became known as Supreme Intelligence, and displayed the appearance of a perfect fully-ripened vidyadhara.[9]

He then charmed Mandarava, a qualified dakini who was the daughter of Tsuklakdzin the king of Sahor, and brought

---

9. According to the mahayoga tantras, the tantric path has four levels of attainment: When a practitioner perfects the path of the vase empowerment, they become a fully-ripened vidyadhara, which means that although their mind has become the deity they still inhabit a body of karmic ripening. When they perfect the path of the secret empowerment they become a vidyadhara with mastery of longevity. When they perfect the path of the third empowerment they become a mahamudra vidyadhara. When they perfect the path of the fourth empowerment they become a vidyadhara of spontaneous presence.

her as an accomplishment support mudra to Maratika Cave. They performed life-accomplishment for three months, during which time the protector Amitayus actually appeared, empowered them, and blessed them so that they were no different than him. Amitayus gave them a billion life tantras. Guru Rinpoche achieved the siddhi of a vidyadhara with mastery of longevity and attained a vajra body beyond birth and death.

He then went to the land of Sahor in order to tame it. He went begging, and the king and ministers attempted to burn him in a fire. The place of execution became a lake of sesame oil. In its center was a lotus flower. Seated atop the lotus were the father and mother, Guru Rinpoche and Mandarava. By performing this miracle he caused everyone in that land to have faith in him. He brought them all to dharma and placed them on the level of irreversibility.

He then returned to Uddiyana in order to tame that kingdom. While begging, he was recognized. The evil minister whose son he had killed and others tried to burn him in a sandalwood fire. The site of execution became a lake. In its center, seated on a lotus flower, were the father and mother, Guru Rinpoche and Mandarava. In order to symbolize the liberation of beings from samsara, he miraculously appeared to be wearing a garland of skulls. He therefore became known as Padma Skull Garland. He remained in Uddiyana for thirteen years, serving as the king's chaplain and establishing the whole land in dharma. He bestowed the ripening empowerments and liberating instructions of the *Assembly of Dispensations: An Ocean of Dharma*. The king, queen, and all others with karma achieved the supreme state of a vidyadhara. Guru Rinpoche became known as Padmaraja.

As predicted in the *Sutra on Magical Display*, Guru Rinpoche then emanated the bhikshu Indrasena in order to tame King Ashoka. He established Ashoka in irreversible faith. Ashoka then erected ten million stupas containing relics of the tathagata in a single night.

Guru Rinpoche also removed and skillfully subdued several powerful tirthika kings who were harming the dharma. One king tried to serve Guru Rinpoche poison. He threw it into the Ganges River, causing its water to rise up. He then danced in the sky, and therefore became known as Powerful Garuda Boy.

He also displayed many other forms and names, such as the master Saroruha, who discovered the *Hevajratantra*; the brahmin Saraha; Dombhi Heruka; Virupa; and the great Krishnacharya. He went to the great charnel grounds, such as Complete in the Body, and taught guhyamantra to the dakinis. He received the life-essence of all external and internal aggressors and made them protectors of the dharma. While doing so he became known as Rays of Sunlight.

When five hundred tirthika teachers menaced the dharma at Vajrasana, Guru Rinpoche defeated them all in both debate and magic. When the tirthikas then tried to cast evil spells, the dakini Tamer of Mara offered Guru Rinpoche forceful mantra, with which he reversed the tirthikas' spells and brought down a shower of meteorites that liberated the tirthika teachers and burned their village. He entered those left alive into the Buddhadharma and raised aloft the victory banner of dharma, becoming known as Lion's Roar. Up to this point he maintained the appearance of a vidyadhara with mastery of longevity who had completed the path and exhausted the three depletions.[10]

10. The three depletions are desire, rebirth, and ignorance.

He then went to Yanglesho Cave at the border of Nepal and India. With the support of Shakyadevi, the daughter of the Nepalese king Vasudhara, Guru Rinpoche began the accomplishment of the supreme siddhi by means of Shri Heruka. Three powerful rakshasis attempted to stop him by preventing any rainfall for three years and causing both sickness and famine. Guru Rinpoche sent a message to his gurus in India, asking them to send him dharma that overcomes obstacles. They sent him so many tantras and agamas of Vajrakilaya that they had to be carried by two people. As soon as they arrived, the obstacles disappeared of themselves. Rain fell, and the sickness and famine ended. Both the father and mother—Guru Rinpoche and Shakyadevi—achieved the supreme siddhi. He thus became a Mahamudra vidyadhara. Seeing that although the practice of Shri Heruka brings great siddhi it is vulnerable to many obstacles and therefore requires the practice of Vajrakilaya just as a merchant needs a bodyguard, Guru Rinpoche composed many sadhanas combining these two practices. He also bound by samaya the sixteen Kilaya guardians and all the other male and female spirits, making them all protectors of the dharma.

At various other times Guru Rinpoche taught dharma appropriate for various dispositions in the islands surrounding Uddiyana called Humuju, Sikojhara, Dhamakosa, and Rugma; in outlying regions such as Tirahuti; and in places such as Kamarupa. He helped many beings using common siddhis, such as by causing water to appear where it was lacking and by diverting excessively great rivers underground. When Buddhism was menaced by three self-arisen images of the tirthikas' gods—one each in eastern, central, and western India—he destroyed them through the power of Vajrakilaya. When the large Buddhist community in the Kancha area was attacked by the armies of a Durushka king, and all his soldiers were embarked in ships, Guru Rinpoche made the threatening gesture. All five hundred ships sank, and the threat from the Durushkas was ended.

Although it is unclear exactly when Guru Rinpoche went to the land of Droding, he did subdue the dakinis, non-humans, and people there. He caused them to build temples. His traditions of Hevajra, the *Secret Moondrop Tantra,* Heruka, Hayagriva, Vajrakilaya, Matrika, and other systems of teaching, study, and practice of the four tantras have flourished down to the present. According to the histories of those traditions, it was from Droding that Guru Rinpoche departed for the southwestern island of rakshasas.

These accounts come from authentic Indian sources and are

well known. It is generally said that he remained in India for three thousand six hundred years, serving the dharma and beings. However, it appears that the learned explain this figure either as the number of half-years or as merely denoting a large number of years.

In order to tame Tartary and China Guru Rinpoche emanated kings with supercognition and powerful yogins. In the land of Shangshung he emanated a self-arisen boy called Tabihritsa who disseminated the instructions of an oral lineage of the Great Perfection, bringing many fortunate practitioners to the achievement of bodies of light. His diverse activity in different lands with different languages, placing all sorts of people on the path to liberation, has been immeasurable.

He came to Tibet in the following way: The dharma king Trisong Detsen was an emanation of the bodhisattva Manjushri. When he was in his twentieth year he gave rise to the intention to spread the holy dharma. He invited the abbot Shantarakshita from India. The abbot taught the dharma of interdependence and the ten virtuous deeds. When Trisong was in his twenty-first year he attempted to lay the foundation of a monastery. The gods and spirits of Tibet prevented the construction from going forward. At the instruction of the abbot, the king sent five messengers to invite Guru Rinpoche. Guru Rinpoche knew it was time for him to go to Tibet, and traveled from Nepal to Tibet. He miraculously visited every place in Tibet, including Mangyül, Ngari, Ü, Tsang, and Kham. He bound to samaya the twelve earth goddesses, the thirteen mountain gods, the twenty-one upasakas, and all the other powerful non-humans. He received their life-essences.

He met the king Trisong Detsen at Red Rock Tamarisk Grove. They then proceeded to Mount Hepo, where Guru Rinpoche bound all spirits by his command. He laid the foundation of Samye Monastery and built it. All the gods and spirits assisted the construction, so that five years after the work began it was completed. Pal Samye Mingyur Lhundrup Monastery was designed to resemble Mount Meru surrounded by the four continents, the subcontinents, the sun, the moon, and an enclosing wall. It included three "islands" for the three queens.[11] When Guru Rinpoche consecrated the monastery, five amazing signs of blessing appeared.

Because the king then wished to have dharma translated in order to establish the teachings, intelligent Tibetan children were trained as translators. Other scholars were invited from India. The "seven test subjects" undertook renunciation in the presence of the abbot Shantarakshita.[12] The sangha of renunciates gradually grew. The abbot Shantarakshita; Guru Rinpoche; other panditas; and translators such as Vairochana, Kawa Paltsek, Chokro Lui Gyaltsen, and Shang Yeshe De translated into Tibetan all the Buddha's teachings of sutra and tantra as well as the major shastras explaining them. Vairochana, Namkhay Nyingpo, and others were sent to India. Vairochana received the Great Perfection from Shri Singha. Namkhay Nyingpo received the dharma of Heruka from Humkara. They both gained siddhi through their respective practices and spread them to Tibet.

The king Trisong Detsen requested that Guru Rinpoche bestow the ripening empowerments and liberating instructions of the vajrayana. Guru Rinpoche opened the mandala of the eight dispensations at Samye Chimphu and ripened the king and eight of his subjects. Each of those nine disciples received one of the dispensations and achieved corresponding siddhi.[13] Guru Rinpoche also gave immeasurable uncommon profound dharma of the three yogas to the king, the princes, the twenty-five disciples, and other worthy persons at Lhodrak Karchu, Shotö Tidro, and other places.

It is said that Guru Rinpoche stayed in Tibet for one hundred and eleven years. If we assume that this number refers to half-years, it means that Guru Rinpoche arrived in Tibet when Trisong Detsen was in his twenty-first year and remained in Tibet for several years after the king's death at sixty-nine.

11. *Pal Samye Mingyur Lhundrup* means the "Glorious, Inconceivable, Unchanging, and Spontaneously Arisen." The main chapels within the Samye Monastery complex, aside from the central temple, are called Lings or islands.

12. The "seven test subjects" were the first seven Tibetans to undertake renunciation and become monastics. They were regarded as test cases: if they were able to keep their vows, Tibet was destined to host a monastic sangha; if they failed, Tibet would not receive the vinaya. The seven passed the test, and Tibet has held the vinaya ever since.

13. The eight dispensations are the eight mandalas of Manjushri Yamantaka, Hayagriva, Heruka, Amrita, Vajrakilaya, Matrika, Forceful Mantra, and Mundane Propitiation. When presented as one super-mandala, a ninth dispensation, that of Guru Vidyadhara, is included.

Then Guru Rinpoche, it is said, departed for the land of the rakshasas. So he clearly remained in Tibet for fifty-five years and six months: forty-eight years during the lifetime of Trisong Detsen, and seven years and six months after his death. While he was in Tibet, evil ministers of the king who were frightened of Guru Rinpoche's power asked that he be sent away. He then appeared to leave Tibet, flying away from a pass in Mangyül, after having stayed at Samye for eight years. It was, however, only an emanation that left. In reality the master and his royal patron were communicating secretly. Guru Rinpoche, accompanied by Yeshe Tsogyal and other disciples with karma, traveled all over Tibet, leaving not so much as a horse's hoof-print's amount of land that he hadn't walked on.

He blessed all the snowy peaks, mountains, and lakes as places of accomplishment, including the twenty snow-covered peaks in the Ngari region; the twenty-one sites of accomplishment in Ü and Tsang; the twenty-five great sites in Kham; the three kings among hidden valleys in the west, center, and east; the five valleys; the three settlements; and the single island—each of them including a root site, its branches, their flowers, and their fruit.

Knowing that the king's great nephew, an emanation of a mara, was going to suppress the dharma, Guru Rinpoche made many predictions about the future to Trisong Detsen. The master and his royal patron decided to conceal terma so that the dharma of guhyamantra would not disappear, so that it would not be corrupted by sophists, so that its blessing would not diminish, and so that future disciples would continue to have access to it. They concealed the hundred termas of the king's spirit, the five great heart termas, the twenty-five great profound termas, and innumerable others, some named and some unnamed. Guru Rinpoche predicted the time of discovery, the tertön, and the karmic inheritor of each of the termas.

At Mönka Nering Lion's Fortress and the rest of the thirteen Tiger's Lairs Guru Rinpoche arose in a terrifying form of wild wrath and bound all the major and minor aggressive spirits to samaya. He entrusted them with the protection of dharma. At that time, he became known as Dorje Trolö.

For the sake of the faith of future generations he left innumerable miraculous imprints in rock, such as the imprint of his body at places such as Dorje Tsekpa in Bumtang; his handprint at places such as Chukmo Sky Lake; his footprint at places such as the White Rock of Paro; and both his and Yeshe Tsogyal's handprints and footprints in many sites of accomplishment.

When the prince Murup Tsenpo conquered the monastery of Bhatahor and returned with the spoils of victory he was followed by the king-spirit Shingjachen. Guru Rinpoche displayed the form of the Wrathful Guru, bound the king-spirit to samaya, and appointed him the guardian of temple property.

After the passing of Trisong Detsen, Mutik Tsenpo became king. Guru Rinpoche convened a Great Accomplishment Gathering of the *Assembly of Dispensations* at Tradruk, where he entrusted that profound dharma to the prince Lharjey. Guru Rinpoche predicted that the prince would be a tertön for thirteen lives and tame many beings.

The number of Tibetan disciples tamed by Guru Rinpoche is inconceivable. However, the earliest group of his principal disciples consisted of twenty-one people, the intermediate group of twenty-five, and the later groups of seventeen and twenty-one disciples each. There were also the eighty disciples from Yerpa who accomplished bodies of light, the hundred and eight meditators of Chuwori, the thirty mantrins of Yangdzong, the fifty-five realized ones of Sheldrak, the twenty-five dakinis, the seven yoginis, Amay Jangchup the Spirit-Commander, Gyü Jangchup Shönnu, Rokben Namkha Yeshe, Nyang Deshinshekpa, Pangjay Tsentrom, Shami Gocha, Ngapmi, Ngapdray, Chay Gyamtso Drak, Dray Sherap Drak, and others. Families such as Lang, Ngok, Kön,

Rok, Gö, Pang, So, Zur, Nup, Gyü, Kyo—in which many of the great masters of the new translations have been born, and which have produced unbroken successions of siddhas—are all descended from disciples of Guru Rinpoche.

When the time for Guru Rinpoche to depart in order to tame the southwestern rakshasas was approaching, the king, ministers, and people of Tibet tried to delay him, but were unsuccessful. He gave each of his disciples extensive individual instructions and kind advice. He then left from a pass in Gungthang, riding on either a lion or a horse. Surrounded by a vast display of devas presenting offerings, he went to Chamaradvipa. He removed the king of the rakshasas, Raksha Tötreng, from his residence on the peak of the Glorious Copper-Colored Mountain, and took his place. He emanated the inconceivable array of the Lotus Light palace. He emitted an emanation in each of the eight islands of rakshasas to reign as their kings and teach dharma such as that of the eight dispensations. He saved the lives of the people of Jambudvipa.

Guru Rinpoche presently lives as someone at the end of the final path, a vidyadhara of spontaneous presence, a regent of Vajradhara. He will remain here, unchanging, until this world is empty. He constantly thinks compassionately of Tibet and benefits it through emanations. Even when the dharma of the vinaya has been destroyed, his emanations will continue to appear in every community of mantrins. Many worthy persons will accomplish the body of light. It is said that when the victor Maitreya comes to this world, Guru Rinpoche will emanate the bodhisattva Tamer of All Beings, who will teach the dharma of guhyamantra to the worthy.

This was a partial account of his deeds based on the experiences of ordinary disciples.

If I describe merely a seed of the lives of the principal heart-children and dharma heirs of this great master, this second Buddha, they were the king Trisong Detsen, the rest of the twenty-five disciples, and the five heart-consorts.

King Trisong Detsen

At the glorious retreat of Samye Chimphu Guru Rinpoche opened the mandala of the eight dispensations, the Sugatas' Assembly. When he bestowed the empowerment, each of the twenty-five disciples present offered a flower made from ten measures of gold to the mandala. Each of them then received the dispensation of the deity on whom their flower landed, and gained siddhi. They therefore became known as the Twenty-Five Siddhas of Chimphu, the Lord and Subjects.

During the ceremony spirits attempted to test Guru Rinpoche by causing a landslide. Guru Rinpoche exclaimed, "HUM!" The landslide reversed itself and the rocks took the form of the syllable HUM. Nowadays, the site is called HUM-like Rock.

According to Chögyal Tashi Tobgyal Wangpo De, an emanation of Trisong Detsen, King Trisong Detsen (who was Guru Rinpoche's heart-son and the "Lord" among the Twenty-Five, the Lord and Subjects) was predicted in the *Manjushri Mulatantra* by the name, Good Light of the Earth. Trisong was born four generations after Songtsen Gampo, his ancestor. His father was May Aktsom. His mother was the Chinese noblewoman Kongjo. He was born on the eighth day of the first month of spring in the Male Water Horse Year under the constellation Pushya.[14] Until his seventeenth year he mainly prepared for kingship. During that year, his potential for holiness awoke and he conceived the idea of building a great monastery. He discussed his intention with Gö, one of his ministers who was a Buddhist, and others and allowed them to decide whether or not to build the monastery. They all agreed that it should be built. The great abbot Shantarakshita, who was like a second Shakyamuni for Tibet, was invited to tame the land on which the construction would occur. In order that Guru Rinpoche be invited to Tibet, Shantarakshita pretended to be unable to tame the land. Based on his instructions, Guru Rinpoche was then invited. He brought under his strict control all the vicious spirits in central and eastern Tibet and made them his obedient subjects. Using the mandala of Vajrakilaya, he made the construction site workable. Performing a vajra dance in the sky, he had the foundation dug wherever his shadow landed on the ground. Humans worked on the building by day and non-humans by night. After five years, Samye Mingyur Lhundrup Monastery and its contents were completed without impediment. Guru Rinpoche cast the flowers of consecration and displayed mighty miracles. Based on his predictions, Vairochana, Kawa Paltsek, and Chokro Lui Gyaltsen were brought to Samye and trained as translators. They easily mastered what they were taught. Ba Yeshe Wangpo and the

14. The year of Trisong Detsen's birth is usually said to have been 742 C.E.

others of the "seven test subjects" undertook renunciation. Buddhism had begun in Tibet.

The "ten sutras for the king" and other sutras and tantras were translated. Vairochana and Namkhay Nyingpo were sent to India and received the gift of dharma. Especially, Kawa Paltsek, Chokro Lui Gyaltsen, and Ma Rinchen Chok were sent as envoys to invite the mahapandita Vimalamitra. Vairochana, who had gone to Tsawarong, returned to Tibet. A hundred great panditas gathered together, including Shantarakshita, Guru Rinpoche, and Vimalamitra. Vairochana, Kawa Paltsek, and Chokro Lui Gyaltsen—the principal translators—and a hundred and eight assistant translators established the complete teachings of the Buddha in Tibet by translating, studying, teaching, and listening to the tripitaka, the tantras, and the shastras that explain them. Their kindness and achievement are inconceivable.

In the histories of the kama lineage, such as the *Explanation of Concealment*, it is written that Guru Rinpoche only bestowed the empowerment of Shri Guhyasamaja on the king and ministers, taught *A Garland of Views*, and had the king conceal many writings about dharma and forceful mantra. However, this is just an account of the experience of common disciples. To his worthy uncommon disciples, the king and others, Guru Rinpoche taught countless tantras, instructions, and applications of the innumerable forms of the three roots and the dharmapalas. These included gurusadhanas, instructions on the Great Perfection, sadhanas of Mahakarunika Avalokiteshvara, and sadhanas of the eight dispensations practiced individually and together. As decided by the master and his patron, most of these teachings were sealed as profound terma for the benefit of the future.

In particular, when he received empowerment in the great mandala of the eight dispensations, the *Sugatas' Assembly*, in Red Rock Cave at Samye Chimphu, the king's flower landed in the middle. Guru Rinpoche gave him the secret name Powerful Divine Flower of Brahma. The king received the dispensation of the Supreme Heruka, the *Sugatas' Assembly*. He gave rise to the wisdom of spontaneous presence in unwavering samadhi. He heard the sutras from the abbot Shantarakshita and realized prajnaparamita. He wrote many shastras, such as *Validity of the Perfect Teachings* and a commentary on the *Hundred Thousand Stanza Prajnaparamitasutra*.

Trisong sent an army of one hundred and twenty million emanated soldiers to India to remove relics of the tathagata from the Lotus Stupa. He also built a hundred and eight temples. This dharma king is unique in being the single chariot that brought the bright sun of Buddhism to this cold and snowy land. King Trisong Detsen was Manjushri in the form of a human ruler. His immeasurable bodhichitta and activity have been of peerless benefit to Tibet.

There are varying accounts of the time of the king's passing. For example, in his *Great Biography* it is written that he passed away in his fifty-ninth year. In any case, he has taken continuous pure rebirth since then. From his perfect fruition he has emitted Nyangral Nyima Özer, the emanation of his body; Guru Chöwang, the emanation of his speech (these two were the first great tertöns); Ngari Panchen Padma Wangyal, the emanation of his mind; Naysarwa Dongak Lingpa Khyentse Wangchuk and Pal Tashi Topgyal, the emanations of his qualities; and the Fifth Dalai Lama Dorje Tokme, the emanation of his activity. Although these are the best-known, his emanations are said to be countless. For example, there are said to have appeared seven emanations of each of his body, speech, mind, qualities, and activity.

Briefly put, most tertöns have been declared to be the emanations of either King Trisong, his sons, or the great translator Vairochana, all of whose deeds are therefore inconceivable. As for the dharma king's sons, there are different accounts of them. The standard version is that there were three: the eldest son Mutri Tsenpo, also called Munay Tsenpo; the middle son Murum Tsenpo, also called Lhasay

Damdzin Rölpa Yeshe Tsal; and the youngest Mutik Tsenpo, also called Saynalek Jingyön. All three sons were close disciples of Guru Rinpoche. It is said that Munay Tsenpo's emanations include both Drikung Chögyal Rinchen Puntsok and subsequently Yongey Mingyur Dorje.

Murum Tsenpo is sometimes called the Translator Prince. It is said that he was both learned and accomplished, and that he dissolved into light at the end of his life. In any case, his many emanations include the vidyadhara Sangye Lingpa, Lhatsün Ngönmo, Shikpo Lingpa Ösal Gyuma, and Chokgyur Dechen Lingpa. Mutik Tsenpo's emanations have included Guru Jotsay and others.

Mutik Tsenpo had five sons. Among them, Ralpachen preserved the rule of dharma and revised the earlier translations, using contemporary Tibetan. He also spread the holy dharma widely by building the Stone Temple of Wönchang and so forth. Another of Mutik's sons was Prince Lharjey, also known as Ngakchang Chokdrup Gyalpo. He was recognized by Guru Rinpoche to be an emanation of Tsuklakdzin, the king of Sahor. Prince Lharjey became an especially close heart-son of Guru Rinpoche, and received from him the *Assembly of Dispensations: An Ocean of Dharma*. Some have said that Prince Lharjey was the immediate rebirth of King Trisong Detsen. Prince Lharjey passed away at a young age, but because of Guru Rinpoche's wondrous compassion he was reborn as the first of all tertöns, Sangye Lama; as the translator Gya Dorje Zangpo; as Nyima Senge of Mangyül; and as twelve tertöns in succession, starting with Ugyen Lingpa and up to Chöje Lingpa. His thirteenth successive birth as a tertön is said by some to have been Garwang Chimay Dorje and by others to have been the vidyadhara Jikme Lingpa. However, it is clearly stated in Guru Rinpoche's vajra prophecies that Prince Lharjey's thirteenth successive birth as a tertön is the crown ornament of all the learned and accomplished in this land of snows, the lord of the seven transmissions, our precious noble guru Padma Ösal Dongak Lingpa. That is certain.[15]

15. Padma Ösal Dongak Lingpa is one of the names of Jamyang Khyentse Wangpo (1820-1892).

Nupchen Sangye Yeshe

Among the twenty-five disciples, Nupchen Sangye Yeshe Rinpoche was born in Rongyül to the Nup family. When Guru Rinpoche bestowed the empowerment of the eight dispensations, Nupchen's flower landed on Yamantaka, the dispensation of body. He practiced at the Fortress of Drak and saw the faces of all the deities.[16] He became able to display manifest signs of accomplishment, such as penetrating rock with his kila and using the sun and moon as cushions. He went seven times to India and Nepal, and received the dispensations of the *Mayajala*, the anuyoga sutras, and atiyoga. From the Nepalese Vasudhara, Nupchen received many

16. In most cases in this book the word fortress refers to a practice cave or hermitage.

instructions on direct action and performed much forceful activity.[17]

In particular, when King Langtarma was persecuting Buddhism, it was this master who frightened the evil king. The king summoned Nupchen and asked him, "What magical power do you have?"

Nupchen replied, "Look at the magical power that comes from just reciting mantras!"

He then raised his hand toward the sky, making the threatening gesture. Above his pointed forefinger appeared nine stacked iron scorpions, each the size of a yak.

Seeing them, the king was terrified and said, "I will not kill Buddhist mantrins! You may practice Buddhism!"

Then Nupchen said, "Now look at this magical power!" He then summoned lightning with his pointed forefinger. The lightning struck a nearby cliff, shattering it.

The king was even more frightened and said, "I will never harm you or your retinue!" Nupchen was released. It is evidently due to Nupchen's kindness that the white-robed, long-haired mantradharins were never harmed. He was therefore of great service to Buddhism.

Nupchen achieved the state of a vidyadhara with mastery of life, and is said to have lived into the reign of King Palkhorchen. At the end of his life, having ripened his son Yönten Gyamtso, the "fifteen virtuous dharma siblings," and his other disciples, Nupchen departed for Changlochen. He was a great chariot of the kama lineage of the early translations. Many tertöns have been his emanations, including Dumgya Shangtrom Dorje Öbar and Ugyen Drime Kunga.[18]

17. "Direct action," *abhichara*, is the liberation of obstructors.

18. The best-known recent tertön who was an emanation of Nupchen was the great tertön Barway Dorje (1836-1918). Barway Dorje was still relatively unknown at the time this book was written. It must have been written before 1892, as Jamyang Khyentse Wangpo was still alive while Jamgön Kongtrül was writing it.

Gyalwa Chokyang

Ngenlam Gyalwa Chokyang was born in Penyül in central Tibet to the Ngenlam family. He undertook renunciation in the presence of the abbot Shantarakshita, and was one of the "seven test subjects," the first monastics in Tibet. Gyalwa Chokyang is renowned as having been extremely ethical. In the *Explanation of Concealment*, when it lists those considered the "nine best men" of that time, it says:

> Those with the best morality were Ngenlam and Lhachung.

Gyalwa Chokyang's flower landed on Hayagriva, the dispensation of speech. He practiced at Wentsa and gained might in the three perceptions.[19] A loudly neighing horse's head emerged from his crown. As he achieved the state of a vidyadhara with mastery of longevity, he was still alive during the reign of King Palkhorchen. Maben Jangchub Lodrö, who had been killed by cannibals in western Tibet, was reborn as a king spirit and was harming King Palkhorchen. Gyalwa Chokyang performed a King Spirit Ransom ritual, and Palkhorchen regained his health. Gyalwa Chokyang then concealed part of the ransom device as terma at Karchu. It is said that it was later discovered by Khampa Darberchen.

Gyalwa Chokyang's emanations include Guru Tseten Gyaltsen, Gyatön Padma Wangchuk, and others. The world-famous mahasiddha Karma Pakshi also declared himself to be an emanation of Gyalwa Chokyang.[20]

---

19. The three perceptions referred to here are the mental, visual, and tactile perception of a deity.

20. All of the Gyalwang Karmapas are considered to be emanations of Gyalwa Chokyang.

The Bhikshu Namkhay Nyingpo

Namkhay Nyingpo was born to the Nup family in eastern Nyal, in a place called Nyang Karda Shambu. He undertook renunciation in the presence of the abbot Shantarakshita, and remained a bhikshu. When he received empowerment from Guru Rinpoche his flower landed on Perfect Heruka, the dispensation of mind. He achieved signs of siddhi, such as traveling on the rays of the sun. After being thoroughly trained in translation, he went to India and met many panditas and siddhas, such as the master Humkara. He received many empowerments and instructions, and then returned to Tibet. Because of being slandered by the Bönpo ministers, he lived for a while at Karchu in Lhodrak.

Once, while Namkhay Nyingpo was living in a cave called Red Rock near his birthplace, his younger brother, who was a worldly man, came to see him. He complained to Namkhay Nyingpo that he lacked the necessary seeds for planting crops. Namkhay Nyingpo said to him, "If you, a man of the world, have no seeds to plant, how could I, a hermit, have any? Nevertheless, cast these upon your fields and pretend you're planting. How embarrassing!" Saying that, Namkhay Nyingpo gave his brother a sack of pebbles. His brother did as he had been told, and his fields produced crops superior to those of others.

At another time Namkhay Nyingpo flew from the Red Rock Cave to the peak of Mount Upright, also in eastern Nyal. On his journey, he dropped his mala while flying over a field in eastern Nyang. He miraculously extended his arm from the sky so that he could retrieve the fallen mala from the ground where it had landed. Where his five fingers touched the ground, five flowers sprang up. The dakinis of the five families and the goddesses of the four elements built five stupas in which they enshrined the five flowers. These stupas still exist today.

Once, while Namkhay Nyingpo was living in the Red Wall Cave on Mount Upright, a large group of rowdy young men came from nearby to tour the mountain, carrying a lot of food and drink. When they encountered the bhikshu, they offered their provisions to him as a ganachakra. When they were about to leave, he gave each of them a few red pebbles and said, "These are a blessing." Most of the young men threw their pebbles away, but one of them poured his into his quiver. When he later took an arrow out of the quiver, he found that the pebbles had turned into turquoise. Realizing that the pebbles given him by the master bore siddhi, he told the others. They regretted throwing their pebbles away, and went back to the master to ask for more siddhi. However, the master was not within his cave; only a red wolf was there.

The cave therefore became known as Red Wolf Cave. It is said that some of the turquoise pebbles were given individual names, such as Six Red Skulls, Eight White Roots, and Four Starlike Eyes.

Another story about Namkhay Nyingpo tells that every morning a certain woman would offer him a bowl of yogurt. One day, the master filled the yogurt bowl with pebbles and returned it to her. Knowing that it bore siddhi, she brought the bowl of pebbles back to her home. After a few days she looked at the bowl, and saw that all the pebbles had turned into turquoise.

Namkhay Nyingpo practiced in caves, such as the Cavern of Splendor at Karchu in Lhodrak, and saw the faces of many yidams. He achieved the state of a vidyadhara of Mahamudra, and therefore went to the celestial realm without abandoning his body. His many emanations include several tertöns, such as Jangchub Lingpa Palgyi Gyaltsen and later the vidyadhara Tsewang Norbu. The life of his consort Shelkar Dorje Tso, who also accomplished the celestial state, is clearly related in the *Guru Ocean of Jewels* discovered by Padma Lingpa.

The Translator Nyak Jnanakumara

Nyak Jnanakumara was born in either Yarlung Sherpa or Chö. His father was Nyak Takdra Lhanang. His mother's name was Suza Gönkyi. From birth, Jnanakumara had a mole on his throat shaped like a double vajra. He was given the name Gyalway Lodrö. He undertook renunciation and completion in the presence of the abbot Shantarakshita. As Jnanakumara was inconceivably intelligent, he translated a great deal of dharma of both sutra and tantra. From his masters Guru Rinpoche, Vimalamitra, Vairochana, and Yudra Nyingpo he received their four rivers of dispensation. That is why it is said:

The vajrayana teachings of the early translations first descended to Nyak.

He mainly gained realization through the practice of Vajrakilaya, and accomplished miraculous powers. His lineage of practice, called Nyak-Style Vajrakilaya, was widespread for a long time. When Guru Rinpoche bestowed the empowerment of the eight dispensations, Jnanakumara's flower, like that of King Trisong Detsen, landed on the central Supreme Heruka. Jnanakumara received the secret name Drime Dashar and the dispensation of qualities, Amrita.[21] He practiced at the Crystal Cave in Yarlung. The water of siddhi that he miraculously created there still flows.

Nyak also practiced at Yerpa together with Ngenlam Gyalwa Chokyang. It is said that when Nyak attained siddhi there he transformed himself into a raven and flew to his friend Gyalwa Chokyang, who recognized him. Nyak then turned himself into a small camel, circumambulated Gyalwa Chokyang three times, and reportedly said to him, "My practice has gone well!"

Sometimes Nyak is not included among the eight inheritors of the eight dispensations. For example, Tashi Tobgyal Wangpo does not include him in that list. I have included him here following the account of the eight dispensations in the Assembly of Sugatas. In any case, Nyak was a great holder of the teachings of the three yogas. His disciples include the "eight glorious sons," such as Sokpo Palgyi Yeshe. His nephew lineage was also very active.[22] Nyak's emanations apparently include Yartö Ramo Shelmen; Nyi Ösal, the physician of Jarong; and other emanated tertöns.

21. *Drime Dashar* means "Stainless Moonrise."

22. Monastics often bequeath their lineage to one of their nephews.

Yeshe Tsogyal, the Emanation of Sarasvati

Yeshe Tsogyal's birthplace and the names of her parents vary in different sources. If we follow the *Testament of Padma*, her father's name was Namkha Yeshe and her mother's was Nupmo Gewa Bum. According to the same source, Tsogyal was born to them in the large village of Drak. Her family was Kharchen. The footprints she left in rock as a child and her small soul-lake are still there.

At first she was one of King Trisong's queens. He presented her to Guru Rinpoche as an offering for empowerment, and she became Guru Rinpoche's consort. There are, however, varying accounts of how she first met Guru Rinpoche. During the empowerment her flower landed on the mandala of Vajrakilaya, the dispensation of activity. She saw the faces of the deities of that mandala and achieved siddhi, through which she subdued a parasitic spirit that had been afflicting her family. She practiced reviving the dead, and gained the ability to bring back to life the corpses of those killed by violence.

Yeshe Tsogyal received countless profound dharmas from Guru Rinpoche in different great accomplishment sites. For example, she received the profound dharma of the *Dakinis' Heart Essence* in Shotö Tidro. She practiced what she received and achieved a high level of accomplishment. When Shata—a minister who had obstructed her study and practice of dharma when she was young—was born in hell, Tsogyal went there to free him. In front of the iron hell-building in which Shata was imprisoned, she created the mandala of the peaceful and wrathful ones called *Emptying Hell to its Depths*. This caused the iron building to fall apart. She freed Shata and all the other beings trapped in it, and emptied hell once.

Yeshe Tsogyal collected all the inconceivable secret dharmas taught by Guru Rinpoche. She benefited beings in Tibet for two hundred years, and then went to the terrestrial Glorious Copper-Colored Mountain without abandoning her body. She remains there as Guru Rinpoche's consort, and is like our mother and a wish-fulfilling jewel in her peerless kindness to beings in Tibet. Although there appear to be varying accounts of the year of her passing, I have followed the best-known version here.

Most of the concealment of Guru Rinpoche's teachings as terma was done by this wisdom dakini. Her activity is boundless. She has continued to guide, predict, empower, and support great tertöns, and has emanated the consorts of many of them. Her direct emanations also include great female tertöns who departed for the celestial realm without abandoning their bodies, such as Jomo Menmo and the dakini Kunga Bum. As this indicates, she is unimaginably wondrous.

Drokmi Palgyi Yeshe

Palgyi Yeshe was born to the Drokmi family in the highland nomad region.[23] He became a skilled translator, and translated a lot of sutra and tantra, such as the *Matrika Tantra*. When Guru Rinpoche bestowed the empowerment of the eight dispensations, Drokmi's flower landed on the mandala of the Highest Heruka.[24] He therefore received the dispensation of the matrikas of existence. Drokmi actually saw the mandala of Blissful Existence and became able to employ all the matrikas of appearance and existence as servants.

Drokmi took Shampo Gangra in western Tibet as his practice place. He concealed as terma there the spirit-stone of the great god Shampo. It was made from fifteen jewels of humans, devas, and nagas. All the space within the length of one horse-tail surrounding it was filled with its warmth. It is said to have been discovered later by Kalden Dorje.

As Drokmi lived as a great mantradharin, both the line of his descendants and of his nephew have produced many accomplished mantradharins and translators. His family line still exists nowadays.[25] The great emanated tertön Rashak Chöbar was apparently an emanation of both Drokmi and the great translator Vairochana, and other emanations of Drokmi have appeared at various times, such as Karak Dechen Lingpa.

---

23. *Drokmi* means "nomad."

24. Perfect Heruka, Supreme Heruka, and Highest Heruka are different deities, although one in essence. Perfect Heruka is the principal of the mandala of mind. Supreme Heruka is the principal of the mandala of qualities. Highest Heruka is the principal of the Matrika mandala. Matrikas are wrathful female deities.

25. In all cases in this book other than in the translator's sidenotes, *nowadays* and similar expressions refer to the time at which the book was written, the late 19th Century.

Lang Palgyi Senge

Palgyi Senge was born to the visionary Lang family. His father was Amay Jangchup Dreköl. When Jangchup Dreköl was in his eighth year, he visited Uddiyana. He also subdued rakshasas and was twice invited to Ling by King Gesar in order to subdue the four great demons of the four directions. He could employ spirits as servants.

Palgyi Senge's mother's name was Lady Kalden. He was the eldest of three sons born to his parents. He had inconceivable miraculous and magical powers. In particular, he became a heart disciple of Guru Rinpoche. When Palgyi Senge received empowerment, his flower landed on the mandala of Mundane Propitiation, and he received the dispensation of the Aggressive ones. He became able to employ all Aggressive spirits as servants and attendants. At the accomplishment site of Paro Taktsang he saw the faces of the deities of the mandala of the bhagavat Tamer of All the Aggressive, and achieved the two siddhis.[26]

The Neudongpas, such as Desi Pamodrupa, were descended from the visionary Lang family. Palgyi Senge's emanations include the emanated tertön Ratön Tobden Dorje and others.

26. Tamer of All the Aggressive is the principal of the mandala of Mundane Propitiation.

The Great Translator Vairochana

Vairochana was born to the Pagor family. His birthplace differs in different sources. In the *Testament of Padma* Vairochana is said to have been born in Nyimo. However, in the *Great Image*, a biography of Vairochana, it says that he was born at the confluence of the Nyang and Tsangpo rivers. This clearly refers to the land on the eastern side of the river that flows nowadays by the Samdruptse Palace, where there is a village called Zangkar. It is said that there are clear footprints in stone there that were left by Vairochana as a boy.

Vairochana's father's name was Pagor Dorje Gyalpo. Pagor

Hedö is said to have been Vairochana's uncle, although in the *Testament of Padma* it is said that Hedö was his father. Vairochana's mother's name was Drenkaza Drönkyi. Even as a child, Vairochana exhibited miracles, such as flying back and forth between the high mountains of his birthplace.

He undertook renunciation in the presence of the abbot Shantarakshita as one of the "seven test subjects." He was given the name Vairochanarakshita, Utterly Illuminating Guardian. Vairochana became the greatest of translators. No one among all earlier and later scholars in this land of Tibet can withstand comparison to him. At the command of the dharma king Trisong Detsen, Vairochana went to India, accompanied by Tsangben Lekdrup. Vairochana met twenty-five great panditas, such as Shri Singha, and heard much profound dharma of guhyamantra.

In particular, from Shri Singha he heard all the teachings of the Great Perfection, especially those of the mind class and the expanse class. Through practicing these, Vairochana achieved wisdom no different than Shri Singha's. He then practiced speed-walking, and miraculously returned to Tibet without difficulty.

When Vairochana thereafter became a teacher of King Trisong, evil ministers sought to sow discord between them. Because of their conspiracy, and also through Vairochana's previous aspirations, he went to Gyalmo Tsawarong. He caused Buddhism to shine like the sun there. In particular, Tsangben Lekdrup had been reborn there as Yudra Nyingpo. Vairochana taught him, and Yudra became his greatest disciple. Eventually Vairochana returned to central Tibet and continued to perform great deeds for Buddhism there.

When Vairochana received the empowerment of the eight dispensations from Guru Rinpoche, his flower landed on the mandala of Forceful Mantra, so he received the dispensation of the Aggressive. He was also a great collector of Guru Rinpoche's teachings, such as the eight dispensations of the

Assembly of Sugatas, and is praised for having achieved the same wisdom as Guru Rinpoche. Vairochana saw the face of Powerful Black One and achieved the siddhi of the eye of wisdom.[27] He liberated opponents of dharma through forceful mantra. In particular, there is a story that he caused the queen Margyenma to contract leprosy and that she was cured through the compassion of Guru Rinpoche. The naga that Vairochana set upon the queen is said to still possess people nowadays. However, because it was contaminated by contact with Queen Margyenma it is mute and cannot prophesy. Its propitiation is therefore based on other means of divination.

These first nine disciples are called the eight or nine Holders of the Dispensations. The great translator Vairochana is also regarded as one of Guru Rinpoche's three greatest Tibetan disciples. These three are called the Lord, Subject, and Companion. The Lord was King Trisong Detsen, the Subject was Vairochana, and the Companion was Yeshe Tsogyal. Because Vairochana, as Guru Rinpoche's foremost heart-son, received the dispensations of most of the profound dharma he taught, his emanations include countless known and unknown tertöns throughout all Tibet. These include Vairochana's body emanations, the great tertöns Dorje Lingpa, Kunkyong Lingpa, Chokden Dongak Lingpa, and Trengpo Sherap Özer; his speech emanation, the vidyadhara Terdak Lingpa; and his mind emanation, Rongtön Dechen Lingpa. The details of how Vairochana has brought about unimaginable benefit to the dharma of the early translations and to beings will be clear in the histories of the termas later in this book.[28]

27. Powerful Black One is the principal of the mandala of Forceful Mantra.

28. With typical modesty, Jamgön Kongtrül did not mention here that he was the best-known modern emanation of Vairochana, nor did he mention his own revelation of terma in this book.

Gyalmo Yudra Nyingpo

Yudra Nyingpo was born in Gyalmo Tsawarong, in the capital of King Dosher. He became a disciple of the great translator Vairochana and achieved consummate learning and attainment. Yudra is counted as one of the hundred and eight translators of that period. He received the upadesha *Garland of Views* and other dharma from Guru Rinpoche. Yudra also displayed miracles such as transforming his body into a golden vajra. He mastered the view of the supreme vehicle, the Great Perfection, and became a great chariot of its teachings, especially those of the mind and expanse classes.

Yudra's emanations include Dharmashri the translator of Mindröling and many others who have served the dharma well. Some of his emanations have been tertöns, including Draksum Dorje Tokme, also known as Tendzin Daö Dorje.

Nanam Dorje Düdjom

Dorje Düdjom was born in Tsangrong to the family of the minister Nanam. Dorje Düdjom was, while young, one of Trisong Detsen's Buddhist ministers. He later entered the gate of mantra in the presence of Guru Rinpoche and eventually became a great mantradharin. Dorje Düdjom was one of the disciples who achieved siddhi through Vajrakilaya. The mark left by his kila in solid rock at the hermitage on Mount Hepo is still visible.

When the abbot, master, and king consecrated Samye, Dorje Düdjom saw them in his wisdom. He penetrated solid rock with his kila and, as he had control over wind and mind, passed through the tiny hole he had made in the rock and arrived at Samye. The hole in the rock that he traveled through is still there nowadays. Dorje Düdjom performed countless amazing miracles, such as flying around the four continents in the sky. His place of accomplishment, Red Rock Hermitage, is well known; it is at the border of the great Tsangpo Valley and the upper nomad country.

Dorje Düdjom's main emanations have been a succession of great vidyadharas, including the Vidyadhara Vulture Feathers, who discovered the Northern Termas; Jamyang Lama; and the vidyadhara Lekdenje. It is evident that other tertöns emanated by him, such as the Nepalese Ahum, some of them concealed and some of them known, have continued to appear down to the present.

The Acharya Yeshe Yang

Yeshe Yang was one of the scribes who wrote down the profound terma writings of Guru Rinpoche. He is one of the eight people of the time who were renowned as clear, correct, and learned scribes. This can be ascertained from:

> Denma Tsemang's writing is clear and correct.
> Acharya Yeshe's writing is large, thick, and easy
>   on the eyes.
> Shelkar Gönkhyi's writing is easy to read.

In any case, Yeshe Yang was one of those disciples who achieved siddhi and the miraculous ability to travel to the celestial realms. Although he is sometimes called Ba Yeshe Yang, it is certain that he was known as Acharya Yeshe Yang, and he is often depicted with the dress of an acharya. Yeshe Yang was a renunciate.

The Mahasiddha Sokpo Lhapal

In the past, smiths were called Sokpo; Lhapal was born in a family of smiths. He was a householder, and was able through his attainment to hold dangerous predators by the back of the neck. When Nyak Jnanakumara was looking for a friend to accompany him in the accomplishment of Vajrakilaya, he saw that Lhapal was qualified and trained him. Lhapal therefore gained siddhi through Vajrakilaya. As he subdued Nyak's enemies three times, he became Nyak's closest disciple.

Nanam Yeshe De

The bandhe Yeshe De of Shang was one of the three famous disciples called Ka, Chok, and Shang. He was an excellent translator and was also a mahasiddha with miraculous powers such as the ability to fly like a bird in the sky. He was therefore both learned and accomplished. It appears that he was a renunciate. As he became one of the great holders of Vajrakilaya it appears that his tradition, called *Nanam Vajrakilaya*, was once widespread. Even nowadays some long, intermediate, and short liturgies of this tradition appear still to exist.

Kharchen Palgyi Wangchuk

Kharchen Palgyi Wangchuk was Yeshe Tsogyal's brother. He became a heart-son of Guru Rinpoche. Palgyi Wangchuk gained the ability to liberate any number of aggressors just by brandishing his kila. The story of his liberation of the king-spirit Crystal Gingkara and the story of how he achieved siddhi through Vajrakilaya are found in the histories of the kama lineage. Palgyi Wangchuk was a householder and a lord among holders of vidyamantra. He mastered direct action.

Denma Tsemang

As Tsemang was born in the region of Kamden, he was known as Denma. His actual name was Tsemang. He was an excellent calligrapher, and it appears that his system of calligraphic training still exists. He was also a translator, and was one of the assistant translators among the "three great and three minor translators." Tsemang received much dharma of guhyamantra from Guru Rinpoche. He achieved realization and acquired the retention of all dharma without forgetfulness. It is said that it was Tsemang who wrote down many of the termas, including the *Sugatas' Assembly* of the eight dispensations. I have had the good fortune to see a manuscript of the *Sugatas' Assembly* terma written down by this mahasiddha that is kept at Mawochok in Lhodrak.[29]

29. According to the Eighth Tai Situ Rinpoche, Tenpe Nyinje, the Tai Situpas are emanations of Denma Tsemang.

The Great Translator Kawa Paltsek

Kawa Paltsek was one of the three famous disciples known as Ka, Chok, and Shang. He was born at Kawa in Penyül in central Tibet. His father was Kawa Loden, and his mother was Droza Dzema. Paltsek was predicted by Guru Rinpoche to be one of the emanated translators, and he mastered spoken and written languages as well as translation. He undertook renunciation in the presence of the abbot Shantarakshita, and was one of the "seven test subjects." Paltsek received dharma of guhyamantra from Guru Rinpoche and gained boundless supercognition, including the siddhi of knowing others' minds without impediment. He was the forefather of all Tibetan calligraphers, and his system of calligraphic training is still widespread throughout both central and eastern Tibet. He composed many shastras, including *Discourse on the Precious Supreme Speech*. His nephew lineage has produced many great illuminators of the teachings. It appears that several tertöns, including Drapa Ngönshe, have been his emanations.

Shubu Palgyi Senge

Palgyi Senge's family was that of the dharma king Trisong Detsen. However, Palgyi Senge's branch of the family is said to have been named Shubu after an ancestor who was skilled in Bön, fables, and riddles. In those days, such a person was called a *Shubu of Bön*.

Palgyi Senge was initially one of the king's inner ministers, and was also known then as Shubu Tridring Kangtsen. He was one of the ministers sent to invite Guru Rinpoche. He also became a learned translator under Guru Padma's guidance, and translated instructions on Matrika, Yamantaka, Vajrakilaya, and many other dharmas of the Nyingma tradition. He is among the "eight great scholars of Tibet."

Palgyi Senge achieved siddhi through Vajrakilaya and Matrika. As signs of siddhi he performed such feats as reversing the current of the Ngamshö River by touching the water with his kila, and splitting a large rock by touching it with his kila. There remain traces of his reversal of the river at Chimphu. He wrote:

> As my paternal family is descended from gods, I am the king's equal.
> As my maternal family is descended from the Mu, I am the king's equal.[30]
> As I built the eastern wall of Samye's central temple, I am the king's equal.
> As I built the White Stupa, I am the king's equal.
> As I drew melted butter from an aqueduct, I am the king's better.

30. The Mu was one of the first six Tibetan clans.

His sites of accomplishment appear to have been the Little Valley of Padmaling and other places. A detailed account of Shubu Palgyi Senge's family through the generations can be found in the biography of Shubu Pasang Lekyi Dorje of Lhodrak. It appears that many kalyanamitras who have served the teachings have been born to this family. For several generations after Palgyi Senge, every family member became a powerful mantradharin and gained siddhi through Matrika and Yamantaka. Palgyi Senge's most famous emanation was the tertön Namchö Mingyur Dorje, but it appears that there have been others as well.[31]

> 31. According to Khenpo Karthar Rinpoche, the Thrangu Rinpoches are emanations of Shubu Palgyi Senge.

Bay Gyalway Lodrö

Bay Gyalway Lodrö was a trusted friend of the king, and was initially called Gönpo. He later undertook renunciation and became known as Gyalway Lodrö. He became a learned translator, went to India, received the dharma cycle of Perfect Heruka from the master Humkara, and achieved siddhi. He invaded the realm of Yama with a miraculous army, and rescued his mother from hell. He terrified Yama and his minions with the army he had emanated.

Gyalway Lodrö studied dharma in the presence of Guru Padma and achieved the siddhi of transforming revenants into gold. Several tertöns appear to have discovered gold produced by Gyalway Lodrö's transformation of corpses.

He achieved the state of a vidyadhara with mastery over life, and appears to have remained alive until the time of Rongzom Chökyi Zangpo.[32] There are accounts of Rongzom hearing dharma from him.

> 32. A great master and translator of the Nyingma tradition, Rongzom is considered to be one of the most learned individuals ever to appear in Tibet. He lived in the Eleventh Century.

The Mahasiddha Kyeuchung Lotsa

Kyeuchung Lotsa was born to the Drokmi family. As he learned translation at an early age, he became known as Kyeuchung Lotsa, "Little Boy Translator." He studied and mastered all the dharma of guhyamantra in the presence of Guru Rinpoche. Kyeuchung Lotsa gained the miraculous ability to summon birds with his gaze and threatening gesture.

He was a householder, a long-haired, white-robed mantradharin. It is well known that the lord of the tenth bhumi, the great tertön Düdül Dorje, was his emanation. According to the *Supplication to the Successive Lives of Düdül Dorje*, Kyeuchung's emanations clearly include other tertöns as well.³³

33. The great master Düdjom Rinpoche is the current rebirth of this translator.

Drenpa Namkha

Drenpa Namkha was at first a great Bön priest. He later studied dharma in the presence of Guru Rinpoche, and also learned translation. He gained the miraculous ability to summon wild yaks with his threatening gesture. Drenpa Namkha offered many Bön instructions to Guru Rinpoche, who concealed them as terma. I have seen some of these; they have reappeared in some terma discoveries. Drenpa Namkha undertook renunciation and wore a red hat. He therefore became known as *Ex-Bön Red Head*. Because of this, I think that the custom, evident in some paintings, of showing him wearing a Bön hat is unnecessary. His rebirths have included tertöns such as Bönpo Draktsal and many others. The vidyadhara Trinley Lhundrup is said to have been an emanation of both Nupchen and Drenpa Namkha. It also appears that many emanations of Drenpa Namkha have appeared within the Bön tradition, such as Gyermi Nyiö.

Odren Palgyi Wangchuk

Odren Palgyi Wangchuk was born in Oyukda as the son of Odren Palgyi Jungne. Palgyi Wangchuk became a heart-son of Guru Rinpoche and learned all aspects of guhyamantra. He demonstrated many signs of siddhi, including fearlessly swimming like a fish through great rivers. There exist many dharma practices of the Odren tradition, such as the *Oral*

Lineage Wrathful Guru. It appears that the lineage of the empowerments and transmissions for most of these practices remains unbroken, and also that the family line of Odren Palgyi Wangchuk has survived. Odren Palgyi Wangchuk was a householder.

Ma Rinchen Chok

Ma Rinchen Chok was born in a place called Matso, which is in Penyül in central Tibet. Rinchen Chok is one of the "nine best Tibetans" of his time. It is said:

Ma Rinchen Chok was the most intelligent.

He was also one of the "seven test subjects," the first Tibetans to undertake renunciation at the time of King Trisong Detsen. Ma therefore undertook renunciation in the presence of the abbot Shantarakshita. Ma also realized the view of Nagarjuna, and vanquished the Hoshang in debate. Ma translated oceans of dharma of sutra and tantra. He received empowerment and instruction from Guru Rinpoche, and achieved siddhi. He demonstrated the miracle of pulling solid rock apart as though it were dough and eating it. He achieved the state of a vidyadhara.

Ma's great tradition of the explanation and practice of the *Guhyagarbha* is widely known. He once went to eastern Tibet, pretending to have been banished by the king. While there, he taught Tsukru Rinchen Shönnu. When the tradition Ma transmitted in eastern Tibet later spread to central Tibet, it became known as the "Kham tradition of *Guhyagarbha*."

The great tertön Longsal Nyingpo is said to have been in part an emanation of Ma Rinchen Chok, and it appears that Longsal discovered a profound terma about the four tantras that Vimalamitra had bestowed on Ma.

Lhalung Palgyi Dorje

Lhalung Palgyi Dorje was born at Dramtö Gungmoche in central Tibet. His birth name was Taknyazang. He became a guardian of the border between Tibet and China, and subdued Chinese invaders. He later became inspired by renunciation, and undertook renunciation together with his two brothers in the presence of the master Vimalamitra. He then received the bodhisattva vow from Padmasambhava, and also received all of the empowerments and instructions of mantra. While he was meditating in the White Gorge of Drib, his shawl was carried off by the wind and landed in Yerpa. Seeing that Yerpa was geomantically excellent, he practiced there and gained siddhi and the miraculous ability to pass through mountains and solid rock. He later liberated the evil king Langtarma and benefited Buddhism in many ways. He returned from eastern Tibet and settled at Dentik, where he remained for a long time. At the end of his life, it is said that his body became a mass of light and disappeared.

Langdro Könchok Jungne

Langdro Könchok Jungne was born in the Tanak area of northern Tsang. He was an inner minister of the dharma king, and was known then as Langdro Nangshi. He later undertook renunciation and received the name Könchok Jungne. He mastered translation and was one of the main translators of dharma. He received empowerment and instructions from Guru Rinpoche, practiced, and gained the ability to demonstrate signs of siddhi. He lived as a mantradharin, and had the miraculous ability to bring down fierce meteorite showers, like arrows shot from a bow, just by thinking of it. He became one of Guru Rinpoche's main heart-sons, and was a great lord among yogins. He mastered oceans of guhyamantra. His descendants are the Tanak Drölma family, which still exists. His most famous emanations were the great tertön Ratna Lingpa and the vidyadhara Longsal Nyingpo. If we consider their successive lives and the predictions in their termas, it appears that other tertöns have also been Könchok Jungne's emanations.

Lasum Gyalwa Jangchub

Lasum Gyalwa Jangchub was one of the famous "seven test subjects." He undertook renunciation and completion in the presence of the great abbot Shantarakshita. As he learned translation, he went to India several times and translated dharma of both sutra and tantra. He was a great scholar and reached the other shore of the ocean of learning. From the *Great History*:

Lasum Gyalwa Jangchub was the most learned.

It therefore appears that he was considered one of the "nine best men" of his time. After receiving empowerment and instruction from Guru Rinpoche, Lasum became able to display miracles such as sitting cross-legged in the sky. He was a great lord among siddhas.

Guru Rinpoche, just before he departed for the land of the rakshasas, turned the great dharmachakra of the *Assembly of Dispensations: An Ocean of Dharma*. At this final gathering of disciples, each of those present received the dispensation of one of the twenty-one clusters within the mandala. I will briefly describe this according to the intermediate-length *Supplication to the Assembly of Dispensations* written by Yarje Ugyen Lingpa.

It is said that the dispensation of the complete *Assembly of Dispensations*, both peaceful and wrathful, was given to the prince Lharjey Chokdrup Gyalpo. The dispensation of All-Encompassing Splendor, Buddha Tsaldzok, was given to the prince Mutik Tsenpo and his consort. The dispensation of mind, Perfect Heruka, was given to Namkhay Nyingpo and his consort. The dispensation of Vajramala was given to Acharya Nyima Drak and to Jangchub Nyingpo. The dispensation of Vajrapani was given to Yudra Nyingpo and his consort. The dispensation of Vajra Tsaldzok was given to Dharmabhadra and his consort. The dispensation of Vidyadhara Guru was given to Lekjin Nyima and his consort. The dispensation of Chakrasamvara was given to Yönten Chok and Nanam Yeshe De. The dispensation of Manjushri Yamantaka was given to Sangye Yeshe and Odren Trinjin. The dispensation of Ratna Tsaldzok was given to Pakpa Sherap and Shubu Konglep. The dispensation of Lotus Speech was given to Gyalwa Chokyang and Dorje Düdjom. The dispensation of Hevajra was given to Chokro Luyi Gyaltsen and his brother. The dispensation of Guhyasamaja was given to Gongpa Sal and Chökyi Lhunpo. The dispensation of Padma Tsaldzok was given to Mönmo Tashi Khyidren and her sister. The dispensation of qualities, Supreme Heruka, was given to Jnanakumara and Könchok Jungne. The dispensation of Kalachakra was given to Lui Wangpo and Acharya Salchok. The dispensation of Swirling Space was given to Nyenchen Palyang and Nanam Dingtri. The dispensation of Karma Tsaldzok was given to Kawa Paltsek and Drapa Drumbu. The dispensation of Blissful Fortune was given to Drokmi Palgyi Yeshe and Palgyi Wangpo. The dispensation of activity, Vajrakilaya, was given to Yeshe Tsogyal and Yeshe Salay. The dispensation of Subduer of All the Aggressive was given to Palgyi Senge and Yeshe Tsek. The dispensation of Mighty Black One was given to Vairochana and Denma Tsemang.

In the *Wisdom Assembly of the Yidam*, a terma of Taksham Nüden Dorje, it is taught that the final assembly included seventeen disciples. In *Notes on the Herukakalpa Tantra*, the twenty-five disciples of Chimphu are mostly identified differently. Most sources appear to speak of twenty-seven disciples.[34]

34. The twenty-seven disciples are the twenty-five with the addition of two of Trisong Detsen's sons.

However, as stated earlier, there was a boundless ocean of vidyadhara siddhas in those days, including those who achieved the body of light at Yerpa and at Chuwori. The number of Guru Rinpoche's disciples is inconceivable, so I am unable to mention all of them. Nevertheless, I will supplement the foregoing by describing merely a seed of the lives of Guru Rinpoche's five heart-consorts, who were emanations of the five mothers, the Dhatishvaris.

The life of the dakini Yeshe Tsogyal, an emanation of Buddhalochana, was briefly described earlier. Extensive and clear biographies of her are found in the termas of Drime Kunga and Taksham Nüden Dorje. In brief, she was Dhatishvari Vajrayogini appearing as a human woman. In addition, she devoted her life to the perfect service of Guru Rinpoche and to unimaginable austerity and diligent practice. The inexhaustible, ornamental wheels of her body, speech, mind, qualities, and activity came to equal those of Guru Rinpoche. Her immeasurable kindness to all of Tibet is no different than that of Guru Rinpoche. The flow of her great compassion is unceasing.

Dhatishvari Mandarava

Mandarava was born in the Ratnapuri palace in Zahor to King Tsuklakdzin and Queen Tauki amidst many wondrous signs. Because of the fame of her birth, many kings of India and China competed for her hand in marriage. However, overcome by renunciation, she entered the gate of dharma. Discovering the body of someone who had been born a brahmin seven times in succession, she offered it to her father, who treasured it as a wish-fulfilling jewel.[35]

At around the same time, Guru Rinpoche saw that Mandarava was a destined disciple and began to teach her. The king, fearing that his family would be polluted by this, caused Guru Rinpoche to be burnt alive. By displaying the

35. Consuming the flesh of someone who has been born as a brahmin seven successive times is believed to prevent rebirth in lower states.

miracle of transforming the flames into a lake, Guru Rinpoche placed the king, ministers, and court in resolute faith. The king offered his throne and daughter to Guru Rinpoche, and requested profound dharma from him. Guru Rinpoche showered Mandarava and twenty-one others—the king, his ministers, and other members of the court—with a great rain of dharma: the *Assembly of Dispensations: An Ocean of Dharma*, with its tantras, agamas, and upadeshas. The king and all his ministers achieved the vidyadhara levels.

Taking Princess Mandarava as a mudra, Guru Rinpoche went to the cave of Maratika, which means "the end of death." They practiced the generation and completion stages of the protector Amitayus, and saw his actual face. Amitayus empowered them both; they both demonstrated the attainment of the supreme and perfect state of a vidyadhara with mastery over life, the vajra body of unity.

In such ways Mandarava brought tremendous benefit to beings in India, both directly and indirectly. She also traveled miraculously to Tibet while Guru Rinpoche was turning the great dharmachakra at Tradruk. There, she praised him through symbols and asked him questions. A great deal of this is clear in the *Testament of Padma*. It appears there is also an extensive biography of Mandarava in the *Assembly of Dispensations* discovered by Ugyen Lingpa.

It is said that the Dakini Ornamented by Human Bone, who was encountered by Lord Marpa; the Yogini of the Mountains, encountered by Nyen the Translator; the Queen of Siddhas, encountered by Rechungpa; Maitripa's consort called She with a Stalk from a Banyan Tree; the dakini Niguma; and others were all the wisdom dakini Mandarava displaying different names and forms. They were certainly her compassionate emanations and blessed by her. Mandarava's actual body certainly still exists, as she accomplished the vajra rainbow body.

Mamaki Shakyadevi of Nepal

Shakyadevi was the daughter of Vasudhara, the king of Nepal. Her mother died while giving birth to her, so she was left in a charnel ground along with her mother's body. She was nursed there by monkeys. As she grew up, she developed wondrous physical features, such as webbing between her fingers and toes like that of a swan. Guru Rinpoche saw that she would be a qualified, holy consort. He cared for her and ripened her with empowerment. In the cave of Yanglesho, Shakyadevi was the mudra with whom he accomplished the nine deity mandala of Perfect Heruka. Through the samadhi called Discernment of Appearances, Guru Rinpoche accomplished the state of a Mahamudra vajravidyadhara. Shakyadevi accomplished the siddhi of Mamaki, and finally displayed the vajra rainbow body. In reliance upon Shakyadevi, Guru Rinpoche displayed twenty emanated forms. Especially, she was the first person to whom he spoke of the eighteen types of terma. She has therefore been unimaginably kind to Guru Rinpoche's followers.

Pandaravasini Kalasiddhi

Kalasiddhi was born in the region of drummers in India, in a village of weavers. Both her parents were weavers. Her mother died immediately after giving birth to her, so Kalasiddhi was brought to a charnel ground along with her mother's body. Princess Mandarava took the form of a tigress and nursed her. When Kalasiddhi had grown up, Guru Rinpoche recognized her to be a destined disciple. He took the form of the bhikshu Sukhadeva, which means "god of joy," and cared for her and ripened her with empowerment.

While Guru Rinpoche and Kalasiddhi were living together in the Forest of Webs, practicing the profound path of means, they accepted a young boy from the region of drummers as a disciple. He grew up to become the great siddhacharya Humkara, who is as world-famous as the sun and moon.

I have not seen any account of the dakini Kalasiddhi traveling farther north than Nepal. It is certain that she finally accomplished the body of unity.

Samayatara Tashi Khyidren of Bhutan

Tashi Khyidren was born in Tsaok, in what is now Bhutan. In early childhood, her propensity for dharma was awakened. Symbolically encouraged by dakinis in a dream, Tashi Khyidren went to Lhodrak, where she first encountered Yeshe Tsogyal, who accepted her as a disciple and ripened her with empowerment. She later met Guru Rinpoche at Layak Mönkhar in Bhutan. He gave her profound instructions that condensed the essence, and on their basis she gained siddhi.

Guru Rinpoche took her as his mudra of activity. At Paro Taktsang, when Guru Rinpoche arose in the form of Dorje Trolö, Tashi Khyidren transformed herself at will into a tigress and served as his mount. Together, they again placed all the aggressive spirits of Tibet in samaya. They also concealed countless profound termas. As she was instrumental in such deeds, this dakini is held to be second only to Yeshe Tsogyal in great kindness to Tibet. Finally, without abandoning her body, Tashi Khyidren went to the Glorious Copper-Colored Mountain, where she presently resides.

According to the biography of Yeshe Tsogyal that was revealed as terma by Taksham Nüden Dorje, Khyidren was the daughter of a king in what is now Bhutan named Hamar. While Yeshe Tsogyal was living at Mönkha Senge Dzong, Khyidren met her for the first time and offered her a great deal of honey. Khyidren gradually developed faith in Tsogyal through observing the signs of her siddhi, and began to serve her in every way as best she could. Eventually Khyidren's father, King Hamar, also developed faith in Tsogyal and offered her his daughter. Yeshe Tsogyal changed her name to Tashi Chidren and ripened her with empowerment.[36] While Guru Rinpoche was staying at Önpu Taktsang, he saw that Khyidren possessed all the necessary qualifications to be a vajra karmamudra. At his instruction, Yeshe Tsogyal offered Khyidren to him as a mudra. Khyidren then accompanied Guru Rinpoche in the accomplishment of Vajrakilaya.

They displayed inconceivable signs of siddhi. In particular, Guru Rinpoche arose in the form of Guru Dorje Trolö, and Khyidren took the form of a tigress. In these forms, they placed all the gods and spirits of Tibet in samaya. They emanated a wrathful, dark blue Vajrakilaya who appeared at Paro Taktsang and bound all the gods and spirits of Bhutan, Nepal, India, and the borderlands to samaya. They emanated a wrathful, dark brown Vajrakilaya who appeared at the Taktsang in eastern Tibet and bound all the gods and spirits of eastern Tibet, China, Mongolia, and the eastern borderlands to samaya. These emanations received the heart-vitalities of all of those bound by them.

Elsewhere in the Taksham biography it says that when Yeshe Tsogyal went to Nepal for the last time, she accepted as a disciple a fourteen-year-old girl. The girl's father was a Nepalese called Bhadanna. Her mother was named Nagini. The girl bore the signs of a dakini, and Tsogyal named her Kalasiddhi.

Kalasiddhi accompanied Yeshe Tsogyal on her return to Tibet. Eventually, at Guru Rinpoche's instruction, Tsogyal offered Kalasiddhi to him as a mudra. Together, Guru Rinpoche and Kalasiddhi opened the mandala of the *Guru's Wisdom Assembly*. The dakini Kalasiddhi also became the condition for Guru Rinpoche's plan to conceal terma throughout Tibet. He traveled to the three Taktsangs and throughout all of Tibet with her, and filled all the earth with terma.

36. *Khyidren* and *Chidren* are different names. The first means "leader of dogs" and the other means "leader of all." They are pronounced differently in the central Tibetan dialect, but more or less identically in eastern Tibetan.

After Guru Rinpoche departed for the land of rakshasas, Yeshe Tsogyal finished the work of concealing the termas and continued to guide her innumerable disciples. She lived, according to the Taksham biography, for two hundred and eleven years. Finally, on a mountain peak in Zabulung in Shang, on the tenth day of the bird month, countless viras and dakinis arrived from Chamaradvipa to escort her there. Tashi Khyidren and Kalasiddhi melted into light and dissolved into the right and left sides of Yeshe Tsogyal's heart. Then, without abandoning her body, Yeshe Tsogyal went to Lotus Light.

Part Three
Biographies of Those Who Have Revealed These Teachings

This has two sections:
an account of earth terma,
and an account of mind terma.

Section One
Earth Terma

Thinking of the future benefit of disciples and the teachings, Guru Rinpoche concealed in India, Nepal, and China countless termas containing dharma, wealth, medicine, means of divination, supports, and samaya substances. Especially, in this Himalayan land he taught all the aspects of dharma needed to skillfully tame each disciple, and in particular countless tantras, agamas, upadeshas, and applications connected to the three yogas. All of his teachings were collected by the Lady of Secrets, Dhatishvari Yeshe Tsogyal, who possessed perfect retention. She wrote them down in the symbolic script of the dakinis on paper of the five families. These parchment scrolls were then placed in terma coffers of various materials.[37] These termas were then concealed in their respective locations by Guru Rinpoche and Yeshe Tsogyal, who were sometimes accompanied by their disciples. The custody of each terma was entrusted to its particular guardians.

Yeshe Tsogyal remained in Tibet for more than one hundred years after Guru Rinpoche departed for Chamaradvipa. During that period she concealed innumerable termas throughout all parts of Tibet, completing the work of concealment. The mahapandita Vimalamitra, the father and son dharma kings, the great translator Vairochana, Nupchen Sangye Yeshe, Nup Namkhay Nyingpo, Nyak Jnanakumara, Nanam Dorje Düdjom, Nyangben Tingdzin Zangpo, and

37. In this case, "parchment" is used to translate the Tibetan *shog.ser*, which could more literally be rendered as "yellow paper." However, according to Bardor Tulku Rinpoche, this term refers to paper yellowed with age. I've therefore chosen to use the word parchment, meaning sheets or scrolls of fine paper. The original meaning of *parchment*, "a writing surface prepared from animal skin," is not intended here.

others concealed many profound termas as well.

When the time has arisen for each terma to tame disciples, it has been revealed by its destined tertön. These tertöns have always been those blessed and prophesied by Guru Rinpoche so that they would gain access to the termas and benefit beings. Each of them has been the magical emanation of one of Guru Rinpoche's worthy disciples, reborn through conscious aspiration. They have appeared one after another, born to various families and exhibiting various lifestyles, but always benefiting beings and the teachings.

Although the tertöns of teachings such as those called the Former Termas and the Subsequent Termas have been vast in their activity, undisputed, and very well known, there have also been many tertöns who have discovered minor instructions, as well as tertöns in minor regions who are not well known.[38] Whether they appeared in the past or are appearing nowadays, since they act in accord with dharma and benefit beings, they should be held as authentic. The large number of such tertöns does not make them inauthentic. From the terma prophecy of Drime Kunga:

> There will be masses of tertöns.
> Terma dharma will appear like mushrooms.
> They will not be fruitless.
> They will bring remembrance of me, Uddiyana.

And, from the terma prophecy of Ratna Lingpa:

> In each great land there will be a great tertön.
> They too will bring remembrance of Uddiyana.
> In each small place there will be a minor tertön.
> They too will bring remembrance of Uddiyana.

Many similar predictions are found in other authentic sources. There have also appeared, however, a great many false tertöns with spurious termas. These were predicted as

38. The *Former* and *Subsequent Termas* are those of Nyangral and Guru Chöwang respectively.

well, and are also recorded in history. Honest people with the eye of dharma, who are learned in the sutras and tantras, will through careful examination dispel all doubt.

With that introduction, I will set forth merely the seeds of the lives of the tertöns, taking as my sources the general prophecy of the tertöns in the *Testament of Padma*, revealed by Ugyen Lingpa; and the general prophecies in the termas of Sangye Lingpa, Dorje Lingpa, and Taksham Nüden Dorje. They differ merely in length, and are otherwise in agreement. I will also include accounts of past tertöns who, although not clearly predicted in the above-mentioned sources, are universally accepted as authentic. As for recent tertöns, I will base my accounts on the testimony of Jamyang Khyentse Wangpo, who sees everything with the stainless and unobstructed vision of the pure five eyes, and is praised by the world and its gods for the veracity of his excellent speech.

Sangye Lama

From the *Testament*:

> After eight or ten generations of the king's family,
> In Gyamnak, among the lakes of Latö,
> Famine, sickness, and contagion will strike the people.
> These will be the signs that the time has come to reveal
> The terma concealed at Lowo Gekar.
> The tertön called Sangye Lama will appear.

As predicted there, the first of all the tertöns was Sangye Lama. He was the first of the thirteen rebirths undertaken by Prince Lharjey as a tertön. Sangye Lama was born in the lake region of Latö, during the early part of the life of the great translator Rinchen Zangpo. Sangye Lama lived as a noble mantrin with short hair. He revealed gurusadhanas, Great Perfection instructions, and sadhanas of Mahakarunika from the capital of a pillar in the temple at Lowo Gekar in Ngari. He revealed the *Combined Sadhana of the Three Roots: Everlasting Attainment* from the shoulder of a mountain shaped like Hayagriva. He revealed *Hayagriva Overpowering the Aggressive*, a number of sutra rituals translated from Chinese, and other termas from Tangbar, Chest Rock, and other places. He visited central Tibet and perfectly benefited beings. He also lived into his eighties. It is said that a kila revealed as terma by Sangye Lama was later seen by Chöje Lingpa at the White Lake of Tsari. The family line of Sangye Lama remained in the Latö region for a long time, and the tertön Sangye Bar was born to it.

Because Sangye Lama appeared so long ago, only the reading transmission for a few of his sutra rituals has survived. The lineages of empowerment and transmission, and even copies of the texts of his termas, have not survived. Nevertheless, through the unfluctuating wise vision and compassion of Guru Rinpoche, who knows the three times, and of his disciples; and through their particular concern for their Tibetan disciples at this time of utmost decadence, the unceasing magical compassion of Vimalamitra and King Trisong has appeared as Padma Ösal Dongak Lingpa, the single chariot of the ocean of terma. Because he has been accorded lordship over the seven dispensations, all the profound termas of the hundred tertöns have been placed in his hands either directly or through their lineages. In fulfillment of the repeated opportunities he has received in vajra prophecy, he received the scrolls of the *Answers to Twenty-One Questions on the Combined Sadhana of the Three Roots*, the essence of the emanated tertön Sangye Lama's profound termas. Although he has not published the original terma, he has composed and passed down to us both an activity liturgy and a torma empowerment liturgy according to the meaning of the terma. I have had the glorious good fortune to receive these from him, and have placed them in the *Great Treasury of Precious Terma*. As he has also bestowed these upon the great emanated tertön Chokgyur Dechen Lingpa and other great beings of various traditions, through Padma Ösal Dongak Lingpa's tremendous kindness we enjoy the perfect virtue and wondrous auspiciousness of the reappearance of one of the profound termas of the first of all tertöns, even in this time of utmost decadence.

Gya the Translator

From the next prophecy in the *Testament*:

> The forest on the border of Nepal and Tibet will catch fire.
> Many people will be burnt. This will be the sign that the time has come
> To reveal the terma concealed on Mount Purna.
> The tertön called Gya the Translator will appear.

The tertön Gya the Translator was the immediate rebirth of Sangye Lama. He was born to the Gya family in the region of Dzumlang, on the border of Nepal and Tibet. As he quickly learned several languages he became known as a translator. His actual name was Dorje Zangpo. He lived as a noble mantrin, and was a contemporary of Lord Marpa. He is said to have revealed from Mount Purna and other places the *Essence of the Assembly of Dispensations*, including the guru-sadhanas of the two doctrines and three cycles; the *Stages of the Path of Upadesha*; the *Essential Fragment*; the *Full Presentation of the Channel Sites*; the short treatise called *Padma's Precious Garland*; and other termas. It appears, however, that because so much time has elapsed since then neither the texts of his termas nor their transmission still exist. Nevertheless, as in the case of the termas of Sangye Lama, Padma Ösal Dongak Lingpa, the holder of the seven dispensations, received the actual texts of these termas from the wisdom dakinis. He has revealed from them a wondrous treatise of eight chapters called *Self-Liberated Seeing: The Profound*

Essence of the Gurusadhanas of the Two Doctrines and Three Cycles. He has kindly bestowed its ripening empowerments and liberating instructions on us, and it resides within the *Treasury of Precious Terma.*

Nanampa

The prophecies in the *Great Testament* do not appear to be perfectly chronological in their sequence. Nevertheless, if I follow that book's order, the next one is:

> At Medo in Kham the bird and dog temples will fight.
> This will be the sign that the time has come to reveal
> The terma concealed at Longtang Drölma.
> The tertön called Nanampa will appear.

The tertön Nanampa was an emanation of Vairochana. He was born to the family of Shang Nanampa at the border of the Gegyal and Jangrong areas of eastern Tibet. Another name by which he is known is Drokpa Nanam Tupa Gyalpo. He lived as a common, white-robed mantrin. When he went to the temple of Longtang Drölma, he revealed a great deal of terma from the capital of one of its columns, including many beneficial instructions on medicine, geomancy, and divination. Nowadays only his *Wheel of a Hundred Ransom Rituals* still exists. Recently, our lord guru Padma Ösal Dongak Lingpa received the texts of Nanampa's termas from the wisdom dakinis. Relying on the blessings he has received in clear visions of Uddiyana and his disciples, our lord guru has also received the dispensation of the termas of Nanampa's rebirth, Nyemo Shuyay. These include the text of the *Great Perfection: The Trikaya Blazing Like the Sun and Moon* and the *Instructions from the Ten Sutras of the King.*

Gya Shangtrom Dorje Öbar

From the Testament:

> Latö Chungpa Drilchen will become like agitated water.
> This will be the sign that the time has come to reveal
> The terma concealed at Yupu Dzalhu.
> The tertön called Dumgya Shangtrom will appear.

The tertön Gya Shangtrom Dorje Öbar was the intentional rebirth of Nupchen Sangye Yeshe. From the *Index to the Profound Six Dharmas*:

> May this be found
> At the kalpa's end,
> By someone like me who is not me;
> Who has golden skin and curly hair;
> Who is short, with a white mole on his right
> And a red one on his left;
> Who has white, even teeth
> And a necklace of moles;
> Who will be born in the Year of the Dog or Dragon
> To the family Gya, and will have the name Shangtrom.

In accord with that aspiration made by Nupchen, Gya Shangtrom was born near the spring at Dum in Tsangrong. He lived as a common, householding mantrin. His family name was Gya, and his nickname was Shangtrom. He also became known by his secret name, Dorje Öbar. It is said that he was born in the Dragon Year and that he had curly hair and the other marks described in the quoted aspiration.

At first, Shangtrom was very poor. He became homeless and lived by begging. At the Nyamo Temple on the Tsangpo River he met a yogin who gave him a list of his future termas. Based on that list, Shangtrom revealed his first profound terma from Pungpo Riwoche. According to some accounts,

Shangtrom met the yogin at the spring of Dum, and the yogin both gave him the list and showed him the door to his first terma. In any case, Shangtrom eventually revealed terma from the four sites mentioned in the *Index to the Profound Six Dharmas*—Pungpo Riwoche, Mönmo Tsukrum in Gya, Dorje Drombu in Nyuk, and the Yellow Stupa on the banks of the Tsangpo—and from other places, including Yung Gedza Lhumo, Tadül Traduntsay, Lhodrak Komting, and Samye Chimphu.

His termas included many dharma cycles concerning the accomplishment of awakening, primarily instructions on the mind class of the Great Perfection. In particular, because he possessed the dispensation of forceful mantra, he revealed innumerable instructions concerning Manjushri Ayupatikala, such as the *Ironlike*, the *Iron Scorpion*, the *Magical Weapon*, the *Reversal*, the *Arising*, the *Kingkangs*, the *Molten Iron*, and the collection of instructions known as the *Hundred Neck-Pouches of Nup*. I have received the ripening empowerments, liberating instructions, and supporting transmissions for most of the above-mentioned cycles through the kindness of my holy teachers, such as Mindröling Trichen Dorje Dzinpa Gyurme Yishin Wangyal.

The great tertön Shangtrom was clearly born in the generation preceding that of Jetsün Milarepa. Many siddhas of forceful mantra have appeared among Shangtrom's descendants, and his family appears to still exist in the Tsangrong area. In any case, Shangtrom was the single forefather of all those who have accomplished forceful mantra in Tibet. He was a king among tertöns.

Nyima Senge

Then:

The sky in Mangyül will turn the color of blood.
A rain of blood will fall for eighteen months.

This will be the sign that the time has come to reveal
The terma concealed at Jampa Trin.
The tertön called Surya Singha will appear.

The tertön Nyima Senge was the immediate rebirth of Gya the Translator. He was born near Lake Glory in Mangyül. He lived as a noble mantrin, and studied various treatises on sutra and tantra. From Jampa Trin in Mangyül he revealed a great terma that included gurusadhanas, Great Perfection instructions, Mahakarunika sadhanas, and forceful mantras. However, because of a serious disagreement between his consort and his patrons, he was unable to transcribe most of the terma scrolls. Without having taught them or passed them on, he passed away. Close to his passing, he reconcealed his termas, and several tertöns have recovered some of them.

In particular, one of Nyima Senge's termas included four cycles concerning *Mahakarunika: The Peaceful and Wrathful Ones of the Lotus Family*—a long version, a medium-length version, a short version, and a quintessence version. Of these, the terma text of the quintessence cycle was shown to our lord guru Padma Ösal Dongak Lingpa by the field-born dakini Chandali. He transcribed it, and we have received it from him in its completeness.

Shakya Ö the Teacher from Uru

Then:

The three lowlands will be filled with murderers and
   brigands.
Everyone will hold a shield, a bow, and arrows.
This will be the sign that the time has come to reveal
The northern termas and some lesser termas.
The tertön called Shakya, the Teacher from Uru,
   will appear.

The tertön Shakya Ö, the Teacher from Uru, was born in Uru Penyül. He was clearly an emanation of both Vairochana and Langdro, and held the dispensation of forceful mantra. He lived as an ordinary, noble mantrin. As he studied various treatises of sutra and tantra, he was called the Teacher from Uru. He revealed many termas from Jangdra Duntse, including the *Dark Red Wind Wheel*, the *Reversal*, and the *Twenty Aggressive Ones*. From Yudo Rock he revealed the concise activity of *Play of the Trikaya Guru*. From Rasa Trülnang he revealed a cycle of instructions on the *Wheel of Wind*. Among these, only the concise activity of *Play of the Trikaya Guru* appears to have survived. A short text on *Vajra Fire, the Lord of Secrets* was received by Padma Ösal Dongak Lingpa through the short lineage of blessing. He transcribed it, and I have received it through his kindness.

Bönpo Draktsal

Then:

The White Sky Plain of Paro will be conquered by
  Mongolian armies.
Wearing iron, they will bring pollution and fighting.
This will be the sign that the time has come to reveal
The terma concealed at Bumtang Tsilung.
The tertön called Bönpo Draktsal will appear.

This tertön was born in the Rongsar area of Tsang. As his family was Bönpo, he became known by that title. He was an emanation of both Vairochana and Palgyi Senge, and lived as a mantradharin. As he was tall and strong, he gained the nickname Draktsal.[39] His secret name was Dorje Bar.

At Bumtang Tsilung there was a temple containing bronze images of the Buddhas of the three times. This temple was called the Temple of the Three Jewels by the people of the area. From there, Draktsal revealed a volume of terma called

---

39. *Draktsal* means "Rock Chip."

Experiential Guidance by the Guru. It consisted of Shri Singha's instructions on the completion stage, and contained the Great Perfection instructions of four gurus as well as biographies of the four. The following famous instruction is said to appear in this terma:

> I've never meditated and never been without meditation.
> I've never been without nonmeditation.

These instructions also appear in the *Northern Termas*.

Draktsal also revealed a *Vajrakilaya* cycle and, from Kyetangshing Rock in Shang, the *Auspicious Teaching on Rahula*, which included *Black Turtle: Protection from Hail*, and is so profound that it bore a command seal and life seal. Among Draktsal's many dharma termas, only the reading transmission for the *Auspicious Teaching on Rahula* appears to have survived down to the present. Recently, however, Padma Ösal Dongak Lingpa received—as a dispensation of the short lineage of blessing—wondrous, profound instructions on *Amitayus and Guru Rinpoche Combined* that are in accordance with these old termas.

Nyemo Shuyay

Then:

> At Nyari in Ukpalung, in upper Nyang in Tsang,
> The two doctrines will quarrel and the vapor of dharma
>   will vanish.
> Dharma and people, separated, will be carried off
>   by bandits.
> These will be the signs that the time has come to reveal
> The terma concealed at the Crystal Cave of Nyingdrung.
> The tertön called Nyemo Shuyay will appear.

The tertön Nyemo Shuyay was born at Nyemo in Tsang. As

he was born in a Bönpo family called Shuyay, he was known by that family name. His actual name was Nöjin Bar. It is clear that he was a rebirth of Vairochana. As predicted in the *Terma List* revealed by Bönpo Draktsal, Nyemo Shuyay revealed from the Crystal Cave of Nyingdrung in Rongpo twenty-five Great Perfection tantras, such as the *Chiti Great Perfection Tantra*, and many other termas as well. He offered them to Lord Nyang, and many of the tantras revealed by Shuyay are now found in the *Collected Nyingma Tantras*. The lineage of their transmission still exists as well.

Shuyay became known as Nyemo Shuyay, the Lord of Tantras. He was a renowned, great mantradharin vajra holder. Although his activity was considerable, nowadays only the transmissions of some of the tantras he revealed have survived; his other termas have disappeared. Nevertheless, the dispensation of his terma the *Great Perfection: The Trikaya Blazing Like the Sun and Moon*, a dharma cycle that is both profound and concise, was received by Padma Ösal Dongak Lingpa as rediscovered terma.

Ngödrup the Siddha

Then:

The borders of Dzim will be marked by the three jewels.
Monasteries will appear like unfurled brocade.
These will be the signs that the time has come to reveal
The terma concealed at Riwoche in Tsang.
The tertön called Ngödrup the Siddha will appear.

The tertön Ngödrup the Siddha was an emanation of Vairochana. He was born in Tsang, and lived as a great mantradharin vajra holder. He is renowned for having lived in the human world for three hundred years, and for having achieved the state of a great immortal vidyadhara with mas tery over life. Lord Nyang received the kama transmission of the *Eight Dispensations: The Fortress and the Precipice* from Ngödrup the Siddha, and its lineage has survived.[40] It is also said that Lord Nyang received some of the lists of his future termas from Ngödrup the Siddha.

Ngödrup the Siddha revealed many termas from Riwoche in Tsang. In particular, the dharma king Songtsen Gampo had concealed several sutras, tantras, instructions, and sadhanas of Mahakarunika in the Rasa Trülnang Temple under the feet of an image of Hayagriva and in the left thigh of an image of the naga Kuvera. Guru Rinpoche saw that they were there, and pointed them out to King Trisong, who reconcealed them. The first part of these teachings was then revealed by Ngödrup the Siddha. Their remaining accessories were revealed by Lord Nyang and Lharjey Gewabum. The complete volume of this terma is known as the *Mani Kabum*, and is also called the *Testament of the King*. Although it was revealed by three tertöns, it is considered primarily a terma dharma of Ngödrup the Siddha. Its activity has been vast and unceasing, and it is very well known. I have had the good fortune to receive its complete empowerments, transmissions, and instructions.

Bönpos give Ngödrup the Siddha the name Shötön Ngödrup. It appears that the Bön termas he revealed from behind the image of Vairochana at Komting—the *Three Cycles of Proclamation* and the *Vast Expanse: The Apex of the Great Perfection*—still exist.

40. *Fortress* here refers to the view of the eight dispensations, and *precipice* to the corresponding meditation.

Tsuklak Palge

Then:

China's capital will be occupied by Mongolia.
The teachings will spread; their power will grow.

> These will be the signs that the time has come to reveal
> The terma concealed in the Temple of E in Nepal.
> The tertön called Tsuklak Palge will appear.

The tertön Tsuklak Palge was an emanation of Nupchen. He was born in a town called Sun in Nepal, close to the Tibetan border, toward the end of Sangye Lama's life. Tsuklak Palge lived as a Nepalese mantrin. He revealed terma mostly consisting of forceful mantras from the Temple of E in Nepal. However, the texts and transmissions of this terma disappeared long ago. Recently, through Nupchen's blessing, Padma Ösal Dongak Lingpa received the profound and concise *Seven Sections of Forceful Mantra*, which includes six sadhanas and the protector Mahakala.

In most editions of the above-quoted prediction, the word *Tadzi*, meaning a "herder of horses," appears. However, older editions have the word *Tadzing* in its place, and I consider that to be correct. As both Tawen and Tadzing refer to Mongolia, the meaning of the prediction was that a Mongolian emanation would conquer the capital of China.[41]

41. The predicted Mongolian was Genghis Khan.

Kusa the Physician

Then:

> Latö Tsenyül will grow weapons as crops.
> The nephews of Jambudvipa's king will be oppressed by their subjects.
> These will be the signs that the time has come to reveal
> The southern termas and some lesser termas.
> The tertön called Kusa the Physician will appear.

The tertön Kusa the Physician was a rebirth of Vairochana. He was born in Lhodrak, and lived as an ordinary mantrin and physician. As he gained accomplishment in isolated places, he was also known as Daö the Renunciate and Padma

Kyap the Physician. Kusa is the name of his birthplace. He was also called Kusa the Teacher because he was learned in various treatises. He was a great hidden yogin.

It is said that he opened Parochal Rock, which was shaped like a scorpion's claw, and revealed four terma coffers. From the container shaped like a bell, he drew forth Buddhist terma dharma; from one shaped like a basin, Bön terma; from one shaped like a surgical instrument, medicinal terma; and from one shaped like an astrological chart, terma concerning divination. Nowadays, only the text and transmission of his *Rasayana Using Anise* still exist; I've encountered nothing else from his vast Buddhist termas. The *Black Kila* from among his Bön termas, however, was passed down to Gartön, and its empowerment, transmission, and practice have flourished; it is said to bear great blessing.

Among the three categories of gurusadhana, Great Perfection, and Mahakarunika sadhana, the gurusadhana *Very Profound Embodiment of the Three Jewels* was revealed as terma three times. The earliest of these three was revealed by this great tertön, Kusa the Physician. It was called the *Great Embodiment of All the Three Roots* and was a vast dharma cycle. The dispensation of its quintessence was received by our lord guru Padma Ösal Dongak Lingpa as rediscovered terma.

The second of the three *Embodiment of the Three Jewels* termas was that revealed by Jatsön Nyingpo, Ugyen Letro Lingpa. Known by the name *Embodiment of the Three Jewels*, this cycle is one in which the three roots transform into one another. Our lord guru Padma Ösal Dongak Lingpa received this from both short and long lineages.

The third of the three *Embodiment of the Three Jewels* termas was revealed by our lord guru Padma Ösal Dongak Lingpa in the form of terma scrolls that appeared at the sacred site of Padma Shelri. It is called the *Principal Three Roots: The Heart Essence of the Embodiment of the Three Jewels*. As I have received the root empowerment and transmission of this cycle, it is fitting to assert that I have received all three lineages of the *Embodiment of the Three Jewels*.

Kusa the Physician lived during the early life of Guru Chöwang, and was clearly a contemporary of Yutokpa. Some Bön histories claim that Kusa and Yutokpa were not two different people, but the same person. That, however, is impossible.

Lhabum the Bönpo

Then:

> Wild armies will conquer the higher north.
> The holy dharma in Tibet will split into three.
> Buddhism will be nurtured by kama and terma.
> These will be the signs that the time has come to reveal
> The terma concealed at the border of Tsang.
> Aya Lhabum the Bönpo will appear.

The tertön Lhabum the Bönpo was an emanation of both Vairochana and Drenpa Namkha. He was born in the Tanak region of Tsang, and was a contemporary of Dromtönpa. Lhabum lived as a Bön mantrin. He is also known in the Bön tradition by the name Guru Nöntse. It is well known that Lhabum revealed a great deal of terma—Buddhist terma, Bön terma, medicine, and astrology—from Conch Bowl Rock in Tanak, near the Tsang border. However, among the Buddhist terma only the reading transmission for a minor ransom ritual has survived. Among his Bön terma, the empowerments, transmissions, and instructions for the generation and completion stages of the *Mother Tantra: The Supreme Secret Sun of Compassion*, a vast cycle, have flourished down to the present and are highly valued by masters of the Bön tradition.

Recently, our lord guru Padma Ösal Dongak Lingpa received the dispensation of the gurusadhana, Great

Perfection, and Mahakarunika practices of Lhabum's *Essence of Samvara* cycle as rediscovered terma.

Khyungpo Palge

Then:

> Dharma of the five poisons will appear in U, Tsang, and Kham.
> Dharma teachers with wrong views will cleverly suppress the teachings.
> Calling it "service," they will bind the dharma.
> These will be the signs that the time has come to reveal
> The terma concealed at Bumthang in Bhutan.
> The tertön called Khyungpo Palge will appear.

The tertön Khyungpo Palge was an emanation of Vairochana. He was born at Lhatö in Tsang. His family name was Khyungpo, and his personal name Palge. He lived as an ordinary noble mantrin.

As indicated in prophecies from the past, at the time of Lha Lama Yeshe Ö there appeared eighteen acharyas who, having achieved mundane siddhi, spread the incorrect dharma of engaging in literal union and liberation. It is clear that Khyungpo Palge lived at that time.

In Bumthang Khyungpo revealed both Buddhist and Bön termas, including the *Six Profound Sections*. It is also well known that he revealed a great deal of terma—including teachings on Buddhism, Bön, medicine, and divination—from Mount Hepo. Because of the passing of so much time, I have been unable to locate either copies or transmission lineages of any of his termas. Recently, however, our lord guru Padma Ösal Dongak Lingpa received the dispensation of the quintessence of the *Six Profound Sections*.

Shami Dorgyal

Then:

All the monasteries in Tibet will prepare for battle.
A temple will appear on the red hill of Lhasa.
Lakes of swans and geese will dry up. Meadows will be covered with sand.
These will be the signs that the time has come to reveal
The terma concealed on Mount Hepo in Gegye.
The tertön called Shami Dorgyal will appear.

The tertön Shami Dorgyal was the rebirth of the translator Shami Gocha, and was blessed by the great translator Nyak. Dorgyal was born in Shami Tradu in Shang. Shami was his family name. He lived as a noble mantrin. As he was learned in various sutras and tantras, he was known as Shami the Teacher.

He revealed a vast terma called the *Intended Meaning: the Profound Drop Liberating All Beings*. It is also said that he revealed much other terma, of both dharma and wealth. Because of the passing of so much time, I have been unable to locate either copies or transmission lineages of any of his termas. Nevertheless, it appears that the *Intended Meaning: the Profound Drop Liberating All Beings* was an extensive treatise describing all the vehicles, based on the intended meaning of *Instructions on the Garland of Views*, which is an explanation of the stages of the path according to the Guhyagarbhatantra.

A less extensive version of the same treatise is *Four Cycles on the Garland*, a destined terma of Jetsün Taranatha, as is clearly stated in his secret biography. A concise version was revealed by the mahasiddha Thangtong Gyalpo in the form of terma scrolls at Samye Chimphu. Thangtong Gyalpo also received the extensive version directly from Guru Rinpoche, as well as the intermediate version from the lineage of

Taranatha. He therefore possessed all three versions: extensive, intermediate, and concise.

Our lord guru Padma Ösal Dongak Lingpa has received the dispensation of the essence of the extensive version as rediscovered terma. He has also received the concise version, *Five Quintessential Sadhanas,* as profound mind terma through the blessing of the mahasiddha Thangtong Gyalpo. I have had the good fortune to receive from him the wondrous vajra words of the transcribed text of this.

Dangma Lhungyal

Then:

> False tertöns of false terma will say they are my emanations.
> They will gather around them all those with broken samaya.
> They will fool disciples and teach meaningless dharma.
> These thieves of dharma will spread their corrupt termas.
> Apostates will proliferate like herds of goats.
> Even I, Padmakara, will be saddened and distressed.
> These will be the signs that the time has come to reveal
> The terma concealed by Vimala in the Temple of Sha.
> Vimala's emanation, Dangma Lhungyal, will appear.

One hundred years after Nyangben Tingdzin Zangpo achieved the body of light without remainder, Vimalamitra saw that the time had come to disseminate his profound *Heart Essence*, which had been concealed as terma. Through his miraculous blessing, Vimalamitra took intentional rebirth in Sholung, near Drikung in western central Tibet, as the son of a man named Dangma Gechok. He became known as Lhungyi Gyaltsen, and lived as a noble, short-haired mantrin. He served for many years as the custodian of the Urusha Temple.

During that time, due to a prophecy he received from Vajrasadhu, he revealed from a cave adjacent to the temple the terma that had been concealed there by Vimalamitra, King Trisong, and Nyangben Tingdzin Zangpo. This was the *Great Secret Heart Essence*, also called *Vimalamitra's Heart Essence*. Along with it Dangma Lhungyal found the vast Seventeen Tantras, their protector practices, and their commentaries. He also revealed one hundred and ninety writings of instruction and other texts, all in the original manuscripts. He then received the secret kama lineage from Bay Lodrö Wangchuk. In order that the profound meaning not be left to mere speculation, Dangma Lhungyal practiced, and demonstrated the attainment of a high level on the path.

Fifteen years after retrieving this profound terma, Dangma Lhungyal went in search of a fit vessel for these instructions. In upper Nyang, he met a man called Chetsün Senge Wangchuk, to whom he imparted the seven stages of instruction. Dangma also imparted them soon thereafter to Karak Gomchung, who was liberated by them. Not long after that, Dangma Lhungyal passed away. When he did so, the sky became filled with rainbows, and his remains produced countless relics. In that way, he achieved the wisdom of manifest awakening while leaving remnants of his physical aggregate. He was the king of all tertön siddhas.

Later, Dangma's disciple, the great Chetsün, was accepted as a direct disciple by Vimalamitra. As instructed by Vimalamitra, Chetsün revealed the texts of the *Four Profound Volumes* from Chimphu. Chetsün then meditated for seven years in the mountains of Oyuk Chigong, and passed away without any remaining aggregates.

Chetsün taught Shangtön Tashi Dorje, who practiced these instructions and then revealed the remaining *Heart Essence* teachings from Lion Rock at Oyuk and from Chimphu. That is why this *Great Heart Essence* is known as the collected terma of three tertöns.

The dispensation of these complete instructions descended

to the omniscient Drime Özer, who was the actual reappearance of Vimalamitra.[42] Through his vast *Seven Treasuries*, such as the *Treasury of the Supreme Vehicle*; and through his profound two *Heart Quintessences*, he filled the Himalayan region with this teaching's ripening empowerments, liberating instructions, and supporting transmissions. All of these have flourished down to the present day, and I have received them.

42. Drime Özer and Dorje Ziji are two of the many names of the omniscient Longchenpa.

Drapa Ngönshe

Then:

> Jing and China will become like scattered nests of ants.
> This will be the sign that the time has come to reveal
> The terma concealed in the three islands of the queens.
> The tertön called Drapa Ngönshe will appear.
> He will cover the earth with a hundred and eight monasteries.
> He will build a great temple in Drada.
> He will govern the temple built by the king.

The tertön Drapa Ngönshe is known to have been an emanation of Shubu Palgyi Senge, but he was also an emanation of Vairochana. He was born in the Male Water Rat Year of the first cycle, at Yorudra Khyiru, to the family line of Chim Dorje Treuchung.[43]

43. The year was 1072 C.E.

As his predisposition to holy dharma awoke within him during his youth, he went to the dharma college at Samye and undertook renunciation in the presence of Yamshu Gyalpo Ö, a successor to the great abbot Lumay. Drapa Ngönshe acquired his name from his birthplace, Dra, and from his vast knowledge of the abhidharma.[44] His actual renunciation name was Wangchuk Bar.

44. Drapa Ngönshe means "man from Dra who knows the abhidharma."

From above the door to the central temple of Samye, Drapa Ngönshe revealed the *Secret Sadhana of Red Jambhala* and the *Tantra and Sadhana of Yaksha Dorje Düdül*. In particular, as predicted by the protector Shanglön, Drapa Ngönshe revealed the manuscripts of the *Four Glorious Tantras of Medicine* as translated by the great translator Vairochana. He brought them out from a column in the middle storey of the central temple of Samye three hours after midnight on the full moon day in the first autumn month in the Male Earth Tiger Year.[45] He copied the manuscripts and put them back where he had found them. He kept his copies secret for a year, and then gave them to Kutön Tarma Drak, the kalyanamitra from Yarlung, who passed them on to Yutok Yönten Gönpo, who was like a second Baishajyaguru for this Himalayan region. The benefit and activity that have resulted from these tantras are unimaginably great and wondrous.

Drapa Ngönshe accomplished Jambhala and received the siddhi of the acquisition of gold. He used this to build the great and glorious dharma college of Drathang in Dra, and many other monasteries as well. He served as their abbot, and as the abbot of Samye's college, and was thus a great kalyanamitra.

The empowerments and transmissions for the two yaksha sadhanas mentioned above, and the explanation and transmission lineages for the *Four Tantras of Medicine* have continued unbroken, and we have received them completely. Our lord guru Padma Ösal Dongak Lingpa has also received the dispensation for a profound and concise *Sadhana of Red Vajrapani* that was originally a terma of Drapa Ngönshe.

Rashak the Great

Then:

> I, Uddiyana, will emanate a physician in eastern Nyal.
> A herd of meditators on the essence will gather around
>   Dakpo the Meditator.
> This will be the sign that the time has come to reveal
> The terma concealed at Chimphu Komting.
> The tertön called Rashak, skilled in ransoming, will appear.

45. The year was 1098 C.E.

The nirmanakaya Rashak the Great was an emanation of both Vairochana and Drokmi Palgyi Yeshe. He was born to the Nyen family in the upper nomad region. He became known by the names Rashak Chöbar and Sönam Dorje. In his youth he studied ransoming rituals and medicine, and became learned in both. He was also a great yogin of mantra, and became an immortal vidyadhara.

From Paro Tsal Rock he revealed the tantras and instructions of the *Mamo Gangshar*, profound dharma that raised the terminology and practice of the Matrikas of Existence to the status of an independent tradition. He also revealed the *Great Book of the Matrikas of Existence*, the *Matrikas' Great Ransom Effigy of the Four Continents*, the Bön terma called the *Nine Ransom Effigies of Vast Creation*, treatises on medical diagnosis, sadhanas of powerful mundane beings, and many other termas.

Nowadays the *Ten Secret Ransom Effigies* cycle is very well known. The lineage of the *Mamo Gangshar Chenmo* became very rare, but I diligently searched for it and have received its complete empowerments and transmissions from both long and short unbroken lineages. This is yet another example of my good fortune. The source of the instructions which have come down from Jetsün Milarepa concerning Tseringma and her four sisters was a terma text actually given to the Jetsün by Rashak the Great, as is explained in authentic histories of the terma tradition.

Nyangral Nyima Özer

Then:

A time of unrest will appear throughout the land.
Mantrins will practice magic; laymen will try to repel it.
The killing of a thousand people will be rewarded with
    statues and scripture.
People will be led from one place to another.

These will be the signs that the time has come to reveal
The termas concealed at Sinmo Barjay and Komting.
The king's emanation, Nyangral, will appear.

Guru Rinpoche also predicted:

There will be five kingly tertöns with a thousand subjects.

He predicted five kingly tertöns and three supreme nirmanakayas. The first of the five kingly tertöns was Nyangral Nyima Özer, who was the intentional rebirth of the dharma king Trisong Detsen. Nyangral was born in the Male Fire Dragon Year of the second cycle at Dzesa Sergön in Lhodrak.[46] His father was Nyangtön Chökyi Khorlo, and his mother was Padma Dewa Tsal.

From early childhood, Nyangral exhibited countless wondrous signs. In his eighth year he had visions of the bhagavat Shakyamuni Buddha, Avalokita, Guru Rinpoche, and others. For one month he remained immersed in visionary experience. In particular, one night he saw Guru Rinpoche astride a white horse, with the steed's four feet supported by dakinis of the four families. Guru Rinpoche bestowed the four empowerments with a vase, causing Nyang to undergo three experiences that were like the sky splitting, the earth moving, and a mountain shaking. Based on these experiences, Nyang did various strange things, causing everyone around him to think he had become insane.

He received the empowerment of Hayagriva from his father, practiced at Jöpu Gangra, and saw the deity's face. His copper kila neighed like a horse, and he left handprints and footprints in rock.

As prophesied by dakinis, Nyang went to Mawochok Rock, where the wisdom dakinis gave him the name by which he has been known ever since, Nyima Özer. Guru Rinpoche appeared to him as a yogin called Wangchuk Dorje, gave him lists of his termas as well as a letter of instructions, and advised him. Nyang also acquired the terma lists of Drapa

46. The year was 1136 C.E.

Ngönshe and Rashak the Great. He then went to the terma site Sinmo Barjay. He stayed there for one night. On the next day, a woman who was an emanation of Yeshe Tsogyal appeared, leading a white mule. On the mule's back were two coffers. She unloaded one of them—the one covered in tigerskin—and offered it to Nyang. He also found the site's terma door, and brought out from it a great deal of terma, including a copper coffer, a clay vase, a statue, samaya substances, and jewels. From the copper coffer Nyang revealed the *Mahakarunika Cycle* and the *Peaceful and Wrathful Guru Cycles*. From the clay vase he revealed the *Protector Cycle* and teachings on magic. From the tigerskin coffer appeared an extensive *Dakini Cycle*.

Then a merchant gave Nyang a statue's broken forefinger. Inside he found a terma list. Using it, he revealed two coffers from behind the image of Vairochana at Komting. One of the coffers was brown and one was gray. Within the brown coffer appeared the tantras, agamas, and upadeshas of the *Eight Dispensations: the Assembly of Sugatas*. Within the gray coffer appeared supports of Hayagriva's body, speech, and mind, as well as samaya substances. Nyang also revealed many other termas from such sites as Samye Chimphu and Sky-Ladder Owl Rock, as well as from various isolated places, mountains, and temples.

Nyang studied under many masters, including his father, the great Nyangtön; Gya the Meaningful Madman; Shikpo Nyima Senge; Malka Chenpa; and Tönpa Khache. From them he learned a great deal of both the causal vehicle and mantra. He practiced the *Sadhana of the Trikaya Guru* for three years, during which time he directly met Guru Padma and received much teaching from him. While Nyang was practicing the *Sadhana of the Guru's Mind* at Pearl Crystal Collar Cave, Yeshe Tsogyal appeared to him and gave him a copy of *Answers to the Dakini's Hundred Questions*. She then brought Nyang to the Shitavana charnel ground in India, where he received the complete general and specific empowerments, tantras, and upadeshas of the eight dispensations from Guru Rinpoche and the eight vidyadharas who hold them.

Nyang married a woman named Jobuma, who was an emanation of Yeshe Tsogyal. They had two sons: Drogön Namkha Özer, and the Avalokita emanation Namkha Pal.

When Ngödrup the Siddha visited his area, Nyang told him about his *Eight Dispensations* terma. Ngödrup told Nyang that he held the kama lineage of the *Fortress and Precipice*. Nyang received this from Ngödrup, and thus united the streams of the terma and kama lineages of the eight dispensations. Ngödrup the Siddha also gave Nyang the five scrolls of the *Mahakarunika Cycle* that he had revealed in Lhasa, and said to him, "You are the holder of these."

While Nyang was performing an amrita accomplishment ceremony, a goddess of herbal medicine appeared and offered him a fresh arura fruit with its leaves. He also displayed countless miracles, such as moving through space without uncrossing his legs and walking without his feet touching the ground.

Nyang devoted his entire life to meditation, accomplishment, and teaching. The activity of his termas since his time has equaled space in its extent; Nyang's impact has been inconceivable.

In his sixty-ninth year, the Year of the Male Wood Rat, he withdrew the array of his body amidst many wondrous miracles, and went to Sukhavati in the form of a white HRIH emitted from his heart.[47] He predicted the appearance of emanations of his body, speech, and mind. Chak the Translator attempted to cremate Nyang's remains, but was unable to light the cremation fire. The remains later burst into flame spontaneously. All those present saw many wonders, such as an eight-year-old boy surrounded by dakinis exclaiming HA RI NI SA within the cremation chamber. The cremated remains also produced extraordinary relics.

The mahapandita Shakyashri and his retinue were invited to

---

47. The year was 1204 C.E.

preside over the main funerary observances, and were offered a vast amount of gold. Nyang's sons requested the mahapandita's permission to undertake renunciation in his presence, but he refused them, saying, "You, like your father, are great bodhisattvas. I cannot bring an end to a family line of bodhisattvas. You will bring more benefit to beings as you are."

Because of Shakyashri's extensive praise of both Nyang and his dharma, Nyang became as famous in Tibet as the sun and moon. Although Nyang had already been widely acknowledged as an undisputedly authentic great tertön, whatever incorrect ideas those of the Sarma traditions may have had about him were dispelled by the mahapandita's endorsement.

Nyang's greatest disciple was his son, Drogön Namkha Pal. He was the inheritor of all his father's teachings and received the dispensation of all of his ripening empowerments and liberating instructions. Namkha Pal's son was an emanation of Manjushri called Loden Sherap. Loden Sherap's son was an emanation of Vajrapani called Düdül. In that way, the line from Nyang's son onward became the succession of the nirmanakayas of the three families predicted in his termas.

Nyang's many disciples included the five inheritors of dispensation: his two sons, Nyö Drakgyal, Shikpo Dutsi, and Menlungpa Mikyö Dorje. They and other disciples spread Nyang's teachings all over Tibet, so that the activity of Nyang's dharma has remained all-pervasive down to the present.

Although it would be fitting to describe the life of this great tertön in more detail, extensive biographies of the successive lives of Nyang and his sons and accounts of his revelations already exist. They may be found in the appropriate section of the index to the *Nyingma Tantras*. Fearing writing at excessive length, I have just set forth their briefest essence here.

Nyang's profound termas are as great as an ocean. Those that still exist include the biography of Guru Rinpoche called *Copper Island*, the *Sadhanas of the Peaceful and Wrathful Gurus*, *Mahakarunika Who Tames Beings*, *King Tradition*

Mahakarunika, the *Five Deity Jinasagara*, the *Eight Dispensations: the Assembly of Sugatas*, the *Great Dakini Sadhana* and the *Sadhana of Krodhikali*, the *Four-Armed Terma Protector* and its *Warfare Prevention Ceremony*, and the *Dharmapala Matrika of the Charnel Grounds*. I have supported this tradition a little by diligently seeking out and receiving their extensive empowerments and transmissions, by sponsoring the reprinting of the nine volumes of Nyang's *Eight Dispensations* and some of his other termas, and also through repeated approach practice and assemblies of great accomplishment.[48]

48. Approach, close approach, accomplishment, and great accomplishment are four stages in the practice of any yidam.

Wönsay Khyungtok

Then:

> The king of Purong will search for gold in central Tibet.
> Clans will be scattered and fight over land.
> These will be the signs that the time has come to reveal
> The terma concealed at Drompa Gyang.
> The tertön called Wönsay Khyungtok will appear.

The tertön Wönsay Khyungtok is said to have lived at the time when the king Jangchup Ö levied a poll tax on Tibetan monastics in order to gather the gold needed to bring Lord Atisha to Tibet. The year and place of Khyungtok's birth are unclear in early accounts of his revelations. However, if other early writings are correct, he was born near Latö Lhatse to a family of Bön lamas called Wönsay. His name was Khyungtok Tsal, and he lived as a Bön mantradharin.

It is well known that through Vairochana's blessing Khyungtok revealed a large body of profound terma—including Buddhist, Bön, medical, astrological, and magical teachings—from the Rulak Drompa Gyang Temple. Because it was so long ago, however, I have been unable to find copies or lineages of any of his Buddhist or Bön termas. Recently, Padma

Ösal Dongak Lingpa received the dispensation of part of Khyungtok's *Immortal Heart Essence of Samantabhadra* as a rediscovery.

In any case, Khyungtok benefited beings throughout his long life, which he lived as a hidden yogin. It is evident that his dharmic influence was less than it might have been because he remained an ordinary village mantrin. At the end of his long life, it is clear that people witnessed his body dissolve into light and become a white letter A, which dissolved into the sky.

It is certain that this Khyungtok was the one predicted in the Testament. However, Bönpos refer to the Vidyadhara Vulture Feathers as Wönsay Khyungtok, and it appears that his *Indian Life Empowerment* and *Life Accomplishment of Drenpa Namkha*, which come from his *Iron Treasury of the North*, are still widely practiced in the Bön tradition.

Later, at the time of the vidyadhara Chöje Lingpa, there appeared in Latö a tertön called Takmo Wönsay Khyungtok. He received the lists and prophecies concerning his termas, and is considered an authentic tertön. It seems, however, that his activity and benefit of beings were not vast. A little about his life will appear later in this book.

Ramo Shelmen

Then:

> Even those who've not been to India will be called translators.
> All the wise and chaste in Tibet will be cast out of the land.
> A new regime, Mongolian patronage, will arise.
> It will be like a conch shell, white without and black within.
> Tibet's merit will decrease steadily.
> These will be the signs that the time has come to reveal

The terma concealed at Lotus Crystal Cave.
The tertön called Ramo Shelmen will appear.

The tertön Ramo Shelmen was an emanation of Nyak Jnanakumara. He was born in Ramo Menchuka in western Yarlung. He lived as an ordinary mantrin and physician. Ramo Shelmen was his nickname; his actual name was Yeshe Zangpo. He revealed gurusadhanas, Great Perfection teachings, Mahakarunika sadhanas, and a *Vajramritasadhana* from Piled Lotus Rock at the Crystal Cave of Yarlung, which was also a terma site of Ugyen Lingpa. Ramo Shelmen also revealed teachings on medicine from Clear Light Fortress near the Menchu River.

Although Ramo Shelmen revealed a large amount of profound terma, he publicly emphasized the practice of medicine, and it seems that his dharma activity was not vast. Nevertheless, he indirectly placed hundreds of thousands of beings on the path to freedom, and it is clear from the prophecies among his termas that everyone who put any of his medicine in their mouths achieved liberation within seven lives. I therefore regard his achievement as unimaginably wondrous. A hot spring appeared where he performed an amrita accomplishment ceremony. This spring, known to dispel all illness and demonic harassment, still exists and has tremendous blessing. A stupa was built where some of the amrita he created dissolved into the ground; circumambulation of it frees one from sickness, although nowadays it is just a mound on the ground.

One winter Ramo Shelmen performed an amrita accomplishment ceremony in his residence in Yarlung at which medicine goddesses and dakinis visibly gathered. He concealed some of the powdered amrita substances in a nearby rock, and a wondrous medicinal tree grew there. For many years this amazing tree continued to flower in winter, at the time of year when the amrita accomplishment had been performed. The *Secret Remedy for Dropsy*, a medicinal technique that comes from Ramo's termas, has been used continuously down to the present, and its correct application is still known. I have witnessed the unimaginable benefit this brings to beings. It is said that the use of onions in treating dropsy is also derived from this terma. Other than these medical recipes, no copies or transmissions of Ramo's termas survived the long period between his time and ours. After their disappearance, however, the dakinis offered our lord guru Padma Ösal Dongak Lingpa the Sanskrit text of the *Three Cycles of Vajramrita*, which our lord guru translated into Tibetan as a rediscovered terma. The words and meaning of this treatise are wondrous, and it has the majesty of unbroken blessing. Our lord guru has kindly bestowed its ripening empowerments and liberating instructions on us, and I have done a few things in service to this tradition including the performance of its approach and accomplishment and the composition of supplementary writings in aid of its dissemination.

Guru Chökyi Wangchuk

Then:

> During the Sakya regime, Mongolian armies will invade Tibet.
> The suffering then will be worse than in the lower realms.
> Many people will die in defense of independence.
> Beings will be trampled into the earth.
> These will be the signs that the time has come to reveal
> The terma concealed at Sky Ladder in Karchu.
> The tertön called Chökyi Wangchuk will appear.

The second of the tertöns called the "five kings and the three supreme nirmanakayas" was the precious guru Chökyi Wangchuk.

When the dharma king Trisong Detsen was reborn as Lord Nyang Rinpoche, he achieved the final fruition, buddhahood, the level called "lotus free from attachment." Chökyi Wangchuk was his subsequent emanation of speech.

He was born in Lhodrak, to a family that had continuously possessed magical power since the time of King Trisong. Chökyi Wangchuk's father was Pangtön Drupay Nyingpo. His mother, Karza Gönkyi, was a descendant of dakinis. Chökyi Wangchuk was born at sunrise on the fifteenth day of the first month of spring in the Year of the Monkey amid great, wondrous miracles.[49] At the time of his birth a copy of the *Recitation of Manjushri's Names*, written in gold ink, was being recited. He was born at the moment the name Chökyi Wangchuk was read, and was therefore given that name. Even before Chökyi Wangchuk's birth many mahasiddhas, including Drikung Kyopa and Shang Rinpoche, had predicted to his father that he would have an extraordinary son.

Chökyi Wangchuk began to learn to read and write in his fourth year. He went on to study exhaustively all aspects of knowledge and culture, including even the *Great Treatise on Thread-Cross Ransom Rituals*. He received countless instructions from his father; from the lord Tsurtön, the protector of beings, and his son; and from many other gurus of the Sarma and Nyingma traditions. These included the sutras; the Sarma and Nyingma traditions of guhyamantra; the ripening empowerments, liberating instructions, and explanation lineages of the kama and terma traditions; Pacification; Severance; the Six Dharmas; Mahamudra; and the Great Perfection. In between receiving these, he practiced their respective approach and accomplishment phases.

During his thirteenth year he had a vision in which Arya Tara led him to the top of a crystal palace where he met Vajrasattva and a dakini with four faces. From her four faces issued prophecies of how he would spread the teachings and tame those difficult to tame.

During his eighteenth year Chökyi Wangchuk received the bodhisattva vow and other teachings from the great Sakya

---

49. The year was 1212 C.E.

Pandita. Chökyi Wangchuk dreamed at the time that he went to Five-Peak Mountain in China and met Manjushri there. Manjushri gave him extraordinary instructions, and Chökyi Wangchuk gained the certainty that he had received the essence of all dharma.

He acquired a terma list that had originally been discovered by Drapa Ngönshe. Using this list, in his twenty-second year Chökyi Wangchuk found a further list at Layanyin Sky Ladder. He was given the key to the terma door by the terma protector—a nine-headed naga—and a wisdom dakini appearing as his mother. He opened the door to the terma enclosure and found inside it a vulture the size of a garuda. Riding on this bird, Chökyi Wangchuk ascended through thirteen levels of space. Above them all he came to a tent of swirling rainbow light, within which he met the Buddha Vajrasattva, who bestowed upon him the empowerment of awareness-display and blessed him with a vase of amrita.

Returning to the terma site indicated in the list he again opened its door and found a cubit-sized, cast metal image of a nine-headed naga and a copper reliquary. Within the naga image he found the *Four Cycles of Instruction*; within the reliquary he found the *Hundred and Eight Upadeshas*.

Chökyi Wangchuk's father accepted the authenticity of these dharma termas, and advised his son to complete the practices of gurusadhana, Great Perfection, and Mahakarunika; and to not widely disseminate the application practices. The lord Tsurtön, the protector of beings, also declared his approval.

This was the first of the eighteen great terma revelations—nineteen including his mind terma—of Chökyi Wangchuk. He listed them as follows:

(1) Sky Ladder, (2) Red Rock, (3) Hayagriva's Feet,
(4) Mönkha Teng, (5) Hayagriva, (6) Wentsaygo,
(7) Red Yamari at Ko, (8) Hayagriva, (9) Dromchö Pass,
(10) Saykar, (11) Long Grey Cave, (12) Thumb Rock,

(13) Aryapalo Ling at Samye, (14) Iron Kila, (15) Bumthang in Bhutan,
(16) Temple of the Stars, (17) Rongdrak, (18) Hawo Snows,
And (19) the self-concealed ultimate terma:
Through karma I, Chöwang, encountered these.

As described in the *Dream of the White Horse*, the *Dream of the Black Hat*, and his other writings on the subject, in the Earth Rat Year, Chökyi Wangchuk traveled in a vision to Lotus Light in Chamaradvipa.[50] When he arrived there, Guru Rinpoche and an assembly of vidyadharas were performing a great accomplishment ceremony, and gave him countless empowerments, instructions, and prophecies.

Chökyi Wangchuk performed many miracles such as simultaneously displaying six bodies, flying through the sky, and leaving handprints and footprints in rock. He was therefore venerated not only by Nyingmapas; even the omniscient Pak Ö, Chö Ö, and Butön Rinpoche praised him, saying, "Guru Chökyi Wangchuk is a peerless mahasiddha!"

Chökyi Wangchuk clearly remembered thirteen successive lives, starting with the dharma king Trisong's immediate rebirth as the deva Boundless Light and culminating in his life as Nyangral. Chökyi Wangchuk received the homage of devas including Indra. All of the spirits of Tibet venerated him as their guru. His fame shook the world. He built two temples: Tsongdü Gurmo and Samdrup Dewa Chenpo. He also discovered an image of Shakyamuni that was similar to the Jowo of Lhasa. The image that he found had once been concealed by Arya Nagarjuna. After its initial recovery, Guru Rinpoche brought it to Tibet and concealed it on Mount Hepo. The tertön brought it to the Layak Guru Temple, which became his principal seat. While he lived there, all the great lamas of Tibet, and all its people of high rank, touched his feet.

His descendants have included a succession of extraordinary individuals such as Padma Wangchen, an emanation of

50. The year was 1228 C.E.

Langdro the Translator; and Nyal Nyima Özer. Chökyi Wangchuk's main disciples included Menlungpa Mikyö Dorje, who was a great scholar of all the Nyingma teachings, both kama and terma; the Nepalese Bharo Tsukdzin; the "nine worthy disciples"; and Mani Rinchen of Kathok, who went to a pure realm without leaving his body behind.

Chökyi Wangchuk's disciples and their followers all achieved the high level of siddhas. Their wide dissemination of his profound dharma, and especially his *Mahakarunika Cycle*, in India and Nepal and throughout all of Tibet led to a succession of these teachings that still exists.

When he had completed his great and wondrous deeds, Chökyi Wangchuk passed away and went to the great palace of Lotus Light in his fifty-ninth year while displaying unimaginable miracles.

Starting from his time, whenever two mantrins would meet on a road they would ask one another, "Are you of the former or the latter terma tradition?"[51] In this way, Chökyi Wangchuk was a great chariot of the profound termas. This siddha was a king among all tertöns. His extensive autobiography describing his body, speech, mind, qualities, and activity still exists both as text and transmission. Its essence can be found in the *Index to the Nyingma Tantras*. What I have written here is no more than a seed of his life.

The eighteen termas he revealed include *Guru Guhyasamaja* and four other gurusadhana cycles, along with their accessories; *Mahakarunika: The Quintessence*; the *Emptier of Samsara to its Bottom*; the *Great Perfection: The Union of All Buddhas*; the *Eight Dispensations: The Complete Secrets*; the *Sky-Ladder of Dawn*; *Black Hayagriva*; *Perfect Heruka: The Essence of Great Bliss*; *Wrathful Vajrapani Who Roars Like a Lion*; *Vajrakilaya: The Razor*; the *Wild Rishi Loktripala*; and the *Glorious Neutral Protector*.

We have diligently sought out and received the empowerments and transmissions of all of these, as well as those of

51. The *Former* and *Subsequent Termas* are those of Nyangral and Guru Chöwang respectively.

Chökyi Wangchuk's minor termas and his collected writings, and have performed some of their approach and accomplishment practices.[52] As these two terma traditions—the former and the latter—are like the roots of all other terma, I pray that all great holders of the Nyingma teachings receive, transmit, and practice them. By doing so, you will fan and relight the coals of the teachings!

52. "We refers to Jamgön Kongtrül and Jamyang Khyentse Wangpo in this sentence.

Guru Jotsay

Then:

> The drums of war will pound at Raven Castle.
> Cowards will throw gold dust into the water.
> These will be the signs that the time has come to reveal
> The terma concealed at Copper Rock.
> The tertön called Guru Jotsay will appear.

The tertön Guru Jotsay was, according to the predictions in his termas, an emanation of Prince Mutik Tsenpo. It is clearly stated in the terma predictions of Sangye Lingpa that Guru Jotsay was Sangye Lingpa's preceding birth, in which case Guru Jotsay would appear to have also been an emanation of Prince Murup Tsenpo. In any case, Guru Jotsay was a unified emanation of their united compassion. He was born in Nyeda in eastern Kyi to a family of ordinary mantrins. As he lived as an ordinary mantrin, he acquired the nickname Guru Jowo; his actual name was Tsewang Darpo.

During his youth he was poor and worked as a shepherd and goatherd. Upon maturity he discovered a terma list. This led him to an accomplishment cave of Guru Rinpoche's. The cave was behind a small nunnery at a place now known as Copper Rock, but then called Red Rock Copper Sky Fortress. This is behind a five-peaked mountain in eastern Kyi.

From the cave Jotsay brought forth about thirty volumes of profound terma; wondrous, inexhaustible, ever-increasing relics of the Buddha; a hundred and eight images of Guru Rinpoche; and all the kilas used by Guru Rinpoche during the Vajrakilaya accomplishment he performed at Samye in order to tame the earth there. These kilas had multiplied over time, so that there were more than five hundred of them at the time of their discovery.

Guru Jotsay entrusted most of this vast terma, including both dharma and supports, to the king of Gyere, Rinchen Wangyal, who was descended from the Buddhist rulers of Nyö. Not very much benefit for beings occurred through Jotsay's dharma termas, but the relics have brought endless benefit. There is no doubt that most of the principal kilas discovered by Guru Jotsay are now at Ngödrup Ding in Tölungda. Many other kilas, said to be from Guru Jotsay's terma, have appeared up to the present. I have found no copies or transmissions of any of his terma dharma other than his brief *Ishvara's Wind Lasso* and his *Ransom Ritual Using a Hundred Pieces of Meat and a Hundred Pieces of Dough*. As a sign that our lord guru Padma Ösal Dongak Lingpa has received the dispensation of all termas, he has revealed as rediscovered terma Jotsay's *Confession and Offerings to the Peaceful and Wrathful Ones*, which is based on the *Tantra of Confession*.

Padma Wangchuk

Then:

> The Tachu River will flow into the Drichu inside a temple.
> Sholung will be menaced by fire.
> Weapons will fall like rain in Palmo Palthang.
> These will be the signs that the time has come to reveal
> The terma concealed at Gangbar Cave.
> The tertön called Padma Wangchuk will appear.

The tertön Padma Wangchuk was born to the Gya family in

western Jang. As he was learned in sutra and tantra he was known as a teacher. Padma Wangchuk was his actual name. This great emanated tertön lived as a renunciate, and was one of two emanations of the great translator Gyalwa Chokyang. From a boulder marked by a joy swirl within the great Gangbar Cave in western Eyül, Padma Wangchuk revealed a vast amount of terma including gurusadhanas; Great Perfection instructions; Mahakarunika sadhanas; samaya amrita that liberates through taste; and *Overpowering the Aggressive*, a sadhana of the Panjara Protector composed by Guru Rinpoche and accompanied by instructions. Both the text and the transmission of that cycle are still available as part of the *Sakya Protector Volume*.

I had not encountered any of Padma Wangchuk's termas other than those concerning the Panjara Protector when recently the precious lord Padma Ösal Dongak Lingpa received from dakinis the terma text of Padma Wangchuk's wondrous, profound, and concise *Generation and Completion of the Guru Red Chakrasamvara*. He has transcribed this as rediscovered terma. I have received it from him, have formed a connection with it through practice, and have served its activity slightly by writing needed supplements.

Doben Gyamtso

Then:

A little man of grass will be born at the Silma Pass.
A crystal boulder will burst forth at the Mön Pass.
These will be the signs that the time has come to reveal
The terma concealed at Yama Pagong.
The tertön called Doben Gyamtso will appear.

The tertön Doben Gyamtso was a rebirth of the prince Chokdrup Gyalpo, the fourth of thirteen such rebirths as a tertön. Doben was born to the Yonpo Dorjak family on an island in a lake in the nomad country. As he lived as a mantrin-monk, he was called Doben, a combination of *Do*, from Dorjak; and *ben*, monk. His name was Gyamtso Ö, and he was clearly a disciple of Zur Pakshi Shakya Ö.

From Mutik Pamagong in the upper nomad country, Doben revealed gurusadhanas and Great Perfection instructions. From Drakyangdzong he revealed a cycle of teachings on forceful mantra. Although his termas were many, I have not found any existing copies or transmissions of them. Recently our lord guru Padma Ösal Dongak Lingpa received the essence of Doben's gurusadhanas as a rediscovered terma.

It appears that the prophecy quoted above refers, in describing "the signs that the time has come," to the establishment of an active accomplishment community at the Silma Pass by Lord Montsewa of the Barawa lineage; and to the appearance of an accomplishment community of the Aro tradition of the Great Perfection at Mön pass in Lhodrak. These both occurred during the early life of Dorje Lingpa.

Rakshi the Teacher

Then:

> All the people of Tibet under the king's rule
> Will lose their food and clothing to the Mongolians.
> An elder, a general, will come from Mongolia.
> These will be the signs that the time has come to reveal
> The terma concealed at the border of Tibet and Mustang.
> The tertön called Rakshi the Teacher will appear.

The tertön Rakshi the Teacher was a rebirth of Lang Palgyi Senge, and was born in the Nyal region. He evidently lived as a mantrin. It is said that he revealed a large amount of terma, including teachings on Buddhism, Bön, medicine, and astrology, from terma sites at the border of Tibet and Mustang. However, it is evident that he was born around the time when the Sakyapas ruled three of Tibet's provinces. Because he lived so long ago, neither copies nor transmissions of his termas remain.

According to the omniscient Tenpe Nyinje, the above prophecy refers to the tertön Padma Rikdzin of Puwo Rashi. Ratön Tobden Dorje declared that it referred to himself. In any case, since both Padma Rikdzin and Tobden Dorje were authentic tertöns, I will write a little about their lives as well.

The Physician from E in Jarong

Then:

> Genghis, the upper jaw of the land, will bite off the lower jaw.
> Many will flee. The land will be empty and ruined.
> These will be the signs that the time has come to reveal
> The terma concealed at the border of Tibet and Lhodrak.
> Nyi Ösal, the physician from E in Jarong, will appear.

The physician from E in Jarong was born in Eyül, the source of knowledge, in Jarong. He was one of two emanations of Nyak, the great translator, and lived as an ordinary mantrin and physician. His name was Nyi Ösal. It is known that from Dzarongbhi at the border of Tibet and Lhodrak he revealed termas concerning the Great Perfection and medicine, and that from Koro Rock in Lithang he revealed many lists of sacred places throughout Jambudvipa. However, no copies or transmissions of his termas exist nowadays. It is also apparent that because Nyi Ösal lived as a modest noble mantrin he engaged in no teaching activity.

A medicinal spring that arose from discarded medicine made by Nyi Ösal at Nupdo in Tsangrong is still there. This is just one example of his amazing miracles. He was able to prolong the lives of many people who were near death, and became known as a physician-siddha.

Nyi Ösal revealed from E Rock in Jarong the great Nyak's copies of four cycles concerning the *Great Fortress and Precipice of Amrita Medicine*: an extensive cycle, an intermediate one, a concise one, and a quintessential one. Although Nyi Ösal never disseminated these, the precious lord guru received the quintessential cycle as a rediscovered terma. It is so profound and complete that it could elevate the entire tradition of Amrita Qualities. He has not yet disseminated it, but the gurusadhana cycle from his mind terma the *Immortal Arya Tara's Heart Essence* is identical except for one being in verse and one in prose. It is therefore clear that the lineages of these two termas have been combined into one.

Dragom Chödor

Then:

> The times will get worse year by year.
> Abbots will give public empowerments in towns.
> They will secretly copulate like dogs or pigs.
> Civil wars will be waged with poison.
> These will be the signs that the time has come to reveal
> The terma concealed at Butsal Serkang.
> Dragom Chökyi Dorje will appear.

The tertön Dragom Chödor was the rebirth of Khyungnak Shakya Dar, the fifth rebirth of Prince Lharjey. Khyungnak was a tertön who discovered teachings on dharma, medicine, and especially astrology. His rebirth, Dragom Chödor, the sixth rebirth of Prince Lharjey, was born in Dranang and lived as a mantrin—hence his nickname Meditator from Dra.[53] His name was Chökyi Dorje. From Butsal Serkang he revealed a cycle concerning the powerful deity *Wrathful Guru* and many teachings on Mundane Propitiation, including the *Pekar Activity Tantra*, his sadhana, and means of compelling him. However, neither copies nor transmissions of these exist

53. *Dragom* means "Meditator from Dra."

nowadays. Our lord guru appears to have received the *Three Stages of Instruction on Kila the Wrathful Guru* as a rediscovered terma.

I have heard that the vidyadhara Chokgyur Lingpa once said that termas that Dragom Chödor revealed to meditation communities in eastern Tibet produced some activity for a while, but eventually disappeared.

Yakchar Ngönmo

Then:

> The Buddha's teachings will become distorted.
> False dharma called *Pebble Great Perfection* will appear.
> False medicine called moon, made from lacquer, will appear.
> A *Beacon Illuminating the Cycle of Sixty Years* will appear—
> A system of Tibetan astrology that contradicts all the tantras.
> Much false dharma will appear, called terma
> Yet lacking the provenance of terma.
> These will be the signs that the time has come to reveal
> The terma concealed at Oyuk Yakde.
> The tertön called Yakchar Ngönmo will appear.

The tertön Yakchar Ngönmo was an emanation of the great translator Vairochana. He was born to the Trachung family of Bön mantrins in a place called Töngur, near Colorful Yak Tongue in Oyuk. He evidently lived as a mantrin. Yakchar Ngönmo was his nickname; his actual name was Dorje Bum.

From Colorful Yak Tongue Rock he revealed terma concealed by Vairochana that included Buddhist gurusadhanas, Great Perfection instructions, Mahakarunika sadhanas, and many minor sadhanas; as well as Great Perfection teachings of the Bön tradition. Although Yakchar Ngönmo discovered so much terma, both Buddhist and Bön, no copies of his termas exist nowadays because of the length of time that has passed. He reconcealed at Yerpa Rock one of the minor sadhanas among his profound termas: the *Sadhana of Tara Who Protects From All Danger*, together with its applications. It was later rediscovered by Rongpa Düdül Lingpa, who again concealed it. The text of this terma finally reached the hands of our lord guru Padma Ösal Dongak Lingpa, who transcribed it and kindly bestowed it upon us. I have composed a sadhana, an empowerment liturgy, and a war-prevention ritual for it. It is evident that if the masters and leaders nowadays who search so desperately for means of averting adversity were to perform a war-prevention ritual such as this even once, the blessing would be especially great.

Drum and Karnak

Then:

Buddhism throughout Tibet will become laughable.
Each worldly householder will make up their own dharma.
They will say, "Drunkenness and licentiousness make no
 difference."
They will call every cold wind a demon from above.
The heinous will nurse the sick.
Each person will hold an astrological chart.
Herds of foolish people will repeat the sayings of the glib.
These will be the signs that the time has come to reveal
The terma concealed at Mönka Paro.
The tertön Drum and the one called Karnak will appear.

The tertön Lama Drum and the patron from Paro known as Karnak appeared together as teacher and patron. Drum brought a lacquer reliquary out from the beak of a brown statue of a garuda in the Paro Kyerchu Temple. Within it was the *Exorcism Pit of the Sky: The Forceful Mantra of the*

Razorlike Wild Planet. It appears that both copies and the transmission of this have survived down to the present. As it is said that the powerful planetary magic performed by the vidyadhara Kumaraja was this system, it is clear that Drum and Karnak lived long ago. It is unclear in previous histories of terma whether Drum revealed any other terma dharma.

Lhatsün Ngönmo

Then:

> Amid fivefold failure, people will no longer trust themselves.
> Spirits will spread virulent diseases.
> There will be no way to prevent illness.
> A third of the dharma's blessing will vanish.
> These will be the signs that the time has come to reveal
> The terma concealed at Ushangdo.
> The tertön called Lhatsün Ngönmo will appear.

The tertön Lhatsün Ngönmo was an emanation of Prince Damdzin. He was born at Samye as the son of Lhatsün Bodhiraja, who was descended from the family of King Trisong's mother. As they were noble mantrins of divine descent, they were called Lhatsün.[54] Ngönmo was a nickname; Lhatsün Ngönmo's actual name was Rikpay Gyamtso Loki Trengwa. As he was very learned in the tripitaka, he convened a great dharmachakra at Samye. He also invited Nyima Drak, known as Patsap the Translator; and Shuke Tarma Dorje, who was learned in Arya Nagarjuna's system of Guhyasamaja. Together, they translated, taught, and studied many general and specific dharmas of the sutras and tantras. Lhatsün did a great deal for the teachings.

He revealed many termas from the central temple of Samye, from behind the main image of Vairochana there, and from other places. From his retreat cave at Drakyang Dzong he

---

54. *Lhatsün* means "Noble Deity"

revealed a cycle of beneficial teachings on protection from virulent contagious illness, poison, and magic. It is said that he also found a list of all the termas in Tibet. In particular, as the prophecy quoted above clearly describes, he revealed the instructions called the *Seven Cycles of Pacification* from Ushangdo Rock. He later reconcealed them at the door to the great accomplishment cave at Drakyang Dzong. They were eventually rediscovered there by the great emanated tertön Chokgyur Dechen Lingpa, who offered the terma scrolls to Padma Ösal Dongak Lingpa, who transcribed them. They form a wondrously profound and complete treatise, and I have received their ripening empowerments and liberating instructions. As commanded by them, I have provided a few written clarifications of these instructions.

Nyima Drakpa

Then:

> People will wear mismatched clothing.
> Dharma will also become mismatched.
> The designs drawn by virtue will become mere traces.
> These will be the signs that the time has come to reveal
> The terma concealed at the Triple Rakshasi Fortress
>   of Kham.
> The Khampa called Nyima Drakpa will appear.

Nyima Drakpa, the tertön from Dakpo in western Kham, was born in the western part of eastern Tibet. He was clearly a rebirth of Lhalung Palgyi Dorje. The Rakshasi Fortress of Kham is behind Gampo Dar Mountain in Dakpo. Like a hidden valley, the Triple Rakshasi Fortress—which includes three sites called Rakshasa Fortress, Rakshasi Fortress, and Vajra Fortress—is very hard to get to. It is clearly described in the biography of Dungtso Repa.

From the Triple Rakshasi Fortress Nyima Drakpa revealed

many cycles concerning direct action, including *Yamantaka: The Play of the Secret Moon*, the *Yama of Activity Wearing Monkeyskin*, and the *Seven Cycles of Forceful Mantra*. However, because of this tertön's coarse behavior, he passed away accidentally. For that reason, as well as because he appeared so long ago, I have found no existing copies or transmissions of his termas. Nevertheless, our lord guru has received the dispensation of the *Seven Cycles of Forceful Mantra* as rediscovered terma.

Later, other great tertöns have appeared bearing the crown of the name Nyima Drakpa, such as the emanation of Khön Luwang Sungma. Their lives are well known.

Padma Ledrel Tsal

Then:

> The eight dangers will grow like the antlers of a buck.
> Its merit exhausted, central Tibet will be menaced by wild men.
> These will be the signs that the time has come to reveal
> The terma concealed at Dakpo Danglha Rock.
> The princess will appear as Rinchen Tsuldor.

The tertön Rinchen Tsuldor, also known by his secret name Padma Ledrel Tsal, was the fifth of the five consecutive pure rebirths of Princess Padma Sal, the daughter of King Trisong. He was born in the Female Metal Hare Year, in Nyenrong Dritang at the border of Tibet and Mustang, to a family descended from Nyangral Nyima Özer. He was known during his life as Tsultrim Dorje, the name he received when he undertook renunciation.

During Padma Ledrel Tsal's sixteenth year, an old monk who was an emanation of Guru Rinpoche gave him a terma indication scroll. During his twenty-first year he received from the tertön Rinchen Lingpa the list and prophecy that were among the scrolls Rinchen Lingpa brought out from Dritang Koro Rock. During Padma Ledrel Tsal's twenty-third year, he revealed the extraordinary and profound dharma cycle called the *Great Perfection: The Dakinis' Heart Essence* from Danglung Rock in Dakpo. He also revealed many other dharma termas and cycles concerning forceful mantra and dharma protectors, such as the *Wheel of the Embodiment of All Gurus*, *Vajrapani Who Subdues All the Aggressive*, the *Three Mighty Deities of Hayagriva*, *Yamantaka's Kingkangs: Sealing Enemies' Mouths*, the *Planet*, and the *Realm Protectors*.

On his way back from the terma site, Padma Ledrel Tsal was hosted by a mantrin of Thorn Valley in upper Nyal. The mantrin's son, who accompanied the tertön when he continued his journey, was Gyalsay Lekpa Gyaltsen.

Saddened by how little faith the people of his birthplace had in him, Padma Ledrel Tsal went to central Tibet, accompanied by four disciples. While residing at Samye Chimphu he received a prophecy from Vajravarahi, based on which he went to Lhasa and met the Third Gyalwang Karmapa, Rangjung Dorje. The Karmapa had also received a prophecy from the dakinis, and therefore received the empowerments and transmissions of the *Dakinis' Heart Essence* using the original terma scrolls.

Over time, Padma Ledrel Tsal transcribed his terma dharma, and gave all of its empowerments and transmissions to Gyalsay Lekpa and the nirmanakaya Rinchen Lingpa.

In his twenty-fifth year, due to adventitious circumstances, Padma Ledrel Tsal passed away at Nyal Gyadro Latse, which is near Jarmay Chingkar. During his cremation, everyone present saw a blue woman wearing bone ornaments emerge from his head and fly into the sky. Numerous images of Vajravarahi and other relics were found among his ashes. For seven days after his cremation the entire valley was filled with rainbow light. In these and other ways he inspired beings. In accordance with prophecies, he did not widely benefit beings in that life; it was a time for him to practice secretly. Because his activity for beings' benefit was unfinished at his death, his next birth was as the omniscient Drime Özer, who widely disseminated the *Heart Essence* teachings.

The omniscient Karmapa Rangjung Dorje received the lineage of words of the *Dakinis' Heart Essence* again from Gyalsay Lekpa, and disseminated it widely. He entrusted it to four principal disciples, including Yungtön Dorje Pal, who spread it throughout central, western, and eastern Tibet; Mongolia; and China. Its lineage survives today. This fulfilled the following prophecy from the *Root Tantra of Penetrating Sound*:

> A bodhisattva on the levels
> Will spread this to the oceans.

The essence of the profound termas of this great tertön is the *Great Perfection: The Dakinis' Heart Essence*. It is one of the two original *Heart Essences*. I have received its complete ripening empowerments and liberating instructions according to both of its distinct lineages: the lineage of the Gyalwang Karmapa Rangjung Dorje and that of the omniscient Longchenpa. I have also received the empowerments, transmissions, and instructions of Padma Ledrel Tsal's the *Three Mighty Deities of Hayagriva* and *Vajrapani Who Subdues All the Aggressive*.

Tseten Gyaltsen

Then:

> Things will deteriorate; some disciples will die violently.
> A stone stupa will be damaged, along with its parasol and dharmachakra.
> These will be the signs that the time has come to reveal
> The terma concealed at Mönka River Cave.

The tertön called Tseten Gyaltsen will appear.

The tertön Tseten Gyaltsen was one of two emanations of Gyalwa Chokyang. He was born at Narthang in Mönla Motö. He was known by the names Guru Tseten Gyaltsen and Chökyi Lodrö, and lived as a bhikshu vajra holder. He was a great kalyanamitra, and was widely learned in both sutra and tantra.

As clearly predicted in the prophecy quoted above, Tseten Gyaltsen revealed terma from the Glorious River Cave on Little Rock Mountain in Mön. This mountain is shaped like a dancing goddess; the cave is like her secret place. The profound and extensive terma he revealed there, which had been concealed by the dakini Yeshe Tsogyal, included sadhanas of the peaceful and wrathful Guru Rinpoche as well as applications of those sadhanas.

Although that was his principal terma, Tseten Gyaltsen also revealed from various places such termas as *Vajra Armor: Protection from Weapons*, *Tara: A Garland of Utpalas*, the *Great Perfection: Self-Liberated Sameness*, *Amitayus*, *Chakrasamvara*, *Mewatsekpa*, *A Hundred Means of Rasayana*, the *Sealed Prophecy*, *An Extensive Guide to Sites and Terma in Zabulung and Other Places*, and *Instructions on Dhritarashtra*, which he revealed from Rong Dzalungmo.

It seems that the empowerment and transmission lineages for most of Tseten Gyaltsen's many termas still existed at the time of the vidyadhara Terdak Lingpa and his disciples. I have heard that the transmission of *A Hundred Applications of Hayagriva* from Tseten's the *Peaceful and Wrathful Guru*, the transmission of *Instructions on Dhritarashtra*, and the lineage and practical instructions for *Vajra Armor: Protection from Weapons* still exist nowadays. Other than those, however, even copies of his termas are difficult to find now.

Meben Rinchen Lingpa

Then:

All central Tibet will unite in fear of Mongolia.
An evil emanation of Mara will spread the teachings.
These will be the signs that the time has come to reveal
The terma concealed at Drintang Koro Rock.
The tertön called Rinchen Lingpa will appear.

The tertön Meben Rinchen Lingpa was an emanation of both the Indian pandita Prajnakara and the great translator Vairochana. He was born in the Year of the Ox in Loro Karpo. His father's name was Dorje Gödor Bum. His mother's name was Balmo Yangbum.

While playing as a young child, Rinchen Lingpa left the imprint of his body in a boulder. He entered the gate of dharma, and was given the name Rinchen Gyalpo Pal Zangpo. He completed the study of the causal vehicle at the College of Vairochana at the seat of Tingpa the Translator in eastern Nyal. He then received the instructions of Rechungpa from a lama at Loro Drukral Monastery. As he practiced these, innumerable signs of attainment arose.

Rinchen Lingpa then went to Lhasa on pilgrimage. One night he dreamed that a white man said to him, "Tomorrow you will achieve your aim!" On the next morning Rinchen Lingpa met the yogin called Kunga the Bodhisattva of Tengpo, who said that he had come from Dingri in Latö. The yogin questioned Rinchen Lingpa extensively, and then handed him a list of his termas. Based on the list, Rinchen Lingpa discovered a brown lacquer coffer in an accomplishment cave at Koro Rock in Drintang. The coffer, which had five compartments, contained a large amount of dharma terma and samaya substances. From the eastern compartment Rinchen Lingpa revealed the *Five Special Instructions*. In the southern compartment he found the *Five Jewels of Sadhana*. In the western compartment he found the *Five Jewels of Interdependence*. In the northern compartment he found the *Five Jewels of Forceful Mantra*. In the central compartment he found the *Five Lists and Prophecies*. From a rock shaped like a dharma source in the same place he revealed the *Manjushri Nagaraksha Cycle*.

Rinchen Lingpa practiced one-pointedly, developing experience and realization, and encountering innumerable pure appearances. Especially, he went to the Glorious Copper-Colored Mountain, where he was accepted as a disciple in a wondrous manner by Guru Rinpoche.

Then Rinchen Lingpa revealed from a black boulder in India both the *Great Perfection: Total Liberation at Once* and the *Peaceful and Wrathful: Perfect Great Bliss*. After that, from a rock shaped like a five-pronged vajra at Shawuk Tago, he revealed the *Three Sealed Instructions*. These consist of: the *Sealed Sadhanas*, which are sadhanas of the three roots accompanied by instructions on their implementation; the *Sealed Completion Stage*, which contains instructions on both the gradual and instantaneous completion stages; *Instruction on the Non-Duality of the Two Stages*, which is accompanied by supplementary oral instructions; and the *Sealed Prophecies*, which include general, specific, and particular prophecies. As instructed in his termas, he replaced each terma with the scrolls of the preceding one.[55]

Rinchen Lingpa lived to the age of eighty, and during his long life he completed his activity. He did a great deal: He revealed further profound terma from both Tsaritra and Kongpo, gained accomplishment through practice, became an heir to the profound dharma of Padma Ledrel Tsal, and actively benefited others. His emanations have appeared in succession. The first was the nirmanakaya Shönnu Lhundrup, who was born into the family of Rinchen Lingpa's nephew. Although Shönnu Lhundrup also revealed terma, he unfortunately passed away while young. His rebirth was Gyaltsen Palzang, whose rebirth was Chöwang Lhundrup. These

---

55. Tertöns are required either to replace the terma parchment with something else or replace the parchment itself in its place of concealment after it has been transcribed. It is said that this is to ensure that the region not suffer depletion through the removal of the terma.

three successive emanations were primarily of the Nyingma tradition.

Chöwang Lhundrup's rebirth was the great being Tsuklak Trengwa. Starting with him, and up to and including the present ninth supreme nirmanakaya Tsuklak Nyima, this being has continuously been a peerless holder of the accomplishment lineage of the Karma Kagyu.[56]

Although Rinchen Lingpa's profound terma the *Five Cycles* clearly brought great benefit to beings, only the empowerments, transmissions, and instructions for the *Manjushri Nagaraksha Cycle* have survived continuously down to the present day. Nevertheless, Rinchen Lingpa's *Ayusadhana: A Vase of Light* is practically identical in words and meaning to Rechen Paljor Zangpo's *Life-Increasing Arrow*. In addition, Rechen Paljor Zangpo received the termas of Rinchen Lingpa from the nirmanakaya Gyaltsen Palzang, which effectively combined the two lineage-streams of the two ayusadhanas into one.

Long after receiving the above-mentioned lineage, our lord guru Padma Ösal Dongak Lingpa acquired a copy of the *Great Perfection: Total Liberation at Once*, as was predicted in the prophecies within that cycle. The great tertön Rinchen Lingpa then bestowed its ripening empowerments and liberating instructions upon him. Our lord guru also revealed the gurusadhana and the Mahakarunika sadhana from the *Five Cycles of Sadhana* as rediscovered terma, and has through his great kindness shared them with us.

The Nirmanakaya Ugyen Lingpa

Then:

> A king with ripened conduct will appear in Yarlung.
> A pig will dig in the ground; Mongolia will consume Tibet.
> A hundred and eight fortresses will appear.
> These will be the signs that the time has come to reveal

56. These rebirths of Rinchen Lingpa are the Pawo Rinpoches of the Karma Kagyu.

The terma concealed in the Crystal Cave.
The tertön called Ugyen Lingpa will appear.

The nirmanakaya Ugyen Lingpa was the seventh rebirth of Prince Chokdrup Gyalpo. He was born at Yarje in Yoru Dranang during a Female Water Pig Year to a family of remarkable mantrins.[57] He lived as a noble mantrin, and became skilled in his youth in magic, medicine, and astrology. During his twenty-third year he discovered a list of his termas within the Red Stupa at Samye.

57. The year was 1203 C.E.

At the back of the Crystal Rock of Yarlung are rocks shaped like piled lotuses. Among them is the wondrous Crystal Cave where the great Uddiyana performed amrita accomplishment. This cave has self-arisen images of the peaceful and wrathful deities, and its doorway is guarded by an image of Rahula. It was from this image that a great mass of profound terma burst forth.

From the image's upper faces Ugyen Lingpa revealed guru-sadhanas, Mahakarunika sadhanas, and Great Perfection instructions. These included the *Generation Stage: The Peaceful and Wrathful Gurus of the Two Doctrines and the Three Cycles*, *Mahakarunika: The Padma Heart Essence*, the *Ayusadhana of the Great Perfection*, and other Great Perfection cycles of the atiyoga, chitiyoga, and yangtiyoga.

From the image's lower faces he revealed the yidam cycle the *Great Assembly of Dispensations: An Ocean of Dharma*, which has one hundred and thirty-two sections. From the image's throat he revealed the *Peaceful and Wrathful Assemblies of Dispensations*, the *Dakini Krodhikali*, and the *Neutral Protector Cycle*. From the image's heart he revealed the *Great Testament of Padma*.[58] From the image's serpent tail he revealed many tantras, sadhanas, and applications concerning various wisdom protectors; teachings on medicine; and profound instructions on guarding the dharma. From the image's arms and the end of its tail he revealed instructions on arts and crafts.

58. The *Great Testament of Padma* is the source of the prophecies quoted at the beginning of each biography in this section.

From the Upper Turquoise Rock at Dra, Ugyen Lingpa revealed terma including the *Great Exposition of the Stages of the Path of Guhyamantra*, *A Brief Biography of Padma*, the *Clear Testament of Pacification*, and the *Quintessence of Interdependence*.

From various terma sites at Samye he revealed the *Five Testaments*. From the stone stupa of Zurkhar he revealed *Mahakarunika: Supreme Light of Wisdom* and the *Glorious Protector: Tiger Rider*. From the Tiger's Lair at Onpu he revealed the *Wrathful Guru* and the *Dharmapala Cycle*. From the Great Rock of Drachi he revealed the *Yamantaka Ayupati Cycle*. His terma dharma is said to have filled more than one hundred volumes. The *Assembly of Dispensations* alone filled more than thirty volumes. It is said, however, that he was unable to transcribe many of the scrolls and reconcealed them for future discovery. He also discovered a great number of statues, samaya substances, and wealth terma. In sum, he revealed twenty-eight great termas along with their associated discoveries.

However, when he was preparing to give the great empowerment of the *Assembly of Dispensations* for the first time at Tradruk Jamtö, his first presentation of dharma, Ugyen Lingpa uttered a prophecy. A few of his words aroused the fierce opposition of Tai Situ Jangchup Gyaltsen in Neu Dongtse. This altered the tertön's interdependent circumstances to such an extent that he was forced to flee to the border of E and Dakpo. Soon thereafter, Ugyen Lingpa passed away in a place called Small Mind adjacent to E.

His body was brought to Dakpo and preserved at the Footprint Temple. Later, the ruler of Kurap heard that Ugyen Lingpa's body would bestow liberation through taste because of his seven most recent births. The ruler had the body partially cremated, and then tasted the ashes. He became exhilarated and miraculously rose a cubit into space. Nowadays, most of Ugyen Lingpa's remains are preserved in their original container at Yarlung Tsetsok. Ugyen Lingpa's descendants mostly live in Draptsangka. Their service to dharma is unclear, but they have all demonstrated signs of attainment, and therefore appear to be a wondrous family lineage of vidyadharas.

Of Ugyen Lingpa's terma dharma, it is evident that the lineages of the empowerments and transmissions of the *Supreme Light of Wisdom*, the *Wrathful Guru*, the *Ayusadhana*, and the *Tiger Rider* existed up to the time of the vidyadhara Terdak Lingpa. I have not seen evidence that these lineages exist nowadays. The lineages of the transmissions of the *Crystal Cave Testament of Padma*, the *Five Testaments*, and the *Quintessence of Interdependence* still exist, and I have received them.

Especially, as clearly predicted in the prophecies within Ugyen Lingpa's termas, an old copy of the condensed essence of the *Great Assembly of Dispensations* fell into the hands of our lord guru Padma Ösal Dongak Lingpa. He also transcribed parts of it from the symbol script of the dakinis which appeared to him. We have been fortunate enough to receive its ripening empowerments and liberating instructions, which he bestowed completely on a single occasion. I have performed its approach and accomplishment, and have served it by writing the necessary supplements. I have slightly increased its activity by including it in the *Great Treasury of Precious Terma*.

This cycle, Ugyen Lingpa's *Assembly of Dispensations*, is not merely a gurusadhana given the label *Assembly of Dispensations* because it includes the eight dispensations. It presents the twenty-one group mandala of the *Assembly of Dispensations* exactly as it is described in the great biography and elsewhere. It is therefore wondrous and utterly trustworthy.

Our lord guru also revealed Gya the Translator's *Guru of the Two Doctrines and Three Cycles* as rediscovered terma.

Aside from some difference in length, it is identical to the corresponding profound terma of Ugyen Lingpa. This rediscovery may therefore be considered to include the lineage streams of both termas. As our lord guru also revealed the *Continous Yoga of Day and Night*, another part of Ugyen Lingpa's *Assembly of Dispensations*, he has revealed the essence of Ugyen Lingpa's termas concerning gurusadhana, the Great Perfection, and Mahakarunika. He has revived the fire of dharma.

The Omniscient Longchenpa

Then:

> The charnel grounds of Sahor will spill their contents into Tibet.
> A dog will dig out a skull from beneath a stupa.
> These will be the signs that the time has come to reveal
> The terma concealed at Samye Chimphu.
> The tertön called Drime Özer will appear.

The tertön Drime Özer, the omniscient Longchenpa, was in absolute truth an emanation of the master Vimalamitra. Vimalamitra promised that one of his emanations would appear in Tibet every hundred years, when his *Heart Essence* teachings were about to be adulterated by speculative thinking. Drime Özer was one of these emanations. From the *Great Tantra of Penetrating Sound*:

> Afterward, it will be held by one with supreme intelligence.[59]

As clearly predicted, Drime Özer was really an emanation of the mahapandita Vimalamitra. Out of necessity, he was the rebirth of Padma Ledrel Tsal, who was the nirmanakaya of Princess Padma Sal, the daughter of King Trisong. From the prophecies among the termas of Padma Ledrel Tsal:

> After that, you will spend some time in sambhogakaya realms.

This is definitely a prediction of the great omniscient Longchenpa, who was the immediate rebirth of Padma Ledrel Tsal.

Longchenpa was born in a village in western Yoru as the twenty-fifth lineal descendant of Ökyi Kyilkorchen, the lord of Ngenlam, a relative and contemporary of the master Gyalwa Chokyang. Longchenpa's grandfather was named Lhasung and accomplished the rasayana of amrita. Lhasung had a son known as the master Tensung who was learned in the five sciences and had mastery of yoga. Tensung was Longchenpa's father. Longchenpa's mother was known as Dromza Sönam Gyenma. He was born in a pasture on the tenth day of the month Phalguna in the Year of the Earth Monkey of the fifth cycle.[60]

As soon as he began to speak, it became evident that Longchenpa was a holy being. He learned to read and write in his fifth year just by being shown how. In his seventh year he began to receive from his father the empowerments, transmissions, instructions, and ritual training for Lord Nyang's *Peaceful and Wrathful Guru* and his *Eight Dispensations: The*

---

59. One of Longchenpa's names was Tsultrim Lodrö, Morality Intelligence.

60. The year was 1308 C.E.

Sugatas' Assembly. He also learned and mastered medicine and astology.

In his twelfth year Longchenpa undertook renunciation at Samye in the presence of the abbot Samdrup Rinchen and the master Kunga Özer. He received the name Tsultrim Lodrö. He studied the vinaya and gave original explanations of it that brought him the reputation of great learning.

In his nineteenth year Longchenpa went to Sangpu Neutok, where he studied the *Abhisamayalankara* with its commentaries as well as treatises on valid cognition under the guidance of the master Tsengönpa and especially under Ladrangwa Chöpel Gyaltsen and Shönnu Rinchen. Longchenpa gained consummate knowledge of these subjects. From the master Shönnu Gyalpo he received the *Mulamadhyamaka* and the *Madhyamakavatara*. From the great Wanglo he received explanation of the *Abhidharmakosha*, the *Abhidharmasamucchaya*, and the five profound sutras such as the *Samadhirajasutra*. He also learned poetics and the other common disciplines. He then began to visit various colleges of scripture and reasoning. His inconceivable wisdom caused him to be known as *Erudite Man from Samye*.

During this same period Longchenpa received empowerments, instructions, and explanations of mahayoga, anuyoga, and atiyoga from the master Shönnu Döndrup at the Drepung Denpal College, as well as the *Guhyasamajatantra* and the charyatantras. From the master Tashi Rinchen he received *Chakrasamvara*, the *Path and Result*, the six branches of yoga, pacification, and teachings on the mind class of the Great Perfection. From Shönnu Dorje he received the Kadampa teachings. From Tingma Drakö he received many cycles of profound terma, including the *Eight Dispensations: The Sugatas' Assembly*. He studied under more than twenty teachers, including the Third Gyalwang Karmapa Rangjung Dorje and the Sakyapa Sönam Gyaltsen, and learned most of the teachings of sutra, mantra, and upadesha that existed in

Tibet at that time. He also became learned in all conventional areas of knowledge such as astrology.

After he accomplished the deities Achala, Sarasvati, and White Vajravarahi, Longchenpa exhibited a tremendously powerful intellect. He was continuously blessed by Arya Tara, and received her assurance of siddhi.

In his twenty-seventh year Longchenpa, instructed by his yidam, entered the presence of the great vidyadhara Kumaraja, from whom he received a vast amount of the amrita of dharma, both ripening empowerments and liberating instructions. Principally, Longchenpa received from Kumaraja the empowerments, tantras, and instructions of the great *Heart Essence*.

After receiving these, Longchenpa lived for seven years as an absolute renunciate, devoting himself entirely to accomplishment. During these years he was blessed by many gurus and deities. He achieved the level of the great maturation of awareness, and visited sambhogakaya realms.

The protector Shenpa Sokdrupma offered Longchenpa the terma texts of the *Dakinis' Heart Essence*, and he was blessed by Guru Rinpoche and Yeshe Tsogyal. He thus received the dispensation of these instructions too.

Longchenpa then composed his three *Further Quintessences*. These are mind terma, although they are presented as composed shastras, and by writing these Longchenpa became the principal gatherer of the dharma of the two *Heart Essences*. In support of this, he also wrote the *Seven Treasuries*, the *Three Chariots*, and many other treatises. His writings are considered to be the king among all mind terma. As Jangdak Tashi Tobgyal wrote:

The omniscient Drime Özer is peerless
In his opening of the door to the treasury of wisdom.

In this way, Longchenpa extensively turned the dharmachakra of the instruction class of the Great Perfection. His lion's roar filled this Himalayan region, and his lineage remains undiminished to this day. His kindness is inconceivable.

In his fifty-sixth year, the Female Water Hare Year, on the eighteenth day of the month Paushya, Longchenpa passed into the state of manifest awakening amid innumerable signs and miracles at the great charnel ground in the forest of Chimphu.[61]

The particular meaning of the prophecy from the *Testament*, quoted above, is that Longchenpa discovered three terma scrolls, such as the *Luminosity of the Four Beacons*, at Samye Chimphu. Because of his perfect realization, Longchenpa did not need to reveal much earth terma, but he did reveal and transcribe these three scrolls. Nowadays they are included in the *Wisdom Assembly of Samantabhadra*, a five-part terma of Longchenpa's immediate rebirth, Padma Lingpa.

I have gone to great effort to receive the ripening empowerments, liberating instructions, and supporting transmissions of Longchenpa's mind termas, the three *Further Quintessences*; the transmissions and instructions of his *Seven Treasuries*, his *Trilogy of Rest*, his *Dispelling Darkness in Every Direction*, and all of his other writings that survive. In particular I have received from Dorje Ziji, the second omniscient one, experiential instruction in the great *Heart Essence*, combining the mother and son.[62] I have formed a connection with it through practice, have written a brief but clear book of instruction on it, and have instituted its practice in the meditation college at the Kunzang Dechen Ösal Ling retreat. I have done a little to serve these teachings.

Recently our lord guru received the dispensation of the *Profound Essence of the Dakinis*. It is both profound and concise, and includes the three stages.[63] It is the quintessence of the *Further Quintessence of the Dakinis*. I have had the good fortune to receive it.

61. The year was 1364 C.E.

62. In this case the name Dorje Ziji refers to Jamyang Khyentse Wangpo, although it was also one of Longchenpa's names. The mother and son *Heart Essences* include the two original *Heart Essences* taught by Vimalamitra and Guru Rinpoche (the mother *Heart Essences*) and the three *Further Quintessences* of Longchenpa (the son *Heart Essences*).

63. The three stages are the generation stage, the completion stage, and the Great Perfection.

Rokje Lingpa

Then:

The thorns of squabbling will summon invasion.
An emanation of Mara will shake the earth.
These will be the signs that the time has come to reveal
The terma concealed at Yambu Lagang.
The one called Ugyen Rokje Lingpa will appear.

The tertön Rokje Lingpa is called Chöje Lingpa and Wönjay Lingpa in some testaments. He also referred to himself as Dakpo Chöje Lingpa. He was the twelfth rebirth of Prince Lharjey as a tertön, and was born in Lukardong in the province of Dakpo. His father, Dorje Drakpa, was the fifteenth lineal descendant of Lharjey Nyichung, Lord Gampopa's younger brother.

Rokje Lingpa was known during his life as Chöje Dzamling Dorje and as Deway Dorje. Although Lord Zangpo Dorje held Rokje Lingpa to be the rebirth of Dakpo Shapdrung Rinchen Dorje, Shamar Yeshe Nyingpo recognized him as the rebirth of Rechung Puktrül Chimay Wangpo and named him Daway Wangpo Tenpe Salje. In his sixth year Rokje Lingpa was brought to his predecessor's seat. He undertook renunciation in the presence of the elder Jamyang Drakpa, and completion in the presence of the Ganden Tripa Lozang Dargyay, receiving the name Ngawang Lozang Chöying Pal Zangpo. He soon became a great kalyanamitra, mastering many Indian and Tibetan treatises on sutra and tantra.

As his predecessors had worn their hair long, Rokje Lingpa wore long hair even though he was a bhikshu. He therefore became known as Long-Haired Bhikshu. Throughout his early life he maintained pure conduct and carefully followed all the observances of the vinaya. Later, after revealing profound terma and during the latter part of his life, he took Dechen Trinley Tsomo, the immediate rebirth of the yogini

Ugyen Butri, as a mudra. She gave birth to the wondrous reincarnation of Drukchen Rinpoche, but unfortunately his life was short.

Until his twenty-fifth year, Rokje Lingpa lived at Yarlung Rechung Puk, the seat established by the mahasiddha Tsangnyön Heruka. From the elder Jangchub Lingpa and Geshe Dönden he received all of the empowerments, transmissions, instructions, and ritual training of his own tradition, as well as other dharma of sutra and tantra and various sciences. He achieved the pinnacle of learning. He also trained his mind and practiced, displaying consummate realization.

Although Rokje Lingpa never actually met the Eleventh Gyalwang Karmapa Yeshe Dorje, he received the transference of his blessing and directly saw the nature of Mahamudra. He also received the empowerments of many of the vidyadhara Taksham Nüden Dorje's profound termas, as well as their complete entrustment, from Taksham himself. Through receiving these, his realization of the Great Perfection became complete. He therefore regarded these two masters—the Eleventh Karmapa and the tertön Taksham Nüden Dorje—as his root gurus.

This is how he received the dispensation of profound terma:

The tertön of Takmo called Pönsay Khyungtok offered Rokje Lingpa both prophecy and a terma list. Then Rokje Lingpa went to the area of Ön, where he encountered clear indications of the presence of terma and revealed the *Sadhana of the Guru's Four Bodies* and lists of the termas at Yambu Lagang and Songtsen Bangso. He also discovered another list at Ushangdo, and went to Yambu Lagang and Songtsen Bangso, where he revealed several profound termas. He did not, however, transcribe them, but reconcealed most of them for future discovery.

He later came to feel that it was time to benefit beings through profound terma, and therefore offered his seat to its other tulkus. Rokje Lingpa then undertook a lifestyle of utter renunciation and traveled to such places as glorious Tsaritra, where he devoted himself to meditation. While he was doing so, the prophecies and lists of terma that he had previously received became clearer and clearer. Based on them, he revealed the *Combined Sadhana of the Immortal Three Roots*, wondrous life water, and other terma from the Undefiled Rainbow Cave. He then revealed *Perfect Heruka* and *Vajrakilaya* from the Poisonous Lake of Nine-Headed Karek; the *Gurusadhana of the Profound Path: the Heart Jewel* from Vulture Basin in Puwo; *Guru Vidyadhara* from the lake in Makung Valley; and *Mahakarunika, Kshitigarbha,* and *Red Jambhala* from the Döchu Temple. He also revealed *Dorje Trolö, Vajrachanda the Lion's Roar, Krodhikali,* and other termas, most of which he transcribed.

The transmission lineages for Rokje Lingpa's visionary revelations, his *Collected Sadhanas: A Garland of Rubies*, and most of his collected works have survived down to the present, and I have received them.

Rokje Lingpa practiced a great deal of meditation, approach, and accomplishment, such as when he spent three years meditating in the Upper Valley of Braided Flowers in Kongpo.

His principal dharma heirs included great gurus such as the Twelfth Gyalwang Karmapa Jangchub Dorje, Shamar Palchen Chökyi Döndrup, Trewo Chökyi Wangpo, Drikungpa Könchok Trinley Zangpo, Dakpo Shapdrung Tulku Lhundrup Ngedön Wangpo, and the omniscient Drukchen Paksam Wangpo. There were many others as well, such as Tsupri Drupchen, Lhopa Drupchen, and Ratön Topden Dorje, who was his single innermost heart-son. Rokje Lingpa also appears to have formed a slight dharma connection with the vidyadhara Padma Trinley and Minling Gyalsay Padma Gyurme Gyamtso.

At the end of his life Rokje Lingpa traveled to Padmakö with the intention of revealing its hidden valley. He reached the area, but soon thereafter departed for the realm of Lotus

Light during the month of Phalguna in his forty-fourth year. His well-known nirmanakaya, Jikten Wangchuk, was born to the Gachak family of Kongpo. It is evident that his hidden emanations have also continued to appear down to the present day.

A detailed and clear account of this lord's life can be found in his extensive autobiography, his guides to sacred places, the account of his parinirvana by Gampopa Zangpo Dorje, and other sources. Here, I have set forth merely a seed of his life.

The Great Tertön of Mindröling

Then:

> This land will be filled with bad dharma, outlaws, and samaya breakers.
> The realms of gods and humans will resound with bad news.
> These will be the signs that the time has come to reveal
> The terma concealed at Shaük Tago.
> The one called Ugyen Terdak Lingpa will appear.

The tertön Terdak Lingpa or Padma Garwang Gyurme Dorje

was a speech emanation of the great translator Vairochana. He was born in Yoru Dranang Dargyay Chöding in central Tibet. His father was the vidyadhara Trinley Lhundrup, an emanation of Nupchen Sangye Yeshe and a great sun illuminating the Nyingma dharma. Terdak Lingpa's mother was Lhadzin Yangchen Drölma, a rebirth of Shelkar Dorje Tso. The lotus of his marks and signs bloomed in a Male Wood Dog Year.[64]

From an early age he demonstrated inconceivable holiness. When he offered the fruits of his crown to the great Fifth Dalai Lama, he received the name Ngawang Padma Tendzin. The Dalai Lama foresaw and predicted great virtue in the young boy's future.

From his holy father, Terdak Lingpa received the three vows and all the profound dharma his father could bestow, like the contents of one vase being poured into another one. His other principal teachers were Sungtrül Tsultrim Dorje and the great Fifth Dalai Lama, but Terdak Lingpa studied under more than thirty masters of the Sarma and Nyingma traditions. From them he received so much dharma that the list of the teachings he heard fills two volumes.

He meditated at Samye Chimphu; at his own seat, Mindröling Monastery; and at other places of accomplishment. He displayed progressive realization of the four empowerments, and reached a high degree of accomplishment.

Through his immeasurable turning of the dharmachakra and his establishment of Okmin Ugyen Mindröling, which is like the Lotus Light Palace of this Himalayan region, Terdak Lingpa became the primary source of the streams of teaching and accomplishment in the Nyingma tradition.

This is how he received the dispensation of profound terma:

In his eighteenth year he revealed without obstacle the first of all his termas, the *Heart Essence of the Vidyadhara Guru* and its accompanying samaya substances, from Red Rock Yama Lung. Then from Okar Rock in Ngamshö Jingda he

64. The year mentioned here is 1634 C.E., but Düdjom Rinpoche Jikdral Yeshe Dorje, in his *History of Nyingma Dharma*, gives the year of Terdak Lingpa's birth as 1646, the Fire Dog Year.

revealed the *Great Perfection Heart Essence of the Three Masters: The Profound Meaning of Ati*, the *Heart Sadhana of Vajrasattva*, and the *Red Wrathful Guru*. Flying like a garuda, he revealed the *Manjushri Yamantaka: Conqueror of the Aggressive* cycle from a rocky peak like a victory banner on the north side of the Crystal Cave of Yarlung. From the Wisdom Circle of Great Bliss, Shaük Tiger Gate in Mön, he revealed in public the *Profound Path: Mahakarunika the Embodiment of All Sugatas* and its accompanying supports and samaya substances.

He performed the requisite accomplishment of each of his termas. While doing so he was blessed and accepted by Guru Rinpoche, father and mother, and had inconceivable visions. Upon the release of their command seals, he bestowed the ripening empowerments and liberating instructions of each of his termas, began to teach them widely, and composed ritual liturgies for them. His activity based on his profound termas flourished.

His dharma heirs and disciples included the great Fifth Dalai Lama; the vidyadhara Padma Trinley; Sakya Trichen Kunga Tashi, Tsedong Shapdrung, and many other great beings from the seats of the Sakyas; great holders of the Kamtsang tradition such as Gyaltsap Rinpoche and Treho Choktrül; the Drikungpa Könchok Trinley Zangpo; the Taklungpa Tendzin Sishi Namgyal; the omniscient Drukchen; Gampo Choktrül and his family; Chamdo Gyalwa Pakpalha; the nirmanakaya of Ngawang the Great; and most other famous gurus of this Himalayan region.

In eastern Tibet, his disciples included Dokhampa Ngawang Kunga Tendzin, Katok Gyalsay, the Second Dzogchen Rinpoche, and most of the Nyingma lineage holders. There were very few that did not bow to his feet.

Terdak Lingpa's elder brother, Gyalsay Tenpay Nyima, began to form a dharma connection with him but did not live long. Terdak Lingpa's foremost heart son was his younger brother, the great translator Dharma Shri, who was an emanation of Yudra Nyingpo. Other close disciples included Terdak Lingpa's son Padma Gyurme Gyamtso, Yishin Lekdrup, Rinchen Namgyal, and his daughter Mingyur Paldrön.

It is due to the vast activity in teaching and accomplishment of the magnificent fellowship formed by this master and his disciples that the kama and terma lineages of the early translations have survived down to the present day. It appears that there is no authentic lineage of these teachings that did not pass through them.

Having for the time being completed his inconceivably secret deeds, on the morning of the second day of the second month in the Wood Horse Year, his sixty-ninth year, Terdak Lingpa appeared to depart for the great terrestrial realm of Lotus Light amid wondrous signs.

This great and holy being was very kind both directly and indirectly to all dharma, both that of the Sarma tradition and that of the Nyingma tradition. Especially, through both his own efforts and his encouragement of others, he prolonged the life of fragile lineages such as the Jonangpa, Shangpa, Pacification, Severance, and Bodongpa lines. In particular, when the lineages of the study and practice of the kama teachings of the Nyingma tradition were close to disappearing like little streams in winter, Terdak Lingpa put tremendous, undeterred effort into their preservation. He enriched them with his excellent composition of many sadhanas, mandala rituals, and fine commentaries. He revived the excellent Nyingma teachings of the *Guhyagarbha*, the *Sutra of the Wisdom Assembly*, and the Great Perfection through teaching, accomplishment, and work. His activity insured their survival and prevalence down to the present.

Terdak Lingpa's collected works fill thirteen volumes. They are authentic shastras, and include his liturgical arrangements for the greatest old termas such as those called the *Former* and *Latter Termas*. I have gone to great effort to receive all of the ripening empowerments and liberating instructions from all his works, and have done so with unreserved faith and great appreciation. I have practiced and taught Terdak Lingpa's own termas to the best of my ability, and have instituted the regular accomplishment of both his liturgical arrangement of the *So Tradition Perfect Heruka* and his own Vajrasattva terma. I have done a little for his tradition, and it is my aspiration to continue to do so for the rest of my life.

It would have been fitting to include a more extensive biography of this lord, except that his outer, inner, and secret biographies, as well as accounts of his revelations of terma, already exist and possess both excellent provenance and great clarity. Therefore, and because I fear verbosity, I have abbreviated this account to a partial description of the essence of his deeds.

My essential point is that it is due to the kindness of this great and noble lord, his brother, and his descendants that the unmistaken teaching, practice, and activity of the Nyingma tradition of guhyamantra have survived and flourished. The wondrousness of this alone is sufficient to render his kindness and his mark on the teachings unequaled by anyone. I therefore pray that all great beings who care for the dharma not devote themselves solely to minor teachings of profound dharma, but spread this venerable tradition, this great treasury of dharma, and thereby raise aloft the vajrayana teachings of the Nyingma translations.[65]

65. Jamgön Kongtrül was an emanation of Terdak Lingpa.

Padma Kunkyong Lingpa

Then:

Kharak and Lakha will spy on one another.
This will be the sign that the time has come to reveal
The terma concealed at the White Stupa.
The one called Ugyen Kunkyong Lingpa will appear.

The tertön Padma Kunkyong Lingpa was an actual reappearance of Vairochana. He was the immediate rebirth of the tertön Dorje Lingpa. Kunkyong Lingpa was born in a Male Fire Rat year at Lhapu Bidzing in Shang. His father was Pawo Gyaltsen Gönpo; his mother was an emanation of Tara named Demchok Palmo.

From early childhood Kunkyong Lingpa remembered many of his previous lives and knew dharma without it having been taught to him. His behavior was beyond that of a child, and his holiness was extremely evident. He repeatedly saw Guru Rinpoche and his disciples, and received from them profound prophecies and instructions on his future revelation of profound terma. In his fourteenth year he acquired a list of his profound termas, and soon began to reveal them. As he wrote:

I, Ugyen Kunkyong Lingpa,
Am the rebirth of eight Lingpas.
I clearly remember thirty-three lives.
I have gained power by practicing guhyamantra
  mahayana dharma.
Through previous training I know it now without study.

And:

In my tenth year I saw the nature of awareness.
I never behaved like a child.
In my thirteenth year I met Lord Uddiyana.
He prophesied my termas and instructed me.
In my sixteenth year I discovered five profound termas
And Uddiyana's empowerment implements at Dorje
  Kye Rock.

And, from his *Account of Revelations*:

In the Horse month of the Ox year, based on the terma list I had found at Shoto, I, Padma Kunkyong Lingpa, went to Dorje Kye Rock near Zabulung in Yeru Shang.

> Amidst a large crowd I flew like a bird across an abyss.
> The terma door opened of itself, revealing a large cave of accomplishment.

He entered the cave and found a colorful Vajrakilaya mandala from which he took twenty-one kilas, Uddiyana's empowerment crown, other implements, and a stone vase filled with boiling life-water. Especially, from a stone image of Rahula, one arrow-length in height, he revealed many outer, inner, and secret sadhanas as well as teachings on forceful mantra. From the image's nine faces he took the *Heart Essence of Uddiyana*, the *Sadhanas of the Trikaya*, and the *Outer, Inner, and Secret Sadhanas of the Peaceful and Wrathful Padma*. From the upper body and arms of the image he took the *Eight Dispensations of Great Accomplishment*, the eight tantras on forceful mantra and the accomplishment of power that are collectively called *Hitting the Crux of Enemies and Obstructors*, and three hundred minor applications of protection and reversal. From the image's heart he took the *Heart Essence of Vajrasattva* and the *Dakinis' Heart Essence Tantra*. From the serpent tail he took teachings on dharmapalas such as the *Ekajati Cycle* and the *Rahula Cycle*.

To the left of that cave he found another cave, so large that it was like an entire valley. From that second cave he took three stone coffers and a laquered reliquary sealed with wax. From them he revealed the *Ten Cycles of the Great Perfection*, the *Clear Expanse: Mother and Son*, the *Krodhikali Cycle*, many prophecies, and several termas that Dorje Lingpa had reconcealed for future rediscovery.

Kunkyong Lingpa was assisted during all this by the upasaka and other guardians of that place. In particular, Ekajati granted him her assurance through many prophecies and much advice. During that whole time the dharmapalas appeared in the form of many emanated women, yogis, monkeys, tribesmen, and children. They assisted by carrying the termas into the midst of the assembled crowd. This caused all present to trust Kunkyong Lingpa's revelations. His fame spread.

He then spent three years transcribing the terma scrolls, and then as instructed replaced the originals at the discovery site. The night he did so, he found another terma list, and therefore went to Samye to reveal the terma concealed in the White Stupa. He opened the terma door and revealed a great deal of dharma terma, a list of further termas, the flesh of a brahmin, supports of blessing such as relics of Buddhas, and many teachings on forceful mantra capable of either saving or destroying Tibet. It appears that he put most of these back where he found them.

As Kunkyong Lingpa became famous he began to be known as the Heroic Tertön of Lhapu. His renown spread everywhere and his activity steadily increased. His disciples included his five sons such as Wangchen Nyida Zangpo and his two holy regents. These seven achieved the same wisdom as Kunkyong Lingpa. Many other holy beings of various traditions received his dharma and samaya substances, including Dorje Chang Kyenrab Chöje, the translator Gö Shönnu Pal, the translator from Trukang, the omniscient Tsultrim Gyaltsen, and the omniscient Balu Metokpa.

Kunkyong Lingpa often demonstrated unimpeded supercognition, such as when he met the mantradharin of Lo, Ngakchang Jamyang Rinchen Gyaltsen. Upon meeting him, the tertön prophesied the appearance of the mahapandita of Ngari and his brother as the mantradharin's sons.

Having completed his life and activity, Kunkyong Lingpa passed into the great peace of the dharmadhatu in his eighty-second year. Of his ocean of profound termas, the empowerment, transmission, and instructions of the *Heart Essence of Vajrasattva* became widespread. They have survived down to the present, and I have received them correctly.

Chokden Gönpo

Then:

> A fortress will appear at Nyimado in eastern Nyang.
> A hundred and sixteen generals will gather in Chalung.
> These will be the signs that the time has come to reveal
> The terma concealed on the bank of the Tsangpo at Yeru.
> The one called Ugyen Dongak Lingpa will appear.

The tertön Dongak Lingpa Chokden Gönpo was an emanation of Vairochana and the rebirth of Kunkyong Lingpa. He was born in Chonglung in Lhodrak. His father was of the Gya family and was named Sum Dargyay. His mother was named Yumbu Chungmen.

As Chokden Gönpo was born he recited the syllable DHIH. From infancy he was wild, independent, and very intelligent. He learned to read and write without being taught. As a child he pretended to give empowerments, teach dharma, and translate. He also left footprints in stone.

His mother died in his seventh year. His stepmother did not care for him well, and he suffered for several years. Eventually he became a monk at Kyungtsang Monastery and received the upasaka vow and other dharma from Chöje Tsangpa. As he remembered many of his previous lives he acquired the nickname Rebirth.

When he entered retreat at Drob Monastery he was blessed by Guru Rinpoche and became exhilarated with meditation experience. He revealed a list of termas, some scrolls, and some blessed supports from within a boulder. Guru Rinpoche cleansed him of obscurations and taught him much dharma through symbols. The minor tertön Dzinpa Sönam, a disciple of Padma Lingpa from Chak Jangchup Ling, gave him another terma list and offered him service. Dzinpa Sönam also taught Chokden Gönpo much dharma.

At that time Karchen Kunga Drakpa was at Samye. When

he met Chokden Gönpo he gave him a prophecy. Chokden Gönpo received *Mahakarunika: The Supreme Light of Wisdom*, the *Assembly of the Guru's Wisdom*, and other teachings from Kunga Drakpa. Chokden Gönpo spent most of his time in accomplishment, but in between retreats he went to Tsaritra and experienced many pure appearances and much interdependence. He also revealed a secret terma in Kongpo and benefited beings in Dakpo.

Chokden Gönpo went to meet the vidyadhara Padma Lingpa. Their encounter was like the reunion of father and son. Padma Lingpa took loving care of Chokden Gönpo and decided that he was an emanation of Dorje Lingpa. He therefore became widely known as the nirmanakaya of Dorje Lingpa. Padma Lingpa also gave him much dharma, many samaya substances, and many terma scrolls. He encouraged Chokden Gönpo to reveal the profound terma hidden at Yeru on the bank of the Tsangpo River. However, because Chokden Gönpo's consort Achay Dorje delayed him, he did not reveal it.

Nevertheless, the king of Ngari Gungthang, the Dakpo Tsele vidyadhara Sönam Namgyal, and others invited Chokden Gönpo to both eastern and western Tibet. Most of the chieftains of central Tibet and Tsang also venerated him. In Lhasa he performed a ritual in order to avert invasion. During it a torma caught on fire and flew into the sky. Through his display of miracles, Chokden Gönpo's dharma and material activity expanded greatly.

In his thirty-fifth year he built the Drukral Temple at Benshung and installed within it a golden image of Guru Rinpoche that was twenty-seven fists high. He had the intention of causing the teachings to spread widely, but he had spoiled the interdependence of the revelation of profound terma. As a result, Benpa Kyungtsangpa and other malicious people brought about his death through violence. Chokden Gönpo's work remained unfinished.

It is well known that Dongak Lingpa was his rebirth.

Dongak Lingpa revealed a few termas but did not benefit beings. Dongak Lingpa's rebirth was Yangdak Gyamtso, who founded Baka Sangngak Chöling in Puwo. Yangdak Gyamtso's nirmanakaya was the vidyadhara Chökyi Gyamtso, who benefited beings greatly. He was a dharma heir of Jatsön Nyingpo and a guru of both Karma Chagme and Dzogchen Padma Rikdzin. His emanations have continued to appear down to the present, and his son Tenpe Jungne later settled in Chongye and was very active. Tenpe Jungne was learned, and achieved siddhi. His *Visionary Sadhana of the Three Roots Containing All the Profound* was of great benefit to beings. Its lineage of empowerment and transmission survived down to the time of Terdak Lingpa and the Fifth Dalai Lama.

Tenpe Jungne's rebirth was the nirmanakaya Dongak Jungne, who appeared in Yönpo in the upper nomad country. It is unclear whether or not Dongak Jungne discovered any profound terma, but he did bring about immeasurable benefit for beings. He erected a beautiful three-story temple in his homeland, complete with supports, that still exists.

As described above, the tertön Chokden Gönpo missed his opportunity to reveal profound terma, and there is therefore no lineage of any that stems from him. However, Padma Ösal Dongak Lingpa received the dispensation of his *Five Fierce Deities of Hayagriva* in a vision. This is a concise and wonderful treatise. As he bestowed it upon me in particular, I have formed a connection with it through approach and accomplishment in recognition of my good fortune. I have also placed it in the *Great Treasury of Precious Terma*.

Ugyen Tenyi Lingpa

Then:

> Armies will camp on the nine islands in the nomad lakes.
> Two thirds of Tsang will be killed in war.
> These will be the signs that the time has come to reveal
> The terma concealed in the Temple of Divination.
> The one called Ugyen Tenyi Lingpa will appear.

The tertön Ugyen Tenyi Lingpa, also known as Padma Tsewang Gyalpo, was born at Tashi Ding in Jazang, in Tsangrong. His family was wealthy; his father was called Chieftain Norbu, and his mother Queen Kyi. Tenyi Lingpa is believed to have been an emanation of the princess Nujin Salay, arisen through the blessing of the great translator Vairochana.

Tenyi Lingpa undertook renunciation in the presence of Sangye Palzang, the abbot of Chölung. In upper Kyetsal in Drayül, Tenyi Lingpa studied the sutras. From Serdok Panchen he received training in Prajnaparamita and logic, which he mastered. At Ralung Pökya he received Mahamudra and many other teachings of the Drukpa Kagyu from the dharma lord Chokdenpa. While doing so, Tenyi Lingpa received prophecy in dreams.

Based on this prophecy he went to the Blue Robe Temple in Oyuk. From a riverbank near the temple he revealed a list of profound termas. Following the list, he went first to Zabulung in Shang. From a site there now called Seven Termas he revealed a life vase, its water boiling. Then from the Cave of Good Thoughts he revealed the *Dakinis' Clear Expanse* and samaya substance made from flesh of the seven-times-born. From Pungpo Riwoche he revealed *Yamantaka Containing All Forceful Mantras*. Especially, from a secret terma site at Tsepung he revealed his principal profound terma, which is known as the *View Containing the Wisdom of All Buddhas*.

It is a vast terma, and contains fifteen sections, each called a *Collection of Wisdom*.[66] He also extracted much profound terma from the Stone Stupa of Zurkar, Aryapalo, and Trazang Mountain, and revealed some termas that the tertön Tseten Gyaltsen had concealed for rediscovery at Paro Taktsang.

Tenyi Lingpa benefited beings greatly in Ü and Tsang. In particular, the king of Ngari Gungthang venerated Tenyi Lingpa as his guru, and his activity therefore flourished there. During that period Tenyi Lingpa publicly revealed the *Varahi Profound Seal* teachings which the vidyadhara Gödem had concealed for rediscovery at Palbar Mountain in Mangyül. This caused all to trust him, and he became renowned as an undisputedly accomplished tertön. His activity spread from Ngari throughout all Ü and Tsang.

Tenyi Lingpa's principal dharma heirs were Tsangpa Tsedak and Rongpa Tsedak. Starting with them, the lineages of the empowerments and transmissions for his termas flourished up to the time of the vidyadhara Terdak Lingpa. It seems that nowadays only the *Varahi Profound Seal* teachings survive. However, I have had the good fortune to receive the complete empowerments, transmissions, and instructions of that cycle.

I have heard that the ripening empowerments and liberating instructions of Tenyi Lingpa's *Collection of Wisdom* teachings connected to the Bön tradition still exist within that tradition.

It is evident that Tenyi Lingpa passed away in his fifties. His funeral ceremonies were performed by his dharma heir, Tsangpa Tsedak. Because this tertön had once been the daughter of the great dharma king Trisong Detsen, an image of Tenyi Lingpa containing some of his relics was installed at Khamsum Zangkang Ling.

---

66. This term, *dgongs.'dus*, needs to be translated differently dependent on usage. When referring to a mandala of deities, it means an "assembly of wisdom." When referring to teachings on the view, it means a "collection of wisdom." What must be understood, however, is that since the deities and their wisdom are never regarded as separate from one another, both usages converge in practice.

Dorje Lingpa

Then:

> A herd of pigs will gather in upper Kuyül.
> Little forts will appear on every strategic mountain.
> The passes and roads will become dangerous and blocked.
> People will live off their herds.
> These will be the signs that the time has come to reveal
> The terma concealed at Kongpo Buchu.
> The one called Ugyen Dorje Lingpa will appear.

The third of the kings among tertöns was Dorje Lingpa, an actual reappearance of the great translator Vairochana, emanated for the benefit of the teachings. He was born in a Male Fire Dog year at Dranang Wentsa in central Tibet to a family of mantrin vajra holders.[67] His father's name was Kutön Sönam Gyaltsen. His mother's name was Karmo Gyen.

Upon birth Dorje Lingpa was given the name Ugyen Zangpo. From infancy he demonstrated unimaginable wonders and signs of holiness. In his seventh year he became a shramanera in the presence of the omniscient Traba Shakya at Pangshong Lhari. Starting then, Dorje Lingpa received consummate training in sutra, tantra, the Sarma tradition, and the Nyingma tradition under Traba and other gurus.

In his thirteenth year Dorje Lingpa saw Guru Rinpoche's face seven times. In reliance upon the terma list found among Guru Chöwang's revelations, Dorje Lingpa revealed from the back of the Tradruk Jomo his first terma. This included a sadhana of the three roots accompanied by one hundred and eight minor sadhanas, terma lists, forceful mantras, writings on rasayana, and prophecies.

In his fifteenth year Dorje Lingpa opened the terma door at Okar Rock in Jingda. Behind it was an enormous accomplishment cave. Guru Rinpoche actually came there, arranged a mandala, and empowered him. He gave Dorje Lingpa the

67. The year was 1346 C.E.

transmissions for each of his terma scrolls along with many terma objects. These included a representation of Guru Rinpoche, four volumes belonging to the Guru himself, a hundred scrolls, four vases of vitality water, an amulet filled with samaya substance, and more.

From these, Dorje Lingpa revealed the *Testament of a Hundred Chapters*, the *Great Perfection Father Tantra Vast Expanse of the View*, the *Great Perfection Mother Tantra Brilliant Expanse of the Sun*, the *Dakinis' Quintessence Conjoined Sun and Moon*, the *Son Tantras of the Tenfold Heart Essence*, the *Four Assemblies*, and the *Eight Supplements*.

Then, from Pearl Crystal Heights, Dorje Lingpa revealed the *Ten Instructions on Practice*. In the Vitality Water Cave at the Maitreya Temple of Bumthang he received vitality water from Yeshe Tsogyal herself. Starting with these revelations, Dorje Lingpa revealed a series of termas including dharma medicine consecrated by Guru Rinpoche at Yangleshö, the spirit-turquoises of both the dharma king and Yeshe Tsogyal, wish-fulfilling jewels, and numerous dharma cycles and forceful mantras. In all, he revealed forty-three great termas and a hundred and eight minor ones.

While extracting terma at Chimphu, Dorje Lingpa met Guru Rinpoche thirteen times. At Chuwori Dorje Lingpa emanated two forms of himself and simultaneously revealed two different termas, both publicly. He left footprints in stone there that were a cubit long. In Nyen Cave at Fire Lake in Zabulung, Dorje Lingpa was hosted by both Thanglha and Gangkar Shamay. Many great gods and spirits of Tibet gathered and convened a great accomplishment assembly of the Eight Dispensations. Dorje Lingpa then bestowed empowerment on all the participants. He visited, in emanation, the eight great charnel grounds and met the eight vidyadharas. He received from them instructions on the eight confidences.[68]

Whenever Dorje Lingpa extracted terma Guru Rinpoche, Yeshe Tsogyal, Vairochana, and other masters would actually

68. The eight confidences are the views of the eight dispensations, such as the Four Wheels of Yamantaka, the Three Neighs of Hayagriva, etc.

appear, empower him, and instruct him. Through Dorje Lingpa's wondrous display of miracles, everyone was freed from the chains of doubt and placed on a level beyond reversal. He left many imprints of his body and feet in stone. Each of the terma coffers from Zabulung, Kharchu, and Shotö contained a hundred and eight empowerments, consecration ceremonies, liturgies of fulfillment and confession, fire offering ceremonies, and means of imprisoning demons. As these indicate, Dorje Lingpa did a great deal to ensure the wellbeing of all Tibet.

His dharma termas are both vast and profound, especially his gurusadhanas, Mahakarunika, and Great Perfection. He also discovered wondrous images such as the statue of Vajrasattva he removed from Pungpo Riwoche, and the Eleven-Faced Avalokita and Sandalwood Tara he removed from the capital of a pillar in Lhasa. He recovered samaya substances such as flesh of the seven-times-born and dharma medicine; wealth terma such as wish-fulfilling jewels; and Bön teachings such as the *Golden Spoon of the Great Perfection* and the greater, intermediate, and lesser *Oral Lineages of Tapitsitra*. He also found teachings on both medicine and astrology, and his activity in those disciplines was extensive.

Dorje Lingpa's biological son Chöyingpa was an emanation of Nupchen Sangye Yeshe. It seems that their descendants continue down to the present in Bhutan.

It is said that Dorje Lingpa offered his *Yamantaka* cycle and *Five Jambhalas* cycle to Rolpe Dorje, the Fourth Gyalwang Karmapa.

Dorje Lingpa's main seat was at Lingkhor, but he also resided in Lhodrak, at Paro in Bhutan, and at Nye Monastery in Zanguk. In each of these places he benefited beings vastly.

Although his most famous name was Dorje Lingpa, he was also known as Padma Lingpa, Kunkyong Lingpa, Yungdrung Lingpa, and Manjushridharmamitra.

Having completed his service to beings, Dorje Lingpa composed his *Final Testament and Great Prophecy* in his sixtieth year and then, amid wondrous signs, appeared to pass away at Draklong. His remains were preserved for three years. During that time, his body would occasionally speak or recite stanzas of dedication. At the end of the three years his body was cremated, and produced many images of deities and other relics. His right foot flew out of his cremation stupa with a snapping sound and was kept by his heart disciple Tashi Jungne. Dorje Lingpa's left foot, which also emerged from the fire, was kept by Asanga of India.[69] It is said that the many relics which appeared among Dorje Lingpa's ashes continued to increase miraculously for centuries afterward.

Although Dorje Lingpa's lineage was originally widespread in both Lhodrak and Bhutan, it seems to have almost died out. Nevertheless, our lord guru sought it with great exertion, and has received the dispensations of both long and short lineages of the *Great Perfection Father Tantra Expanse of the View*, the *Great Perfection Mother Tantra Brilliant Expanse of the Sun*, the *Non-Dual Tantra Heart Essence of HUM*, the *Guru's Assembly of Dispensations* and *Yidam's Assembly of Dispensations* from the *Four Assemblies*, *Mahakarunika Who Protects from All Bad Rebirths*, *Jinasagara*, and the *Oral Lineage of the Wrathful Guru*. I have had the good fortune to receive these from him.

There has been discussion as to whether the great emanated tertön Dorje Lingpa's indications and terma sites correspond to those found in the prophecy from the Testament that I quoted above. However, there can be no dispute that he was the third of the five kings among tertöns, or that he was one of the twelve great Lingpas.[70]

---

69. Not the famous Indian writer, but an Indian disciple of Dorje Lingpa's with the same name.

70. Lingpa can mean a person as great as a continent. The name is said to have been given by Guru Rinpoche to those tertöns, such as the twelve Lingpas, who were destined to be like great continents in the world of the terma teachings. The twelve Lingpas correspond to the four continents and eight subcontinents of the Buddhist world. Jamgön Kongtrül was a rebirth of Dorje Lingpa.

Sangye Lingpa

Then:

> Two factions will fight at Gyerphu in Tsang.
> A herd of pigs will gather at Rulak Tsuphu.
> These will be the signs that the time has come to reveal
> The terma concealed at Chimyül in Kongpo.
> The one called Ugyen Rinchen Lingpa will appear.

This tertön, the second Rinchen Lingpa predicted in the *Testament*, was definitely Sangye Lingpa. This is clearly indicated by the prediction here of one of his terma sites, and Sangye Lingpa himself affirmed this in his *Great Autobiography*.

Sangye Lingpa was an emanation of Prince Damdzin Rölpa Yeshe Tsal. He was born in the lower valley of Yülung, above an accomplishment cave of Guru Rinpoche's in the Nyangpo area of Kongpo. Sangye Lingpa's father was an emanation of Hayagriva known as Khamshik Taklung the Crazy. His mother, who was blessed by the mother Vajravarahi, was a qualified dakini named Ahum Gyen. Sangye Lingpa was born amid wondrous signs in the Male Iron Dragon Year at Threefold Vajra Rock.[71] He was given the name Rikdzin.

In his fifth year Sangye Lingpa received the upasaka vows from the abbot Shönnu Pal, and had a vision of Avalokita. He learned to read and write just by being shown the letters, and quickly became learned. His father soon died however, and his mother took another partner who disliked the boy. While Sangye Lingpa was suffering because of this, he received a prophetic instruction from a red woman. Accordingly, he went to Longpo Drong Sarda, where he entered the presence of Rölpe Dorje, the Fourth Gyalwang Karmapa. He then went to the monastery of Changchup Ling near Tsaritra, where he undertook renunciation in the presence of the abbot Changchup Dorje and the master Shakya Yeshe. He received

71. The year was 1340 C.E.

the name Sangye Zangpo, which is why when he later revealed profound terma he became known as Sangye Lingpa. Sangye Lingpa also heard much dharma from his abbot and master.

When Karmapa Rölpe Dorje was about to return to central Tibet, he said to Lama Changchup Dorje, "Give me this nephew of yours."[72] Changchup Dorje complied, and the Karmapa was delighted and predicted that Sangye Lingpa would guide many beings to liberation. When they reached Lhasa, Sangye Lingpa saw the faces of both Avalokita and Guru Rinpoche. These were the first of many repeated visions of them that he would have through the ensuing years.

Sangye Lingpa vowed to practice for three years. Then Lama Changchup Dorje passed away, so Sangye Lingpa went to see the learned and accomplished Lama Chökyi Lodrö in Tsaritra, and became his heart son. When Lama Chökyi Lodrö went to central Tibet, Sangye Lingpa entered retreat in the upper valley of Lhundrup Teng. While he was in retreat, the great terma protector Tsengö offered Sangye Lingpa three scrolls. These included a terma list, prophecies, instructions on how to accomplish his termas, and other advice. Lama Chökyi Lodrö supported Sangye Lingpa, and he was able to perform the terma accomplishment properly. He received empowerment, prophecy, and the permission to reveal terma from Guru Rinpoche and his entourage of dakinis.

In accordance with the prophecies he had received, Sangye Lingpa revealed his first terma from the Great Cave of Puri on the twenty-fifth day of the first month of autumn in the Wood Dragon Year.[73] This contained the texts and instructions of the *Guru's Wisdom Assembly*, which is the intermediate *Assembly of Dispensations*, and is unique among all the termas revealed in Tibet. Along with it Sangye Lingpa also revealed a *Mahakarunika* cycle. He presented these to Lama Chökyi Lodrö, who received them with delight and practiced them, becoming Sangye Lingpa's first dharma heir.

Starting that year, Sangye Lingpa began to reveal terma

---

72. Apparently Sangye Lingpa was his abbot's nephew.

73. 1364 C.E.

from many sites including Karzuk Cliff, Jeworing, Tsechen Rock, Longpo Jangde Bumpa, Langpo Kada Cliff, and Karteng Cliff in Kyen. The termas he revealed include the *Heart Essence Vajrakilayasadhana*, the *Curse of the Black Tortoise*, *Black Hayagriva*, the *Very Secret Unsurpassable Mahakarunika*, and substance termas including pills of samaya substances, images of Guru Rinpoche, a copper vase filled with gold, an iron kila, and twenty-one relics of the Tathagata that multiplied miraculously.

While Sangye Lingpa was in Chimyül in Kongpo in order to reveal terma, the tertön Drime Lhunpo came there because of a prophecy he had received from dakinis. Together, the two tertöns revealed terma containing *Blue-Robed Vajrapani*, the *Magic of Nine Racing Mönpas*, and the bodhichitta of Guru Rinpoche and Yeshe Tsogyal.

At Puri Rinchen Barwa, Sangye Lingpa revealed an Avalokita cycle. At Vulture Basin he revealed another *Mahakarunika* cycle, a rasayana cycle, and *Ishvara's Wind Lasso*. The prophecy concerning Changchup Lingpa Palgyi Gyaltsen came from this terma. Sent to search in Lhatö, he encountered the tertön and gained faith in him.

In Tsaritra Sangye Lingpa revealed a *Sadhana of the Naga King Drinzang*. At the White Sands of Gyer he revealed the *Ayusadhana of the Joined Moon and Sun*. At Shinje Badong in Gyal he and Drime Lhunpo revealed *Yamantaka Ayupati: Magic Causing Unconsciousness* and an activity kila of Guru Rinpoche's known as *Enough Just to Brandish It*. In an accomplishment cave of Guru Rinpoche's Sangye Lingpa revealed the *Concise Essence of the Great Perfection*. At Damdul in Kongpo he revealed the *Six Root Tantras of the Wisdom Assembly*. At Samye Chimphu he revealed a wonderful image of Guru Rinpoche. At Orshong Lungdrom he revealed the jewel called Takshadep and a set of dakinis' jewelry. In all, between his twenty-fifth year and his thirty-second, Sangye Lingpa revealed eighteen great termas and innumerable minor termas. It is impossible to list them all.

Whenever he revealed terma there were rains of flowers, tents of rainbow light, the sound of music, and the visible presence of dakinis.

As prophetically instructed by Vajravarahi with an entourage of thirteen dakinis, Sangye Lingpa precisely catalogued the *Guru's Wisdom Assembly*, dividing it into thirteen volumes. This same division is still used nowadays.

From its prophecies:

One billion people will achieve stability in the generation stage.
Eight hundred thousand will reveal manifest signs of accomplishment.
Ninety thousand will be liberated in the undefiled illusory body.
Ten billion will achieve at least one siddhi.
Those who plant the seed of liberation will be beyond reckoning.
This will be continuous, not all at one time.

As indicated by that detailed prophecy, the *Guru's Wisdom Assembly* became so widespread that there were said to be twenty distinct great streams of its lineage and dispensation. Sangye Lingpa's other termas were also held by countless dharma heirs. His principal dharma heir was the Fourth Gyalwang Karmapa, Rölpe Dorje. Other heirs were Shamar Kachö Wangpo, the Great Lord of Nedong, the holy Sakya guru Sönam Gyaltsen, Yakde Panchen, Joten Khenchen Sönam Zangpo, and the Drikung Dharmaraja.

Innumerable great personages and lamas were Sangye Lingpa's disciples. In particular, when the great Yung Lo Emperor of the Ming Dynasty invited the Fifth Gyalwang Karmapa Deshin Shekpa to China, he requested in his invitation letter that the Karmapa bring with him "an immaculate dharma terma of Padmakara, the siddha from Uddiyana." The Karmapa accordingly brought with him the profound dharma of the *Guru's Wisdom Assembly* along with a wondrous blue vase and a golden vajra of samaya. When Deshin Shekpa offered these to the emperor, he is said to have been so delighted that he immediately offered the Karmapa a seal and special robes.

From Sangye Lingpa's biological son Yeshe Dorje and his principal disciple Jakhyungwa Palden Senge sprang the lineages of his descendants and disciples respectively. Both lineages have produced many learned and accomplished beings. Sangye Lingpa's termas, especially the *Guru's Wisdom Assembly*, passed down through the earlier and later Tsele Rinpoches and the earlier and later Ta Lamas of Kham. Nowadays his termas fill all of Tibet; their practice is extremely widespread. It is evident, therefore, that this emanated tertön is peerless in his expansion of Guru Rinpoche's activity.

After building Dechen Samdrup Monastery in Nyimpu, Sangye Lingpa made it his main seat. When he performed amrita accomplishment there, extraordinary signs and miracles occurred, and it seems that the substance lineage of his amrita still exists.

Having done beings and the teachings immeasurable good, Sangye Lingpa dissolved his wisdom into the dharmadhatu at Changchup Ling Monastery on the thirtieth day of the third month in the Male Fire Rat Year, his fifty-seventh year.[74] His immediate rebirth was born at Nelmeu to a father named Döndrup Gyalpo, but he died young. His subsequent rebirth, the nirmanakaya Sangye Palden, was born at Longpo Gying and was brought to his seat. It is said that he did beings and the teachings a great deal of good. After him, there has been no particular line of recognized incarnations, although it seems that Sangye Lingpa's descendants still exist.

This great emanated tertön's termas are as vast as an ocean. I have received his *Testament of Puri*; *Guru's Wisdom Assembly*; *Three Precious Cycles of Mahakarunika*; *Tsechen Kila*; *White, Red, and Black Manjushri*; *Secret Garuda*;

74. 1396 C.E.

Stainless Confession Tantra; and his *Ayusadhana of the Joined Moon and Sun*. I have received all of the empowerments for his termas that currently exist. I have done the approach, accomplishment, and great accomplishment of the *Guru's Wisdom Assembly* several times. I have served that cycle by commissioning, at the encouragement of others and because of my own devotion, the printing of the complete liturgy of the *Guru's Wisdom Assembly* and by writing necessary supplements. I have also commissioned three sets of paintings of the deities and protectors of the *Guru's Wisdom Assembly*: one set consisting of fifteen paintings, one of eleven, and one of nine. I have also commissioned a complete and fine printing of the *Guru's Wisdom Assembly*'s thirteen volumes. While establishing a good and extensive connection with this tradition, I have made the aspiration that I and all who form any connection with it be accepted by Guru Rinpoche and receive his blessing in every one of our lives.

Padma Lingpa

Then:

> The foundation at Pig Mountain in Gö will conceal a fortress.
> Poison will be sold at Takdru in Latö.
> These will be the signs that the time has come to reveal
> The terma concealed at Fire Lake.
> The one called Ugyen Padma Lingpa will appear.

Ugyen Padma Lingpa was the fourth of the five kings among tertöns. He was the fifth and last of the five pure rebirths of Princess Padma Sal, the daughter of Trisong Detsen. He was born in the Male Iron Dog Year amidst wondrous signs at Bumthang in Bhutan to the Nyö family.[75] His father's name was Döndrup Zangpo, and his mother's name Drongmo Paldzom.

75. The year was 1370 C.E.

As Padma Lingpa was the immediate rebirth of the omniscient Drime Özer, holiness was awakened within him from an early age. He knew both letters and crafts without being taught. Especially, on the tenth day of the first autumn month in the Monkey year, at the Place of the Six Syllables, Guru Rinpoche revealed his face to Padma Lingpa and blessed him.[76] He placed a guide to one hundred and eight termas in his hands.

76. The year was 1380 C.E.

Accordingly, in his twenty-seventh year Padma Lingpa revealed the first of all his termas, the *Clear Expanse of the Great Perfection* cycle, from a swirling pool known as Blazing Lake adjacent to Naring Rock. In the presence of a large crowd Padma Lingpa, carrying a torch, walked into the pool and disappeared under its surface. When he reappeared from the pool his torch was still burning and he was carrying a large terma coffer, the size of a pot, under his arm. Everyone who witnessed this was amazed and filled with faith. As a result his undisputed fame covered the earth like the light of the sun and moon.

At Samye Chimphu he revealed the *Great Perfection: The Wisdom Assembly of Samantabhadra*. At other terma sites he revealed the *Great Perfection: The Lesser Son Non-Dual Tantra* cycle, *Guru Ocean of Jewels*, *Mahakarunika: The Torch that Dispels Darkness*, the *Eight Dispensations: The Mirror of the Mind*, *Kila the Razor*, and his *Amrita Accomplishment* cycle. He therefore revealed not only the Great Perfection, gurusadhana, and Mahakarunika, but also the three cycles of *Dispensation, Kila, and Amrita*.

Padma Lingpa also revealed *Vajrapani: The Tamer of the Vicious* and the lesser *Vajrachanda* cycle; the greater, intermediate, and lesser *Wrathful Guru* cycles; the *Vajra Garland Vitality Teachings*; *Jewel Application: The Accomplishment of Vitality*; the *Three Black Deities*; and termas concerning minor activities. Along with his many dharma termas, Padma Lingpa also revealed vast amounts of samaya substances and the three types of supports, including those that bestow liberation through taste, the flesh of the seven-times-born, and the statue called Padma Guru.[77] In particular, the Temple of Kyerchu, which is similar to the Paltsap Sumpa Temple, was buried and concealed until this tertön excavated it. It is now visible to all.

Padma Lingpa revealed wealth terma such as three of Trisong Detsen's soul turquoises, called Blazing Gem, Blazing Mountain, and Red Mansion on the Hill. He also revealed undamaged garments worn by Yeshe Tsogyal, a mirror called Reveals the Distant, and other fine and precious termas belonging to the dynasty of the dharma kings.

Although Padma Lingpa received a guide to one hundred and eight termas, he was only able to reveal about half of them. When the tertön was dying his son supplicated him for permission to reveal the rest of them. Padma Lingpa told him, "It will be hard for you to reveal terma dharma, but if you keep pure samaya and pray to me it is possible that you might find a few." Accordingly, it is said that Padma Lingpa's son Dawa did reveal a few termas.

Padma Lingpa's deeds were inconceivably wondrous. He prophesied that in the future he will become the Buddha Vajragarbha in the realm Lotus Array, and that all connected to him will be born in that realm and become disciples of that Buddha.

About Padma Lingpa's heart sons and disciples, from a prophecy within his termas:

Ten thousand will be karmically connected.
Two thousand will be connected through aspirations.
Eleven will be connected through the profound point.
Seventeen will hold the mandala.
Three sons of the heart will appear.

Accordingly, among his inconceivably many disciples, the principal ones were the six nirmanakayas; the six mahasid

---

77. The three supports are representations of the bodies, speech, and minds of Buddhas.

dhas; the six great sons who revealed signs of attainment; the three heart sons whose wisdom equaled his—Joden Khenchen Tsultrim Paljor, Nangso Gyalwa Döndrup, and Tulku Chokden Gönpo; and Padma Lingpa's four biological sons, who were emanations of the lords of the three families. Among them his son Dawa, an emanation of Avalokita, possessed inconceivable blessing and power. As he achieved his father's wisdom, his activity was vast. Dawa was praised and revered as a guru by many great and holy beings, including the Great Lord of the Sakyas, Drikung Rinchen Puntsok, Shamar Könchok Yenlak, and Pawo Chögyal Döndrup. Dawa was respected by all the great men of Ü, Tsang, and Bhutan. He benefited other beings tremendously. Nevertheless, as he lived as a hidden yogi, his dharma lineage never became widespread.

Through the activity of two peerless dharma lords—the nirmanakaya Natsok Rangdröl, the ornament of the teachings; and Umdze Döndrup Palbar—and that of Padma Lingpa's speech emanations and the nirmanakayas of his heart sons, who starting with the seven incarnations who left miraculous relics have appeared continually down to the present day, his lineage has spread throughout Bhutan and both central and eastern Tibet.

The lineage of the empowerments and transmissions for Padma Lingpa's termas remains unbroken. I have received his *Gurusadhana*, *Great Perfection*, *Mahakarunika*, *Eight Dispensations* (both collectively and individually), *Vajrapani Vajrachanda* (both the greater and lesser cycles), *Vitality Accomplishment*, *Wrathful Guru* cycle, *Three Black Deities*, and various minor applications. I have taught these to the best of my ability.

Jatsön Nyingpo

Then:

> Two or three panditas will come to Tibet
> From Ghanaru and Vinasa in India.
> They will venerate the Jowo Shakyamuni in Lhasa.
> These will be the signs that the time has come to reveal
> The termas concealed in northern and southern Kongpo.
> The one called Ugyen Letrö Lingpa will appear.

The tertön Letro Lingpa, also called the vidyadhara Jatsön Nyingpo and the mantradharin Humnak Mebar, was a great bhikshu vajra holder, one person known by three names. He was the fruitional emanation of the compassion of Nyangben Tingdzin Zangpo, who was the greatest of the hundred and eight disciples of Guru Rinpoche who achieved immaculate bodies of light.

Jatsön was born at Varuna Sky Grove in Kongpo as the son of Chökyong Gönpo, his father; and Namlang Butri, his mother, under the constellation Pushya in the Female Wood Bird Year.[78] From infancy he remembered his predisposition for dharma, and learned letters in his third year merely by being shown them. During his childhood he left many handprints and footprints in stone.

From the age of twelve until his twentieth year he studied. In particular he mastered medicine. During those years he repeatedly encountered Guru Rinpoche in reality, in visions, and in dreams. Driven by renunciation and intense sadness, his mind became one-pointedly focused on dharma alone. He came to regard all samsaric places and companions as like a pit of fire. He fled to dharma and entered the presence of the dharma lord Mipham Tashi Lodrö.

That lord had dreamed that a few women brought him an old stupa constructed by Guru Padma, saying to him, "This needs to be reconsecrated." When he reconsecrated the stupa

78. The year was 1585 C.E.

in his dream, it blazed with light. Mipham Tashi Lodrö therefore saw that Jatsön was worthy, and permitted him to undertake renunciation, giving him the name Ngawang Chögyal Wangpo. He also gave him innumerable guhyamantra empowerments, transmissions, and instructions. After receiving these, Jatsön devoted his time to one-pointed practice.

From other masters such as Dakpo Shabdrung Norbu Gyenpa, the omniscient Drukchen, and the peerless Lhatsewa Jatsön received practically all the dharma of sutra and tantra of the kama and terma lineages of the Sarma and Nyingma traditions. In particular, he undertook completion in the presence of Lhatsewa, becoming a bhikshu.

For seventeen years Jatsön Nyingpo raised the victory banner of accomplishment in sealed retreat. During those years he received repeated prophecies of terma. He ignored them until, when he had completed a hundred million recitations of Vajrapani's mantra, he was encouraged by the dharma lord Mipham Tashi Lodrö.

On the tenth day of the first month in the Male Iron Monkey Year, Jatsön Nyingpo revealed the first of his termas.[79] This was a cast iron image of a garuda, the size of a baby bird. Within it he found a terma guide in the handwriting of Yeshe Tsogyal. Accordingly, from the Iron Gate at Hom Gorge in Draklung he secretly removed the *Very Profound Embodiment of the Three Jewels*. He then completed the accomplishment of that terma and maintained secrecy for the requisite period of time.

At such sites as Buchu in Kongpo; Jangtrandze, a sacred place in Jönpalung; Nyemo Lhari; the abode of the sangha at Kongtrang; and the Urusha Temple he revealed many profound termas such as *Mahakarunika*; *Hayagriva, Varahi, and Guru Wish-Fulfilling Jewel*; the *Essence of the Definitive Meaning: The Peaceful and Wrathful Ones*; the *Vajra of Meteoric Iron Ayusadhana*; *Dorje Trolö*; the *Glorious Protector Maning*; and many guides to sacred places. Although the *Embodiment of the Three Jewels* and a few

79. The year was 1620 C.E.

others were secret termas, most of his revelations were public.

Jatsön Nyingpo had boundless supercognition and miraculous abilities. He was able to easily see what was hidden from others and cross rivers and abysses without difficulty. In particular, when Jatsön was about to reveal the terma of Nyemo Lhari, Pratiwa of Kongpo and other spiteful people were guarding the terma site with an army because they feared that the terma's removal would deplete the earth's richness. The tertön, enraptured, mounted his horse. It galloped straight up a rock face as smooth as a mirror, reaching a place only accessible to birds and leaving hoofprints in the rock. In an instant, Jatsön Nyingpo removed the terma and rode away. The soldiers were so terrified by this display of yogic prowess and great miraculous ability that they all gained faith in him.

Jatsön's magical power and force were unimaginably great. He did much for the wellbeing of all of Tibet, as well as particular regions, by controlling samaya-spoilers and averting invasion. He accepted many fortunate people as disciples and gave them the amrita of ripening and liberation of many types of dharma from the kama and terma lineages of the Sarma and Nyingma traditions. This lord was noble in his behavior, and never departed from the conduct of a bhikshu. He lived as a complete renunciate and encouraged his disciples to do so as well. He caused them to participate in the true path.

Jatsön Nyingpo founded a practice community at Bangri Jokpo, a high, isolated, and sacred place that he had revealed himself. It remains active to this day, and is held by both nephew and emanation lineages. Jatsön's first dharma heir was Gampo Shapdrung Norbu Gyenpa. Once the gate of Jatsön Nyingpo's activity was opened, people gathered around him from all of central and eastern Tibet, including the Tenth Gyalwang Karmapa Chöying Dorje; Shamar Chökyi Wangchuk; Gyaltsap Drakpa Döndrup; Drikungpa Chökyi Drakpa; Drukchen Paksam Wangpo; Ngaki Wangpo, the vidyadhara of Dorje Drak; Tsele Natsok Rangdröl; Lhatsün Namkha Jikme; the vidyadhara Trinley Lhundrup;

Kangyurwa Gönpo Sönam Chokden; Puwo Baka Tulku Rikdzin Chökyi Gyamtso; Kunga Gyamtso, the siddha of Derge; the great tertön Düdül Dorje; and Tala Padmamati.

Jatsön Nyingpo's activity and influence spread all the way to the great eastern ocean, and continues undiminished today. I have increased this activity. I have received his complete six volumes of terma as well as his collected works. I have taken his termas in general and especially the *Very Profound Embodiment of the Three Jewels* as the essence of my daily yoga of generation and completion, and have received signs of their blessing. I have composed writings in support of his termas, including essays of instruction and the *Great Guide to Approaching the Embodiment of the Three Jewels*. I have had these printed, as well as the *Essence of the Definitive Meaning: The Peaceful and Wrathful Ones* and its accessories. I have established its continuous observance as the tenth-day practice and offering in front of the great golden relics of our lord protector, Vajradhara Padma Nyinje Wangpo.

In summary, although this tertön's interdependence was the worst among the four types described—excellent, intermediate, poor, and very poor—his bodhichitta and training were extraordinary. Because he perfected the practice of his own profound termas, his terma dharma—especially the *Embodiment of the Three Jewels*—has spread throughout all of the Sarma and Nyingma traditions, as anyone can see. Throughout the history of Jatsön's dharma lineage, many practitioners appear to have achieved the body of light. During the lifetime of Lord Sönam Topgyal alone, two people did so at Dakpo.

Having completed his activity, Jatsön Nyingpo consciously demonstrated how to pass into a great pure realm in his seventy-second year at Bangri Jokpo, openly displaying signs and miracles.[80]

Although there have been five tertöns who have worn the crown of the name Letro Lingpa, and all of them have been

80. The year was 1656 C.E.

authentic tertöns, it is universally known that the prophecy in the *Testament of Padma,* including the identification of terma sites, refers only to Jatsön Nyingpo.

Samten Dechen Lingpa

Then:

> Here in Tibet there will be a hundred and eight so-called kings.
> Because of the karmic connection between the snow and the lion
> Worldly people will lack even a moment's happiness.
> These will be the signs that the time has come to reveal
> The terma concealed at Jar Rock.
> The one called Ugyen Samten Lingpa will appear.

The tertön Ugyen Samten Dechen Lingpa was an emanation of both Drokmi Palgyi Yeshe and Yudra Nyingpo. He was born at Longpo Jimgang, and lived as a mantradharin vajra holder. It is clear that he founded Dechen Ling at Nyangkha in Kongpo.

At the White Rock of the Jowo in eastern Jar, Samten Dechen Lingpa revealed the *Profound All-Inclusive Three Roots* cycle. He also revealed the *Subduing All the Vicious* cycle, which is one of the nine great traditions of the *Eight Dispensations*; the *Glorious Four-Faced Protector*; the *Protector Realm-Guardian Father and Mother*; and other cycles. It appears, however, that Samten Dechen Lingpa's dharma lineage eventually became rare. Nevertheless, our lord guru recently revealed the tantras, agamas, and upadeshas of the *Eight Dispensations: Subduing All the Vicious* as rediscovered terma, and I have had the good fortune to receive it from him.

Although it is unclear exactly when Samten Dechen Lingpa lived, some historical sources indicate that he appeared during the later life of Sangye Lingpa. Chöje Lingpa and others have interpreted the prediction of Samten Dechen Lingpa as a prediction of Taksham Nüden Dorje, who appeared later. This is also correct, but I have presented it as a prediction of Samten Dechen Lingpa because that was the original and widespread reading of it. You may learn about the great tertön Taksham from the seed of his life that will appear below.

Shikpo Lingpa

Then:

> Because of designs drawn on felt with vermilion
> Famine will occur in Nupkyi Sekpalung.
> This will be the sign that the time has come to reveal
> The terma concealed at Garuda Nest Rock.
> The one called Ugyen Shikpo Lingpa will appear.

The tertön Shikpo Lingpa Gargyi Wangchuk was an emanation of Prince Damdzin. Shikpo Lingpa was born at Tölung Nangtse in central Tibet, not far from where the two Jowo images reside, on Sunday the twenty-third day of the tenth month in the Male Wood Monkey year under the constellation Purva-Phalguni.[81] His father's name was Namkha Wangchen Puntsok; his mother's was Tsewang Tenma. As he was born to a ruling family, his birth occurred in the Golden Palace of Nangtse.

In his fifth year Shikpo Lingpa requested hair-cutting and renunciation from the lord Menchupa Namkha Rinchen. Namkha Rinchen refused the request, saying, "Cutting this boy's hair would do the cutter no good! I will give you the vows of mantra instead, and will name you." He gave him the name Namkha Tsewang Gyalpo.

In his twenty-first year Shikpo Lingpa performed the accomplishment of terma. He dreamed that someone told him, "Your termas are at Garuda Nest Rock. Here is a list of

81. The year was 1524 C.E.

them," and gave him a book wrapped in yellow silk. Looking at the book, he found that it was a precise terma list. When he awoke, the list remained clearly in his mind, so he wrote it down.

In the evening of the tenth day in the fourth month of that year, Shikpo Lingpa and six attendants rode to Garuda Nest Rock. They reached the entrance to its secret caves at sunrise, which Shikpo Lingpa recognized as auspicious. The rope needed to climb to the upper secret cave was broken; there was no way to get to it. Shikpo Lingpa entered the cave miraculously and searched for signs of terma. He discovered a smooth, long stone one cubit in width, with a flaming jewel drawn on it in calcite. By removing the stone he opened the terma door. The cavity was filled with powdered charcoal. Within it lay an octagonal clay terma coffer. Inside the box were the *Assembly of Victors Ayusadhana* cycle, samaya substances from the seven-times-born, vitality water, and many other termas.

At Zangyak Rock, the Stone Stupa of Zurkhar, the Urusha Temple, Shotö Terdrom, Lhasa, Samye Monastery, and other sites Shikpo Lingpa revealed the *Seven Profound Deity Cycles*, *Mahakarunika Who Liberates from Samsara*, the *Secret Heart Essence of the Great Perfection*, *Hayagriva the Naga Tamer*, the *Wrathful Wheel of Blazing Meteoric Iron*, *Twenty-Five Ways to Prevent Invasion*, and much other terma dharma. He also found many images and supports, and much samaya substance.

There was known to be a prediction that Shikpo Lingpa would be a contributor to the *Wisdom Assembly* terma tradition. Accordingly, he performed excellent service to that tradition at Nyimphu. In general, he emphasized the practice of the earlier kama and terma teachings. He therefore became a lord of all the Nyingma teachings of great secrecy, both kama and terma. His vast activity in study and teaching made him a vital source of dharma.

Shikpo Lingpa's main disciples were the omniscient

Könchok Yenlak, Sakya Dakchen Kunga Rinchen, Tsedong Dakchen Kunga Samdrup, and Drukpa Shapdrung Mipam Chögyal. His lineage was held by innumerable disciples who came from Kham, Kongpo, Dakpo, Enyal, Bhutan, Tsang, and central Tibet. He prolonged the life of the great secret Nyingma teachings. This great tertön, along with Sokdokpa Lodrö Gyaltsen and Gangra Lochen, caused all of the kama and terma Nyingma teachings to become widespread. The survival of these teachings down to the present is due to this tertön's kindness.

Having completed his activity, he demonstrated the dissolution of his wisdom into the dharmadhatu amid wondrous signs in his sixtieth year, at the new moon of the second month in the Sheep year.[82] The lineage of Shikpo Lingpa's termas has lately become quite rare. Nevertheless, this tertön predicted the appearance of eight disciples named Padma to his dharma heir Padma Gyaltsen. Because of those eight disciples—Tala Padmamati and the others—Shikpo Lingpa's lineage has survived. I have gone to great effort to receive its ripening empowerments and liberating instructions, have served it by writing texts, and have spread its activity a little through teaching.

82. The year was 1583 C.E.

Dechen Lingpa

Then:

> Central Tibetans will gather at Targo Field.
> A fortress called Meyar will appear near Mount Hepo.
> These will be the signs that the time has come to reveal
> The terma concealed at Karak Cave.
> The one called Ugyen Dechen Lingpa will appear.

The tertön Dechen Lingpa was born in Drushül Salt Valley at the foot of Soaring Garuda Mountain. His father's name was Paljor Gyaltsen; his mother's name was Padma Tso. Dechen

Lingpa was born in the Male Water Dog year.[83] His family was the Ker, and it is said that his father was related to the great vidyadhara Ratna Lingpa. It is well known that Dechen Lingpa was an emanation of Drokmi Palgyi Yeshe.

In his seventh year Dechen Lingpa saw the five wisdom dakinis. While playing he left a clear footprint in stone. In his fifteenth year he met Guru Rinpoche, who blessed and empowered him. Encouraged by Guru Rinpoche's prediction, Dechen Lingpa extracted the *Sadhana of Manjushri Yamantaka*, various substances, and a kila from Great Garuda Rock on the tenth day of the monkey month in the Water Horse year.[84] He extracted many other termas from that site as well as from Design Rock, the Accomplishment Cave of Namkha Nyingpo, the Secret Cave of Zilchen, the Great Cave of Gangbar, Protector Face Rock, Medicine Water Long-Eared Red Rock, Domtsang Chakrasamvara Cave, Datsa Zer Cave, the back of the Vairochana of Komting, Benpa Langrong, the Red Spring of Benpa, Karak Cave, Nawo Cave in Lhodrak, Tamshül Rock in Lhodrak, Black Rakshasi Rock, Ezarpo Rock, Erong Trap Pass, Rainbow Rock, Life-Path Glorious Mountain, and other terma sites.

From these places Dechen Lingpa removed statues, supports of body; terma scrolls, supports of speech; scepters, supports of mind; samaya substances that liberate through taste; vitality pills, and many other termas. It is even said that he discovered a complete Sanskrit copy of the *Hundred Thousand Stanza Prajnaparamitasutra*. Accounts of his discovery of the *Wish-Fulfilling Mirror: Instructions on Vitality*, of his extraction of the *Eight Dispensations: Conquering the Vicious* from Jomo Karak, of his revelation of the *Five Cycles of the Realm Guardians*, and of many of his other revelations can be found in his *Accounts of My Termas*.

It was predicted that he would live until the age of seventy-eight, as follows:

Your life will end in your seventy-eighth year.

---

83 The year was 1562 C.E.

84. The year was 1582 C.E.

You will pass away near Crystal Rock.
Conceal your remains as terma in Lhasa,
Then complete the extraction of terma at Kongpo Buchu.
You will do this with a wisdom body, not a karmic body.

However, because Dechen Lingpa did not follow the indications in his prophecies, this prediction was not fulfilled; he passed away in his thirty-first year due to accidental conditions. Although his termas predicted many dharma heirs, he was unable to gather some of them because he did not control interdependence. He did encounter both Jangchup Lingpa Natsok Rangdrol and Karpo Tendzin Norbu, but Dechen Lingpa's lineage and benefit for beings never became widespread.

Dechen Lingpa was reborn at Kongpo Buchu. The rebirth was brought back to Dechen Lingpa's seat by his disciples. He offered the first fruits of his crown to the Ninth Karmapa and studied with many masters including the great tertön of Trengpo, Shikpo Lingpa, and Drikungpa Chögyal Puntsok. He received many empowerments and transmissions for the kama and terma teachings of the Sarma and Nyingma traditions of guhyamantra, and became a great holder of the teachings. He was unable, however, to reveal any profound termas, and passed away in his thirty-ninth year amid wondrous signs. His nirmanakaya was born in Melpo in Bhutan, and it is said that there were three successive rebirths.

Dechen Lingpa's principal terma was the *Dakinis' Wisdom Assembly*. Its treatises, tantras, and upadeshas were gradually revealed by his three successive rebirths. They are said to have filled six volumes, but it seems their lineage has not survived. It appears that the lineage of the *Wish-Fulfilling Mirror: Instructions on Vitality* survived for some time, but nowadays even copies of it are not to be found. I have received the reading transmission of Dechen Lingpa's *Vitality Vase of Medicinal Amrita*. It seems that Chokgyur Lingpa's *Essence of the Dakinis' Wisdom Assembly*, which I have also received, could be considered to have come from the same stream as Dechen Lingpa's *Dakinis' Wisdom Assembly*. Especially, our lord guru Padma Ösal Dongak Lingpa acquired the actual terma scrolls of Dechen Lingpa's *Dakinis' Wisdom Assembly* as rediscovered terma. He revealed their essence, and I have had the good fortune to receive that as well.

These forty-seven emanated great tertöns, starting with Sangye Lama and concluding with Dechen Lingpa, are those actually predicted in the Great Testament. I have therefore written fully about their lives, based on whatever sources I could find. Many of the prophecies are out of historical sequence; I will explain below the order of these tertöns' appearance. In writing about their lives I have not altered the order of the prophecies found in the *Great Testament of the Crystal Cave* itself.

In the hundred and seventeen chapter *Testament*, a terma of Sangye Lingpa, it states that Sangye Lingpa would appear before Ugyen Lingpa, and gives the signs of his appearance. There is no mention of a second Rinchen Lingpa. At the end of the prophecy, the tertön Mingyur Dorje and the signs of his coming are predicted.

In another version of the *Testament* we find:

The tertön called Dorje Trolö will appear.

This prediction, which also gives the signs of his appearance, is held by the learned to refer to the great vidyadhara of Ngari, whose secret name was Dorje Trolö.

In the *Testament* of Düdül Dorje, there are many other predictions, such as that of the five essence tertöns. There is therefore no final consensus about these predictions.

Many other great and minor tertöns, not mentioned in these prophecies, have appeared. I will primarily write now about those whose lineages I have received, basing my account on previous histories of dharma. I will begin with Gyaben Dorje Ö.

Gyaben Dorje Ö

The tertön Gyaben Dorje Ö was born at Nyangro in Tsang toward the end of the period of Early Dissemination. He lived as a mantradharin, and was known by the nickname Aku Tönpa. In later life Dorje Ö became discouraged by his service to his lineage, and went to Kharchu in Lhodrak to practice. On the way, while passing through Yardrok Ridge, he met Drokmi Palgyi Yeshe and his sons. Then he continued on to Kharchu and, while practicing, received a prophecy. Based on it he went to the deep cave at Arrow Feather Rock and found the *Most Profound Rasayana of Ever-Crying*. Through its implementation he accomplished rasayana of life and body; he regained a youthful form. Although it is said that he lived for three hundred years, it seems certain that this figure refers to half years.

The transmission and practical instructions for this practice still exist. I have had the good fortune to receive them, and have included their texts in the *Great Treasury of Precious Terma*.

Guru Humbar

Guru Humbar was born to a Bönpo family in Takde. He lived as a mantrin. He discovered the *Rahula Keta Cycle*, extremely profound and effective teachings on forceful mantra, in the heart of the image of Shri Hayagriva in the Toling Temple in Ngari. He gave it to Takde Drakpa Gyaltsen, who offered it to the Purong king Lha Lama Yeshe Ö, who was pleased with it and gave it to Lokya Tönpa of Gyerpu. Its instructions have been transmitted continuously since then, and I have received them.

Lhatsün Jangchup Ö

Lhatsün Jangchup Ö was born in the royal family of Lha Lama Yeshe Ö, and was his nephew and successor. He lived as a bhikshu and became learned in all sutra and tantra as well as translation. By inviting Lord Atisha to Tibet, Lhatsün Jangchup Ö was of tremendous kindness to all of Tibet. Within a column at Samye he found the *Sadhana of the Brother and Sister Putras*, extraordinary instructions combining invocation, exhortation, and termination into a single practice. This sadhana is known as the *Column Sadhana*. Jangchup Ö gave it to the translator Rinchen Zangpo, from whom it has been passed down. Its text, the transmission of which remains uninterrupted, is included in the *Protector Volume* of the glorious Sakya lineage.

The two kings Lha Lama Yeshe Ö and Lhatsün Jangchup Ö left a tremendous imprint on Tibet. During their reigns the temples built by the early dharma kings, such as those at Lhasa and Samye, were restored; the Ushangdo Temple, which had burned down, was entirely rebuilt; the Golden Temple of Toling was built; and many panditas were brought to Tibet, causing a revival of Buddhism in this land.

Atisha

The glorious lord Atisha Dipamkara Shrijnana was a great scholar and siddha. He became famous throughout both India and Tibet; the three levels of existence are filled with his renown. He was an emanation of both the Buddha Amitabha and Guru Padma. He was the very embodiment of bodhichitta, and his kindness to all of Tibet was tremendous. As his life story is well known I will not write much about it here.

Encouraged by a prophecy he received from Arya Tara, and invited by the king of Tibet, Atisha came to this land of snows. He disseminated and entirely revived Buddhism here. In Lhasa, he received a prophecy from a natural yogini who was masquerading as a madwoman. Based on her prophecy, Atisha found three scrolls in a space three feet deep within an ornamental column. These three scrolls contained the *Great Testament of the Dharma King Songtsen Gampo*; *Brilliant White Silk*, a history written by Songtsen's queens; and the *All-Bestowing Moon*, a history written by Songtsen's ministers. As the terma guardians were strict, Atisha had four people, including the yogin to whom he transmitted the terma, transcribe the scrolls on the very day of their discovery. It was felt necessary to reconceal the original scrolls that same night, and it is said that only a fragment of the original scrolls was kept.

Lord Atisha passed this terma on to a disciple called the Great Yogin, who gave it to Jayülwa, who gave it to the custodian of the Lhasa Temples as the terma described the great qualities of Mahakarunika. It is said that the first transcribed copy, written with gold ink on blue paper, was placed with Atisha's remains after his death, and that the scrolls themselves were reconcealed in a clay statue of Hayagriva in a temple annex.

It is also said that Atisha discovered other termas in India, such as the *Ritual for Raising the Victory Banner of the Five Ushnishas*, which he is said to have found in the Lotus Temple in Bheta.

Shangtsün Tarma Rinchen

Shangtsün Tarma Rinchen was born at Puhrang in Ngari around the time of Atisha's presence in Tibet. He revealed the *Secret Sadhana of Remati the Self-Arisen Queen*. This has been passed down and, since Lord Dusum Khyenpa, she has been the principal protectress of the Karma Kagyu.

Rongzom Chökyi Zangpo

Rongzom Chökyi Zangpo was the reappearance of Vairochana, and was the greatest mahapandita who ever appeared in this land of snow-covered mountains. It is known that he revealed several profound termas, but it is uncertain whether their lineages survived. Recently, however, our lord guru Padma Ösal Dongak Lingpa received the wondrous *Secret Sadhana of the Dakini Kurukulle* as rediscovered terma, and I have had the good fortune to receive it from him. The great Rongzom Chökyi Zangpo's life story is well-known; there is no need for me to write of it here.

Dorbum Chökyi Drakpa

Dorbum Chökyi Drakpa was an emanation of Ugyen Drupay Nyingpo, who was so blessed by Guru Rinpoche during his presence in Tibet that they became inseparable. Dorbum Chökyi Drakpa was born in Ngari to an affluent family that had, at the time of his birth, just sponsored an edition of the *Vajrachedikasutra* and the *Hundred-Thousand Stanza Prajnaparamitasutra* written in gold ink. He was therefore named Dorje Bum.[85] His monastic name was Chökyi Drakpa. A prophecy among his termas says:

> A disk of light with a rim like a peacock feather.

Dorbum Chökyi Drakpa had a disk-shaped mark like the pattern on a peacock feather on his forehead. He revealed the *Root Cycle of the Great Vase of Medicinal Amrita* from the heart of an image of Hayagriva the Subduer of the Aggressive in the Northern Border-Taming Temple at Traduntse. He also brought supplements to that cycle out from beneath a stone image of Maitreya and revealed the *Cycle of the Small Vase of*

---

85. *Dorje Bum* means "Vajra Hundred Thousand."

Amrita from the heart of an image of the Panjara Mahakala.

The lineage of the empowerments, transmissions, and instructions for these cycles has survived undiminished, and they have produced unexcelled benefit to this Himalayan land.

Sangye Bar

The tertön Sangye Bar was born to the family line of Sangye Lama. It is said that he revealed cycles concerning Fierce Vajrapani and Hayagriva; the root text of the *Stages of the Guhyamantra Path*, along with its instructions; the *Sadhana of the Four Great Kings;* the *Jewel Garland of Dakinis;* and other termas from Latö Kachu, Lowo Tangbar, and other places. However, as he appeared so long ago, his lineage has not survived.

Setön Ringmo

The terma guide used by the master of forceful mantra called Setön Ringmo came from Lhatsün Ngönmo. Lhatsün gave the terma guide to two monks and sent them to find the terma. The two monks, however, were killed at the foot of Paro Cliff in the south by the people who lived there. The guide was lost and came into the hands of Setön Ringmo. Using it, he is said to have revealed the *Little Hindu Tantra of the Seven Activities*, along with its instructions, from a deep cave in the Red Rock of Paro. This terma, an uncommon cycle of teaching on forceful mantra, had been concealed by Guru Rinpoche in order to protect the dharma. However, I've seen no evidence that its lineage has survived.

Gya Purbu

Gya Purbu was born in Lhodrak to the Gya family. His name was Purbu Gön. He lived as a white-robed mantrin.

Guru Rinpoche had combined the essence of tantras such as the *Sky-Iron Vajra Tamer of Naga*s and the *Vajrachanda Heart Tantra*, and taught it to King Trisong Detsen for his protection. The king concealed these teachings as terma at Genay in Bumthang and at Paro Kyerchu. Both concealments were revealed by Gya Purbu. One came to be named after its place of concealment and is called the *Poisonous Blood of Bumthang*. The other was named after its magical power, and is called the *Iron Stem*. As these two termas were combined into one, they are nowadays called the *Combined Iron and Bumthang*.

They were passed down from the tertön and eventually came to the Vidyadhara Vulture Feathers. They were passed down by him and were eventually received by Jangdak Wangpoi De, who composed several writings for their practice. The lineage of the *Rasung Blessing*, and of the transmissions and instructions for all these texts, has survived undiminished, and I have received it.

Geshe Dranga Dorje Kundrak

Geshe Dranga Dorje Kundrak revealed the dharma cycle of the *Glorious Black Protector Riding a Tiger* from Dorje Drombu in Nyuk. This was eventually received by Tsarchen Rinpoche, and is nowadays the main protector of Ngor Ewam Tartse Monastery. However, only the blessing ritual has survived; the terma text itself has not.

Lharjey Nupchung

Lharjey Nupchung was born as the son of Nup Yeshe Gyamtso at Kulung in Tsang. Nupchung lived as a mantrin, and is said to have acquired tremendous magical power through forceful mantra. From Koting in Lhodrak he revealed Nupchen's ultimate teachings on forceful mantra, the *Fiery Razor Reversal Cycle*. He gave it to Shangtrom and others, from whom it has been passed down. It is still used by the vajra holders who guard the Nyingma teachings.

The glorious Drikung Chökyi Drakpa, mainly through practicing this cycle, came to be directly accepted by Manjushri Yamantaka. He therefore widely disseminated its ripening empowerments, liberating instructions, and various branches. This cycle is therefore known as the *Drikung Reversal*. I have received its complete lineage.

Gyatön Tsöndru Senge

The mantradharin Gyatön Tsöndru Senge was born to the Gya family. He was an emanation of Nupchen Sangye Yeshe. He revealed the *Yamantaka the Lord of the Tomb, Long-Armed Butcher, Dorje Draktsen*, and *Jowo Adrak* cycles—means of exterminating enemies of dharma within seven days—from the Tiger's Lair at Paro Red Rock. I have seen no evidence that his Yamantaka cycle has survived, but his Draktsen cycle seems to be a main protector of the glorious Drukpa Kagyu.

Chetsün Senge Wangchuk

Chetsün Senge Wangchuk was born as the son of Che Tupay Wangpo in Nyangro Nyentse. In youth Chetsün Senge

Wangchuk perfected learning. He met the master Dangma Lhungyal, and received from him at Kharak the complete teachings of the Great Perfection. After the passing of his master, Chetsün concealed the old terma texts as three reconcealed termas in Langdro Chepa Takdra, Oyuk, and the upper valley of Jar. While moving about and practicing meditation, Chetsün received in a dream the prophetic instruction of Vimalamitra that he should go to Samye Chimphu, which he did. There, the terma guardians offered him the *Four Profound Volumes of the Heart Essence*. Carrying these books, Chetsün then went to the rim of mountains in outer Oyuk.

While he was there, Vimalamitra came to him and remained for two weeks, bestowing upon him all of the empowerments and instructions of the *Heart Essence*. Chetsün then meditated in that place for seven years and achieved the rainbow body. He then bestowed the complete instructions on the nirmanakaya Shangtön.

Chetsün lived for a hundred and twenty-five years. At the end of his life, he dissolved into light in the sky.

Thirty years after Chetsün concealed the *Heart Essence* teachings as terma at Oyuk, they were recovered by Chegom Nakpo of Narda. He practiced them and taught them to others. Shangtön Tashi Dorje recovered the *Secret Unsurpassable Cycle* from the door-like White Rock of Jarphu. It is also said that Shangpa Repa recovered other instructions concealed by Chetsün from Langdro Chepa, and disseminated them.

In these ways the kama lineage of Vimalamitra's instructions, the *Great Secret Heart Essence*, the *Tilaka Secret Cycle*, has come down from Be Lodrö Wangchuk. The terma lineage comes from the discoveries of five tertöns. All of these as well as the vast *Seventeen Tantras* with their commentaries—eighteen with the *Tantra of the Fierce Black Protectress*—and the hundred and ninety instructions along with the *Four Profound Volumes of the Heart Essence* were widespread in the past.

Nowadays, however, only the complete teachings of the Eighteen Tantras, some of the instructions, and the *Four Profound Volumes of the Heart Essence* have survived. I have received them.

Especially, when our lord guru Ösal Trülpe Dorje was in his twenty-fourth year he went to the area of Oyuk Shukpa Ling in Tsang, near the Khandro Chigong Mountains.[86] While there, our lord guru remembered the occasion on which the great Chetsün passed into a body of light. He clearly remembered the place, time, teacher, retinue, and the turning of the dharmachakra by Chetsün before his passing. Our lord guru wrote down the teachings Chetsün gave then. These are profound, concise, wonderful, and full of blessings, and are called the *Three-Part Writing on the Five Expanses, the King of Instructions, the Profound Essence of Omniscient Vimalamitra*.

Our lord guru has discreetly bestowed this on the Fourteenth Gyalwang Karmapa Tekchok Dorje, the great tertön Chokgyur Lingpa, and other great beings. In particular, he first kindly bestowed its ripening empowerments and liberating instructions on me. I have therefore formed a connection with its practice, have served it through the composition of clear and brief texts for its empowerments and instructions, and have taught it to others as much as I could.

86. Ösal Trülpe Dorje is yet another of Jamyang Khyentse Wangchuk's many names.

Sarben Chokme

The tertön Sarben Chokme was a rebirth of Shelza Drönkyi, one of Guru Padma's consorts. Sarben Chokme was born near Paro in Bhutan. He lived as a mantradharin. He revealed the *Manjushri Great Perfection Cycle* and its accessories from a rock with embedded turquoise in the Glorious Lion's Cave at Takstang. As this cycle later became the principal Peaceful Manjushri sadhana used by Yamantaka Ayupati practitioners, it became widespread. I have received its empowerments.

Nyen the Translator

Tarma Drak, the Translator of the Nyen family, was a descendant of Nyenchen Palyang. He was born at Shaptö in Tsang. He went to India and mastered linguistics and logic. From Vajrasanapada, the Yogini of the Mountains, and other masters he received much dharma and many protector cycles. As it was Nyen who revealed the *Glorious Four-Faced Protector Cycle*, this is nowadays called the *Nyen Protector*.

This practice cycle was concealed by Guru Rinpoche in a rock face with ledges to the north of Palmo Palthang. By revealing this, Nyen united the streams of kama and terma teaching concerning this protector. He gave the kama teachings to Lama Namkha Upa, who gave them to Jetsün Tsewa Chenpo, who made this a principal protector of the glorious Sakya tradition. It is said that Nyen gave the terma teachings to the nirmanakaya Rashak the Great, but I do not know if their lineage has survived.

Nyen revealed the Kurukulle sadhana called the *Golden Heart Essence of the Glorious Goddess* from the left breast of a clay statue of Ekajati that was beneath an image of Kurukulle to the north of Vajrasana in India. This cycle is nowadays one of the *Three Little Red Cycles* among the *Thirteen Golden Dharmas of the Sakyas*. Although these are not considered Nyingma teachings, because of their connection to other revelations I have written briefly about them here.

Shakya Zangpo

Shakya Zangpo, also known as Shakya Ö, was a teacher in Lhasa. He was a rebirth of the mantradharin Shakya Ö. From a buttress on the Rasa Trülnang Temple he revealed the sutrayana part of King Songtsen Gampo's collected writings.

It seems that what he discovered was the sutrayana component found nowadays within the *Mani Kabum*.

Shakya Zangpo also revealed the particularly profound *Wheel of Black Wind*, teachings on magic drawn from the *King of Agitators Tantra*. This was much used by practitioners of forceful mantra, but I have not seen any evidence that its lineage has survived. Among Shakya Zangpo's minor discoveries are the *Play of the Trikaya Guru: Protection from Contagion* and *How to Banish the Five Inborn Gods*. I have received these.

Recently, our lord guru Padma Ösal Dongak Lingpa revealed Shakya Zangpo's *Vajrapani the Vajra Blaze* as rediscovered terma. I have received the amrita of its ripening empowerments and liberating instructions, and have served it through composition.

Zangri Repa

The guru Zangri Repa was born in Latö Chungpa. He became a disciple of Lord Rechungpa. His name was Gotön Wangchuk Dorje, although he is better known as Zangri Repa because he practiced at Zangri. He was one of Lord Dusum Khyenpa's teachers.

From the foundation of a small yellow building in the Black Charnel Ground of Yerpa Zangri Repa revealed the guide to Yerpa called *Divine Prophecy*. Its transmission survived for some time, but nowadays there do not even appear to be copies of it.

Nyalpo Josay

Nyalpo Josay, also known as Nyaltön Nakpo, is said to have discovered the instructions of the fierce Brahmin mantrin Amoli that Guru Rinpoche had concealed in the vase of the

Black Stupa of Samye. These instructions were known both as the *Combined Sadhana of the Three Supports* and as the *Tsangshukma Cycle*. They appear to have been lost.

Sangye Wangchen

Sangye Wangchen of Nyemo Gyagong Mountain was born in Nyemo. He lived as an ordinary mantrin. He revealed the *Secret Sadhana of Hayagriva*, and bestowed it on Kyergangpa Chökyi Senge at the command of Guru Rinpoche. Starting then, it gradually became as famous as the wind for its extreme profundity, and is known as the *Kyergang Hayagriva*. It has spread throughout all traditions, and I have received its empowerment and the transmissions of many of its earlier and later literature.

Chupa Tokden

The tertön Chupa Tokden was born at Norbuling, adjacent to a river in Gyalmorong. Because he lived without activity or direction, he came to be called Tokden.[87] His actual name was Gendun Gyaltsen.

There is a mountain in Gyalmorong called Sertö Drongri. It is associated with the great local spirit Draklha Gonpo. Within a north-facing cave on this mountain's side Chupa Tokden saw three lacquer coffers. He took one of them and found within it the *Glorious Protector Ganapati Source of Siddhi Cycle*, which had been concealed as terma by Vairochana. By receiving the unbroken kama lineage of the extensive *Secret Razor Cycle* from the dharma lord Gendun Gyaltsen he combined the kama and terma streams into one. He bestowed them on the Black Lama of Miklung, also known as Gendun Gyaltsen. Since then, this has been a principal protector of the Kathok lineage of the Nyingma

---

87. *Tokden* means "One with Realization."

tradition, and is renowned for its great power. Its empowerments, transmissions, and practical instructions have been passed down unbroken, and I have received them.

Bakhal Mukpo

The nirmanakaya Bakhal Mukpo was an emanation of Prince Damdzin, and was born in Lhodrak around the time of Lord Nyang. Bakhal Mukpo lived as a mantrin. As he had a brown face, he was nicknamed Tulku Mukpo Dong, Nirmanakaya with a Brown Face, and became known as Bakhal Mukpo, Brown Cow Kidney.

It is said that from Khalarongo Rock in Mangyül he revealed a biography of Guru Rinpoche describing his birth from a womb; the supplication *Removing Obstacles on the Path*, along with a commentary; and a concise *Vajrakilaya Cycle*. Nowadays, the supplication has spread to all traditions, and it appears that copies of the biography still exist.

In recent times the nirmanakaya Chokgyur Dechen Lingpa revealed the *Sadhana of the Guru's Heart: Dispelling All Obstacles*, including its liturgies, instructions, and applications. I have received its profound and extensive ripening empowerments and liberating instructions. It seems that the stream of its blessings and those of Bakhal's terma could be considered to have been combined into one.

Prince Mekhyil

Prince Mekhyil was born in southwestern Tsang into the family of King Trisong Detsen. He lived as a noble mantrin of royal descent, and was the predicted rebirth of the meditator Haminatha, a Bhutanese disciple of Guru Rinpoche. From a column in the northern Traduntse Temple he revealed the *Sadhana of Hayagriva Ekavira*, the *Life-Wheel of the King*,

Compelling Pehar, and *Compelling the Aggressive*. The lineage and practice of the *Life-Wheel of the King* became widespread for a while, but eventually even copies of its text became unavailable. Recently, our lord guru Padma Ösal Dongak Lingpa received an old copy of it in the context of the dakinis' entrustment seal. Through the blessing of Guru Rinpoche and his disciples, he has circulated it as rediscovered terma. He has kindly bestowed it on me.

Drugu Yangwang

Drugu Yangwang was an emanation of the great king Trisong Detsen. He was born in Drugu in Kham, and lived as a great vajra holder and mantrin. He was known by the names Yangwang Ter and Dorje Tershay Tsal.

There is a saying, "Nyemo Shuyay Nöjin Bar held the dispensation of tantra. Nyangral Nyima Özer held the dispensation of agama. Drugu Yangwang held the dispensation of upadesha and forceful mantra." These three lived at the same time.

Drugu Yangwang revealed the *Powerful Black Sun and Moon* cycle of instructions, which can overcome all external and internal forces, from Red Rock Tamarisk Grove. Its empowerments, transmissions, instructions, and implementation have survived down to the present, and I have received all of them.

In particular, Drugu Yangwang revealed the great tantra, instructions, and applications of *Hayagriva the Liberator of All the Aggressive* from a flame-shaped rock at Paro. Eventually these teachings disappeared, until even their name was forgotten. Finally, however, Padma Ösal Dongak Lingpa, an emanation of King Trisong, received an old copy of this vast cycle—including its tantra and sadhana—in the context of the dakinis' entrustment seal. He also revealed some of its instructions as rediscovered terma through the blessing of this great tertön. I have received all of these from him, and have formed a bit of a connection with this cycle through composition, approach, accomplishment, and great accomplishment.

Sumpa Jangchup Lodrö

Sumpa Jangchup Lodrö was born in the area of eastern Tibet called Markham, the "Third Southern Region" among the "Three Ridges." He was called Sumpa after his birthplace, "Third." His actual name was Jangchup Lodrö. His completion name was Sönam Gyaltsen. He was an emanation of Guru Rinpoche's mind, and held the dispensation of a lord of profound terma.

According to some accounts, when Guru Rinpoche was about to return to India from Tibet the king of Tibet offered him a golden begging bowl filled with amrita. According to other accounts, he offered him a golden mandala on which were arranged eight turquoises the size of pigeons. In any case, the instructions requested by the king at that time were the *Wind-Wheel of the Twenty Aggressive Ones*, a means of eradicating those with broken samaya by casting them to the wind.

Sumpa Jangchup Lodrö revealed these instructions together with their accessories from beneath the toe of an image of Vajrapani at Samye. He also revealed some brief writings from the forehead and heart of an image of Maheshvara at Samye. Some of what he found there was contained in a copper tube four finger-widths in length.

Nowadays these teachings are known as the *Aggressive from Kham*. They have spread all over central, southern, and northern Kham, and have survived undiminished. Nevertheless, I have not received them up to now.

Taklungpa Sangye Wönpo

Taklungpa Sangye Wönpo was born into the Taklungzi family. His birth occurred on top of a donkey shed in Kham Yangshö. When his umbilical cord was cut, a sound like a guitar string was heard, and within it, many stanzas of dharma. He was given the name Könchok Se. In his fourth year he was brought to central Tibet. He undertook renunciation and was named Drakpa Pal Özer Zangpo. He achieved completion in his twentieth year in the presence of the abbot Galungpa. He returned to Kham and founded the glorious Riwoche Monastery. His achievements in construction of temples and the like are great.

This lord revealed from a terma at Nine Beards Rock in Tsang, a practice place of Zurchungpa, the practice of Guru Rinpoche surrounded by the eight Gauris and a vajra and bell that had been Guru Rinpoche's scepters. This vajra and bell were kept for a long time at the Tsangpo Gogu Retreat in western Kongpo as its inner support. About other termas he recovered, he wrote:

> From the side of Gyawodong Rock
> I revealed seventeen dharmas like my heart.
> Especially, I revealed Black Yamantaka.
> From Gardzong Rock I revealed thirteen.
> From Lungmodza I revealed a vase.
> From Utse Nangwa Rölpa,
> Gönpo Rawa, Ngalok Dzong,
> And other places I revealed much terma dharma.

From among these, I have received the complete *Mind Sadhana*. I have placed it, along with a liturgical arrangement, in the *Great Treasury of Terma*.

Nyalpa Nyima Sherap

Nyalpa Nyima Sherap was born in Nyal. He was a disciple of Zangkar the Translator, Pakpa Sherap. He studied and became very learned in yogatantra. He founded monasteries in both western and eastern Nyal, and installed images of the Buddha Vairochana in many temples. Because of his extensive turning of the dharmachakra of yogatantra, it became extremely widespread during his lifetime. He was of great benefit and kindness to the yogatantra teachings. His main residence was at Tsangpo Dong.

From the annex of the Jagöshong Temple he revealed an image concealed there by the minister Lhazang Lupal, a large silk banner depicting Vaishravana known as the Jongyülma, and the *Sadhana of Vaishravana Bearing a Red Spear*. The lineage of the latter remains unbroken.

Trophu the Translator

Trophu the Translator, Nup Jampay Pal, was born as the son of a powerful mantrin of the Nyingma tradition known as Rozen Nakpo. Trophu was of the Pamodru Kagyu tradition, and founded the Trophu Kagyu, one of the eight secondary divisions of the Kagyu. His learning and attainment were unimaginably great. He invited three pandita siddhas to Tibet: the mahapanditas Shakyashri, Buddhashri, and Mitra the Yogin. He also created a great image of Maitreya, twenty-eight fathoms in height, which bestowed liberation through being seen. His imprint on the teachings has been as great as that of any of the scholars or siddhas of Tibet.

This great translator revealed from Vulture Basin the seven-chapter *Tantra of the Yaksha Vaishravana Bearing a Mace* that had been translated by Nyak Jnanakumara, along with a commentary by the mahapandita Vimalamitra on the ayusadhana taught in its last chapter.

These two Vaishravana cycles—that of Nyalpa and this one of Trophu—are fully contained within the Sakya *Book of Vaishravana*, and I have received them.

Yeben Yabön

The tertön Yeben Yabön was born to a Bönpo family during the later life of Nyen the Translator. He revealed teachings on forceful mantra, including the *Wind-Wheel Razor of Life*, from the northern Traduntse Temple. The lineage and practice of the *Wind-Wheel* continued until fairly recently, but nowadays I've been unable to locate or receive the transmission of its text.

Balpo Ah Hum Bar

Balpo Ah Hum Bar was born in southern Tsang. He lived as a mantrin, and was clearly predicted to be an emanation of Nanam Dorje Düdjom. Accordingly, from the Red Rock of Paro he revealed profound instructions including the *Great Life-Wheel of Black Jambhala* and the *Ritual for Training Elephants*. These were passed down through the glorious Gawalungpa, and their transmission and practice seems to have continued until somewhat recently, but by our time it had become impossible to locate even a copy of their texts. However, dakinis presented our lord guru with an old copy. He revealed the sadhana and applications as rediscovered terma. I have received them fully from him, and have offered the service of composition.

Ajo Palpo

The tertön Ajo Palpo was born at Zurkhar, near Samye. He lived as a common householder mantrin. From a column in the Bumthang Temple in Bhutan he revealed the *Profound Wheel that Strengthens the Bull of Merit*. It is still practiced by everyone nowadays, and I have received it. It is said that he also revealed the *Sadhana of the Three Tenma Sisters* from Drakyangdzong, and the *Sadhana of Mari Rapjam Dorje Drakmo* from Samye Chimphu, but neither their texts nor their transmissions exist now.

The Three Tertöns

Kyangpo Drakpa Wangchuk, Sumpa Jangchup Tsultrim, and Dre Sherap Lama revealed from Yerpa Sewa Lung the *Very Secret Wrathful Hayagriva Lotus Might Cycle*. They only passed it on once: to Nyaktön Lhabar of Drutsang, using the terma scrolls. Because of the terma's curse Kyangpo contracted leprosy, Sumpa died, and Dre went mad. The terma scrolls fell to the hands of a Hayagriva siddha called Shutön, but he was unable to decipher them. For a long time there was no unbroken, well-known terma lineage of these teachings. Eventually the great lord of siddhas Darcharupa, while at Jomo Nakgyal in Tsang, was given their complete empowerments and transmissions by Guru Rinpoche, who had taken the form of a mantrin called Shangtse Dadrak. Guru Rinpoche said to Darcharupa, "Change the OM in the mantra to HRIH, and practice this!"

The three tertöns, although able to reveal this terma, subsequently experienced obstacles because it was not their karmic destiny to reveal it. The real inheritor of this dharma was the mahasiddha Darcharupa. For that reason, even though Guru Rinpoche had directly given him this dharma,

Darcharupa also sought out Lama Gya of Tanak, who held the original terma lineage, and received it from him. He did this out of respect for the succession of the teachings. Darcharupa therefore came to hold both the kama and terma lineages of this dharma, and since his time its empowerments, transmissions, and instructions have become increasingly widespread. I have received them fully.

The great Darcharupa also gained siddhi through Vajrakilaya. Using a material kila, he totally overcame the enchantments of the tirthika spirit Nanda the Stealer. The kila he used then is now kept at Sera Je College as its principal inner support, and is famous. The protector Rahula directly offered Darcharupa *Rahula's Instructions on Protection and Healing*, which still exist and which I have received.

Nyaktön Lhabar, the only recipient of this Hayagriva terma from the three original tertöns, is said to have revealed a few termas himself, but their number is unclear and it seems that no lineage of them arose. It is also said that he revealed a Bön terma, the *Five Agamas*, and that the three tertöns discovered many Bön termas, including the Bön *Hundred Thousand Stanza Prajnaparamita*, *Treatise on Valid Cognition*, and the *Nine Magical Mirrors*. It appears that copies of most of these still exist.

Dugu Rinchen Senge

Dugu Rinchen Senge was born in central Tibet. He revealed the *Dorje Tsuklak Cycle* of forceful mantra from the Traduntse Stupa in the north. This contained the instructions that Vairochana entrusted to the twenty-five disciples before leaving for Gyalmo Tsawarong. When he did so Vairochana said to them, "Conceal this as terma for the future benefit of the teachings."

King Trisong Detsen accordingly concealed this cycle in the vase of a stupa that had been erected to the northeast of the

Traduntse Temple as a monument to the wise panditas and translators. Two hundred years later, Dugu Rinchen Senge found the guide to this terma at Samye. In a tiger year, he revealed the *Little Letter of Meteoric Iron* and the *Forceful Activity Tantra* from the vase of the Traduntse Stupa. He revealed the *Seven Supplementary Tantras* and their sadhanas from the stupa's base.

However, he failed to perform the necessary self-protection rituals or the *Binding Wheel of Rahula*. Because his offerings to the terma guardians were insufficient, while the tertön and his disciple Tsangpa Rinchen Sherap were in a boat crossing the Lake of the Mother in Tsang, they quarreled and stabbed each other to death. Dadrak, a resident of Yerushang, found the terma parchment after the deaths of the tertön and his disciple. Dadrak gave the scrolls to Ödem, the tertön's daughter. As her karmic propensities were awakened by this, she practiced diligently and gained siddhi. She then deciphered the scrolls. Their lineage still exists, and I have received it enthusiastically.

Tsangring Sherap

Tsangpa Lawa Ringpo, also known as Tsangring Sherap, appears to have revealed several dharma termas, including *Vajra Armor*, a profound protection against sorcery; means of self-protection; means of invisiblity using the nagas of the five families; means of protection from naga ailments and of curing leprosy; means of protection against spirits invoked by sorcery and against malevolent nagas; means to prevent any attack by gods or spirits; means to prevent approach by nagas or earthlords; and means of ending pre-existing sorcery.

Latö Marpo

The nirmanakaya Latö Marpo, also known as Dampa Marpo, revealed the *Rasayana of Great Amrita Cycle* from Scorpion Pincer Rock, a boulder shaped like a lion's coffer, at Paro Rock. From the Black Stupa of Samye he revealed the *Magical Mantras of the Acharya Hewa the Black*. This had originally been discovered on the western slope of Mount Malaya inside a clay statue of Ishvara by the acharya Trala Ringmo. He offered it to Guru Padmasambhava, who concealed it beneath the Black Stupa of Samye. It is said that its presence under the stupa was the reason why that place was dangerous. This profound cycle contains the tirthikas' magical mantras of the dark destroyer of the world known as Dritalma.

From Yerpa Jarawa Latö Marpo revealed the *Guide to Yerpa*, in the handwriting of Queen Kongjo. From Mangkhar Mugulung he revealed instructions on using seven materials to conquer obstructors, instructions powerful enough to crack the hardest rock. Among the many profound termas Latö Marpo revealed, it is evident that the mahasiddha Thangtong Gyalpo practiced his *Rasayana of Great Amrita Cycle* and gained siddhi. In spite of that, I have not encountered its texts.

Jomo Menmo

The emanated great tertön known as Jomo Menmo was one of two authentic dakinis who were the true reappearance of Dhatishvari Yeshe Tsogyal, the Queen of Great Bliss, the collector of Guru Rinpoche's teachings of great secrecy. From the prophecies within her own terma, the *Secrets of All Dakinis*:

> Eventually, the dakinis will entrust this dharma
> To a girl of family, blessed by dakinis,
> Born in a monkey year,

With the hidden name Jomo.
Blessed, she will become realized and naturally freed.
At that time, she will not appear to help others very much,
But all connected to her will reach the stage of great bliss.
They will achieve awakening without remaining aggregates.

As clearly predicted in that prophecy, which is also a concise account of her life, the lotus of Jomo Menmo's emanation bloomed in a Male Earth Monkey year.[88] She was born near Guru Rinpoche's accomplishment cave at Zarmolung, in Eyül. Her father was a mantrin of the Dakpo Kagyu tradition named Dorje Gyalpo. Her mother was a dakini named Padma Paldzom. Her parents named her Padma Tsokhyi. Her family was neither extremely wealthy nor poor. Throughout her early childhood she was cared for lovingly by her parents, but in her fifth year her mother passed away. As a result her father remarried, and Jomo Menmo was made to tend herds and perform other mundane tasks, which caused her to suffer somewhat.

One day in the spring of her thirteenth year, while she was tending the herds near the Secret Cave of Great Bliss, Guru Rinpoche's place of accomplishment at Great Soaring Garuda Rock at Zarmolung in Eyül, Jomo Menmo fell asleep. She was awakened by a beautiful sound that came from the rock. She saw the door to the secret cave open by itself. With transformed perceptions, she entered the cave and found herself in a terrifying charnel ground, amongst dakinis engaged in a ganachakra. Vajravarahi, who was presiding over the feast, said to her, "Daughter of family, you are welcome!"

Vajravarahi then appeared to take a small book from out of the rock behind her back. She placed the book on top of Jomo Menmo's head, ripening and freeing her all at once. Placing the book in Jomo Menmo's hands, Vajravarahi said,

88. The year was 1248 C.E.

"These instructions are the *Secrets of All Dakinis*. If you practice them with extreme secrecy, you will achieve the supreme siddhi."

By receiving that prophecy, Jomo Menmo realized that all things are self-liberated. She became a great realm-born yogini. She took part in the feast gathering. Then the emanated mandala disappeared, and Jomo Menmo returned home.

As her being had been ripened by the amrita of Vajravarahi's blessing, words of dharma began to burst forth from her throughout both day and night. She sang vajra songs and danced vajra dances. She spoke of her unimpeded knowledge of others' minds. A few people developed faith in her, but most others thought that by falling asleep in the mountains she had become bewitched by a menmo, a spirit of the hills. That is why she received the nickname Jomo Menmo.

Appearing discouraged by the attitude taken toward her, Jomo Menmo lost all attachment to her homeland. Intending to wander without direction, she went to Layak Pang village in western Lhodrak, where she met the tertön Guru Chökyi Wangchuk. Just through meeting him, connate wisdom arose effortlessly within her. Guru Chökyi Wangchuk recognized her as one of five qualified consorts prophesied by Guru Rinpoche. He accepted her as a karmamudra. This caused knots in his channels to be loosened, which enabled him to fully comprehend the *Upadesha Mahatantra of the Eight Dispensations: The Complete Secrets*. Although he had previously been unable to decipher this terma, he was now able to translate it into Tibetan. In this way, Guru Chökyi Wangchuk and Jomo Menmo brought each other tremendous good.

Jomo Menmo did not remain at Layak Pang for very long, but while there she received the essence of Guru Chökyi Wangchuk's ripening empowerments and liberating instructions. Finally, he said to her, "Your profound dharma, this book of the dakinis, appears to be the wondrous essence of your practice during your previous birth as the dakini Yeshe Tsogyal. However, now is not the right time to disseminate it among beings. Practice it yourself with extreme secrecy. Wander through all of central Tibet and Tsang. Help beings discreetly by bringing all who meet you to the state of great bliss. In the end, you will attain celestial siddhi without abandoning your body."

She followed his advice. Accompanied by two worthy yoginis, Jomo Menmo traveled through every region of central Tibet and Tsang, all the way to Latö and Dingri. She discreetly and naturally helped beings. Finally, in her thirty-sixth year, on the tenth day of the first month of autumn, she climbed up to the peak of Mount Lhari in Drak. Along with her two companions, she performed a feast offering. All three of them rose into the sky without abandoning their bodies, like great birds soaring through space. They quickly reached the Glorious Copper-Colored Mountain and joined the feast assembly of dakinis there. Their departure was witnessed by herders in Drak, who rushed to the peak of Mount Lhari and found the feast that the three yoginis had left behind. Eating it, the herders achieved natural meditation.

Jomo Menmo's terma, this wondrous great secret, the *Secrets of All Dakinis*, was kept by dakinis for a while, and was not available to ordinary people. Toward the end of this age of disputation, when it was the right time for this dharma to tame disciples, it was rediscovered by the emanated tertön and great vidyadhara Padma Ösal Dongak Lingpa. Through his compassion and aspirations; because of his having been, during his life as Jomo Menmo, a secret companion of Guru Chökyi Wangchuk; and occasioned by the blessing of wisdom dakinis, our lord guru received and revealed this dharma through the great miracle of his perfect recollection of its words and meaning. I wrote it down as he dictated it, and was both fortunate and delighted to be the first to receive its entire ripening and liberation.

Since then I have formed a connection with this dharma through approach and accomplishment, and through performing its great accomplishment and lesser accomplishment several times. I've seen signs of its blessing, so it would be appropriate for any of my followers who have conviction about the great secret to make this the jewel of their hearts and the essence of their practice.

I've written some needed supplements for it, and had all of it printed. I've also given its ripening and liberation many times. I've accomplished a little bit of service to this profound dharma.

The wisdom dakini Jomo Menmo was so little known that early histories of terma do not even mention more than her name. Even the time of her appearance is not given. Here, taking her actual terma prophecies and the words of my lord guru as witness, I have written of her at slightly greater length.

Melong Dorje

The mahasiddha Melong Dorje was born in the upper valley of Drak as the son of a yogin. In his ninth year he undertook renunciation in the presence of the siddha Zalungpa and the abbot Selungpa. In his sixteenth year he realized the nature of things by reciting the *Eight-Thousand Stanza Prajnaparamitasutra* a hundred times. Meditating at Copper Lake, his experience blazed and minor supercognition appeared. He began to wander all over the land, and received many teachings of the Sarma and Nyingma tantras from his thirteen superior teachers and others. In many sacred places he practiced with fierce austerity and saw the faces of deities such as Vajravarahi and of many vidyadharas.

In his eighteenth year he received the *Heart Essence of the Great Perfection* from the delusion-destroyer Senge Gyapa. While engaged in the preliminaries, Melong Dorje saw Vajrasattva's face continuously for six days, all day and night. In dreams he was empowered by Vajrasattva, and achieved perfect realization of the Great Perfection. Because of his great discipline, he was able to engage in the actual conduct of guhyamantra. As he had control over the five elements, his reputation as a mahasiddha spread widely. He planted the victory banner of accomplishment at isolated places such as Kharchu.

Melong Dorje revealed the *Heart Essence of Vimalamitra* from the Further Fortress of Drak. This terma is called the *Further Fortress Heart Essence* after the site of its revelation; the *Heart Essence of Melong* after its tertön; the *AH HUM Heart Essence* after its seals; and the *Collar Pouch of Vimalamitra* after the size of its book. Although it appears that its textual transmission survived until recently, a generation has now passed since its dharma lineage ended.

In his sixtieth year Melong Dorje passed into peace amid many signs that he had reached the primordial place of liberation. His body produced the five types of relics as taught in the tantras.

Recently our precious lord guru received a wondrous short lineage of the *Heart Essence of Melong*. As well, the parchment of the original *Heart Essence of Melong*, reconcealed by the dakini Vajratara, reached my hands. Our lord guru deciphered it, and kindly received its ripening and liberation. We have placed it in the *Great Treasury of Terma*.[89]

The Fortunate Child

Once, in Guge Damdrok in Ngari, a group of children were digging in a large sand dune and discovered a covered stone coffer. When they opened it, they found that it was filled with all sorts of strange creatures, all moving about. All but one of the children died. That fortunate child wisely ran away, carrying the coffer's lid, and was not harmed. A great epidemic occurred in that region, and many people and animals began to die of various types of plague.

The fortunate child found teachings on protection from epidemics in the coffer's lid. He gave people the yantra,

89. The Dzogchen Pönlop Rinpoches are held to be the rebirths of Melong Dorje.

materials, and mantras taught there. All of the plagues ceased immediately. Knowing the profundity of this cycle, the fortunate child gradually disseminated it. It is still considered a profound means of protection, and is known as the *Unified Protection of Guge*. Its transmission and practice have survived, and I have received them. Because the actual name of this tertön is unkown, he has come to be called "the fortunate child."

Drangti Gyalnye Kharbu

I've not seen an extensive account of Drangti Gyalnye Kharbu, but he was one of the nine greatest physicians of Tibet. He was born in the Drangti region, and revealed the *Physicians' Sadhana* and some teachings on healing that had been concealed by Guru Rinpoche and Trisong Detsen in the capital of a pillar in the thirteenth part of the roof of Samye. He is said to have practiced the terma and gained signs of accomplishment. It is said that his terma was passed down through Drangti Jampal Zangpo and others, but nowadays all that has survived from it is the *Empowerment of the Three Brahmin Brothers*, which is included in the *Heart Essence of Yutok*.

The Four Assistants

Gomchen Drukpa, Nyentön Jambhala, Döndrup Senge, and Padma Drakpa were assistants of the vidyadhara Guru Chökyi Wangchuk in his recovery of terma. Of the eighteen great termas that he revealed, the tenth was the *Six Dharmas of the Sekhar*. Guru Chökyi Wangchuk sent Gomchen Drukpa to reveal it. Similarly, the *Manjushri Great Perfection Cycle* that Nyentön Jambhala took from the heart of a statue of Red Yamantaka in the Khoting Temple in Lhodrak is considered to be Guru Chökyi Wangchuk's seventh terma. It is said that Döndrup Senge and Padma Drakpa, called the "two other individuals," helped the other two assistants in their recovery of terma. The transmission of the *Six Dharmas of the Sekhar* still exists, and I have received it.

The Earlier Dungtso Repa

The earlier Dungtso Repa was a rebirth of Gampopa's disciple Kyegom Yeshe Dorje, an emanation of Nyangben Tingdzin Zangpo. Dungtso Repa was born in Yarlung. While young he entered the gate of dharma at Densatil, and was given the name Sherap Gyamtso. He later undertook completion in the presence of Gampo Dorje Lodrö and received the name Rinchen Zangpo.

Dungtso Repa undertook the vow of austerity in the presence of Trülshik Khampa at the Turquoise Lake of Kharak. As instructed by Trülshik Khampa, Dungtso Repa practiced in a hut on top of a small hill beside the lake. Beneath the hut he discovered a list of termas, and went to Gampo to find them. In the ice covering the lower lake of Gampo, at a depth of one cubit, he found dharma terma that had been concealed by Gampopa and Yeshe Dorje together. Within a stone coffer he found an image of a mongoose, and within it a scroll bound with five-colored silk, along with Naropa's empowerment vase and other things. From the scroll Dungtso Repa deciphered the *Wish-Fulfilling Jewel: A Guide to the Mind* and *Instructions on Ejection and Transference*. The *Guide to the Mind* used to be widespread, and nowadays its lineage still exists. I have received its transmission as part of the *Whispered Lineage of Surmang* and its transmission and instruction as one of the *Hundred Instructions of Kunga Drölchok*.

Dungtso Repa created many supports, including the Dungtso Temple that he built at Gampopa's birthplace in

Nyal. It is also said that he presented many material offerings to Tsalpa Drungchen Mönlampa and Kunga Dorje in order to sponsor the distribution of gruel to pilgrims to Lhasa.

Kunga Bum

The dakini Kunga Bum was the second of the two famous emanations of Yeshe Tsogyal, the mother of the victors. She was born at Tashi Dokhar in Ön. Her father's name was Dorje Wangchuk. Her mother was an authentic rebirth of Shelkarza Dorje Tso, and was called Lhakhyi Paldzom. Kunga Bum was born in a monkey year. In her sixth year she offered the first fruits of her crown to Chenga Drakpa Gyaltsen at Densatil. He gave her the name Kunga Bum. She attended many gurus, such as Drakpa Gyaltsen, and received countless empowerments and instructions from the Sarma and Nyingma traditions of guhyamantra. As she devoted herself to practice, she achieved consummate realization. In particular, one evening she heard the words:

> O worthy one with karma, practice for seven years, seven months, seven days, and seven mealtimes in the Cave of Luminosity at Drakyangdzong. You will receive the dakinis' prophecies and will see the celestial realm.

She therefore practiced one-pointedly for seven years in the Crystal Cave of Luminosity at Drakyangdzong. Based on the prophecy of Vajravarahi, she revealed the *Secret Practices of Mother Tantra* and its supplements as terma within that cave. By giving this dharma cycle to many fortunate people throughout Tibet, she ripened and liberated them. In particular, as prophesied within the terma, she bestowed it on Dungtso Repa, the protector of beings. Although it subsequently became extremely widespread, copies of it and the lineage of its transmission became very rare by our time. I eventually found an old copy of it at the Crystal Cave of

Yarlung. The great tertön Chokgyur Dechen Lingpa received its complete ripening empowerments and liberating instructions through the dispensations of recollection and the short lineage of blessing, and began to disseminate it.

The dakini Kunga Bum opened the door to the sacred place of Drakyangdzong while revealing this terma. At that time there occurred rains of flowers and the sound of the music of the dakinis at Dra, Döl, Shung, Kyiyor, Yarön, Lo, Do, Samye, and Zurkhar. Countless lamas, leaders, and spiritual teachers from all over Tibet gathered to receive her teachings.

Once Kunga Bum had completed her activity, she went to Tashi Yangön in Ön. There, in the Hermitage of the Lady's Stupa, she remained in retreat for seven days. Then, amidst inconceivably wondrous signs such as sounds, light, and rains of flowers, she accomplished the vajra rainbow body without leaving her physical body behind.

The Later Dungtso Repa

The later Dungtso Repa was born at Dingmadrin in Latö. His father's name was Shang Könne; his mother's was Drönza Drönkhyi. He clearly remembered his previous life as the earlier Dungtso Repa, and therefore came to be called the Later Dungtso Repa. In his eleventh year he entered the gate of dharma, and began to study both sutra and tantra extensively. In his twenty-third year he entered the presence of Minyak Repa in Kangbule and received from him many empowerments and instructions of the Sarma and Nyingma traditions.

He practiced in many snowy and grassy hermitages, saw Guru Rinpoche's face, and received his prophecies. Based on them, he went to central Tibet and Kongpo. In Ön he met the great Kunga Bum. She accepted him and predicted that he would be her dharma heir.

Dungtso Repa opened the doors to sacred sites such as Vulture Fortress in Bhutan and Rakshasa Fortress in Latö. At

Rakshasa Fortress he revealed the *Guru Sadhana That Fulfills Yearning* and the *Vase of Light Ayusadhana* as terma and disseminated them widely. Especially, from beneath a boulder like a prone tortoise on the shore of Black Mandala Lake behind Gampo Mountain, he revealed the instruction cycle of the *Single Golden Syllable of Black Yangti*. He disseminated this to the worthy and many of them achieved the body of light. He also exhibited unimaginably many wondrous signs of attainment such as leaving the imprints of his hands and feet in stone. He sustained vast activity helping beings throughout Kongpo, Long, and Ral.

The empowerments, transmissions, instructions, and practice of Dungtso Repa's *Black Yangti* have flourished widely down to the present day. I have fully received them.

Vajramati

The Indian tertön Vajramati revealed the *Luminous Spacious Expanse of the Great Perfection* at Lishanti in Nepal. Its applications include a remedy for nagas and earth lords—meditation on and mantra recitation of a dark blue Guru Rinpoche riding on a pig—and the *Tretreho*, a combination of medicine and mantra. They were promised by Guru Rinpoche to be effective protection from contagious diseases in this age of fivefold degeneration. At the time of their revelation, Tsalgung Thangpa Shönnu Samten was visiting Nepal. He met the tertön and brought his terma dharma to Tibet. As had been predicted, they were widely disseminated by a lineage that began with a Lama Paljor. However, nowadays only the transmission of the Blue Wrathful Guru has survived.

Gyalsay Lekpa

Gyalsay Lekpa was an emanation of both the translator Rinchen Zangpo and the lady Shelkarza. As prophesied by the siddha Ugyenpa, Gyalsay Lekpa was born in a Male Iron Tiger year as the son of the physician Wangchuk Gyalpo of the Showo family in lower Sewalung in Nyal. From the earliest age he displayed both great intelligence and mental strength. He relied upon many gurus such as his uncle, the omniscient Shawo, and received much dharma of the Sarma and Nyingma traditions, as well as the sciences. His knowledge and understanding were excellent, his qualities infinite.

In particular, in his twenty-eighth year Gyalsay Lekpa met the tertön Padma Ledrel Tsal, received from him the complete *Great Perfection Dakinis' Heart Essence*, and was prophesied by the tertön to be his dharma heir.

In the Female Fire Snake year Gyalsay Lekpa found a terma guide at Trakchung Dorje Drak in Jar. Six years later, in the Male Water Dog year, he opened the terma door and revealed the *Great Perfection: Cutting Through Samsara All at Once*, the *Mahamudra: Clarifying Buddhahood, Turning Samsara into the Path of Great Bliss*, the *Heart Essence: The Three Posthumous Testaments*, and the *Heart Sadhana: The Combined Practice of Padma Tötreng and the Three Roots*. He also revealed the *Realm Protector Cycle* as terma at Great Majesty Cave in Tsari.

In the Male Water Monkey year, Gyalsay Lekpa's forty-third year, the omniscient Karmapa Rangjung Dorje was invited to Kongpo. During his visit, Gyalsay Lekpa offered him the complete empowerments, transmissions, and instructions of the *Dakinis' Heart Essence*. It is said that he did so using the original terma parchment. He also offered him much other dharma, and received many teachings from the Karmapa, including the *Jatakas*, the *Profound Inner Meaning*, and *Jinasagara*. Their two minds mixed, Gyalsay Lekpa proclaimed and prophesied the Karmapa to be the heir of the *Heart Essence*, saying, "I have given this dharma to its heir."

Gyalsay Lekpa continued to help beings widely, and passed into the dharmadhatu in the Male Fire Horse year, his seventy-seventh year. Although I have not seen evidence of any of his other terma dharmas having survived, I have received the transmission of his texts on divination and cleansing smoke offerings. As well, the practice cycle of the glorious Realm Protector, a guardian of the Karma Kagyu, appears to have mainly come from Gyalsay Lekpa.

Ugyen Zangpo

Ugyen Zangpo was one of the twenty-one disciples of Dorje Lingpa who were also minor tertöns. He was born west of Chökhor Dechen in Bumthang, Bhutan. He revealed such termas as the *Clear Mirror of the Great Perfection* and the *Ayusadhana of the Sugatas' Assembly*.

There was a prophecy that in order to assure the well-being of the four communities in Bumthang it was necessary to both restore the damaged Imprint Temple and create a three-dimensional model of the mandala of the Eight Dispensations.[90] As there arose some doubt as to how to build the mandala, Ugyen Zangpo entrusted his body to the care of an attendant and flew to the Glorious Copper-Colored Mountain in the form of a vulture in order to consult Guru Rinpoche. A week passed before he returned, and the attendant decided to cremate Ugyen Zangpo's body. When Ugyen Zangpo got back, he found that his skull had already been burnt by the cremation fire, and that his former body was no longer of any use. Having no choice, he transferred his consciousness into the body of a young woman from Tsaok who had just died. She deciphered her terma parchments in the Imprint Temple, which she restored. Because she was now female she was prevented by others' prejudice from erecting the three-dimensional mandala, but she painted it on the ceiling of the temple's upper story; it is still there. Her benefit to beings was great, and she was considered wondrous, but her dharma lineage no longer exists nowadays.

90. The Imprint Temple housed an imprint of Guru Rinpoche's body in stone

Sherab Mebar

The tertön Sherab Mebar is said to have been born in Kham. He revealed many profound cycles of instruction. From Gyaliba in Kongpo he revealed the *Great Perfection: Self-Liberated Samsara and Nirvana* and the *Great Perfection: The Combined Three Wrathful Ones*. From Tiger Peak he revealed instructions on Rahula and the *Miracles of Shridevi*.

The *Great Perfection: Self-Liberated Samsara and Nirvana* contained a hundred different languages and scripts. At the beginning of the terma text, written in Tibetan, was:

> May this meet with an omniscient nirmanakaya!
> No one else in degenerate times will be able to
>   decipher it.

The tertön was unable to decipher the rest of the parchment. His disciple Taktsang Repa brought the parchment to many learned and attained people, including the Karmapa Rangjung Dorje, but none of them were able to decipher it. He brought it to a Lama Kunga, who knew sixteen alphabets and thirty languages, but even he was unable to decipher it.

At that time it was well known that the tertön Dorje Lingpa's habits from his life as Vairochana had awakened, and that he consequently understood every language and alphabet perfectly. He was therefore invited to Kongpo. As soon as he saw the parchment, he understood it easily. The wondrousness of this added to his fame, and it seems that he is included in the lineage of these termas.

Sherab Mebar later went to Bhutan, where a chieftain forced him to reveal a terma that was not rightly his. The chieftain died, and the tertön passed away not long afterward. The parchments were reconcealed and eventually revealed by Padma Lingpa. As most of the parchments were damaged he was unable to completely decipher them, so he used the previous tertön's transcription. This terma is said to be the *Little*

Child Cycle: A Non-Dual Tantra of the Great Perfection.

Although the actual lineage of Sherab Mebar's *Great Perfection: Self-Liberated Samsara and Nirvana* has not survived, its text appears to be identical to dharma within Taksham Nüden Dorje's *Wisdom Assembly of the Yidam*. It is therefore appropriate to regard them as two streams combined into one.

Nyida Sangye

Nyida Sangye was a rebirth of the dharma minister Nyima. He was born in Dakpo. He revealed the *Planted Grass-Blade Ejection* instructions from Black Mandala Lake. He gave them to the naga king Tsukna Rinchen and his retinue. It is said that as a result all of the beings living in the lake were liberated.

This tertön appeared to judgmental people to be as aimless as the wind, but in reality he went to the Glorious Copper-Colored Mountain, met Guru Rinpoche, and received extraordinary instructions on ejection from him. These instructions are known as the *Whispered Lineage of Ejection*; there is an essay of instruction on them by the vidyadhara Terdak Lingpa.

Nyida Sangye also revealed a self-arisen image of the eleven-faced Avalokita from the Turquoise Lake in Tsari. It is said to be kept in Nyal nowadays.

It is also said that Nyida Sangye lived, helping beings, for two hundred and twenty years, but I am certain that this is the number of half-years of his life. Karma Lingpa was Nyida Sangye's son, and he helped Karma Lingpa reveal his termas. Karma Lingpa's lineage was also passed on to and by his father. Nyida Sangye's ejection instructions are both extremely profound and very widespread; they appear to have done beings immeasurable good.

The Mantradharin Letro Lingpa

The mantradharin Letro Lingpa was a disciple of the supreme being Dorje Lingpa. He was born in Dola. He revealed the *All Gurus Perfectly Complete* cycle from the Cave of the Dakini at Fire Lake in Zabulung. Some of the materials he found as part of that terma are said to have been passed down by his descendants and are nowadays kept at Drakar Chöding Monastery, but it seems that the lineage of this dharma terma no longer exists.

The well-known *Padma Shavari: A Single Mantra for a Hundred Ailments* appears to come from many termas, including that of Dorje Lingpa, but the *Sadhana of the Red Padma Shavari* was discovered by Letro Lingpa at Yangdzong. It has been received by our lord guru as rediscovered terma and is available.

Zangpo Drakpa

The nirmanakaya Zangpo Drakpa was an emanation of Prince Mutri Tsenpo. Zangpo Drakpa was born in southern Latö. He lived as a bhikshu, and entered the dharma gate of the Kagyu. He gained perfect realization through practicing one-pointedly at Shri in Gyal, the hermitage in Manglam, Gangbule, and other places. While he was at Gangbule Guru Rinpoche appeared to him as a boy wearing a turban and encouraged him to reveal terma, but Zangpo Drakpa considered this to be merely a meditation experience and disregarded it. Guru Rinpoche then emanated as an extraordinary yogin called Nyinam Lagom and gave Zangpo Drakpa a terma list and advice. Based on these, he revealed from the Stonewall Temple at Rulak sadhanas of Hayagriva and Maitreya and the *Instructions Given to the Gungthang King*. In Yönpolung he revealed several sadhanas, including that of

Vajrapani; the *Long, Intermediate, and Short Writings from the Heart*; a guide to sacred places; a terma list; the *Supplication of Seven Chapters*; and the *Wheel of Reversal*.

He brought the terma list and the *Writings from the Heart* to the Vidyadhara Vulture Feathers, who consequently revealed great terma at the Divine Rock of Zangzing. Vulture Feathers also deciphered the *Supplication of Seven Chapters* from the terma parchment and disseminated it throughout all of Tibet. It adorns the throats of everyone in this land, august and lowly; its activity is as vast as space.

Drime Lhunpo

Drime Lhunpo was a rebirth of Acharya Sale. He was born at Orshong in Kongpo amid many wondrous signs on the 15th day of the first month of spring in a Male Water Dragon year.[91] His father's name was Vajrapani; his mother's Padma Tso. Lama Yazangpa prophesied that he would become a protector of beings, a child of the victors, and gave him the name Light of Vairochana.

On the first day of the first month of summer in the year of his birth a list of his termas reached his hands. By his third year he possessed impartial supercognition and was able to explain both without difficulty. Guru Rinpoche and Yeshe Tsogyal revealed their faces to him and bestowed empowerments, blessings, and instructions upon him.

In his thirteenth year he revealed the *Assembled Wisdom of all the Teachings*, relics, samaya substances, and a list of thirty-one termas from the Stupa of Natural Blessing at Gangpa Kyawo in Chim. He undertook renunciation in the presence of the abbot Chökyi Lodrö, and completion in the presence of the Sakyapa Palden Lama. Drime Lhunpo completed the study of the five sciences and became vastly learned in dharma such as that of the Great Perfection.

Lists of one hundred and thirty profound termas reached

91. The year was 1352 C.E.

his hands, and he revealed most of them. Among them, the *Nine Assemblies*, the *Quintessence: Liberating All Beings*, the *Supreme Essence: Liberated Wisdom*, and the *Profound Essence: Self-Liberated Cognition* are the best known. He reconcealed some of his termas for future rediscovery, but those he revealed were inconceivably many. They included a copy of the *Hundred-Thousand Stanza Prajnaparamitasutra* called the *Red Hundred-Thousand* that had belonged to King Trisong and was written with blood from the noses of the abbot Shantarakshita, Guru Rinpoche, and Trisong himself; many wondrous images; and much wealth.

Drime Lhunpo also performed a great ceremony in the service of all the teachings along with the great tertön Sangye Lingpa. Every year in the first month of spring Drime Lhunpo presented vast offerings. In the first month of summer he engaged in thousandfold generosity. In the first month of autumn he created a hundred thousand tsatsas. In the first month of every winter he performed a hundred ganachakras. He established the interdependence for the Fourth Gyalwang Karmapa Rolpe Dorje to become his dharma heir, which brought the Karmapa the greatest joy.

Drime Lhunpo constantly exhibited wondrous signs and miracles that were apparent to everyone. The Buddhas of the ten directions revealed their faces to him, placed their hands on his head, and prophesied, "In the future, in the upper pure realm Immeasurable Natural Qualities, you will become the Tathagata King of Massive Stainless Natural Splendor." After completing his work for the benefit of beings he went to the realm of Lotus Light. His remains and his White Stupa That Moves are still at Tsagong Monastery.

I have received the complete ripening empowerments and liberating instructions of his main terma, the wondrous and renowned *Quintessence: Liberating All Beings*. There seems to be an existing lineage of the practice of his *Red Wind of Karma That Shakes the Three Realms* among practitioners of forceful mantra, but I have not yet received it. It appears that lineages and copies of his other termas no longer exist.

Drime Kunga

Drime Kunga was one of three tertöns who are collectively called the Three Drimes. He was an emanation of Nupchen Sangye Yeshe, and was born amid wondrous signs on the tenth day of a Female Fire Pig year at Red Hall in Drachi. His father's name was Paljor Zangpo; his mother's Gögö Dzomma. His family line was one of good mantrins, and he eventually became a great mantradharin vajra holder.

At first he went to Clearwater in Drachi to study the vinaya. In his twenty-first year he undertook the stages of the training in the presence of the great abbot of Clearwater, and was given the name Sherab Gyaltsen. Based on prophecies by his teacher and the dakinis he practiced at Samye Chimphu, where Guru Rinpoche directly bestowed empowerment and instruction on him. He gave rise to immeasurable experience and realization.

In particular, in his twenty-ninth year, at the top of Lönpo Gul at Chimphu he received a prophecy from Guru Rinpoche, and Yeshe Tsogyal gave him a list of termas. Based on those, during the next year he revealed a vast amount of dharma and wealth terma, including the *Guru Chintamani Practice*, the *Dakinis' Quintessence: The Great Perfection*, and *Mahakarunika: The Supreme Light of Wisdom*, from Lion-Faced Arrow Rock at Chimphu. Along with these extensive cycles of gurusadhana, Great Perfection, and Mahakarunika he revealed their concise essences. He also revealed the *Eight Dispensations: The Crown Jewel*, the *Ayusadhana of Hayagriva's Play*, the *Great Dakini*, and the *Protector Barchung*. He practiced his termas at Chimphu until signs of accomplishment arose.

He helped beings greatly throughout Tibet and Bhutan by

means of his gurusadhana, Great Perfection teachings, and Mahakarunika cycle. Finally he went to eastern Kongpo, where he sent down a great rain of dharma and founded Lhundrak Hermitage, a community of mantradharins. After completing such deeds, he departed for other realms amid wondrous signs.

His seat was passed on to his greatest heart-son, Tsenden Shönnu Sangye. Based upon the prophecies of wisdom dakinis, Shönnu Sangye changed the color of his vestments and those of his community to white. This caused the hermitage to be known as White Lhundrak, and its activity to flourish. It is also said that many of Drime Kunga's descendants have helped beings in Kongpo.

Drime Kunga's profound termas *Mahakarunika: The Supreme Light of Wisdom* and the *Protector Barchung* were once in widespread use, but nowadays I have not found either copies or lineages of their transmission. Drime Kunga practiced the concise cycles of gurusadhana, the Great Perfection, and Mahakarunika that he found, but did not teach or disseminate them. In consideration of the future he reconcealed their parchment at Red Rock Fine Throat. In recent times they were rediscovered by Padma Ösal Dongak Lingpa, who holds the dispensation of the ocean of profound terma, when he discovered his *Mahakarunika: Resting Mind-Itself*. He kept them secret for a long time, but when the interdependence of time and place came about, and with the encouragement of gurus and dakinis, he revealed them and bestowed their combined ripening and liberation upon me.

I have repeatedly performed the approach, accomplishment, and great accomplishment of *Guru Chintamani* and Drime Kunga's *Mahakarunika Jinasagara*; I have received indications of their blessing. They should therefore be treasured as jewels of our hearts. I have written a few necessary supplements in their service.

Ngödrup Gyaltsen the Vidyadhara Vulture Feathers

The tertön and great vidyadhara Ngödrup Gyaltsen was one of three supreme nirmanakayas who were rebirths of Nanam Dorje Düdjom. He was born amid remarkable signs on the tenth day of the month in a Female Fire Ox year at Namolung Hall, in the northern Black Stone Pile area, east of Mount Trazang. His father, Lopön Düdül, descended from an unbroken line of Vajrakilaya siddhas and was also a descendant of King Gesar.

As prophesied, in his twelfth year three vulture feathers grew on top of his head. In his twenty-fourth year five vulture feathers grew there. He therefore became widely known as the Vidyadhara Vulture Feathers. In his youth he perfectly studied, contemplated, and meditated on all of the Nyingma dharma held by his father.

Zangpo Drakpa of Manglam knew that the *Writings from the Heart*, the *Seven Points of Instruction*, and the rest of the eight dharmas which he had discovered in Gyang Yönpolung were necessary for the revelation of the termas concealed at Divine Rock. Zangpo Drakpa brought them to the teacher Sönam Wangchuk, who offered them to the great vidyadhara Ngödrup Gyaltsen. On the eighth day of the waxing phase of the Snake month in the Fire Horse year, Ngödrup Gyaltsen found within three white stelae on the peak of Mount Trazang the keys to the discovery of three great termas and a hundred minor ones. He concealed a terma substitute. He did not conceal the cavity left by his removal of the terma. Nowadays it is known as the Aperture of the Winds, and it is said that on the New Year's Day following the discovery a seedling grew from it and that the descendants of that seedling still grow there.

On the evening of the fourth day in the Sheep month of the same Fire Horse year Ngödrup Gyaltsen revealed the termas concealed in a cave at Zangzang Divine Rock. Divine Rock was a mountain of rock, shaped like a coiled poisonous snake; the cave was in the middle of the snake's body.

The termas were contained in a four-sided blue coffer. Inside, it was divided into five compartments, each of which formed one treasury. Collectively, these profound termas are called the *Gathered Trove of Five Treasuries*. The heart treasury in the coffer's center was brown. It held three scrolls and three kilas, bound by one brown silk ribbon. The eastern white conch treasury contained dharma that transcends cause and result, its wisdom as vast as space. The southern golden treasury contained dharma practices of fourfold approach and accomplishment, as brilliant as the sun and moon. The western red copper treasury contained dharma of extraordinary interdependence, like a sandalwood tree. The northern black iron treasury contained dharma of the pulverization of enemies and obstructors, like a tree of poisonous wood.

Briefly put, innumerable dharma termas and samaya substances emerged from the coffer, starting with the *Penetrating Wisdom of Samantabhadra*. Each of the five treasuries contained a hundred dharma termas, making a total of five hundred termas and their branches. Ngödrup Gyaltsen deciphered them all from their parchment and disseminated them among the worthy. His dharmic fame filled all of Tibet, and his dharma line stemming from his eight sons, eight consorts, and eight disciples remains undiminished today.

Although all of the profound termas that have been revealed over the centuries have been means of ensuring the present and future welfare of all of Tibet, these Northern Termas have spread the teachings, averted invasion, ended epidemics, pacified illness and civil unrest, subdued demons, restored the sovereignty of communities, and tamed sicknesses caused by either the earth or spirits.[92] These termas contain everything anyone could possibly need, including various means of ensuring the welfare of all Tibet in general, and of every part of it individually, from Garuda Valley's Silver Hall in the west to Tara of Space Meadow in the east. They also

92. Northern Termas is the collective name for the termas of Ngödrup Gyaltsen, the Vidyadhara Vulture Feathers.

include guides and keys to the identification of many sacred places such as the seven great hidden valleys. Because of the great good these termas have done all of Tibet, they are renowned as the Termas Like a Minister.

In the latter part of his life Ngödrup Gyaltsen went to Sikkim and opened the door to its hidden valleys. He also became the guru of King Chokdrup of Gungthang, which was beneficial to the welfare of Tibet. Finally, in Ngödrup Gyaltsen's seventy-second year, his deeds complete, his mind dissolved into the dharmadhatu amid many wondrous signs.

Many people from his dharma lineage have achieved rainbow bodies or become siddhas. I have fully received most of his termas that have extant lineages nowadays, including his *Peaceful and Wrathful Guru, Mahakarunika the Tamer of Beings*, the *Great Perfection: Penetrating Wisdom*, the *Self-Arisen Eight Dispensations*, most of his *Dharma of Interdependence*, and his protector cycles.

Palgyi Gyaltsen of Langlo

Palgyi Gyaltsen of Langlo was a prophesied emanation of the bhikshu Namkhay Nyingpo. He was born in western Ngari as the son of Lungtön Jamyang Gönpo. Palgyi Gyaltsen was the name he received when he undertook renunciation. He is also known as Jangchup Lingpa because of his residence, Jangchup Ling.

He traveled through central Tibet and Tsang, and cut through misunderstanding by studying and contemplating. He also received a guide that came from the termas of Guru Tseten Gyaltsen. Using it, he revealed a sky-metal vajra—a scepter of Guru Rinpoche's—and the sacred dharma called the *Treasure of Samantabhadra's Heart* from Deva Rakshasa Lake Rock, west of Palmo Palthang. As the terma's parchment was contained within the various parts of the vajra, it is known as the *Five Cycles: the General Composition* and the four parts of the inner terma—the *Prongs Cycle*, the *Hub Cycle*, the *Hub Cycle Summary*, and the *Prongs Cycle Supplement*.

The terma included both the instruction to create an image to be called Glorious Blaze of Merit for the benefit of all of Tibet, and the terma substances to be placed within it. Jangchup Lingpa created the image exactly as instructed. When he consecrated it, inconceivably wondrous signs of virtue appeared.

There is a wonderful story that Sangye Lingpa revealed a terma that was Jangchup Lingpa's by right, called *Pills Meaningful to See*, along with its index, from the peak of Horse Head Forest Rock Mountain at Vulture Basin in Kongpo. Sangye Lingpa read within the index a prophecy of the appearance of a tertön called Jangchup Lingpa in Latö. He sent a man named Könchok Wangpo to look for him. Sangye Lingpa eventually met with Jangchup Lingpa at the Nyanam Hermitage and gained confidence in him.

Although the activity of Jangchup Lingpa's profound dharma was once extensive, his lineage eventually died out. Then our lord guru Padma Ösal Dongak Lingpa's recollections of having been Jangchup Lingpa's son Samdrup Dorje were awakened; he received the blessing of his close lineage. He kindly bestowed upon me the ripening empowerments and liberating instructions of all of Jangchup Lingpa's dharmas. I have written a few things in their service.

Karma Lingpa

The tertön Karma Lingpa was an emanation of Chokro Lui Gyaltsen. He was born as the eldest son of the mahasiddha Nyida Sangye at Khyerdrup in western Dakpo. Karma Lingpa lived as a mantradharin. His qualities were immeasurable, and he was the very embodiment of unlimited supercognition and activity.

In his fifteenth year the prophecies concerning him and the necessary interdependence came together, and he revealed terma from Gampo Dar Mountain, which resembles a dancing god. This terma included both the *Peaceful and Wrathful Ones: Self-Liberated Wisdom* and *Mahakarunika: The Lotus Peaceful and Wrathful Ones*. He bestowed the *Lotus Peaceful and Wrathful Ones* on all fourteen of his dharma heirs, his major disciples. He bestowed *Self-Liberated Wisdom* only on his son Nyida Chöje, and commanded that it be sealed as a singular lineage for three generations.

As the interdependence between Karma Lingpa and his prophesied consort did not occur, he soon passed away to other realms.

The third inheritor of the *Peaceful and Wrathful Ones: Self-Liberated Wisdom* was Namkha Chökyi Gyamtso, who disseminated it widely. Its activity, including its empowerments, transmissions, instructions, and thousandfold offerings ceremony, has flourished to this day throughout central Tibet, Tsang, and Kham, and especially throughout all of eastern Tibet. I have received it fully, and have formed a connection with it through approach, accomplishment, and so forth.

Palden Jamyang Lama

Palden Jamyang Lama was the rebirth of the great Vidyadhara Vulture Feathers. He was born in western Nyang, in Tsang. From youth he lived at the Nenying College, where he eradicated misunderstanding by studying and contemplating all dharma of sutra and tantra.

Once, when he was visiting Trogang in western Nyang in order to teach, he noticed a large brick on the outer wall of the temple there and thought, "I would like to break that open." He waited until no other monks were present, and broke the brick open. From within it emerged a terma guide. Using it, he revealed the *Combined Sadhana of the Three*

Roots, including its outer, inner, secret, that-alone, and prayer sections, as well as the *Black Liberator Cycle* concerning its protector, from the image of a red tortoise in the Dakinis' Secret Cave on Black Liberator Palace Mountain.

About the number to be liberated by this prayer, the terma says:

> One million five hundred and ninety thousand people
> Will be freed by this prayer.

This profound dharma has brought beings much good throughout Tsang, including areas such as upper and lower Nyang, Shang, Tanak, and Oyuk; its activity has been vast. I have received its ripening empowerments and liberating instructions from an unbroken lineage.

Thangtong Gyalpo

The lord of siddhas Thangtong Gyalpo was an emanation of both Avalokita and Hayagriva. He was Guru Rinpoche appearing as a man born from a womb. Thangtong Gyalpo was born at Olpa Lhatse in western Tsang. Relying on five hundred and one masters, he studied and contemplated dharma to an immeasurable degree. Although he was already a self-arisen great lord among siddhas, out of necessity he received the complete Northern Termas from the ascetic Dönyö Gyaltsen and the dharma of the Shangpa Kagyu from Lama Dorje Shönnu. He demonstrated the attainment of siddhi through the practice of these two traditions.

His yogic discipline enabled him to travel throughout Jambudvipa and its subcontinents, and especially to Lotus Light in Chamaradvipa. He received dharma from Guru Rinpoche and countless other siddhas. Dakinis and dharmapalas placed his feet on their heads. He built many temples at key sites throughout Tibet in order to repel invasion. He bound all vicious gods and spirits under samaya.

He revealed a great deal of profound terma, such as five terma scrolls including the *Ayusadhana: Glorious Gift of Immortality* at Samye Chimphu; the *Very Secret Highest Heart Sadhana* at Drampa Jong; the *Mountain of Precious Treasure Secret Instructions* at Lotus Island on Accomplishment Lake; a scroll ten fathoms long containing the profound meaning of all sutras and tantras at Paro Taktsang in Bhutan; the *Profound Dharma Heart Treasure Cycles* at Guhyamantra Hall in Tsari; and the *Bright Beacon*, a prophecy concerning him, along with the *Sadhana of the Realm Protectors* at Great Majesty Cave in Tsari. He also concealed termas of his own.

By displaying miracles he subdued and led to dharma a sinful tirthika king at Kamata in India and the barbarians inhabiting the borderlands surrounding Tibet. His miracles were countless. He created innumerable amazing supports of body, speech, and mind. His amazing deeds, including the construction of fifty-eight iron suspension bridges and one hundred and eighteen ferries, are well-known.

In his one hundred and twenty-fifth year he departed for the celestial realm in his actual body. When his heart-son Nyima Zangpo keened with grief, Thangtong Gyalpo returned, bestowed extensive final instructions, and then departed for Pal Riwoche.

The mahasiddha of Ngari called Tsultrim Zangpo, who lived into his hundred and thirtieth year and tsansformed his body into a mass of light, and the siddha of Kham called the Felt-Cloaked One both appear to have been emanations of the mahasiddha Thangtong Gyalpo. Down to the present day, many people with karma have continued to be accepted as disciples by his wisdom body.

Thangtong Gyalpo had countless disciples. In particular, there were many who, holding his lineage, achieved the siddhi of longevity. This is because the mahasiddha himself had become a vidyadhara with mastery of longevity. His profound dharma, the *Great Whispered Lineage of Thangtong Gyalpo*, seems to have survived. The *Ayusadhana: Glorious Gift of Immortality* is practiced by all of the Sarma and Nyingma traditions.

In our own time, our lord guru Padma Ösal Dongak Lingpa has been repeatedly blessed and instructed by Thangtong Gyalpo's wisdom body. Based on this, our lord guru has revealed a wondrous dharma, the treasure of his heart, arisen from the expanse of his mind, called the *Heart Essence of the Mahasiddha*. Its root is a profound and extensive gurusadhana cycle, including both generation and completion. Its branches include both five sadhanas concordant with the tantras and the *Stages of the Path of Magical Illusion*, and instructions condensing the tantras, agamas, and upadeshas of the *Eight Dispensations of Accomplishment*. Through our lord guru's kindness, I have received all this from him.

The mahasiddha of Ngari mentioned above received the wondrous *Blessing Supplication of the Six Syllables* from Avalokita himself. The mahasiddha Thangtong Gyalpo bestowed this on our lord guru. I have had the good fortune to receive it from him. As it is amrita for everyone, august and lowly, it would seem fitting for those with bodhichitta to disseminate this meditation and recitation as widely as possible.

Gönpo Rinchen

Gönpo Rinchen was a rebirth of Princess Leksher, who was a daughter of Prince Mutik Tsenpo. Gönpo Rinchen was born at Tamshül in Lhodrak to the Shubu family of Kilaya siddhas. At an early age his dharmic propensities were awakened. In his thirteenth year he received much dharma from the great abbot Vajrapani. He also attended many teachers throughout central and southern Tibet. He engaged in assiduous study, practice, and austerity.

Although he discovered a terma guide at Bumthang Rock, a long time passed before he found the termas themselves.

When he was in his fifties he revealed many dharma termas, including the *Great Perfection: The Heart Essence of Padma*, from Zangyak Rock at Tsona Gorge in Bhutan. He also revealed many other termas from other places, such as Kharmezur, and exhibited countless signs of siddhi. Even the great tertön Ratna Lingpa received much dharma from him.

Gönpo Rinchen performed vast activity for the good of beings in upper and lower Lhodrak, Tsona, and Drushül. He departed for Lotus Light in his eighty-fourth year. It is said that his nephew lineage continues in Drushül; his dharma lineage no longer exists. It is also said that, based on some of the prophecies in his termas, he was also called both Jowo Tsemo and Shubu Chödrak.

Ratna Lingpa

The great emanated tertön Ratna Lingpa was a rebirth of Langdro Könchok Jungne. He was born in Drushül in Lhodrak on the fifteenth day of the first month of autumn in a Water Sheep year as the son of Dodedar the Wealthy, his father; and Sitharmen, his mother.[93] He learned to read and write without difficulty. Starting in about his tenth year he began to have pure visions. Through the power of his previous lives' training, he easily mastered the sciences. He also studied dharma widely.

In his twenty-seventh year he encountered Guru Rinpoche in the emanated form of an actionless yogin of Kham who was wearing yellow robes and hat. The emanation bestowed a terma guide on Ratna Lingpa and advised him. Based on that, Ratna Lingpa revealed twenty-five termas. They include his first terma, the *Sadhanas of the Three Roots*, revealed from Great Garuda Rock in his thirtieth year; the *Sadhana of Hayagriva and Vajravarahi in Union*, revealed from Koro Rock in Drithang; the *Four Assemblies*, revealed from the Sky's Stairway in Lhodrak; the *Peaceful and Wrathful*

93. The year was 1403 C.E.

Guru; *Mahakarunika Guhyasamaja*; and the *Great Perfection: The Brilliant Expanse of the Sun*.

As he wrote in his *Thirteen Storehouses of Writings*, he demonstrated unimaginably great supercognition and miraculous powers, such as the miracles he performed while revealing terma at the Glorious Deep Cave in Kharchu; he encountered Guru Rinpoche twenty-five times; and in visions he traveled to the Glorious Copper-Colored Mountain. He performed a great many Heart Sadhana Assemblies, Medicine Accomplishments, and Seven-Times-Born Flesh Accomplishments. Whenever he did so or gave empowerments or teaching great wonders would occur, such as rainbow light, rains of flowers, and the pervasive fragrance of incense. Obstacles never arose to any of his activity.

As his interdependence was the best, he revealed in one life the termas that would otherwise have been revealed during three lives. He therefore bore three names: Shikpo Lingpa, Drodül Lingpa, and Ratna Lingpa. He ripened and liberated countless beings throughout this land, from Mount Kailash all the way to Queen's Gorge in Kham. His family line and lineage of disciples have both survived, and both have included many fine individuals, starting with his four heart-sons.

Having completed his deeds, Ratna Lingpa departed for the Palace of Lotus Light amid wondrous miracles in his seventy-sixth year.

Although it would be appropriate to write at greater length of Ratna Lingpa's life, the transmissions and texts of his *Great Account of My Revelations* and his visionary *Thirteen Storehouses of Writings* still exist. One can also learn more about his life by reading the extensive biographies written by Yardrokpa Sherap Zangpo and Nyangpo Döndrup Gyalpo.

I have fully received all of the termas of this supreme tertön that have been preserved here in eastern Tibet, including his *Sadhanas of the Three Roots*, his *Peaceful and Wrathful Guru*, his *Four Assemblies* (except the *Profound Path*), his *Great Perfection: The Brilliant Expanse of the Sun*, his

Vajramala Ayusadhana, his *Very Secret Highest Vajrakilaya*, his dharmapala cycles such as the *Neuter Mahakala*, some of his minor termas, and his collected writings. I have performed extensive approach and accomplishment of several of them, including the *Vajramala Ayusadhana* and the *Very Secret Highest Vajrakilaya*. Working with Wontrül Rinpoche—who is a prophesied emanation of Langdro Könchok Jungne and a great treasury of compassion—I have instituted the performance of the vase accomplishment of *Mahakarunika Guhyasamaja* in the main temple at the great seat of Palpung and the great accomplishment of the *Very Secret Highest Vajrakilaya* in the Vajrakilaya temple there. We have made sure that these rituals are performed purely and correctly. I have written new manuals for their practice. In such ways, I have committed myself to this tradition.

Kalden Dorje

The tertön Kalden Dorje was an emanation of Drokmi Palgyi Yeshe. He was born in Nyal and lived as a mantradharin. He revealed a number of termas from Shampo Gang. Among them were eighteen scrolls containing the *Buddhakapalatantra* and *Sadhana*, the *Chakrasamvarasadhana*, and the *Instructions on Severance*. He also found many material termas, including the spirit-stone of the great god Shampo, made from jewels of devas, nagas, and men; and the skull of Drokmi Palgyi Yeshe. His dharma lineage lasted for a while in E and Nyal, and his *Instructions on Severance* were once widespread, but it seems that his lineage no longer exists.

Chokden Dorje

Chokden Dorje was an emanation of both Acharya Sale and

Sale's rebirth Chölo Gönpo. He was born at Gyashö Lagong in a Male Wood Tiger year. He undertook renunciation in the presence of Gyatön Lozang Drakpa, and developed incredible wisdom and signs of siddhi. Once, the chieftain of Jar tried to burn him to death, but was unable to harm him.

Chokden Dorje encountered Guru Rinpoche many times and received his prophecies. Based on them, he revealed the *Great Perfection: The Heart Essence of Hayagriva* from White Rock Divine Water in Nyangpo.

Taksham, Chöje Lingpa, and others held Chokden Dorje's termas in high regard and disseminated them, as is clear in their biographies. I have also received these termas.

Chak Jangchup Lingpa

Chak Jangchup Lingpa was born in one of the valleys of Lhodrak Tamshül. He was a disciple of Padma Lingpa and others. He also revealed a few profound termas, but it does not seem that their lineage has survived. Jangchup Lingpa's seat later received the support of the vidyadhara Trinley Lhundrup and his disciples, and appears to be still inhabited.

The Mantradharin Shakya Zangpo

The mantradharin Shakya Zangpo, the nirmanakaya of Yölmo, was a rebirth of the great Buddhist minister Gö Padma Gungtsen. He was born to the family of the great vajra holder of Drangpo in Drompa Jong in southern Latö. Shakya Zangpo became learned and accomplished in all traditions of guhyamantra—Sarma and Nyingma, kama and terma. He opened the door to the sacred place Yölmo Gangra and revealed a terma there called *Mahakarunika: Liberating Samsara into the Expanse*.

He once went to Samye on pilgrimage. While there he

received the dakinis' prophecy. Based on it, he revealed a scroll containing a guide to the Great Stupa of Bodhanath and instructions on its restoration from the Red Stupa of Samye on the eighteenth day of the sheep month in the Water Monkey year. These prophetic instructions had previously been revealed by Lhatsün Ngönmo from the back of the image of Vairochana at Samye, and subsequently replaced by him after he received the prophetic instruction to do so. What Shakya Zangpo revealed from the Red Stupa was a copy of the scroll, made by Lhatsün and concealed by him there.

After that Shakya Zangpo repaired the dams at Lhasa and received another prophecy, based on which he revealed the terma *Mahakarunika: The Collected Teachings of King Songtsen Gampo*.

As instructed in the prophecy he had found at Samye, Shakya Zangpo met with the great vidyadhara Padma Lingpa, Kongpo Karchen Kunga Drakpa, Drikung Kunga Rinchen, and other holy beings who shared his aspiration to restore the Great Stupa, and received their blessings. Through the good interdependence of this he was able to perfectly restore the Great Stupa. As his restoration of it involved revealing it from underneath a mound of earth, he practically rediscovered the stupa as a terma!

On the stupa's life-tree he found relics of the Nepalese king Özer Gocha, who was seven-times-born. Shakya Zangpo distributed these relics for the good of beings.

He also attended Kongchen Namkha Palden, Metön Namkha Gyaltsen, the vidyadhara Sangye Tenpa, Tsangtön Ugyen Palzang, and other masters. He received the empowerments and instructions of most of the Nyingma teachings, kama and terma, that existed at his time. He practiced them and bestowed them fully on the great vidyadhara of Ngari, his brother, and others. In such a way he prolonged the life of the teachings. He also perfected the forceful activity of direct action. He was of great help to beings in Ngari and Gungthang.

He meditated for a long time at Glorious Blaze Mountain. While there he met the vidyadhara Chokden Gönpo, who bestowed prophecy on him. Accordingly, Shakya Zangpo went to the hidden land of Lotus Garden, also called Yölmo Gangra. He built Tsuda Monastery there, furnished it with supports, and remained there for the rest of his life, engaging in many means of ensuring the well-being of all Tibet. At the end of his life, when he passed into peace, he left a detailed testament. According to it, he would be reborn in the family line of the king of Latö, descended from the bhikshu Nup Namkhay Nyingpo, fourteen generations after Nyangral Nyima Özer. His rebirth was the nirmanakaya Namkha Gyajin, whose nirmanakaya was the principal heart-son of the vidyadhara Ngaki Wangpo, Tendzin Norbu, also known as Topden Shukchang Tsal. He made Thupten Dorje Drak his seat, and was very kind to the teachings.

Drodül Letro Lingpa

Drodül Letro Lingpa was an emanation of both the translator Rinchen Zangpo—one of the hundred and eight great translators of the early period —and Shelkarza. He was born in western Nyal to the Nyi family amid wondrous signs. His father's name was Paljor Gyalpo; his mother's was Tashi Lhamo.

He experienced boundless pure appearances. Especially, he first received a list of profound termas in his sixteenth year. In his eighteenth year he offered the fruits of his crown to the peerless Namkha Gyalpo at Chölung Riwoche, and received the name Namkha Dorje. He received and practiced the profound instructions of the Barom Kagyu. Especially, he met the vidyadhara Padma Lingpa and resolved all misunderstandings through hearing and thinking. His being was ripened by profound instruction. Drodül Letro Lingpa is considered to be one of the three heart-sons of Padma Lingpa, the one called Dorje of Nyal, who was predicted to be an emanated tertön.

Accordingly, in his twenty-first year he was encouraged by the Protectress of Mantra, Ekajati. He went to Domtshang Valley in Bhutan. In the Cave of Yeshe Tsogyal there he performed a Hayagriva ganapuja, and wisdom dakinis directly bestowed the terma guide. He went to the Cave of the Moon. Amid wondrous apparitions, he revealed his first terma.

He subsequently revealed terma from such places as the Tiger's Lair at Paro, the Glorious Deep Cave in Kharchu, the Water Temple in Lhokye, the Dakinis' Secret Cave, Drakyangdzong, the Glorious Secret Treasury Cave of the Blazing Sun and Moon, the Dakinis' Ledge, Samye Chimphu, the White Stupa, Shampo Gangra, and Slender Rock. The termas he found include *Mahakarunika: Lamp Illuminating the Truth*, the *Very Secret Highest Eight Dispensations*, the *Profound Heart Essence of Samantabhadra*, and countless other dharma termas, cycles of forceful mantra, samaya materials, and supports.

In his practice places he performed many great accomplishments of deities including the Peaceful and Wrathful Guru, the Eight Dispensations, and Vajrakilaya. He also performed many medicine accomplishments, seven-times-born pill accomplishments, and torma accomplishments. He ripened and freed vast numbers of disciples, and remained active to the end of his life. His nephew Lhayi Dawa, who possessed excellent realization, also helped countless beings.

It is said that Drodül Lingpa was reborn several times. Especially, his descendants were all mantradharin vajra-holders for some time. His dharma line was once widespread, but it does not seem that it has survived. Nevertheless, our lord guru received a short lineage of *Mahakarunika: Lamp Illuminating the Truth*, and I have received its complete ripening and liberation.

Jampal Dorje

Jampal Dorje, the tertön from Mangrong, was an emanation of Nanam Dorje Düdjom. He revealed the *Mahakarunika: Liberating All Beings* cycle from Yerpa. It appears that the lineage of its empowerments and transmissions lasted until the time of the great tertön of Mindröling.

Jampal Dorje founded Ngesang Dorje Ling at Tsang Gangra. This seat was subsequently held by Nyida Drakpa, the dharma heir of Shikpo Lingpa; his nephew, the great translator Ngaki Wangpo; and his nephew, Shenpen Dorje. After that the seat was awarded by the great Fifth Dalai Lama to Tratsangpa Lochok Rikpe Dorje.

Padma Wangyal Dorje

Padma Wangyal Dorje, the mahapandita of Ngari, was the ninth rebirth of Prince Lharjey and a mind emanation of the king Trisong Detsen. He was born at Lowo Tang in a Female Fire Sheep year. His father was the greatly learned and accomplished Jamyang Rinchen Gyaltsen, who was both of royal descent and a rebirth of Lord Marpa. Padma Wangyal Dorje's mother was called Drocham Tromgyen. He was given the name Padma Wangyal.

In his eighth year he became an upasaka. He generated bodhichitta in his father's presence, and received from him the kama teachings of the Nyingma tradition, especially the *Guhyagarbhatantra*, the sutras of anuyoga, and the Great Perfection. He studied these to perfection. He performed many approaches and accomplishments, achieving signs. From the acharya Norten Zangpo he received the vinaya, the sutras, and the Kadampa teachings.

Beginning in his twentieth year he studied a hundred great textual traditions, including the Middle Way, valid cognition, and the *Prajnaparamita*. He became widely known as a kalyanamitra who deserved that title.

In his twenty-first year he received the ripening empowerments and liberating instructions for the Red Yamantaka and other deities from Jamyang Chökyong, Tsultrim Pal, and others. He performed approach and accomplishment and saw the face of the wrathful Manjushri.

Especially, in his twenty-second year he received the complete transmission of the kama and terma teachings of the Nyingma school from his holy father. When Padma Wangyal subsequently performed the *Sadhana of the Eight Dispensations*, his father experienced extraordinary visions that caused him to encourage and praise his son, referring to qualities that became evident later in his life.

In Padma Wangyal's twenty-third year he twice received the *Path and Result* from the Translator of Lowo. In his twenty-fifth year he undertook complete renunciation at Samdrupling Monastery in the presence of Sönam Lhundrup, the great abbot of Lowo, an emanation of Manjushri Sakya Pandita.

From then on, Padma Wangyal maintained the discipline of an utter renunciate, including eating only once a day. His practice of the vinaya was so correct that he became the foremost vinayadharin of his day.

From the above-mentioned great abbot; from Namgyal Palzang, the mahapandita of Guge; and from Jamyang Lodrö he received teaching on linguistics and logic as well as many empowerments and tantras of the Sarma tradition of guhyamantra. Mastering all these, he came to wear the crown that is the title "mahapandita."

He received many of the Northern Termas from Shakya Zangpo, the tertön from Drangpo.

In brief, Padma Wangyal went to great effort to re-ceive most of the empowerments, tantras, and instructions of the Sarma and Nyingma Traditions of guhyamantra that existed in his day. He also performed their approaches and accomplishments.

He traveled to Nepal and studied there with many Nepalese and Tibetan gurus. While meditating on pilgrimage in Nepal he had countless pure visions.

Starting in his thirty-eighth year he began to rain down a vast shower of dharma of the Sarma and Nyingma Traditions without distinction. The resolution to restore the diminished dharma lineages of the Sarma and Nyingma Traditions throughout central Tibet arose in his heart. After receiving the permission of his father and the officials of Lowo, he traveled through Zangzang Lhadrak. Accompanied by his younger brother Lekden Dorje, Padma Wangyal reached central Tibet. He visited the emanated temple of Lhasa and received prophecies there. Based on them, he went to receive the Ngok mandalas and Ngok's *Red Yamantaka Cycle* at Shungdreshing from Ngoktön Sönam Tendzin and Shalu the Great of Drathang.

When Padma Wangyal visited Samye, the habits from his life as the dharma king Trisong Detsen were awakened. He performed a great accomplishment of the *Eight Dispensations: The Assembly of Sugatas* in the middle temple and accepted the Guru of Lhodrak as a disciple. He also received the *Wisdom Assembly of the Guru* from Trengso Ugyen Chözang and Kongchen Namkha Palzang.

Padma Wangyal meditated at Drakyangdzong and Chimphu, where he saw the faces of many deities. The eighth lineal descendant of Guru Chöwang invited him to Lhodrak. Padma Wangyal restored the diminished dharma lineages there. He filled Lhodrak with his great kindness.

This lord received the *Eight Dispensations: The Assembly of Sugatas* twenty-five times. He regarded the last of these as the most satisfying, in that the source was pure, definitive, and powerful: at the White Monastery of Lhodrak, Padma Wangyal received the *Eight Dispensations: The Assembly of Sugatas* from the peerless mahasiddha, the noble Namkhay Naljor.

In particular, the way Padma Wangyal revealed profound

terma was as follows: In his forty-sixth year he revealed terma from a secret coffer concealed among the four outward-facing figures that formed the statue of Vairochana in the upper temple at Samye. This terma included the *Later Assembly of Dispensations: The Assembly of All Vidyadharas* and the *Sadhana of the Seven-Chapter Supplication*. He deciphered most of this terma, and it has remained widespread down to the present. I have received it all.

With the vidyadhara Lekdenje as go-between, Padma Wangyal invited Rinchen Puntsok, the tertön of Drikung, to join him at Samye. These three masters together reconsecrated Samye Monastery, which was of great benefit to all Tibet. That is an example of the countless things Padma Wangyal did for beings and the teachings while in central Tibet.

Finally, in his fifty-sixth year he departed from Önmönthang for the Glorious Copper-Colored Mountain.

The life of this holy being was one of inconceivable learning, accomplishment, and impeccability. This is evident in his versified autobiography; here I have merely summarized it.

Among his innumerable achievements his composition of *Ascertainment of the Three Vows*, which is brief yet remarkably inclusive, was an act of unimaginable kindness. This shastra continues to adorn the throats of those who hold the teachings of the Early Translations down to the present. Padma Wangyal was a renowned and great chariot of the kama and terma teachings of the Early Translations. He illuminated them and benefited them in many direct and indirect ways.

His immediate rebirth was the Lord of the North, Tashi Topgyal, whose biography will be found below.

Mingyur Letro Lingpa

Mingyur Letro Lingpa, Kunga Palzang, was a rebirth of Shelkarza Gönkhyi. From the *Assembly of All Vidyadharas:*

Four tertöns will bow to him.
They will each reveal my holy, profound dharma as terma.

Mingyur Letro Lingpa was one of those four tertöns. He was born at Gyam in west-central Tibet. He became both a master and disciple of Drikung Rinchen Puntsok. He was also a dharma heir of the tertön from Ngari, the great vidyadhara Lekden.

The four tertöns predicted above revealed the *Profound Dharma of the Four Assemblies*, terma materials, *Profound Protection from the Planet*, and *Invincible Environment* from Changeless Dharma-Source Rock. They were passed down through Rinchen Puntsok, the four tertöns' dharma heir. Although these termas were once widespread, their transmission has not survived.

The wondrous little text of the *Profound Dharma of Fierce Padma* came to our lord guru as rediscovered terma. I have received its ripening and liberation, and saw while doing so extraordinary signs of its blessing. For example, while giving the empowerment our lord guru wrote the mantras on the surface of a mirror. Later, it became evident that the mantras had spontaneously engraved themselves into the mirror's surface.

Namchak Mebar

The tertön Namchak Mebar was a combined emanation of the great master Humkara and Prince Mutri Tsenpo. He was born at Drikung in west-central Tibet. His father was the dharma king Tenpe Gyaltsen of the Kyura lineage of the Guge kings. Namchak Mebar was born to his mother Sönam Drönma amongst wondrous signs in a Female Earth Snake year.

His dharmic habits awoke in his youth. Even then he was amazing, and remembered many previous lives. In his eighth year he undertook renunciation at Pamodru in the presence of

Chenga Chökyi Drakpa Rinpoche and received the name Rinchen Puntsok Chökyi Gyalpo. He studied the traditions of sutra and tantra perfectly with Chenga Rinpoche, the Mahapandita of Ngari, and the latter's brother.

He practiced in many places, including Shotö Tidro, and mixed appearances and mind into inseparable equality. He was placed on the great dharma throne of the protector Jikten Sumgön and engaged in vast activity both spiritual and secular.

While Rinchen Puntsok was living at Tidro the yogin Vajranatha came from India and gave him the *Instructions of Jatavira on Bhuprana*. Encouraged by the dakinis' predictions, Rinchen Puntsok changed his costume to the white robes of a yogin. This opened the door of profound interdependence, and he received at that time the *Instructions on the Wish-Fulfilling Supreme Light* in a vision. He also acquired a terma guide. Based on it he revealed the five wondrous pages of the *Holy Dharma of Very Profound Wisdom* from the Great Feast Hall of Tidro. He immediately entered retreat. During the night of a tenth day, he went to the Glorious Copper-Colored Mountain in a vision, received empowerment and extensive guidance from Guru Rinpoche, and took part in a ganachakra. From then onward he became a lord of the kama and terma teachings of the Sarma and Nyingma traditions.

As Rinchen Puntsok was both greatly learned and accomplished, his way of explaining texts was superior to that of others. He emphasized the *Former* and *Latter Termas*, the nine traditions of the Eight Dispensations, the *Four Branches of the Heart Essence*, and the writings of the omniscient Longchenpa.

After completing such deeds Rinchen Puntsok departed for the great palace of Lotus Light.

His disciples lived all over Tibet, all the way from Ngari and Ladak in the west to Dokham and Hor in the east, and throughout the four parts of central Tibet and Tsang.

Foremost among them were Rinchen Puntsok's physical and dharma son Chögyal Puntsok, who was a rebirth of Tsuklakdzin, the king of Zahor. Chögyal Puntsok took his father's seat. Down to the present day, its tradition combining the Sarma and Nyingma schools remains undiminished. All holders of the Drikung lineage hold the lineage of the study and practice of the *Holy Dharma of Very Profound Wisdom*, and I have received most of it.

Sherap Özer

Trengpo Drodül Lingpa Sherap Özer was an emanation of the great translator Vairochana. He was born amongst wondrous signs on the tenth day of the month of Ashadha in a Male Earth Tiger year, in Ngomchen in the north, to the Tri and Sam families. From an early age he had unfabricated revulsion, compassion, and great intelligence. His mahayana disposition was awakened.

In his eighth year he became an upasaka in the presence of the master Tsultrim Özer, and received the name by which he is best known, Sherap Özer. He then undertook renunciation in the presence of Dorgyalwa, a disciple of Serdok Panchen. He studied the treatises on the vehicle of attributes as well as the *Guhyasamajatantra* for six years with the Ganden Tripa Tendarwa. He studied the tantras of the Sakya tradition and the *Kalachakratantra* with Dorgyalwa. His studies completed, Sherap Özer caused the drum of his throat to resound in the colleges of the vehicle of attributes. When he did so, no one could respond to his learning and reasoning. He became known as a great kalyanamitra.

In his eighteenth year he met Drikung Rinchen Puntsok, and felt faith beyond control. When they discussed dharma, the two of them—the master and the disciple—gained trust in one another. Sherap Özer received from Rinchen Puntsok countless teachings including the profound dharma of the

Drikung Kagyu and Karma Kagyu; the collected tantras of the Sarma and Nyingma schools; the mahayoga, anuyoga, and atiyoga tantras with their explanations; and all the kama and terma Nyingma dharmas along with their practical instructions, especially the *Dakinis' Heart Essence*.

As commanded by his guru, Sherap Özer turned the dharmachakras of sutra and tantra, including all the Buddha's teachings, amidst an ocean of the sangha. He based his presentation on the fivefold Mahamudra, taught the *Vajra Speech of a Hundred and Fifty Stanzas*, and expounded the view of the *Single Intention*. He thereby fulfilled his guru's wishes and brought his sangha to wondrous realization.

Sherap Özer lived within the virtues of training; he abandoned distraction and unnecessary activity. He practiced in solitude for eight years. In particular, he meditated for three years in the Piled Jewels Cave of Accomplishment on Drok Mountain. Inconceivably great signs arose; he acquired countless gates of samadhi.

During that time, on the tenth day of the month Ashadha in the Female Fire Sheep year a dakini with the appearance of a Bhutanese woman gave him a skullcup filled with liquor. He drank it, causing him to see Guru Padmaraja amidst white light. Guru Rinpoche instructed him, and based on that Sherap Özer revealed the *Essence of Liberation: Self-Liberated Wisdom* and supports of body, speech, and mind from that terma site.

Thereafter in Lhasa he revealed as terma relics of the Tathagata, substances that liberate through taste called *Sealed by Aḥ*, and other remarkable supports and samaya substances. In all, he revealed profound terma from six locations. He deciphered the terma parchment together with Drikung Rinchen Puntsok Rinpoche, and then performed the terma accomplishment at Zingwa Tiger Head.

While he was doing so, he had a vision in which he went to Lotus Light and encountered Guru Rinpoche and Yeshe Tsogyal in the form of Guru Mahasukha. They empowered

Sherap Özer and instructed him. He seemed to remain there for one month.

In Trengpo he and Drikung Rinchen Puntsok received the *Wisdom Assembly of the Guru* and much other dharma from Nyima Gyaltsen, a dharma heir of the *Wisdom Assembly*. As requested by the people of Trengpo, Sherap Özer then made Trengpo his seat.

Sherap Özer remained in retreat at Dorje Drak for three years. During that time he again saw Guru Rinpoche, who told him, "Nowadays you are the only one who correctly understands the view. Explain it clearly!"

He therefore wrote the *Bright Beacon of the Guru's Words*, a profound and concise shastra. By this time everyone known to be learned and realized praised him and drank the amrita of his profound dharma. When he practiced the *Dakinis' Heart Essence*, the *Very Profound Wisdom*, and the *Essence of Liberation* and gave their empowerments and instructions, seven thousand people would attend the public empowerments. There were always wondrous signs such as rainbow light and rains of flowers. Sherap Özer had the eye of dharma; his supercognition knew no bounds.

Through the sponsorship of Hor Sönam Topgye, Sherap Özer founded Pangye Palri Tekchen Ling and filled it with supports. His dharma activity filled central, western, and eastern Tibet.

On the tenth day of the sixth month in his sixty-seventh year, the Year of the Water Monkey, Sherap Özer wished to pass into peace. However, his physical son Karma Kunzang, together with his daughter-in-law and grandchildren, prayed that he live. In response he remained alive for three additional days. On the morning of the thirteenth day of the month he withdrew his emanated display into the heart of the great vira Skull Fragment in the city of Mahasukha Shantapuri.

There is a wonderful biography of Sherap Özer including the story of his termas, consisting of ten chapters, written by Chöje Kunzang.

I am fortunate to have received the unbroken ripening empowerments and liberating instructions of the *Essence of Liberation*.

The Great Vidyadhara of Ngari

The great vidyadhara of Ngari was an emanation of Nanam Dorje Düdjom. He was born as the son of Jamyang Rinchen Gyaltsen, a great mantradharin of the divine family line of Ngari Lowo. The great vidyadhara was also the younger brother of the mahapandita of Ngari.

As predicted in the termas of Kunkyong Lingpa, the great vidyadhara was given the name Lekden Dorje. In certain testaments there appear predictions of "the tertön Dorje Trolö." The signs of the time for revelation in these predictions match those of the great vidyadhara, as clearly predicted in his termas.

Lekden Dorje received many empowerments and teachings from his father, and completed approach and accomplishment. He saw his father as Great Splendor Supreme Heruka, and had many other visions of the three roots. He received many prophecies and developed immeasurable qualities. Knowing that Shakya Zangpo, the mantradharin of Drangpo, had been his guru in many lives he took him as his root guru. He also attended many learned and accomplished masters of Tibet, from Ngari all the way to Kongpo, and became the lord of an ocean of kama, terma, and upadesha dharma. He employed dharmapalas as servants and thereby mastered the four actions.

Together with his elder brother, the mahapandita of Ngari, Lekden Dorje revealed the *Assembly of All Vidyadharas* cycle from a concealed coffer within the Vairochana statue in the central temple of Samye. Although the mahapandita indicated that the dharma heir of this cycle was to be Drikung Rinchen Puntsok, he was unable to impart it to him; it was from

Lekden Dorje that Rinchen Puntsok received it completely. In the *Assembly of All Vidyadharas* there is the prediction:

Four emanated tertöns will bow to him.

These were Drikung Rinchen Puntsok, Mingyur Letro Lingpa, Nesar Khyentse Wangchuk, and the vidyadhara Lekden Dorje.

In particular, Lekden Dorje revealed as his own terma the profound and extensive cycle of the *Nine-Headed Wrathful One* from Önpu Taktsang. He opened the door to the sacred place of Sikkim and revealed the wondrous cycle of the *Amritakundalin Ayusadhana* from Divine Mountain Jewel-Essence Rock. It is said that he also revealed many other profound termas, including sadhanas of the peaceful and wrathful forms of Manjushri, of Mahakarunika, and of Vajrapani.

He compelled the yaksha Tsimara, a guardian of the property of Samye, to become gentle. In such ways, it is said that he exhibited a degree of magical power that has never been exceeded.

During his later life he sat on the lion throne at Sangngak Tekchok Ling and indefatigably engaged in the holy deeds of empowerment and teaching. His disciples were countless, from the greatest and best-known holders of the Sarma and Nyingma lineages to the most humble inhabitants of mountain caves. He lived into his hundred and thirteenth year, nurturing the dharma of teaching and accomplishment, and passed into the dharmadhatu without illness at Sangngak Tekchok Ling. The preparation of a support for his relics and all the other duties connected with his passing were performed by the dharmaraja Wangpo'i De.

Of his termas, *Mahakarunika: Liberating Samsara into the Expanse*, the *Wrathful One: Self-Luminous Wisdom*, the *Ayusadhana*, and the instructions of the *Trikaya Guru* have survived unbroken, and I have received them.

Matiratna

The tertön Matiratna was an emanation of Kharchen Palgyi Wangchuk. He is said to have been born at the border between Domey and Tashel. He revealed the cycle of the *Wrathful Goddess, the Tamer of Mara* from sindhura water in Shelkok Thangshing. He also revealed a gurusadhana and other termas. Even today, his monastery and lineage flourish.

The story is told about this tertön that because of the interdependence of his previous lives he had but scanty provisions. Accordingly he prayed to Guru Rinpoche and received a prophecy that to the east, at Shakra Karmo, there was a golden mule to be revealed as terma. He went there to reveal it and found a little wax mule with bits of gold the size of peas on its back. If he had taken it as a support for the accomplishment of wealth and performed the terma practice he would have gained wealth equal to the gold that a mule could bear upon its back. Unfortunately, the tertön became discouraged and gave rise to slight wrong views. He therefore spoiled the interdependence and passed away in poverty.

I have not seen a detailed account of his life. The cycle of the *Wrathful Goddess, the Tamer of Mara* is widespread in Domey. I have received its empowerments and transmissions, as well as those of his *Wish-Fulfilling Jewel Who Embodies All Gurus*.

Tsering Dorje

Tsering Dorje of Dongkar Lakha was a rebirth of Salwe Drönma, a female servant of Princess Nüjin Sale. He was born in the south, near Paro. From the terma site Red Rock, north of Nyangrotsi Nesar, he revealed the *Great Perfection Chiti Cycle*. From behind the statue of the Great Mother at Nesar he revealed as terma six pills made from the flesh of the seven-times-born, each pill the size of the first egg laid by a large bird. Tsering Dorje also revealed many termas from Paro in the south. He helped beings tremendously throughout the south and in both Nyangshap and Tanak. His subsequent rebirth and his son Kalden Dorje also helped beings immeasurably. The dharma of *Chiti* is famous because all of its practitioners have achieved bodies of light. It's ripening empowerments and liberating instructions remain unbroken, and I have received them.

Khyentse Wangchuk Dongak Lingpa

Khyentse Wangchuk Dongak Lingpa, also known as Nesarwa, was an emanation of both the dharma king Trisong Detsen and Langdro the Translator. He was born to the Asha family of Tsi Nesar in a Male Wood Monkey year amid wondrous signs at Tongpodong in Tsang. His father was Tongpön Namkha Dorje; his mother was Tseten Budren.

From an early age he displayed unassailable wisdom and tremendous faith, devotion, and compassion. His behavior was always holy; he never behaved like an ordinary child. He was inconceivably amazing. He clearly remembered receiving the four round empowerments of *Guru Guhyasamaja* in his first year from Jetsün Gorumpa. He sometimes spontaneously spoke in Sanskrit. Even before learning to read, he spontaneously recited a poem of praise to the lord of yogins Virupa.

He learned reading, writing, and the sciences without difficulty. In his eighth year he undertook renunciation in the presence of Tsarchen Vajradhara Kunga Lekpe Jungne. He was given the name Khyentse Wangchuk Tenpe Gyaltsen Pal Zangpo. He received an ocean of dharma from Tsarchen Vajradhara, Gorumpa, and other teachers. He performed many approaches and accomplishments, and meditated one-pointedly on the vajrayoga and other completion stage practices.

In his twentieth year he undertook completion. He was an exemplary monastic; all of his behavior was pure.

While he was in retreat he was visited by Manikanatha, a yogin who had accomplished immortality, the son of a king of Kakota in western India. From Manikanatha Nesarwa received a sadhana of Guru Padma's trikaya, a Vajravarahi blessing derived from the *Abhidhana*, and instructions on bhuprana. Manikanatha carried with him as a practice support an image of Guru Padma in royal attire; this image was so impressive that one would never tire of looking at it. Seeing the image, Nesarwa realized that the sadhana of Guru Rinpoche that he had just received from Manikanatha was the same as a terma of Ratna Lingpa, and that the existence of an Indian image of Guru Rinpoche in royal attire disproved the false accusation that this form of Guru Rinpoche was merely an emanation of Pehar that appeared only in Tibet. Nesarwa immediately lost his previous negative attitude toward the Nyingma tradition and strongly regretted his denigration of it. He committed himself to receiving, studying, teaching, and disseminating all of the kama and terma dharma of the Nyingma tradition, and to adopting its view as his own. From then on he delighted in yogis and the behavior of Indian siddhas. He spontaneously became able to read the Nagari and Kashmiri scripts.

He completed his study of the vehicle of attributes at Tanak Thupten, and then received all of the Sakya teachings and especially all of the instructions of the whispered lineage, such as the *Explanation for Disciples of the Path and Result*, from Lord Tsarchen. He was empowered as a lord of the teachings.

In response to a prophecy Nesarwa went on pilgrimage to Dramgyang. He later said that he observed both the location of terma there and signs of its time of revelation; he did not describe revealing it. Because of his residence at a college of the vehicle of attributes, and because of samaya-contamination, he was unable to reveal very much terma. However, it is said that he did reveal one volume of wondrous instructions, including some concerned with lightning and hail.

He received many Nyingma teachings from Setra Zangpo and the great vidyadhara of Ngari. His dharma activity of disseminating both the Nyingma and Sarma teachings was boundless. His service to the dharma was vast, and included sitting on the dharma throne of the great seat of Shalu and thereby restoring the waning doctrine of the omniscient Butön.

Nesarwa passed to other realms in his forty-fourth year. Starting with his nephew Wangchuk Rapten and the great emanation of Tsarchen, the great sun of dharma called Gönpo Sönam Chokden, Nesarwa's display of emanations has continued down to the present. I have received the instructions on bhuprana which have come down from him.

Karma Guru

Karma Guru, also known as Chögyal Wangpo'i De, was a prophesied emanation of the qualities of the dharma king Trisong Detsen. He was born in western Yeru. His father was Namkha Rinchen, the great scion of the royal line of Minyak. Karma Guru's mother was Chökyong Dzomchen. He was born in a Male Iron Dog year amid extraordinary signs. Jetsün Kunga Drölchok named him Pal Tashi Topgyal Wangpo'i De and gave him a longevity empowerment.

From many learned and accomplished masters of various traditions, including Jetsün Kunga Drölchok, Lochen Ratnabhadra, Nupgönpa Jampa Chökyi Gyaltsen, the vidyadhara Lekden Dorje, and Drikungpa Chögyal Rinchen Puntsok, Karma Guru received vast amounts of sutra, tantra, Sarma, and Nyingma dharma. His knowledge became boundless.

In particular, he received and held all the lineages of the termas that had been revealed up to his time that are mentioned in his *Supplication to the Tertöns*. He acquired all of their various samaya substances. He mastered the four actions, and utterly eradicated enemies with his magical power.

His first revelation was of a guide to many termas, substances that liberate through taste, and a ruby amulet. He revealed these from the Aryapalo Ling Temple at Samye. Then, in the sight of a large crowd, he flew like a bird over the face of Tsangrong Lhanglhangma Cliff and revealed the *Trikaya Embodiment of All Families* and the *Karmaguru* cycle. After that he revealed the *Triple Essence of Mother Tantra*, samaya substances, and a kila from the Golden Stupa of Jöpa in Lhodrak. It seems that he also revealed various other termas as well.

His dharma activity and display of signs of siddhi throughout central Tibet, Tsang, Lhodrak, eastern Tibet, and Kongpo were unimaginably great. He traveled all the way through eastern Tibet to Haka Lingtse and placed many beings, both august and lowly, on the path to liberation.

In the evening of the twenty-first day of the middle month of spring in the Year of the Earth Tiger, his fifty-third year, he dissolved his mind into the dharmadhatu in front of the Great Stupa of Jamling.

The empowerments and transmissions of his three above-mentioned terma dharmas have remained unbroken, and I have received them.

Ngaki Wangpo

The vidyadhara Ngaki Wangpo was the immediate rebirth of the great vidyadhara Lekden Dorje. His father was Chögyal Wangpo'i De. His mother, Lhacham Yishin Wangmo, was a descendant of the royalty of Zahor. Ngaki Wangpo was born in a Male Iron Dragon year amid wondrous signs. He offered the fruits of his crown to Drikungpa Chögyal Puntsok and received the name Ngawang Rikdzin Dorje Chögyal Tenpe Gyaltsen Pal Zangpo. His being was also ripened by bodhichitta on that occasion.

Ngaki Wangpo received all of his lord father's dharma, like the contents of one vase being transferred into another. He therefore became like an ocean of the kama and terma Nyingma dharma. He lived as a mantradharin with the three vows, a great vajra holder. He engaged one-pointedly in approach and accomplishment in many sacred places such as the Crystal Cave of Yarlung, and saw the faces of many deities. He employed vajradharmapalas as servants and had peerless magical power, as indicated by the fact that he intimidated even the great dharmapala of Samye. He also had vast supercognition.

He twice traveled all the way to Haka Lingtse in China, greatly helping beings. The first time was in his youth, when he went there as his father's attendant. The second time he went there he did so as a teacher, accompanied now by his own entourage.

Ngaki Wangpo took Thupten Dorje Drak as his primary seat, and his deeds of the three wheels flourished there.

Finally, after granting his final instructions to his heart-son Yölmo Tulku Tendzin Norbu, Ngaki Wangpo withdrew his rupakaya into the dharmadhatu without apparent illness on the tenth day of the month Chaitra in the Earth Hare year. When his remains were cremated there were many wondrous signs; white rainbow light swirled about and white flowers the size of crane eggs rained down. The duties connected with Ngaki Wangpo's passing, including the creation of a support for his relics and the recognition of his nirmanakaya Padma Trinley, who was born at Namseling, were performed by the great vidyadhara of Yölmo.

Although it is certain that Ngaki Wangpo was a chakravartin of profound terma, in Shazukpa Tashi Namgyal's *History of Terma* it is written:

> Although Ngaki Wangpo did discover a few profound termas, he never revealed them because of his great appreciation for earlier termas.

Similarly, from the *Testament of Padma*:

> Sometimes they will not reveal them, but keep the dharma of old termas.

That is what Ngaki Wangpo did. In his upholding, keeping, and dissemination of the old termas that he had received from his father, he was peerless. He was the single life-tree of the Nyingma guhyamantra dharma.

Garwang Letro Lingpa

Garwang Letro Lingpa of E Pechok was an emanation of the minor translator Könchok Ö, and was also the tenth rebirth of Prince Lharjey. He was born to the nephew line of the nephew of the vidyadhara Ratna Lingpa, the family line of the translator Kerda Khorlo Drak, at Pechok in the forested valley of E. He undertook renunciation in his sixth year and engaged throughout his youth in amazing behavior.

In his seventeenth year he revealed countless termas, supports, and samaya substances from the Piled Lotus Crystal Cave of Yarlung. These included *Mahakarunika Who Frees from Samsara*, the *Seven Profound Yidams*, the *Formless Dakinis' Dharmas*, the *Yidam White Vajravarahi*, the *Eight Dispensations: The Fortress and the Precipice*, *Amitayus*, and the *Four-Armed Protector*. To do so he miraculously flew like a bird up to the Piled Lotus Cave, which was unreachable on foot both then and long afterward. Everyone present was amazed.

Over time he revealed many termas from the side of Ode Gungyal Mountain and other sites that included the *Guhyasamaja Ayusadhana*, the *Vajra Knot*, *Krodhikali*, the *Neuter Mahakala*, the *Tiger Rider*, the *Realm Protectors*, and *Trak the Artisan* (a continuation of a terma of Ugyen Lingpa). Garwang Letro Lingpa perfectly heard, contemplated, and meditated upon countless instructions of guhyamantra of the kama and terma traditions. As his signs of siddhi and supercognitions were boundless, he came to be revered by great people such as the leader of the Ching Taktse community. He helped beings greatly throughout central Tibet, the nomad country, E, and Dakpo. It is also well known that it was Garwang Letro Lingpa who offered the list of the termas of Garuda Nest Rock to the vidyadhara Shikpo Lingpa.

Garwang Letro Lingpa lived to a great age. Both his family lineage and his dharma lineage lasted for a long time in E Gangpo Pechok. Among his termas, it appears that his *Singhamukha* cycle and other teachings were received from him by the vidyadhara Terdak Lingpa, but their lineage does not exist now. However, our lord guru revealed Garwang Letro Lingpa's *White Vajravarahi: The Wheel of Wisdom* as rediscovered terma. Through his kindness I have received its complete ripening empowerments and liberating instructions; I consider myself fortunate in this too.

Yongdzin Ngawang Drakpa

The precious tertön Yongdzin Ngawang Drakpa was born to the family line of the great omniscient Longchenpa at Kunzang Ling in Paro. He perfectly heard, contemplated, and meditated upon the secret unsurpassable instructions of the Great Perfection. He gained the ability to display signs of having mixed awareness and appearances, such as flying in the sky like a bird. It is said that he revealed as terma a *Dark Red Wrathful Guru with Garlands of Flame* cycle and life-water, but it does not seem that their lineage survived. In any case, Yongdzin Ngawang Drakpa was a greatly learned and accomplished master, and it appears that Lama Sokdokpa took him as one of his main root gurus.

Tashi Tseten

Tashi Tseten was a mantradharin of the Chak community in Langpo. At his place of accomplishment, which he called the Glorious Copper-Colored Mountain, he revealed a profound cycle of gurusadhana. It seems that at some point it became fairly widespread. Nowadays I have not seen either existent copies or transmission lines of most of it, but I have received its extraordinarily profound and brief *Ayusadhana* through the kindness of our lord guru.

Tashi Tseten lived at the same time as the vidyadhara Jatsön Nyingpo. They were each other's dharma heirs, and received teachings from each other. The tertön Düdül Dorje also praised Tashi Tseten as one of his greatest root gurus, calling him "my supreme father Mangayu."[94] It is therefore certain that he was an authentic tertön.

94. "Mangayu" is a Sanskrit translation of Tashi Tseten.

Padma Rikdzin

The tertön Padma Rikdzin was certainly the eleventh rebirth of Prince Lharjey. He is also said to have been an emanation of both Vairochana and the vidyadhara Padma Lingpa. He was born at Zhi in Puwo, and therefore became known as the Tertön from Zhi.

He revealed a *Peaceful and Wrathful Guru* cycle and other termas from Sky Iron Rock on Mara Mountain. He revealed the *Secret Sadhana of the Guru's Wisdom Assembly: A Mala of Jewels* from the silk crown ribbon on the body of the Powerful Black One of Dülung. He also revealed many teachings such as *Chiti: The Completion Stage of the Guru*, samaya substances, the flesh of the seven-times-born, and images from places including Drakyangdzong, Kharchu in Lhodrak, the Sky Steps, and Zabulung. He opened the door to the sacred place Makunglung in Puwo.

Padma Rikdzin offered his termas to the Tenth Karmapa Chöying Dorje, the Seventh Shamarpa, and others and appointed them as his dharma heirs. As he lived at the same time as the vidyadhara Jatsön Nyingpo, Padma Rikdzin was also one of Jatsön Nyingpo's dharma heirs. When Tsele Natsok Rangdröl was very young, Padma Rikdzin accepted the fruits of his crown, named him Kechok Padma Lekdrup, and offered him the empowerments and transmissions of some of his termas. It appears that his termas became somewhat widespread. Although his lineage was held at Puwo Bakha Sangngak Chöling and other monasteries, I have not heard that the empowerments or transmissions of his termas still exist. I have received through the kindness of our lord guru Padma Rikdzin's wondrous and extraordinarily profound and brief *Multi-Colored Vajra Garuda* cycle.

Padma Rikdzin's next rebirth was the vidyadhara Chöje Lingpa, the twelfth rebirth of Prince Lharjey. In Chöje Lingpa's autobiography there are extremely clear accounts of his life as Padma Rikdzin, based on his recollection of past lives.

Düdül Lingpa

The tertön of Rongpa known as Düdül Lingpa was an emanation of Gyalwa Chokyang. He was born at Tsangrong Dumra. He first lived at the college of lower Kyetsal and studied the tripitaka. Then he practiced the profound and secret Nyingma teachings and began to display unstoppable signs of siddhi and control of prana. He revealed many profound termas and his activity flourished a bit, but in the end the kingspirit Lhazang interfered and Düdül Lingpa passed away accidentally. It appears that his dharma lineage did not continue.

In any case, as the great tertön of Mindröling and others considered Düdül Lingpa to be authentic, it appears that he was. Although I have not received his actual termas, I have received his *Tara Who Protects from All Danger*, which our lord guru received as a rediscovered terma.

Düdül Lingpa's subsequent rebirth was Zungkhar Tekchen Lingpa.

Düdül Dorje

The tertön and great vidyadhara Düdül Dorje was the ultimate rebirth of Drokben Kyeuchung Lotsa. He was clearly predicted in about thirteen previous termas. Düdül Dorje was born on the shady side of the area known as Silver Uplands, near the palace of the great dharma king of Derge, in eastern Tibet. His father, who was of the Ling family, was a learned physician named Lukyap. His mother was named Boluma. He was born in a Female Wood Hare year.[95]

95. The year was 1615 C.E.

His father taught him reading, writing, and medicine. In his sixth year he began to have visions, and at an early age he went to live at the dharma college of Pal Lhundrup Teng. He offered the fruits of his crown to Kunga Gyamtso, a siddha of Derge who was an emanation of the Vidyadhara Vulture Feathers. He received the name Kunga Sönam Chöpak. He also left a footprint in a boulder that is still there, behind the eastern entrance to the great assembly hall at Lhundrup Teng.

While Düdül Dorje was studying the treatises of the glorious Sakya tradition at that college, he developed a desire, as strong as the thirst of the parched, to seek the essence of wisdom. He therefore went to practice in Muksang, where he received much profound dharma such as the Great Perfection from his master Könchok Gyaltsen. Düdül Dorje practiced, and realization burst forth within him.

He then went to central Tibet. At Nyangpo he met the mahasiddha Tashi Tseten, from whom he received many empowerments and instructions. At White Rock Divine Water Düdül Dorje forsook food, living entirely on rasayana. While there, he perfected the profound path of the channels, energy, and essence.

Because of the interdependence of his initial entry through the gate of dharma, Düdül Dorje visited the Sakya and Ngorpa seats in Tsang and received the *Sacred Words of the Path and Result*. During his journeys throughout Tibet he also touched the feet of the vidyadhara Jatsön Nyingpo at Bangri, and received all of the empowerments and instructions of his termas.

Especially, it was at around that time that Düdül Dorje received prophecies indicating that he was destined to reveal terma. He went to Puwo, and at Turquoise Lake Palace he diligently practiced Ratna Lingpa's *Very Secret Insurpassable Vajrakilaya*. While there he dreamed that he was brought by dakinis to the Glorious Copper-Colored Mountain. He seemed to remain there for twenty-eight days, during which time he received complete empowerment and instruction, as well as prophecy of his termas, from Guru Rinpoche. This is clearly related in Düdül Dorje's autobiographic *Majestic Might of Pure Visions*.

Düdül Dorje then went to meet the glorious Ugyen Tendzin. Ugyen Tendzin evaluated Düdül Dorje based on his dreams and was extremely pleased with him. With the utmost respect he proclaimed Düdül Dorje to be a vajracharya. From then on Düdül Dorje lived as a great vajra holder and mantradharin.

His first revelation of profound terma began with his acquisition of a terma guide. In his twenty-ninth year he took the dakini of family Padma Kyi as a karmamudra. This enabled him to discover the terma guide at Turquoise Lake Jewel Rock, and to reveal the *Holy Dharma Including All Wisdom* from the Secret Cave of Great Bliss at Puwo Döchu. As this cycle is his principal terma, he taught that all his subsequent revelations were its branches.

Then, successively, he revealed the *Holy Dharma: The Nirmanakaya's Heart-Essence* and its protector cycle, the *Realm Protectors*, from Tsapdro Rock. He revealed the

Profound Meaning: The Secret Heart-Essence, *Shri Chakrasamvara*, and the *Four-Armed Protector* from Puri Dakdzong Cave. He revealed the *Heart-Essence Combined Sadhana of Amitayus, Perfect Heruka, and Vajrakilaya* along with their individual sadhanas and the protectresses *Ekajati* and *Self-Arisen Queen* from the Crystal Enclosure of Puri. He revealed the *Guide to the Hidden Land of Padmakö* from the north face of Puwo Döchu. He revealed the *Yidam Yamantaka: Red, Black, and Vajrabhairava* from Ziltrom Karyak Mountain in Derge. It appears that he only transcribed the *Sadhana of Peaceful Manjushri* section of the latter cycle.

Düdül Dorje revealed the *Glorious Four-Faced Protector* cycle and the *Mahadeva Sadhana* from Japu Iron Stake. He revealed the *Guru's Assembly of Vidyadharas*, the *Hot Red Ayusadhana*, and the protector cycles *Shanglön* and *Pomra* from the central temple of Samye. He revealed the *Whispered Lineage: The Wish-Fulfilling Crown Jewel* from the upper story of the western annex to the Rasa Trülnang Temple. It appears that he did not transcribe the latter cycle.

He revealed the *Peaceful and Wrathful Deities of Magical Illusion*, the *Eight Dispensations*, and their protectors from Blazing Sky-Iron Mara Mountain in Puwo. A yogin with a conch mala revealed the *Glorious Protector Tiger-Rider* cycle from the Stupa of Rastakdo and offered it to Düdül Dorje.

As is clearly set forth in Düdül Dorje's *Account of My Termas*, he also revealed many other profound termas from sites including Yama's Face at Turquoise Lake, the Secret Cave of the Vidyadharas, Serak Butte, Mist Fortress, and Tashö Mandala Valley. He opened the way to many sacred places in both central Tibet and its border areas, including the hidden land of Padmakö. Along with the above-mentioned termas he revealed countless images, scepters, and samaya substances.

In sum, Düdül Dorje is said to have had the dispensation of a hundred termas and a thousand substances that liberate through taste; he revealed most of them.

In his forty-second year he was invited to return to the college of his youth by the Derge Lama Jampa Puntsok and his nephew. Düdül Dorje built a Conquest of Maras Temple at his former college, thereby fulfilling the prophecy that he would help both the dharma and the government of Derge.

Düdül Dorje visited the great Nyingma seats, all the way to Kathok Vajrasana Monastery, and accepted many fortunate disciples at each of them. He lived and meditated for a long time at Takpu Drakring in Nop, near Dzing Namgyal; the small house he stayed in is still there.

He went to Lingtsang, and formed a good connection of patronage with the ruler of Ling. When Düdül Dorje performed the vase sadhana of *Mahakarunika the King of Space*, inconceivably wondrous signs arose; the vase he used still exists.

He was successively invited to, and visited, Barkham, Upper Ga, Barma Lhateng, and Riwoche. He helped beings and the dharma immeasurably in these places.

In particular, Düdül Dorje met Namchö Mingyur Dorje at Porney Rock. They formed a good connection and received one another's dharma. They were introduced to one another by the mahasiddha Karma Chagme, on whom Düdül Dorje cast flowers of praise.

Düdül Dorje's principal dharma heirs were Lhatsün Namkha Jikme, the vidyadhara Longsal Nyingpo, Baka Tulku Chökyi Gyamtso, Dzogchen Padma Rikdzin, Kunzang Khyapdal Lhundrup, and the mahasiddha Padma Norbu. His dharma heirs were innumerable, and included many of the great vajra holders of eastern Tibet. Especially, his son Norbu Yongdrak and his descendants have maintained his dharma lineage without impairment, and as a result we have received it completely.

At the end of such deeds, and after roughly indicating the gate to the hidden land of Padmakö, Düdül Dorje departed, amid countless miracles such as sounds, light, and rains of flowers, for the great palace of Lotus Light in his fifty-eighth year, the Year of the Male Water Rat.[96] Most of his body dissolved into light, leaving only one cubit of remains. This was cremated, and became a heap of the five great relics and shariram.

Several emanations of Düdül Dorje have appeared; the most famous of them was Sönam Deutsen, the son of the vidyadhara Longsal Nyingpo. Sönam Deutsen's successive emanations have been, and continue to be, seated on the lion throne at Kathok Vajrasana Monastery.[97]

Longsal Nyingpo

The tertön and great vidyadhara Longsal Nyingpo was an emanation of Könchok Jungne, the translator of Langdro. As clearly prophesied in the termas of the vidyadhara Düdül Dorje and others, Longsal Nyingpo was born in a place called Jepa, part of the Rawa area, near Kawone. His father was the mantradharin Kunga Döndrup. His mother, who was blessed by White Tara, was called Könchok Drönma. Longsal Nyingpo was born in a Female Wood Ox year.[98]

He soon received a Wrathful Guru empowerment from the lord of siddhas Tenpa Gyamtso, as well as the name Wangdrak Gyamtso. He learned to read in his seventh year just by being shown the letters.

As his propensity for holy dharma, including renunciation, awoke vividly in his youth, he fled to the dharma in his twenty-second year and went to Kathok Monastery. On his way there he visited Gaje Khamshong Monastery, where he received many empowerments and instructions from the lord Chökyong Gyamtso. After reaching Kathok, he received experiential instruction in the *Great Perfection: Penetrating Wisdom* from the peerless Könchok Gyaltsen and mastered the natural state.

Longsal Nyingpo then returned to his birthplace and began to live in solitude in places such as Chölung Hermitage. He

---

96. The year was 1672 C.E.

97. As is evident in the *Autobiography of Düdjom Lingpa*, the great master Düdjom Rinpoche is a rebirth of Düdül Dorje.

98. 1625 C.E.

made a firm commitment to practice with austerity equal to that of Jetsün Mila Shepa Dorje. Doing so, he saw the faces of the ocean of deities of the three roots. He employed the wisdom and karma dharmapalas as servants. Gods, spirits, and place-lords offered him their life-essences. He reached a high degree of siddhi.

In particular, the way he inherited the dispensation of profound terma was as follows: In about his twenty-eighth year he began to receive many prophecies and indications of terma, but he ignored them. He then received the prophetic instruction to go to meet the great tertön Düdül Dorje. Accordingly, he went to Puwo and entered the presence of that great vidyadhara, who became very fond of him and gave him many empowerments and instructions, including his recently revealed profound termas. Düdül Dorje also prophesied that Longsal Nyingpo would receive the siddhi of terma. Not long thereafter, the vidyadhara Düdül Dorje told Longsal Nyingpo to return to his homeland, which he did.

While Longsal Nyingpo was engaged in approach and accomplishment in the Vast Sky Hermitage, in his thirty-second year, the Year of the Male Fire Monkey, a red-brown yogin wearing bone ornaments gave him a terma guide.[99] Longsal Nyingpo became certain that the yogin was an emanation of Guru Rinpoche, and so he performed the terma accomplishment prescribed in the guide for two years. As a result, he revealed the first of his termas from the Changeless Vajra Rock of Ke on the tenth day of the first month of the Earth Dog year.[100] He extracted this terma secretly. It included both the *Vajra Essence of the Trikaya* and the *Vajra Essence of the Three Roots*. Longsal Nyingpo practiced both of these cycles to perfection.

His second terma was the *Wrathful Guru Blazing Wisdom*, which he revealed from Great Sky White Rock in Litang. His third was *Songtsen Gampo's Whispered Teachings on Mahakarunika: The Crown Jewel*, which he revealed from the side of Tara Rock. His fourth was the *All-Profound*

99. The year was 1656 C.E.

100. The year was 1658 C.E.

Quintessence of the Great Perfection, which he revealed from Ribar Rock. His fifth was *Vimalamitra's Three Profound Cycles of Instruction*, which he revealed from three terma sites in Ke. His sixth was the *Eight Dispensations: The Assembly of All Sugatas*, which he revealed from the Palace of Playful Great Bliss. His seventh was a sky-iron vajra and other supports, which he revealed from a site in Ngogya. His eighth was the *Very Secret Insurpassable Ayusadhana*, which he revealed from Na White Rock Vajra Fortress. His ninth was the *Very Secret Insurpassable Mahakarunika*, which he revealed from Shingo Gangra. His tenth was the *Very Secret Insurpassable Dakini*, which he revealed from the Turquoise Lake of Shingo Gangra. His eleventh was a Bön terma, which he revealed from a Bön sacred place at Shingo Gangra. His twelfth was the *Great Perfection: The Secret Excerpt of the Mayajala*. His thirteenth included both the *Outer, Inner, and Secret Prophecies* and the *Dharmapalas' Forceful Mantra Cycle*; he revealed these from Pawang Bönmo. His fourteenth was a profound terma that he revealed from Ngotik Yungdrung. His fifteenth was the rediscovery of a volume concerning the *Mayajala* that Dampa Deshek had concealed near the Holy Cave of Kathok.

These fifteen termas are called the Sixteen Termas of Longsal Nyingpo. The reason for this is that since the contents of the fourteenth terma are unknown, it is not counted, and since *Vimalamitra's Three Profound Cycles* were revealed from three different sites, they are considered to be three separate termas.

Along with these termas Longsal Nyingpo revealed a large number of statues, fine scepters, and samaya substances that liberate through taste. He transcribed almost all of his termas, and practiced each of them until signs of accomplishment appeared. He reconcealed a few of them.

Although Longsal Nyingpo was originally destined to be only a minor tertön of terma, because of the great scope of his bodhichitta and aspirations, and because of his consummate mastery of generation and completion, he gained the siddhi of becoming a great tertön. He helped beings tremendously.

Longsal Nyingpo is also known by other many names, including Ugyen Dongak Lingpa and Humnak Namkha Dorje.

His miracles were inconceivably many, and included climbing sheer cliff faces on horseback, submerging himself and his horse in lakes, and the many hoofprints left in rock by his horse. He took the life-essence of many aggressive spirits produced by our evil times. He bound them to samaya; and exorcised, banished, and controlled them. In this way he bestowed protection on the people of many regions. The dakini of the king of the Mongols was so inspired by Longsal Nyingpo's miracles that she offered him land for a monastery and her patronage. Many other important people, including the king of Derge, also regarded Longsal Nyingpo as their guru.

He traveled all over eastern Tibet and opened the gates to many sacred places. In later life he lived at Kathok Vajrasana Monastery and engaged in the activity of dharma, reviving the teachings. He also created many supports at Kathok and other seats.

At the conclusion of such deeds, in his sixty-eighth year, on the twenty-third day of the monkey month in the Year of the Water Monkey, he departed for the celestial realm of Lotus Light amid many wondrous signs.[101] His remains became a heap of shariram, amazing everyone.

Longsal Nyingpo's principal lineage holders were excellent and numerous. They included his sons, Sönam Deutsen and his brother; his nephew, Tashi Özer; Kunzang Khyapdal Lhundrup, and Tala Padma Norbu. They spread his dharma throughout eastern Tibet. The lineage of the empowerments and transmissions of his termas and of detailed instruction in his *Vajra Essence* is still widespread; I have received his principal cycles.[102]

101. The year was 1692 C.E.

102. Khenpo Achö of Golok was held to be an emanation of Longsal Nyingpo.

Tendzin Norbu

Tendzin Norbu, the nirmanakaya of Yölmo, was born in the village of Lungye in Kongpo. His father was the vidyadhara Trinley Wangchuk; his mother was called Kunzang Wangmo. Based on a prophecy he received from dakinis, Trinley Wangchuk recognized his son as the rebirth of the nirmanakaya Namkha Jajin, and named him Tendzin Norbu. From infancy Tendzin Norbu remembered previous lives and had supercognition and miraculous powers. In his fifth year he had a vision of Guru Rinpoche riding a lion.

Tendzin Norbu eventually went to central Tibet, where he received the vows of an upasaka from Shamar Chökyi Wangchuk, who gave him the name Karma Thupten Nyingpo Nampar Gyalwe De. He went on to study under many of the great masters of the Karma and Drukpa Kagyu as well as the great translator Gyurme Dechen. He studied the sutras to perfection at colleges such as Nyinling. He was then invited to Nepal by the king of Yambu, who served him with great respect. While he was performing a ceremony of consecration at Swayambu, a rain of flowers fell. He built a new residence for the custodian of the Bodha Stupa. He visited Ngamring College, and received the patronage of the king of Tsang.

On his return journey Tendzin Norbu met the vidyadhara Ngaki Wangpo in Menthang and received from him countless Nyingma teachings. Through that lord's kindness, Tendzin Norbu banished all traces of sophistry from within him and became a pure Nyingma mantradharin.

Tendzin Norbu then went to Mount Palbar in Mangyül and founded a practice community. This precipitated his experience of a number of visions and prophecies. After a few years he was urged in a vision to reveal terma. Accordingly, he revealed a terma guide and a *Dorje Trolö Sadhana* from Yönpolung in Gyang. Bearing a wondrous prophecy found in his terma, he went to central Tibet and showed it to the vidyadhara Ngaki Wangpo, who was pleased and encouraged him. Ngaki Wangpo also gave Tendzin Norbu his offering vessels, three supports, and terma substances, and instructed him to take future responsibility for his seat.

Tendzin Norbu went to reveal the terma concealed on Mount Palbar, but before he arrived there he heard reports that the vidyadhara Ngaki Wangpo had passed away. He therefore returned to central Tibet, allowing the time for the revelation of that terma to pass. He oversaw the funerary rites of his master and watched over his seat for five or six years. During that time he composed *Visionary Moonlight*, an account of the visions that enabled him to recognize Ngaki Wangpo's rebirth. He also revealed a cycle of visionary dharma that he received from dakinis while residing at the Beacon Cave in Blackhorse. It appears that Tendzin Norbu passed away prematurely due to his having spoiled the interdependence of profound terma.

Zangpo Dorje

The nirmanakaya Zangpo Dorje was the rebirth of Dakpo Norbu Gyenpa, who was the rebirth of the omniscient Dakpo Tashi Namgyal, who was universally renowned as an emanation of Padmakara, Vimalamitra, and Gampopa. Zangpo Dorje was born amid wondrous signs in the eastern part of a place called Gangpo in Eyül, the source of knowledge. His father, who was descended from the dharma kings, was a Nyingma mantradharin called Apo Chödze. His mother was called Wangdzin Gyalmo.

Zangpo Dorje was unmistakenly recognized by the vidyadhara Jatsön Nyingpo as the rebirth of Norbu Gyenpa. Dakpo Chenga Rinpoche came to Eyül and offered Zangpo Dorje the upasaka vows and the name Pal Zangpo Dorje Chok Tamche Le Nampar Gyalwe De. He was brought to the great seat of Daklha Gampo and placed on the lion throne of fearlessness.

The vidyadhara Jatsön Nyingpo journeyed especially from Bangri for this. He accepted the fruits of Zangpo Dorje's crown and named him Avadhutipa Gyurme Dorje Gyaltsen Pal Zangpo. Zangpo Dorje also received much dharma from Jatsön Nyingpo both then and later.

Not long after that Zangpo Dorje received the vows of a shramanera and the name Lobzang Trinley Namgyal Ngeton Drupe Shingta Choki De Tön Yongsu Drupa, from the omniscient Lobzang Gyamtso. He also received the bhikshu vows from him, as well as continuous support and assistance. Zangpo Dorje received the Dakpo Kagyu teachings from Dakpo Chenga Rinchen Dorje and others. He also received much dharma of many traditions from Tsele Natsok Rangdröl.

He performed a three-year three-phase meditation retreat at Copper Valley in Gampo. During this he saw many wondrous appearances of luminosity. Especially, he had many visions indicating his ability to reveal profound terma. Furthermore, in Jatsön Nyingpo's terma prophecies there were clear predictions that Zangpo Dorje would complete the work of revelation begun by Jatsön.

Accordingly, Zangpo Dorje first revealed a cubit-long sandalwood kila from the side of Mount Gampo, which is shaped like a meditation hat. In the kila's handle he found a terma guide, and in its blade a brief *Vajrakilaya* liturgy. Based on the terma guide he then revealed the *Great Wrathful Lord of Secrets* cycle and a sky-iron vajra from Colorful Rock in Dakpo Valley. He revealed a terma-kila, the heart's blood of the five garudas, and the ocean-foam of the great garuda from the Accomplishment Cave of Yeshe Tsogyal at Tralung in Bhurpu and the shore of the lower Naga Palace Lake. He revealed an Ayusadhana, life-water pills, and a *Yamantaka Reversal* cycle from White Rock Divine Water. He transcribed most of them.

Zangpo Dorje arranged the interdependence for the Fifth Dalai Lama to become his dharma heir. However, samaya-spoilers with perverted aspirations took the form of the Dalai Lama's attendants and told him various lies. Zangpo Dorje was so thoroughly disheartened by this that he offered most of his termas, both the originals and their copies, to the flames. He also concealed some for future rediscovery. His activity of profound terma therefore ended. Nevertheless, he continued to receive dharma from Terdak Lingpa at Mindröling, he continued to engage in approach and accomplishment in solitude, he continued to ceaselessly turn the Sarma and Nyingma dharmachakras, and he built many supports.

At the end of his life Zangpo Dorje went to Namseling Palace in Bhutan and decided that King Tashi Rapten and his queen would be his next parents. He gave them intensive empowerments and blessings, and left a cryptic prophecy of his rebirth. Then, at that great seat, he demonstrated departure for other realms. He was reborn at Namseling Palace and named Kunzang Ngetön Wangpo. His next rebirth was the tertön Dorje Gyalpo, who was born as the son of Depa Lhagya Riwa, in the royal family of Eyül. It appears that Dorje Gyalpo rediscovered his predecessor Zangpo Dorje's *Great Wrathful Lord of Secrets* cycle.

Garwang Dawa Gyaltsen

The tertön of Ngari, Garwang Dawa Gyaltsen, also known by his secret name Padma Garwang Tsal, was an emanation of Nyak the Translator, Dorje Düdjom, and Namkhay Nyingpo. He was born in a place called Yama in the western mountains of Gungthang in Ngari. He was amazing in many ways from an early age.

In particular, while he was engaged in the approach and accomplishment of the vidyadhara Düdül Dorje's *Mahakarunika* terma on the isolated, turtle-shaped rock ledge called Musey Boulder, three naked, bone-adorned, wisdom dakinis exhorted him with song and gestures. Exhilarated, he flew to a boulder shaped like a coiled black snake, where he was again exhorted by the same three dakinis, the gods of the place, and the guardians of terma.

First, he traveled miraculously to a rock face unreachable by humans and revealed a terma guide. Based on it he revealed the *Heart Mirror of Vajrasattva* cycle, which the great Vidyadhara Vulture Feathers had concealed in the hidden land Happy Valley for rediscovery. Garwang Dawa Gyaltsen disseminated these teachings, and the lineage of their empowerments, instructions, and transmissions still exists; they have been extremely beneficial.

Garwang Dawa Gyaltsen revealed many other profound termas containing dharma, supports, and samaya substances. These included *Avalokita: The Heart Essence of the Three Roots*, which he revealed at Wati Bathhouse; *Padma's Very Secret Stainless Whispered Lineage*; the *Self-Illuminating Dharmadhatu: The Profound Essence*, and *Vajrakilaya*.

His miracles and supercognition were boundless. The great Fifth Dalai Lama, while traveling to Jamata, performed divination to determine whether Garwang Dawa Gyaltsen was an authentic tertön. He also consulted the vidyadhara Terdak Lingpa about this. Based on both his own examination and the testimony of Terdak Lingpa, the Dalai Lama became certain that Garwang Dawa Gyaltsen was authentic. He therefore issued the edict that Garwang Dawa Gyaltsen was permitted to freely benefit beings. This proclamation caused Garwang Dawa Gyaltsen to become unanimously respected and very well known; his benefit for beings was therefore extensive.

Garwang Dawa Gyaltsen's rebirth was the omniscient Chöwang Dorje Dzinpa, the son of the mahasiddha Nyida Longsal. Chöwang Dorje Dzinpa touched the feet of both the vidyadhara Terdak Lingpa and the latter's brother, and lived for a long time at Mindröling. He studied sutra, tantra, and the sciences. Because of his great learning, he composed liturgical arrangements for Garwang Dawa Gyaltsen's termas and disseminated them widely. Even today, holders of their lineage are still living at Sangchö Padma Lhunding in northern Tsang.

Through the kindness of our lord guru, I have received the ripening empowerments and liberating instructions of Garwang Dawa Gyaltsen's *Self-Illuminating Dharmadhatu: The Profound Essence*, his *Avalokita: The Heart Essence of the Three Roots*, his *Heart Mirror of Vajrasattva* cycle, and his *Vajra Knot Ayusadhana*. His *Profound Essence*, Drime Lhunpo's *Ultimate Essence*, and Taksham's *Wisdom Assembly Liberating All Beings* are identical in words and meaning aside from the presence or absence of their source tantra. It is therefore appropriate to regard them as three lineages combined into one. Furthermore, I have heard our lord guru remark that these three are essentially the same as Jatsön Nyingpo's *Heart Essence: The Self-Illuminating Dharmadhatu*, which Jatsön never disseminated.

Yongey Mingyur Dorje

Mingyur Dorje Drakpo Nuden Tsal, a chakravartin among treasure-revealing siddhas, was an emanation of Prince Mutri Tsenpo. He was born in a nomad community called Great Refuge (Kyapche) in the southwest of Zalmogang in Dokham in the Male Earth Dragon Year.[103] His father was the leader of the Yongey clan; his mother was named Bermo. At the time of his birth he exhibited extraordinary marks such as a vajra eye on his forehead.

Eventually his family moved to the vicinity of Dzodzi monastery in Lhatok. While he was living there Kunga Namgyal, the Fourth Surmang Trungpa, visited the area. The tertön offered him the first fruits of his crown and received the name Karma Samdrup. He heard a great deal of dharma from the mahasiddha Kunga Namgyal, Sönam Gyamtso of Dzigar Monastery, and others.[104]

103. The year was 1628 C.E..

104. Dzigar Monastery is a monastery of the Drukpa Kagyu tradition.

As his paternal uncle was a retreat leader at Dzodzi Monastery, the tertön came to be known as Yongey the Nephew. His personality was extremely tranquil and calm, and he was very diligent in meditation and study. As he was skilled with his hands he created many paintings and statues of deities.

Traveling in a large company he went to Jang to meet Chöying Dorje, the Tenth Gyalwang Karmapa.[105] On the way he dug in the earth and found a crescent moon of gold. He discreetly offered it to the Karmapa, who placed it among his supports. On the next day, when the Karmapa showed his supports to the travelers, he held up the crescent moon and said, "This is a terma of the vidyadhara Mingyur Dorje Drakpo Nuden Tsal.[106] Had he found both a sun and a moon, the interdependence would have been supreme!"

None of the travelers understood what he was talking about.

In his twenty-fifth year the tertön accomplished the protector Bernakchen at Dzodzi monastery. One morning while he was doing so he saw the faces of the mahasiddha Karma Pakshi, Guru Rinpoche, and their retinue. They bestowed empowerment, blessings, and instruction on him. He wrote these down; they form the *Gurusadhana of Karma Pakshi*.

In reliance upon it, the tertön removed from a boulder beneath his dwelling a scroll of instructions on the retrieval of his termas. His first terma was discovered in two locations. He entered the lake on Dzodzi Hill and retrieved a rectangular blue terma chest. From the Hidden Lake of Kamgyal he retrieved a container made of copper. From these emerged the *Dorje Trolö* cycle, which includes sadhanas, with applications, of the three roots.[107]

His second terma was discovered at a hidden place, the Divine Rock of Drugu. After excavating solid rock for a month at the terma-site, he removed five scorpion-shaped containers made of cast iron. They contained *Guru*

---

105. Jang is in the easternmost part of the greater Tibetan region. The Tenth Karmapa lived there for much of his life.

106. This is the tertön's full name, as given in the prophecies of Guru Rinpoche. It means "Changeless Vajra Forceful Powerful Energy."

107. Dorje Trolö is one of the eight principal forms of Guru Rinpoche.

Padmavajra: the Mandala of the Ocean of Siddhas, together with its *Five Accessories*.[108]

His third terma was discovered at Chijam in Dzatö. After seven months of excavation and great effort he broke through the rock seals and removed the *Life Sadhana of Conjunct Means and Wisdom*. Nearby he retrieved the brief instruction called the *Life Sadhana of Namkhai Nyingpo*.

During all these discoveries many wondrous signs arose, such as rainbows, rains of flowers, delicious scents, the sound of voices in song, and so forth. The tertön transcribed the dharma he had discovered and gave it, over time, to its inheritors.

It is said that if during this period the interdependence with his destined consort had come together he would have discovered a hundred and eight termas. Because the interdependence was spoiled the tertön cut his long hair and appeared to others to behave like a madman. His seven attending monks fled. Two of them went to Tsurphu to request the help of the Eleventh Gyalwang Karmapa, Yeshe Dorje. He said to them, "Mingyur Dorje is a mahasiddha who has destroyed bewilderment, not a madman. Go back and obey his every command as you did in the past!"[109]

After that, his monks having returned, he lived as a nomad. He wore common clothing and appeared to speak nonsense. However, everything he said was a prophecy of the three times, which he saw clearly through unobscured supercognition. He performed amazing and unrestricted miracles. The power of his blessing was inconceivable; with little effort he cured severe and advanced illnesses and cast out great demons.

It was at this time that the disease of cattle called "rinderpest" first appeared.[110] He overpowered the causer of the disease and started the spread of its benign form. He also engaged in means of, and created the interdependence for, repelling foreign invasion. In these and other ways he was

---

108. Padmavajra is a sambhogakaya form of Guru Rinpoche.

109. Most tertöns have consorts. This is said to be necessary in most cases for them to retrieve their destined termas without mishap. If the tertön fails to meet his destined consort the number of retrievals and sometimes the tertön's lifespan are reduced.

110. Rinderpest remains a common and severe disease of cattle. Yongey Mingyur Dorje's response to it seems to be the earliest recorded use of veterinary immunization.

directly and indirectly of the greatest kindness to the doctrine and to beings. He also opened the doors to several wondrous hidden places.

When Lord Chökyi Jungne was young he visited the nomad country.[111] He met the tertön, who established auspicious interdependence for him, gave him prophecies, and presented to him the complete dispensation of all his termas.

After completing, in that way, the conduct of yogic discipline and his benefit of beings in that life he predicted his subsequent birth. Saying, "It is time to repel the invasion!" he withdrew the array of his form-body in Bamthangpoche while establishing symbolic interdependence through conduct.[112]

His subsequent emanation-body, Kunzang Chökyi Dorje, possessed supercognition and miraculous abilities no different from those of his predecessor. It appears that he also received a few mind termas. That lineage of emanation has continued down to the present, and the continuity of his doctrine is maintained at the monastery founded at the site of the tertön's camp.[113]

The tertön's son, Guru Chödzin, and several of his disciples have produced successive recognized incarnations. They too have engaged in perfect service to the doctrine.

These terma dharmas have benefited beings tremendously. Their principal inheritors, the holders of the black and red crowns and especially the omniscient Chökyi Jungne, dispelled obstacles to the doctrine of the lineage of accomplishment through their practice of them. These termas have therefore been a boon ensuring the continued survival of the doctrine. In particular, as predicted in this lord's termas:

> In Atarong, Tai Situ will wave the vajra copper-knife in the sky.

This occurred as predicted. Our glorious protector guru, Padma Nyinje Wangpo, printed the complete termas and established their practice and observance in all our monaster-

---

111. This is the Eighth Tai Situ Rinpoche, Tenpe Nyinje or Chökyi Jungne (1700-1774), who founded Palpung Monastery and is widely considered to have been one of the greatest linguists of Tibet. His influence on the philosophy and practice of the Karma Kagyu has been immeasurable.

112. The year of Mingyur Dorje's death is unknown. He met the Eighth Tai Situ when the latter was in his twelfth year (this means he was eleven in our terms. Tibetans refer to the year a person is within when giving that person's age; we refer to the years a person has completed). The year of their meeting was 1711, at which time the tertön was eighty-three. We therefore know that he lived until at least 1711.

113. The current incarnation, Karma Gyurme Tendzin Chökyi Dorje, is the seventh and was born in 1975.

ies from Ngari in the west all the way to the border of China in the east.[114] In that and other ways he greatly increased their activity of taming beings. Of all the later termas, Jatsön Nyingpo's *Embodiment of the Three Jewels* and the profound termas of the great vidyadhara Yongey Mingyur Dorje have proven to be peerless in their blessing and great benefit of beings. I have therefore received the complete ripening empowerments and liberating instructions of these termas.[115]

114. Padma Nyinje Wangpo was the Ninth Tai Situ Rinpoche.

115. A longer biography of Yonge Mingyur Dorje exists. Called *Chariot of the Fortunate*, it was written by Tukyi Dorji and Surmang Tendzin Rinpoche.

Kuchok the Actionless

The tertön of Gomde Japa, Kuchok the Actionless, also known as Ngaki Dorje, was a further emanation of the dharma king Trisong Detsen. He was born at Gomde in Nangchen, and lived as an ordinary mantrin. He received much profound dharma from Lho Rinpoche and other holy masters, and began to practice one-pointedly in his youth. Especially, the vidyadhara Yongey Mingyur Dorje prophesied that Kuchok would hold the dispensation of Yongey's *Dorje Trolö* terma, and that Kuchok would also reveal his own termas.

While performing the approach and accomplishment of Vajravarahi, Kuchok received both prophecy and exhortation from terma guardians, but he initially disregarded them. Then, in a vision, he was brought by dakinis into the presence of Guru Rinpoche who, appearing as the mandala of Forceful Mantra, blessed and taught him. As well, both Yongey Mingyur Dorje and Lho Rinpoche assured Kuchok that it would be appropriate for him to reveal terma.

Accordingly, Kuchok went to Japa White Rock, the palace of Mahakarunika, a sacred place where a hundred images of the Buddha Passionless Lotus Eyes appeared spontaneously. He spent three months breaking the thirteen seals of the terma there, and then revealed supports of body, implements, and a lacquer coffer. Within the coffer was an extremely profound *Lord of Secrets: Forceful Mantra* cycle. While practicing this terma Kuchok saw the face of the Lord of Secrets, and external miraculous signs visible to everyone appeared.

There are no accounts of Kuchok revealing any other termas, except that when he revealed the flesh of the seven-times-born he was obstructed by rumor. His lineage, which was inherited by Lama Lodrö Gyamtso and others, still exists, and I have received it. Kuchok's emanations have appeared successively, and still reside at Japa Monastery in Nangchen.

Pönsey Khyungtok

The tertön of Latö Takmo known as Guru Pönsey Khyungtok was a further emanation of the great translator Vairochana. He was born near Lhatse in Tsang around the time of the Eleventh Gyalwang Karmapa Yeshe Dorje, and lived as a noble mantrin. He began by studying sutra and tantra a little according to the Sakya tradition. He then received some of the Northern Termas. While practicing the *Sadhana of the Vidyadharas' Lineage* he received a terma guide.

Based on it, Pönsey Khyungtok revealed the *Great Perfection: The Heart Essence of Samantabhadra* and other termas including gurusadhana, the Great Perfection and Mahakarunika from the shoulder of a rock mountain shaped like a garuda at Yönpo Lung in Rulak Gyang. Based upon a clear prophecy found in the Ayusadhana branch of this terma, he went to central Tibet and met the vidyadhara Chöje Lingpa, who was living in the Cave of Rechungpa. Pönsey Khyungtok openly offered Chöje Lingpa his termas, including their prophecies, and created the interdependence for Chöje Lingpa to become his dharma heir. Later, when the vidyadhara Chöje Lingpa became known as a great emanated tertön, he clearly recounted this in his autobiography. It is therefore certain that Pönsey Khyungtok was a genuine tertön.

However, as he lacked both family and influence, he never disseminated his profound termas. I have therefore written only briefly about him here.

Nevertheless, our lord guru received the blessed short lineage of the *Life-Essence of Wisdom: An Ayusadhana of the Single Hrih,* a profound, complete, and brief accessory of Pönsey Khyungtok's *Great Perfection: The Heart Essence of Samantabhadra.* I consider myself fortunate to have received it from him.

Samten Lingpa

The vidyadhara Taksham Nüden Dorje, also called Samten Lingpa, was the king of all the later tertöns of eastern Tibet. He was born into the Zur clan of mantrins in a nomad community in Parshö in the south. His father was a Severance practitioner named Tashi; his mother was named Lökhyi. Samten Lingpa was born in a Female Wood Sheep year.[116] Wondrous signs surrounded him. By his third year self-arisen wisdom had been born in his heart, and he continuously remained in the gaze of meditation.

From an early age Samten Lingpa had great renunciation, pure perception, and compassion. He therefore abstained from all activities other than dharma. In his eleventh year he received prophecy from dakinis. This was the first of his many visions, and caused him to be unable to distinguish day from night. Because he continuously engaged in vajra song and dance, he was given the nickname Vira. He also touched the feet of several holy gurus and studied a great deal.

In Samten Lingpa's seventeenth year, while he was on his way to a hermitage, he encountered Guru Rinpoche in the emanated form of a yogin with a topknot, a cotton shawl, and a yogic kilt. The yogin gave Samten Lingpa both instructions and advice. Ecstatic, he remembered his previous life as Lhapa Chöjung and told others about this. Everyone started calling

116. 1655 C.E.

him Ugyen Lhapa. At that site, a mountain called Tramo Rock, Samten Lingpa revealed a guide to several profound termas. The year after that he revealed the *Heart Essence of Vajrasattva* and the *Wrathful Kilaya* cycles from a practice cave of Vairochana's at Trikaya Rock in Langlung.

In his twentieth year Samten Lingpa undertook complete renunciation and thereafter lived as a bhikshu. His actual monastic name was Samten Dorje.

Samten Lingpa's second terma included both the *All-Liberating Heart Essence of Padma* and its protector cycle, the *Realm Protectors*. He first revealed their terma guide and introduction from a boulder in the lower valley at Tramo Rock. Based on those, he revealed the actual terma from the practice cave of Vairochana among the Lotus Crystal Caves.

His third terma, revealed from Sokhar Kyok Cave, was vast and included the *Wrathful Fiery Black HUM*, the *Guru and Vajrakilaya Combined*, and the *Dakini Singhamukha*. However, because he was unable to maintain the necessary secrecy and other conditions prescribed in the terma guides, great upheaval occurred after he had transcribed a few sections of the peaceful and wrathful parts of the *All-Liberating Heart Essence of Padma*. Therefore, based on a particular instruction within the terma, he reconcealed all of his third terma except for the *Guru and Vajrakilaya Combined*.

Samten Lingpa's fourth terma was revealed from beneath the pedestal of Vajrapani at Garuda Grove. It was the *Three Sadhanas of the Guru's Heart Like Refined Gold: Peaceful, Wrathful, and Semi-Wrathful*.

His fifth terma was the *Peaceful Secret Essence of Padma*, which he revealed from the Blazing Heart Vitality Fortress.

Samten Lingpa's sixth terma was the *Dorje Drakpo Tsal* cycle, which he revealed from a practice cave at White Rock Divine Water Vitality Fortress.

His seventh terma: Encouraged by the terma protector Ekajati, Samten Lingpa went to Lhotö to meet Lama Kunga Gyamtso. On the way he was hosted by a family called Lathok. While he was staying in their home, the family offered him the volume of the *Essential Practice of Hayagriva*, which was a terma of Chokden Dorje. Samten Lingpa then had a vision in which the mahasiddha Chokden Dorje gave him the empowerments and instructions of that terma. Samten Lingpa thereafter restored and widely disseminated that previously broken lineage.

Samten Lingpa's eighth terma was the *Essential Practice of the Three Roots*, which he revealed from the Secret Cave at White Rock Divine Water.

His ninth terma was the *Intention of Mahakarunika: The Liberation of All Beings*. He revealed it from a heart-shaped boulder on Black Mara Mountain.

Samten Lingpa's tenth terma was the *Biography of Yeshe Tsogyal* in eight chapters, which he revealed from Pakshong Khamdo Rock.

His eleventh terma was the *Great Testament: A Biography of the Guru*, which he revealed from Secret Yanglesho.

Samten Lingpa's twelfth terma was the *Lord of Secrets Who Conquers the Aggressive*, which was directly offered to him by its terma guardian from within the lake at Dombu Gangra.

His thirteenth terma: At the great charnel ground Joyous Grove in Happy Valley in Puwo, there was a hill on which grew many trees. He cut them down, removed the earth and stones beneath them, and discovered an image of Hayagriva and Vajravarahi one story in height. From their place of union he revealed a terma guide. Based on it he then revealed from the throne of Guru Rinpoche and other sites within that charnel ground the tantras, sadhanas, and accessories of the *Yidam's Wisdom Assembly*, which comprised nine volumes.

Samten Lingpa's fourteenth terma was the *Whispered Lineage of Yeshe Tsogyal*, which he revealed from Khrodikali Rock.

His fifteenth terma was the *Wrathful Goddess Conqueror of Mara* cycle, which he revealed from the Tiger's Lair of Dorje Trolö.

Samten Lingpa's sixteenth terma was the *Samaya-Bound*

Brother and Sister cycle, which he revealed from Tsagang Turquoise Rock.

His seventeenth terma was *Mahakarunika: The Heart Essence of Mitra the Yogin*, which he revealed from Maitreya's Sleeve in Dorchu.

With few exceptions, Samten Lingpa deciphered all of these and bestowed them on his principal dharma heirs, including the great tertön Chöje Lingpa, Samten Lingpa's nephew Namkha Dorje, and Peltsa Samten Tendzin. The vidyadhara Chöje Lingpa bestowed them on both the Gyalwang Karmapa and Shamar Rinpoche, and the activity of these termas flourished.

Along with these termas, Samten Lingpa also revealed countless supports of body and mind, scepters, and supports of blessing. For example, if we consider only the kilas that he revealed, they are said to comprise a complete set of the kilas needed for a Vajrakilaya Great Assembly.

Samten Lingpa's main seat was Samten Ling in Partö. Countless people, august and lowly, assembled there from all over Tibet, and he ceaselessly turned the dharmachakras of ripening and liberation for them. He convened Great Accomplishment Assemblies such as Amrita Accomplishment, the creation of samaya substances that liberate through taste, many times. He also engaged in innumerable deeds of conventional virtue.

Having accomplished so much, he finally withdrew his rupakaya into the hearts of Hayagriva and Vajravarahi amidst numerous signs and miracles.

His monastery in Puwo has been maintained by both his emanations and lineage, which is prevalent both there and in Ngomgyu and Shaknying. I have carefully received all of his ripening empowerments and liberating instructions that are presently available, and I dare to call myself extremely fortunate as a result.

Ratön Topden Dorje

Ratön Topden Dorje, also called Padma Tsewang Tsal, was an emanation of Langchen Palgyi Senge. He was born in Gyangtse in Tsang to the family line of the great Ra the Translator, who was a lord of magical power. His family line was an unbroken succession of powerful mantradharins.

Ratön studied to perfection at the Zurde College in Gyangtse. He then entered the presence of the vidyadhara Chöje Lingpa and received from him all the dharma he had, like the contents of one vase being poured into another. In particular, Chöje Lingpa appointed Ratön as the dharma heir of his new termas. Ratön was also the scribe who wrote down the majority of the deciphered parchments of Chöje Lingpa's termas. Ratön remained with his master for a long time and came to understand his wisdom.

Due to unrest in central Tibet, Chöje Lingpa fled to the hidden valley of Padmakö, accompanied by Ratön as his attendant. When Chöje Lingpa was about to pass to other realms he gave Ratön extensive final instructions, saying, "You are the destined heir to this northern part of Padmakö, this place of force called Wild Black Winds. You must construct a dwelling where my illusory body is destroyed, reveal the sacred sites here, and make them clear to people."

Ratön fulfilled his master's final wishes by building a dwelling there after Chöje Lingpa's passing, as well as a stupa containing his ashes. He attempted to accomplish the rest of his instructions as well, but was prevented from doing so by the magic of maras, which disturbed the interdependence among the disciples and monks there.

Ratön discovered a rebirth of Chöje Lingpa and installed him at Drakey Monastery in Puwo. He then returned to Tsang, and thereafter traveled to Kushinagara in India and various borderlands between India and Tibet such as Sikkim. During this journey he traveled exclusively by means of yogic discipline, and acquired a terma guide. Accordingly, at Onpu Tiger's Lair he revealed a *Vajrakilaya* cycle, the *Peaceful Heart Essence of Samantabhadra*, the *Wrathful Supreme Heruka*, and the *Black Hayagriva* cycle. The lineage of this wondrous dharma continues, and I have received it. It is evident that Ratön revealed other termas as well.

In the later part of his life Ratön was venerated by the ruler Pholha Taiji Sönam Topgyal. Ratön engaged in many acts of pacification, enrichment, power, and force for the good of all Tibet and exhibited signs of their success. While Ratön was living in Puwo the Eighth Tai Situpa Tenpe Nyinje received many empowerments and transmissions from him, including the termas of Chöje Lingpa. Ratön's mind and Situpa's mind became inseparable. Ratön was also proclaimed a dharma heir by the Gyalwang Karmapa and Shamarpa, and many great lineage holders such as Nesar Dakwang Kunga Lekpe Jungne and the glorious Sakya Tridzin received the nectar of his teachings either directly or indirectly.

Having completed his life and activity, Ratön departed for Akanishtha, the citadel of vajra array. His nirmanakaya was born in Dakpo to the Physician of Labar, in the family of Abo Chöje's nephew. Ratön's descendants still live in Red Rock Hall in Gyangtse. His lineage is unbroken.

Khampa Rinpoche

Khampa Rinpoche, the renowned Ngawang Kunga Tendzin, was the display of Guru Rinpoche's blessings. He was born at Dekhyiling, below Gongkar Dzong in central Tibet, in the Iron Monkey year of the eleventh cycle.[117] He offered the fruits of his crown to Mipam Chökyi Wangchuk and received the name Ngawang Kunga Tendzin. He relied upon many great masters, including the father and sons of the Drukpa Kagyu, Gampopa Zangpo Dorje, and the great tertön of Mindröling and his brother. He received practically all of the

117. The year was 1680 C.E.

dharma of the Sarma and Nyingma kama and terma traditions. He was also learned in the common sciences, and mastered medicine in particular. He was recognized as the rebirth of Drukpa Karma Tenpel and Umdze Kunga Lhundrup, and was therefore brought to eastern Tibet.

While he was living on top of Mount Zegyal, during a period of his life in which he engaged in dharmic austerity in many isolated retreats, Khampa Rinpoche directly encountered Vimalamitra and received instruction on the Great Perfection from him. Although Guru Rinpoche blessed him and gave him a terma guide and many prophetic instructions, Khampa Rinpoche was unable to reveal much terma because of the conditions present at that time and place. However, he did open the doors to many sacred places and was able to successfully exorcise the possessed. He did reveal a few profound termas, including both supports and dharma. Of these only the *Sadhana of Magyal Pomra*, which Khampa Rinpoche revealed at Dorgyal, still exists; I have received it.

At dawn on a tenth day of the lunar month in the Water Dragon year, Khampa Rinpoche had a vision of Guru Rinpoche, his trikaya, his six families, his eight names, and an entourage of viras and dakinis, as depicted in the Tenth Day Dance.[118] Based on that vision, he combined the *Guru Guhyasamaja* and the *Very Profound Embodiment of the Three Jewels*. This shastra, a mind terma, is called the *Heart Sadhana of Khampa Rinpoche*. At his seat he combined the pre-existing ritual practices of dance, mandala creation, melody, and music with those he received in his vision. He established a wondrous form of Tenth Day Dance, as well as the *Fundamental Dance of Vajrakilaya*. This vast contribution to the practice of elaborate ritual is now known as the *Great Accomplishment Assembly* of Khampa Rinpoche, and has continued down to the present unbroken. From his writings:

118. The year was 1712 C.E.

To provide shade in a time of heat
I gathered five hundred thousand clouds.

For the sake of Tibet, Khampa Rinpoche created five hundred thousand of each of the following: images of Guru Rinpoche's form; Vajra Guru mantras, his speech, carved in stone; stupas representing his mind; copies of the *Seven Chapters*, to represent his qualities; and copies of the *Great Testament*, to represent his activity.

Khampa Rinpoche's deeds were vast, and included the consecration of pills which liberate through taste, great assemblies for the creation of amrita, and the constant turning of the dharmachakras of the kama and terma Nyingma dharma, including the bestowal of the empowerment of the anuyoga-sutras. He was a great vidyadhara of the Nyingma tradition.

His disciples included most of the lineage holders of his own Drukpa Kagyu tradition as well as the omniscient Eighth Situ Chökyi Jungne, the vidyadhara Rölpe Dorje, and countless others.

After achieving so much for the good of beings and the teachings, Khampa Rinpoche withdrew his emanated mandala. His immediate rebirth was Tendzin Chökyi Nyima, a heart-son of lord Chökyi Jungne. Tendzin Chökyi Nyima was supreme among the learned, accomplished, and good. Since then his rebirths have appeared successively and have greatly spread the unified teachings of the Kagyu and Nyingma traditions.

Rölpe Dorje

The great vidyadhara Rölpe Dorje was a mind emanation of both the master Mahahumkara and Khön Lui Wangpo. He was born amidst signs of virtue in southern Dokham, in a small valley called Runang in the Kerong area. His father's name was Tsering Dorje; his mother's was Lhamo. Rölpe Dorje was given the name Könchok Lhundrup.

He grew more quickly than other children, and was more impressive. He possessed unbearable compassion. While still a child he declared himself to be a great vidyadhara afraid of nothing. Simply by invoking the power of the truth he was able to end the illnesses of cattle and bring rain where there had been drought. His unimpeded ability to eradicate problems and help beings caused others to have faith in him while he was still young. In dreams he gained certainty about the meaning of selflessness and thereby naturally came to realize suchness.

From Drung Drupgyü Tenpa Namgyal, Chetsang Rikdzin Sungrap Gyamtso, Khampa Ngawang Kunga Tendzin, and many other wise and accomplished gurus he received countless teachings on sutra, tantra, and the guhyamantra of the Sarma and Nyingma traditions. As he possessed the stainless eye of dharma, he understood how to combine all the profound points of the Sarma and Nyingma traditions into one system of practice, and wrote the *Source of Jewels: An Account of Teachings I Have Received*. This wonderful shastra is a necessity for anyone with an impartially pure outlook toward all the Buddha's teachings.

Rölpe Dorje was perfectly noble in his behavior; he never transgressed the rules of a renunciate, and never allowed the flesh of an animal killed for food to touch his tongue. Through his diligent practice of the yogas of generation, recitation, and completion he repeatedly saw the faces of the master Humkara, Guru Rinpoche, and Yeshe Tsogyal, and received their blessings.

As an indication that he was about to receive the siddhi of profound terma, he first found some pure gold. Then, in a cave he discovered a pleasing sphere of stone, within which he found a terma guide.

At sunrise on the tenth day of the first month of autumn in the Iron Snake year magical parchment appeared before him.[119] It contained a precise account of a lake terma along with its key. Rölpe Dorje was also strongly encouraged by the protectress Remati, and so he began the terma accomplishment. On the evening of the tenth day of the month Saga in

119. The year was 1701 C.E.

the Water Horse year he destroyed a vicious spirit that was trying to prevent him from revealing terma.[120] At dawn the next morning Guru Rinpoche and Yeshe Tsogyal bestowed empowerment, blessings, and extensive instructions on him.

Accordingly, Rölpe Dorje went to Gyamgyal Doti on the tenth day of the fifth month of that year. Amid a great crowd of all kinds of people he entered Great Turquoise Lake. Everyone present saw rainbow light and heard pleasant sounds. A yaksha and a lake goddess offered Rölpe Dorje terma coffers. The lake's nagamara delayed the presentation of other terma coffers, so Rölpe Dorje compelled him through samadhi. After the lake became unbearably bright like the sun and miraculous thunder and lightning occurred, the naga offered Rölpe Dorje the remaining coffers. He carried them through the crowd, causing everyone there to develop irreversible faith.

There were six terma coffers in all, of various shapes such as that of the palace of Guru Rinpoche With Nine Topknots, that of the Glorious Copper-Colored Mountain, and that of an iron scorpion. Rölpe Dorje brought them to the Puntsok Rapten hermitage at the great seat of Dütsi Til and presented offerings before them. On the twenty-second day of that month some of the terma coffers spontaneously opened. The dharma cycles that he deciphered from the parchment within them included the outer, inner, secret, and mother sadhanas of the *Guru Who Embodies All Victors*; extraordinarily profound instructions on the *Dark Red Wrathful Guru*; and a dharmapala cycle.

Again encouraged by prophecy, Rölpe Dorje went to the Vajra Calcite Cave in Kerong and dug through the rock seals for three months. When he performed a fire offering of the four actions in order to remove obstacles to the actual extraction of the terma there, unmoving clouds in the shapes of the four actions appeared.

He revealed a dark red triangular coffer as well as one shaped like a scorpion and another shaped like a vase. Every-

---

120. The year was 1702 C.E.

one present witnessed wondrous signs including rainbows and a rain of flowers when he brought out the coffers. The dharma cycles within them included the *Peaceful and Wrathful Lord of Secrets Who Conquers All the Aggressive*; its mother cycle, the *Red Singhamukha*; and the *Untitled Cycle*.

These two revelations, known as Rölpe Dorje's Lake Terma and Rock Terma, together make up about five volumes.

Rölpe Dorje made Dütsi Til his main seat. He went to Chamdo to meet the great tertön Taksham Nüden Dorje and received from him the complete dispensation of his termas, including the *Wisdom Assembly of the Yidam*. Taksham praised Rölpe Dorje, appointed him as his regent and dharma heir, and presented him with empowerment implements, robes, and many other gifts.

Rölpe Dorje visited Dalung, Drilung, and western Ga; he guided many fortunate beings in those places to higher rebirths and liberation. He subdued many vicious nonhumans and brought them to the training. He visited Jophu Monastery in order to receive the almost extinct *Hundred Empowerments of Mitra the Yogin* and received a pure lineage of their empowerments and transmissions from the supreme guide Yeshe Dorje. As a result, their lineage still flourishes.

Rölpe Dorje was extremely devoted to the teachings, and was prophesied to be the dharma heir of many tertöns. It is evident that, had he lived out his full life span, he would have become the life-tree of both the Kagyu and Nyingma traditions. However, because his teacher Chetsang Rikdzin forbade Rölpe Dorje to accept a mudra, demanding that he remain a renunciate; because Rölpe Dorje himself neglected to enlist the aid of the terma guardian, the great king Pehar, in the transcription of some of his terma parchments; and because of other missed opportunities, Rölpe Dorje began to repeatedly witness signs that dakinis were beckoning him to depart for other realms. After revealing the meaning of symbolic words predicting his final deeds, he began a journey to Tsangshi. On the way, he suddenly passed into peace.

When his remains were cremated wondrous signs arose. His heart, tongue and eyes emerged from the fire undamaged. Garwang Chökyong Namgyal and Tsedrung Karma Tenpel, who had both studied under Rölpe Dorje's teachers, and many other dharma heirs spread Rölpe Dorje's activity. His main lineage holder was his nephew Ugyen Lhundrup, who offered all of the empowerments and transmissions of Rölpe Dorje's termas to the omniscient Situ Chökyi Jungne. Their lineage has remained undiminished down to the present, and I have received their complete ripening and liberation.

Among Rölpe Dorje's termas his *Wrathful Guru* has proven to be the single armor protecting the life of beings by pacifying epidemics caused by fierce spirits in these times of decadence. Its activity has therefore been tremendous.

Rölpe Dorje's successive emanations have held their seat at Surmang Dütsi Til down to the present, and have also held the lineage of his dharma. However, the rebirth of Chetsang Sungrap Gyamtso fell prey to obstacles, ending his emanation lineage. As I have written above, and shall further below, the deeds of tertöns are of such great value that any interference with them is extremely dangerous. If any authentic tertöns should appear in the future, it seems that those who pride themselves on being learned and fine monastics and are fixated on what appears to them to be the good of their lineages should not censor even slightly, based on their own thinking, the vajra prophecies of Guru Rinpoche!

Padma Dechen Lingpa

Rongtön Padma Dechen Lingpa was a mind emanation of the great translator Vairochana. He was born amid good signs at dawn on the tenth day of the middle month of spring in a Water Hare year, in a village called Gongti at the border of the

Ser and Do regions of eastern Tibet.[121] His father's name was Könchok; his mother's was Zungtharma. He was given the name Shakya Thar.

121. The year was 1663 C.E.

In his third year his past habits were awakened and he began to conduct himself only as a guru and helper of beings. He spontaneously sang in verse, including a *Supplication of the Trikaya Guru*. His maternal aunt, an emanation of Ekajati, prophesied that he was destined to be a great being and offered him her faith and respect.

In his thirteenth year he learned to read, and gave rise to sadness for samsara and unbearable compassion for beings. He received a few minor instructions from Lama Yeshe Gyaltsen.

In his twentieth year Padma Dechen Lingpa journeyed on pilgrimage to central Tibet and made extraordinary prayers of aspiration at the sacred places and supports there. He continued to live as a mantrin.

In his twenty-first year he offered Neserwa Lama Yeshe Gyaltsen the three things that please, and received instruction. He bound his being with moral discipline. For seven years he one-pointedly practiced meditation on the channels and energy, Mahamudra, and the Great Perfection. He gained signs of accomplishment and full realization of the nature of things.

In his twenty-fifth year Padma Dechen Lingpa received a prophecy and acquired a terma guide. He secretly went to Queen's Wooded Gorge. From a boulder there called Assembly of a Hundred Thousand Dakinis at the sacred place of Mudo he revealed the *Heart Essence of the Dakinis of the Brilliant Expanse* along with its protector cycle, the *Life Mara*. He kept them secret, and continued to receive countless teachings on the Sarma, Nyingma, kama, and terma dharma from his gurus.

In his twenty-seventh year Padma Dechen Lingpa entered the presence of the vidyadhara Longsal Nyingpo at Kathok. Longsal Nyingpo assured him that they had been connected in many previous lives. He gave Padma Dechen Lingpa uncommon instructions and blessings, and appointed him as his true regent.

In Padma Dechen Lingpa's thirtieth year he met the great tertön Taksham Nüden Dorje, who was visiting Tsen Mountain. Padma Dechen Lingpa received all of Taksham's terma dharma. Their minds merged as one.

Padma Dechen Lingpa also received much dharma, including uncommon whispered lineages, from both Tala Padma Norbu and Kunzang Khyapdal Lhundrup of Red Rock. He undid the seal of secrecy on his *Heart Essence of the Dakinis of the Brilliant Expanse* and bestowed its ripening empowerments and liberating instructions on those two holy beings first, the interdependence of time and place having been fulfilled. His activity and benefit of beings gradually expanded in their area.

Then, based on his terma guide, Padma Dechen Lingpa revealed the *Secret Wisdom Dakini* cycle from the Molten Castle at Trephu Rock Mountain, and the *Essence of the Assembly of Dispensations* cycle from Tsen Mountain Vajra Rock. He deciphered most of them. His main terma should have been the *Dakinis' Wisdom Assembly*, which was concealed on Sow's Head Mountain, but he did not reveal it. It seems that because of this, he also did not reveal a profound terma concerning *Mahakarunika* concealed in the Water Temple of Kongbu.

In later life Padma Dechen Lingpa lived at Tsen Mountain, his main seat. Having achieved immeasurable benefit for beings by forming meaningful connections with wild people who were extremely difficult to tame, he withdrew his emanated display into the dharmadhatu.

Padma Dechen Lingpa's son Padma Wangyal relied upon his father and upon the great tertön of Mindröling and his brother as gurus. Padma Wangyal became greatly learned and attained. His younger brother Chökyong Palden also became learned in Nyingma dharma and achieved signs of siddhi. The Tenth Shamarpa and the omniscient Situ Tenpe Nyinje received Padma Dechen Lingpa's termas from Chökyong Palden.

The main holder of Padma Dechen Lingpa's lineage was his regent, the vidyadhara Tsewang Norbu, from whom both the Drukchen Kagyu Trinley Shingta and Pawo Tsuklak Gawa received these termas. Tsewang Norbu spread the lineage of their empowerments and instructions as far as Ngari, and they have survived to some extent. The lineage of Padma Dechen Lingpa's descendants continued at his seat and maintained his dharma lineage there.

Among all the tertöns who have appeared in eastern Tibet, Padma Dechen Lingpa's terma dharmas possess the most excellent words and meaning. Those with eyes of dharma can see this for themselves. I have diligently received Padma Dechen Lingpa's three termas.[122]

122. Jamgön Kongtrül was a rebirth of Padma Dechen Lingpa.

Padma Chögyal

Padma Chögyal, the tertön of Batser in eastern Tibet, revealed many profound termas, as was witnessed by many. He is renowned for his great blessing and magical power. Even now, his seat has not been abandoned, and it seems his dharma lineage has survived in a scattered form. It seems that the vidyadhara Tsewang Norbu met Padma Chögyal while young and formed a slight dharma connection with him. I have received the much-needed *Red Garuda* cycle which comes from three lineages, one of them Padma Chögyal's.

Padma Wangchuk

Padma Wangchuk, the tertön of Lingtsang Dzong, is said to have been an emanation of the great translator Vairochana. According to Padma Wangchuk, Vairochana's speech emanation, Terdak Lingpa; his mind emanation, Padma Dechen

Lingpa; and his body emanation, Padma Wangchuk himself, were of one mind-stream.

In any case, Padma Wangchuk met the vidyadhara Longsal Nyingpo and received from him both a prophecy that he would reveal earth terma and a terma guide. Padma Wangchuk revealed the *Great Perfection Heart Essence of the Guru* from a rock near the Longthang Drölma Border-Taming Temple. This cycle included sadhanas of the peaceful and wrathful forms of Guru Rinpoche, of Singhamukha, and of longevity. I have seen their texts, and the words appear to be flawless.

Padma Wangchuk is also said to have revealed the *Great Perfection Heart Essence of the Three Roots* from a crack in the doorway to the Trori Ziltrom Cave, a place of the Vidyadharas' Assembly; and *Gurusadhana*, *Great Perfection*, and *Mahakarunika* cycles from the Great Cave of Gyatö Gangbar. Most people consider him to have been an authentic tertön, and he was somewhat active, but he had no well-known disciples. His lineage was carried on by his sons, Ugyen Shenpen and his brother, and it seems that the empowerments and transmissions for his sadhanas of the three roots still exist.

Khyungdrak Dorje

The tertön Khyungdrak Dorje is said to have been an emanation of the translator Yudra Nyingpo. His actual name was Ugyen Puntsok. He began as a disciple of the great tertön Yongey Mingyur Dorje. Later, when Khyungdrak Dorje first received the dispensation of terma, he met the vidyadhara Longsal Nyingpo, who declared him to be an authentic tertön, at Kathok. Longsal Nyingpo also advised him that he needed to perform the requisite terma accomplishment. Khyungdrak Dorje followed this advice and gradually revealed the *Great Perfection Eight Dispensations*, the *Wrathful Jnanabhairava*, and his *Cycle of the Three Roots*. These termas still exist.

Encouraged by a prophecy by Yongey Mingyur Dorje, Khyungdrak Dorje went to the Sangen area, where he was subsequently somewhat active. It appears that he presented to Mingyur Dorje the offerings he received there. It is said that Khyungdrak Dorje had a few disciples, including Lhateng Jamo Tulku and Ga Damtsik Tulku. In any case, he used the offerings he received to sponsor the publication of many volumes of kama and terma teachings, including the *Collected Nyingma Tantras*. He did well. It seems that his image and relics were kept for some time in the temple built at his birthplace.

Tsewang Norbu

The vidyadhara Tsewang Norbu was an emanation of the mind of Nup Namkhay Nyingpo. He was born at Sangen Sowa in eastern Tibet. His father's name was Dupa Ati Gönpo; his mother's was Goza Dorje Tso. Both the wondrous signs at his birth and the supercognition of his maternal uncle, Padma Dechen Lingpa, indicated that Tsewang Norbu was the rebirth of the lord of siddhas Padma Norbu. He was therefore brought to his seat at Nenang and named Tsewang Norbu Dorje Palbar.

Tsewang Norbu easily learned to read and write, and became learned in various sciences and in philosophy. He venerated Padma Dechen Lingpa as his root guru, received many empowerments and instructions from him, and gave rise to good experiences and realization. He received the upasaka vow from Kathok Gyalsay, and many teachings from Chetsang Sungrap Gyamtso of Surmang. Tsewang Norbu lived as a great vajra holder mantradharin.

He traveled through Pukong and reached central Tibet, where he received countless empowerments and transmissions of Sarma and Nyingma guhyamantra from many gurus of many traditions. In particular, Tsewang Norbu received the complete dharma of the Jonang tradition from the dharma lord Kunzang Wangpo and caused its lineage to spread, in which regard he was of incomparable kindness.

With his supercognition Tsewang Norbu saw the three times without obscuration. He left footprints in rock, reversed the flow of waterfalls, and demonstrated many other signs of attainment. Even the ruler Polha Tadzi and his sons developed faith in him and awarded him the rank of Tishri.

If he had been able to meet the tertön Rölpe Dorje, Tsewang Norbu would have established the interdependence for revealing thirteen termas. Because of Rölpe Dorje's sudden passing, Tsewang Norbu never met him and was unable to reveal those great termas. He did, however, reveal a profound and concise *Sadhana of Red Tara* from the Kongbu River and the *Essence Empowerment of the Wrathful Display of Vajrakila* that Rölpe Dorje had reconcealed at Kegyü. Tsewang Norbu is also said to have acquired several terma guides in Tsang. He revealed as visionary dharma and mind terma the extraordinary *Spontaneous Fulfillment of Wishes* sadhana cycle.

Tsewang Norbu performed approach and accomplishment in many of Tibet's places of accomplishment. He founded monasteries in Pukong and Ngari; his benefit of beings in those areas was vast. He visited Nepal three times. During his second visit he restored the Great Stupa of Bodhanath; during his third he restored the Great Swayambunath Stupa. While Tsewang Norbu was doing so, the Gurkha king of Nepal was disrespectful to him. Tsewang Norbu proclaimed the power of the truth to the great gods of Nepal, and the town of Nagakoti caught fire. The queen, princes, and ministers supplicated Tsewang Norbu, and the fire extinguished itself instantaneously. The royal family thereafter had faith in him and listened to whatever he said.

In order to fund his restoration of the Stupa of Swayambunath Tsewang Norbu requested gold from the gods and spirits of Nepal. It is said that they provided him with fifteen human loads of gold, and that he also discovered a vast source of building stone.

While Tsewang Norbu was in Nepal the second time the kings of Ngari and Ladakh went to war with one another. Armies were brought in from western Tibet and Mongolia. The Tibetan government asked Tsewang Norbu to intervene. He did so, a treaty was made between the warring parties, and the armies from western Tibet and Mongolia went home. Through Tsewang Norbu's compassion, the war was completely ended. He then returned to Nepal and continued his restoration of the stupas. Not long after that he passed to other realms at Kyirong. His disciples completed his work of restoration as instructed in his will.

Tsewang Norbu's main disciples were the Gyalwang Karmapa and his spiritual sons, the omniscient Drukchen, and Situ Chökyi Jungne. He had countless disciples throughout western, central, and eastern Tibet, and his dharma lineage has also become widespread. I have received his two minor earth termas and his mind terma.

Tsasum Terdak Lingpa

Tsasum Terdak Lingpa, also called Garwang Namchak Dorje, was an emanation of Nupchen Sangye Yeshe. He was born to the family line of the mahasiddha Langchen Palgyi Senge amid wondrous signs near Zegyal, a sacred place in southwest Nangchen. He received the upasaka vow and the name Tashi Puntsok from a Gelukpa dharma lord who was said to be an emanation of Ngok Loden Sherap. He studied a bit. When the great tertön Taksham Nüden Dorje visited the capital of Nangchen, Tsasum Terdak Lingpa formed a dharma connection with him.

He later went to Drikung and relied upon Könchok Trinley Zangpo as a guru. He received dharma from him, especially detailed instruction on the whispered lineage of Jatavira's prana teaching. He remained there for three years practicing it; experience and realization burst forth from within him. Miracles and supercognition arose effortlessly.

Based on a timely prophecy Tsasum Terdak Lingpa began to engage in the conduct of awareness-discipline. He also visited many sacred places without hindrance. During his journey, based on both a terma guide and prophecy, he first revealed the *Sugatas' Assembly Sadhana of the Guru's Heart* and the *Spontaneous Fulfillment of Wishes* cycle from Samye Chimphu. He then revealed the *Very Profound Padma Heruka* cycle, comprising profound and concise tantras, agamas, and upadeshas, from the Feast Hall of Shotö Tidro. He then revealed the extensive tantras, agamas, and upadeshas of the *Secret All-Surpassing Yidam: The Eight Dispensations* from the Lotus Garden of Powo Gorge; this cycle comprises seven volumes.

He also revealed from various sites of concealment many cycles of empowerment and instruction concerning the boundless three roots, including the *Dark Red Reliquary of Heruka and Kila*, four ayusadhanas such as the *Conquering Death Ayusadhana*, *Mahakarunika Who Conquers Samsara and Nirvana*, *Hayagriva the Essence of the Sun*, *Hayagriva Who Embodies the Strength of All Wrathful Kings*, the *Wisdom Light of Vajrasattva*, the *Very Secret Powerful Wrathful Padma*, his *Dorje Trolö* cycle, *Yamantaka the Fiery Poison Mountain*, *Secret Wisdom: The Supreme Wish-Fulfilling Jewel*, the *Wrathful Dakini Tamer of Maras*, the *Wealth Sadhana of the Guru*, and the *Dharmapala Realm Protector* cycle. Those he deciphered from the parchments make up eighteen volumes. The lineage of their empowerments and transmissions appears to have remained unbroken at Doshül, Khyungpo, and Powo.

Tsasum Terdak Lingpa made Powo Tromzik Ngamchen his main seat. Although he assembled a number of disciples, and his activity flourished, he passed away in his forty-fourth year.

It therefore appears that his deeds remained uncompleted. The observances connected with his passing were well performed by his disciples.

Tsasum Terdak Lingpa had three emanations. The emanation of his body was Rongnyön Ugyen Rikdzin, who lived at the seat at Tromzik. The emanation of Tsasum Terdak Lingpa's speech was Kunzang Chime Norbu, who is said to have appeared in the Gawalung area of Puwo, but there is no evidence of that emanation line having continued. The emanation of Tsasum Terdak Lingpa's mind was the vidyadhara Mijik Dorje, who lived in the Khyungpo region. The body and mind emanation lines have continued down to the present.

Tsasum Terdak Lingpa's main disciple was his spiritual son, the vidyadhara Tukchok Dorje, who passed most of Tsasum Terdak Lingpa's profound termas on to Zungkhar Tekchen Lingpa and others, spreading their lineage. Tsasum Terdak Lingpa also had a few other disciples capable of spreading the teachings, including Könseng Pandita, the lord Kunga Lodrö, and Yeshe Gyaltsen.

Because of the partial similarity of Tsasum Terdak Lingpa's name and that of the great vidyadhara Terdak Lingpa of Mindröling, people have speculated as to whether or not they were disharmonious. However, there is no evidence of any disharmony between them in any of their prophecies, so this speculation is nothing more than mistaking one's own shadow for a carnivorous spirit.

When Tsasum Terdak Lingpa visited Tsurphu to offer his termas to the Gyalwang Karmapa and Shamarpa, he was prevented from doing so by their attendants. He was also of a mercurial disposition, and did not do anything to smooth his way. As a result, he did not fulfill the prophetic instruction to offer his termas to them, but he did nothing that was displeasing to them, and is well known to have been an authentic tertön. I have therefore formed a dharmic connection with him by receiving the essence empowerment from his *Padma Heruka* cycle.

Tukchok Dorje

The vidyadhara Tukchok Dorje Humnak Drodül was an emanation of both Nup Namkhay Nyingpo and Chim Shakyaprabha. He was born in Kyirong, near Samye Chimphu in central Tibet. He entered the monastic college of Palri and became learned in the two traditions. He therefore acquired the nickname Dharma Treasury from Kyirong. His actual names were Ngawang Lapsum and Kunzang Trinley Dorje.

Tukchok Dorje received countless instructions from the mahasiddha Kunzang Rangdröl at Tsupri in Kongpo, especially the *Black Quintessence of the Great Perfection*. Practicing them, he achieved maturation of awareness. Tukchok Dorje also received the complete *Guru's Wisdom Assembly* from Kunzang Rangdröl in the company of the vidyadhara Tsewang Norbu. He was accepted by both the vidyadhara Chöje Lingpa and Ratön Topden Dorje, and received their teachings like the contents of one vase being completely poured into another.

Tukchok Dorje one-pointedly practiced approach and accomplishment in various places. Inconceivable signs of siddhi and pure appearances arose for him. In particular, he manifested skill in wrathful direct action.

He acquired a terma guide, and revealed the *Sadhana of the Five Families of Vajrakilaya* from Önphu Taktsang; the *Three Roots: Hayagriva's Assembly* from the Red Tomb of Chongye; and *Mahamudra: Wisdom that Liberates upon Sight* from Samye Chimphu. He also revealed many other wondrous and profound termas including the *Wheel of Sky-Iron that Conquers the Aggressive* and *Nagaraksha Who Conquers Demons from Below*.

Had Tukchok Dorje established the necessary interdependence with the Baturs by means of the ruler Chingwang, there was an extremely profound prophecy indicating benefit for beings and the teachings. However, that ruler fell under the power of maras. He behaved poorly, and issued commands indicating his displeasure with Tukchok Dorje. Because of the pervasive and negative influence of this, Tukchok Dorje reconcealed his termas for future discovery. He burned those that he had deciphered from the parchments, and thereby spoiled their interdependence. The ruler died by the emperor's command. Not long thereafter, Tukchok Dorje dissolved into the dharmadhatu at Powolung.

I have received a few of Tukchok Dorje's termas, such as his *Nagaraksha*. His main disciples, capable of helping beings, are said to have been four: Tekling Drodön Tarchin; the vidyadhara Jikme Lingpa; Kunzang Dechen Gyalpo; and the mantradharin of Trati, Karma Rikdzin. Karma Rikdzin is said to have been a final birth of Nup Namkhay Nyingpo. The first three of these received the dispensation of their own profound termas. Karma Rikdzin did not reveal terma, but his experiences and realization were perfect, and he was learned in all the sciences and their branches. Through his vast realization he mastered the four actions and was venerated as a guru by many other great lamas and by the rulers of central Tibet and Kongpo. He completed his alotted lifespan and activity.

Drime Lingpa

The tertön Drime Lingpa was an emanation of the translator Gyalwa Chokyang. He was the immediate rebirth of Düdül Lingpa, the tertön of Rong. Drime Lingpa was born at Zungkhar Tekchen Ling to the family of the tertön Dechen Lingpa. At an early age Drime Lingpa offered the fruits of his crown to the Twelfth Gyalwang Karmapa Jangchup Dorje and was given the name Karma Drodön Tarchin. He studied at the Tantric College of Drak, and received many teachings of the Sarma and Nyingma traditions from Lama Nyenpa

Gelek and other holy beings. Especially, Drime Lingpa received the complete empowerments and instructions of the *Great Perfection Heart Essence of Samantabhadra* from the vidyadhara Tukchok Dorje. He practiced it and achieved consummate experience and realization. He spontaneously knew the words and meaning of dharma, and unimpeded supercognition arose. He recollected many of his previous lives, including Melong Dorje, Dechen Lingpa, and Düdül Lingpa. The channel-knots in his throat loosened and a treasury of vajra song burst forth.

Drime Lingpa planted the victory banner of accomplishment in many isolated places, and repeatedly received prophecies of his revelation of profound terma. He was recognized by the vidyadhara Tukchok Dorje as his dharma heir, and also advised that he would receive the dispensation of terma himself. Accordingly, Drime Lingpa revealed the *Ayusadhana of the Immortal Vajra Brilliant Expanse* and the *Source of All Qualities Sadhana of the Guru's Heart* from Drakyangdzong and deciphered them. He also revealed a *Mahakarunika* cycle from the upper Stone Stupa at Zungkhar, but he reconcealed that cycle for future discovery. The Dalai Lama Kalzang Gyamtso bestowed an edict upon Drime Lingpa authorizing him to benefit beings freely.

Drime Lingpa's main dharma heir was Chakzampa Tendzin Yeshe Lhundrup, an emanation of Yudra Nyingpo. The lineage passed down by him and by Drime Lingpa's other disciples has continued unbroken. I have received Drime Lingpa's *Ayusadhana* and his *Padmaraja Gurusadhana* cycle. Drime Lingpa's descendants still live at Zungkhar Lhading

Kunzang Dechen Gyalpo

Kunzang Dechen Gyalpo, also known as Mönlam Dorje, was an emanation of Acharya Palyang. He was born at the foot of White Vulture Pass at Samye. He began to spontaneously engage in tantric behavior such as binding devas and spirits to samaya in his fifth year. He studied at the monastic college at Samye and at Chongye Palri, and received many instructions from the Mahasiddha of Tsupri. Especially, he was cared for by the vidyadhara Tukchok Dorje, whom Kunzang Dechen Gyalpo regarded as his root guru.

In his eleventh year Kunzang Dechen Gyalpo acquired a terma guide. Based on it, in his twenty-sixth year he revealed the *Essence of the Five Families* cycle from Rölbu, a place in between western Kongpo and eastern Dakpo. He then revealed much dharma as well as many supports and samaya substances from Puwo, Gawalung, and the Samye area. He revealed profound instructions on the four means of attraction that had been concealed by Lord Atisha from the Tsechen Tara Temple near Gyangtse. It is said that in all Kunzang Dechen Gyalpo revealed eighteen termas, and that every revelation was accompanied by numerous miracles. He also revealed terma containing wondrous medicinal materials, including the all-victorious arura fruit, from a meteoric iron rock at Zurkhar Cave in Dakpo; but reconcealed it for future discovery due to various circumstances.

Kunzang Dechen Gyalpo was given the rank of Tishri by the regent Demo Rinpoche, and was appointed to perform the taming of the ground before the restoration of Samye. He offered a thousand statues of Guru Rinpoche; they are now housed in the Vidyadhara Temple. When Kunzang Dechen Gyalpo came before the Jowo Shakyamuni in Lhasa, everyone present saw that pea-sized shariram poured forth from the statue's heart onto his head. He also received a remarkable prophecy from the image.

The family line of the glorious Sakyapas had by this time almost disappeared. At the command of Sakya Dakchen Kunga Lodrö, Kunzang Dechen Gyalpo offered ritual service, and scions to this precious family line were born. This is just one example of his many fine deeds.

Chöling Tulku Jikten Wangchuk offered Kunzang Dechen

Gyalpo Drukthang Monastery in Kongpo, and he settled there, making it his seat. He planted the seed of liberation in countless disciples there. Finally, he passed away in order to benefit beings elsewhere. His lineage has survived in a scattered form, and I have received his *Profound Embodiment of All the Three Roots* cycle.

Rokje Lingpa

Rokje Lingpa Drodül Tsal, who appeared in Taurong, was predicted in the termas of Rongtön Padma Dechen Lingpa to be an emanation of the great translator Vairochana. Accordingly, Rokje Lingpa was born soon after the passing of Padma Dechen Lingpa, and appears to have been his rebirth.

From three terma sites in the region of his birth, such as Red Rock Fortress in the Black Valley of Rongdong, he miraculously and secretly revealed three dharma termas collectively called the *Wish-Fulfilling Trilogy*. The principal one of these is *Hayagriva and Vajravarahi: The Blazing Wish-Fulfilling Jewel*. His dharma heirs were predicted in *Hayagriva's Prophecy*:

> Do not openly teach this very profound dharma,
> *Hayagriva the Wish-Fulfilling Jewel*; teach it secretly.
> Vairochana, practice it yourself.
> For the good of the future, conceal it in eastern Rong.
> Your emanation will find it and practice it secretly.
> If he gives it to the bearers of the black and red crowns,
> Emanations of Avalokita and Amitabha;
> To a rebirth of the king, named Zangpo;
> And to others with the eye of dharma,
> Their lives will last and their activity flourish.

However, because of the status of the Dalai Lama Kalzang Gyamtso, the Gyalwang Karmapa, and the Shamarpa; and because of the circumstances of his time and place, Rokje

Lingpa was unable to offer them his termas. When Tai Situpa Chökyi Jungne was traveling to Mongolia, Rokje Lingpa secretly met him and offered him all of his dharma. It is said that this enabled the Eighth Tai Situpa to live out his full life span.

Rokje Lingpa lived secretly and was therefore little known. I have not heard of his termas having been given to beings; in fact, it seems that hardly anyone alive nowadays has even heard of them. Nevertheless, as they were received as a short lineage by our lord guru Padma Ösal Dongak Lingpa, and in consideration of the interdependence of my predecessor, I have fortunately received from our lord guru the empowerment and transmission of the *Ayusadhana* accessory to Rokje Lingpa's *Hayagriva* cycle.[123]

123. Jamgön Kongtrül was a rebirth of Rokje Lingpa. He admits this by referring to him as "my predecessor."

Garwang Chime Dorje

As predicted in writing to the Norbu Döndrup family of western Puwo by the vidyadhara Chöje Lingpa, the tertön Garwang Chime Dorje was born in a village called Kuyül, in the dharmachakra heart region of the hidden land of Padmakö. Garwang Chime Dorje's father was a mantradharin called Könchok; his mother was called Gyaldema. He was born in a Female Water Sheep year. His conception coincided with the passing of Jikten Wangchuk, the nirmanakaya of Chöje Lingpa, at Dakchak.

From an early age Garwang Chime Dorje passed his time in holy conduct. Even the local tribespeople found him amazing. He studied at Bakha Monastery in Puwo. He offered the fruits of his crown to the tertön of Drukthang and received the name Kunzang Özer Garwang Tenpe Nyima. The tertön also predicted Garwang Chime Dorje's future greatness.

Based on a terma guide that he acquired at Bakha Monastery, Garwang Chime Dorje revealed the *Immortal Heart Essence*, life water, samaya substances, and images at the shore of the dark red Blood Lake in the Valley of a Hundred Thousand Dakinis in western Padmakö. He kept his discovery secret for twelve years, during which time he perfected his own practice of it. He first loosened the seal of secrecy by bestowing the complete instructions of the *Immortal Heart Essence* on Gampo Tulku. He later gave them to the omniscient one of Jora and others.

Garwang Chime Dorje journeyed to central Tibet, where he established positive interdependence at the national capital. He also accomplished some service for the teachings. It is said that he revealed many termas at Bachak Shri and other places he visited on his journey, but the only two of Garwang Chime Dorje's termas that have survived are the *Immortal Heart Essence* and the *Flaming Sky-Iron Wheel of Dorje Trolö*.

Garwang Chime Dorje and the tertön of Dakpo together revealed many sacred places such as the navel nirmanachakra in Padmakö. For the good of all Tibet they built many temples and stupas at critical sites, and also performed several great accomplishments at such places.

After caring for many beings of the southern tribal areas through the four means of attraction, Garwang Chime Dorje passed into peace. It is said that his successive emanations have continued to appear in Padmakö. As he appears to have been an authentic tertön, I have received his *Immortal Heart Essence*.

Dorje Tokme

The tertön Dorje Tokme, also known as Tendzin Daö Dorje, was an emanation of Yudra Nyingpo. He was born near Tsochu Darma Rock, one of the three great mountains of Kongpo. His father, whose name was Jamyang, was a mahasiddha of the Dakpo Kagyu.

Dorje Tokme devoted his time exclusively to approach and accomplishment from an early age, and received prophecies from gurus and dakinis. Based on them he revealed the hidden sacred place Tsophu Norbu Köpa. He also revealed several profound termas there, but reconcealed them for future discovery due to negative interdependence. He later met Gampo Tulku and corrected the previous interdependence, enabling him to reveal a terma guide from the Döchu Temple in Puwo. Based on it he revealed the *Web of Light Ayusadhana* from Red Tsen Life-Razor Rock at Pulung. It is said that he also publicly revealed other termas.

Dorje Tokme built a hermitage at Jangling Tsenchuk in Padmakö, where he resided until his passing, having perfected his realization. His consort, who was named Daö Wangmo, was a yogini close to the achievement of a rainbow body; she upheld his lineage. As a result, his *Ayusadhana* has survived. I have received its essence due to the kindness of our lord guru.

Rangdröl Tingdzin Gyalpo

The tertön Rangdröl Tingdzin Gyalpo, also known as Daway Özer, was an emanation of Prince Lharjey. He was born in the uplands of Drak, where the hawthorns grow. His father was the tertön Drime Lingpa; his mother was a dakini of the Nup clan.

When Rangdröl Tingdzin Gyalpo was old enough, his father Drime Lingpa gave him all of the empowerments and instructions of his termas. When Rangdröl Tingdzin Gyalpo was in his sixth year, his father passed away. He therefore received most of the kama and terma Nyingma dharma from his elder brother Padma Tendzin Gyamtso and from Chakzampa Tendzin Yeshe Lhundrup.

In his thirteenth year Rangdröl Tingdzin Gyalpo entered the dharma college of Palri and offered the fruits of his crown to Padma Chöjor Gyamtso, a nirmanakaya of Yeshe Tsogyal. While living at Palri Rangdröl Tingdzin Gyalpo saw boundless pure appearances. For example, Princess Mandarava actually presented him with seven fresh arura seeds. He mastered the study of medicine while there.

In Rangdröl Tingdzin Gyalpo's eighteenth year he acquired a terma guide and received several prophecies, but because he delayed taking a consort the time for the retrieval of many of his destined termas expired.

He then received the complete empowerments and transmissions of the *Essence of Liberation: Self-Liberated Wisdom* from the mahasiddha Ngawang Chödrak. He vowed to practice it for five years at Samye Chimphu; he fulfilled this vow with great austerity. He also practiced his father's terma *Source of All Qualities: A Sadhana of the Guru's Heart* for three years, bringing his practice of it to perfection. When he subsequently visited Lhasa he experienced boundless visions, including traveling to Lotus Light on Chamaradvipa and receiving the blessing of the mahasiddha Thangtong Gyalpo.

Rangdröl Tingdzin Gyalpo then discovered another terma guide at Drinzang Red Rock. He began the journey back to Minister's Throat at Samye Chimphu. On the way he met the Tsogyal nirmanakaya of Palri, who had become aware, through supercognition, of Rangdröl Tingdzin Gyalpo's discovery of a terma guide. Accompanied by an attendant, they completed their journey in the guise of actionless yogins.

Tsogyal Tulku and the attendant went on ahead and prepared to receive the tertön in the White Tent Cave. When Rangdröl Tingdzin Gyalpo arrived they received him with great honor and ceremony. He then revealed as terma a support of Guru Rinpoche's form called the *Great Image that Liberates through Sight*; a support of his speech, the *Peaceful and Wrathful Sadhanas of the Guru's Heart: The Vidyadhara Assembly of All Sugatas*; and twenty-one substances that liberate through taste called *Sealed by Aḥ*. He copied the symbol script and reconcealed the terma parchments as instructed, and then deciphered and transcribed the terma at Yamalung.

Rangdröl Tingdzin Gyalpo kept his discovery secret for

seven years, during which time he perfected his practice of it. He then began to disseminate it to his prophesied dharma heirs. The lineage of its empowerments, transmissions, and instructions still exists. I have received the *Vajra Essence Web of Light Ayusadhana* from the *Vidyadhara Assembly of All Sugatas* and Rangdröl Tingdzin Gyalpo's *Vajrapani the Embodiment of All Wrathful Deities*.

Rangdröl Tingdzin Gyalpo's main disciples included the Eighth Tendzin Rinpoche Khyenrap Tutop, the Fourth Dzogchen Rinpoche, the tertön Tendzin Sherap and his disciples, and many others. He was acclaimed by the government of Tibet as a great emanated tertön, and performed many ceremonies for the good of all Tibet at the government's request. Wondrous stories are told of his deeds. When the central temple at Samye was damaged he proclaimed samaya to the devas and spirits there; no other part of the monastery suffered any damage. When the central temple was rebuilt Rangdröl Tingdzin Gyalpo tamed the ground and consecrated the new construction.

Having perfectly enacted such great deeds for the good of beings and the teachings, Rangdröl Tingdzin Gyalpo departed for the great citadel of Lotus Light. His funerary observances were performed by his sons. His emanation was reborn in eastern Tibet, as predicted by the Fourth Dzogchen Rinpoche, and lived at Chimphu. He spread his predecessor's profound dharma.

Chokgyur Lingpa

The peerless, great emanated tertön Chokgyur Dechen Shikpo Lingpa was an emanation of the glorious prince Damdzin Murub Tsenpo Yeshe Rölpa Tsal. From a prophecy in the termas of Ugyen Drime Kunga:

> Among the passes at Yortö Dra will appear
> An emanation of Padma's mind, an heir to the dharma,
> Bearing the names Ratna and Uddiyana.
> He will reveal the greatest terma dharma.

A prophecy similar in words and meaning to the above appears in the termas of Rongtön Padma Dechen Lingpa.

From the *General Prophecy of Twenty-Five Future Dharma Heirs* in the termas of Ratna Lingpa:

One named Jewel will appear in southern Kham.

As predicted, Chokgyur Lingpa was born near the Dranang Meditation College affiliated with the Yortö community in southern Kham. His father was the mantradharin Padma Wangchuk, a member of the family of Achak Dru, a minister of the king of Nangchen. His mother was named Tsering Yangtso. Chokgyur Lingpa was born amid wonders such as rainbow light on the tenth day of the month Ashadha in a Female Earth Ox year.[124]

From an early age he exhibited the amazing behavior of a holy being. He learned to read and write with little difficulty. He was called Norbu Tendzin at this time.[125] Without anyone telling him to do so, he meditated. When he offered the fruits of his crown to Lho Kunzang Choktrül, he received the name Könchok Tendzin. Until much later, this was the name by which he was known. Könchok is Ratna in Sanskrit, and therefore fulfills the above-quoted prophecies.

In his thirteenth year, while Chokgyur Lingpa was playing at a place called Manika, Guru Rinpoche actually came to him and asked him about the name of that place and such things. Chokgyur Lingpa answered his questions, and Guru Rinpoche prophesied, "This place is called Manika. You are called Norbu Tendzin. This valley is called Aryanang. You will become one of the greatest people in the world." Then Guru Rinpoche vanished like a rainbow.

That year Chokgyur Lingpa undertook the shramanera vow in the presence of Taklung Ma Rinpoche. He also received the blessings and transmissions of the *Hot Red Cord Heart Sadhana* and the *Beautiful Flower Garland Liturgy*, both from the *Guru's Wisdom Assembly*, from the Eighth Pawo Rinpoche Tsuklak Chökyi Gyalpo. While giving these, Pawo Rinpoche earnestly advised Chokgyur Lingpa that it would be good for him to practice them. In essence, Pawo

---

124. The year was 1829 C.E.

125. "Norbu" means Jewel, his name given in the above quoted prophecy.

Rinpoche was entrusting Chokgyur Lingpa with the lineage of terma.

Chokgyur Lingpa also studied at various times with many other masters, including the Fourteenth Gyalwang Karmapa, Drukchen Rinpoche, the Drikung Choktrül, and various abbots and teachers of Surmang Monastery. From his teachers he received countless empowerments, transmissions, and instructions concerning the Sarma and Nyingma traditions of both sutra and tantra; guidance in scholarship; and instruction in ceremonial dance, the creation of sand mandalas, ritual melodies, and the playing of musical instruments. He always seemed to learn whatever he was taught without difficulty.

In his twenty-fifth year Chokgyur Lingpa went to the great seat of Palpung Monastery at the urging of Guru Rinpoche. There, during the Miracle Month of the Water Ox year, he met the Ninth Tai Situ Rinpoche Padma Nyinje Wangpo.[126] Chokgyur Lingpa offered him a kila called Laughing Hayagriva and other termas. Situ Rinpoche accepted them joyfully and told Chokgyur Lingpa that by offering them to him he had both removed obstacles for him and ensured his longevity. He advised Chokgyur Lingpa of the need for him to complete the practice of his termas and to maintain their secrecy for the period indicated in the termas themselves. From the *Secret Prophecy*:

> At that time, your dharma heirs will appear in this way:
> On the peak of a glorious mountain on the left bank of
>   a golden river
> You will meet Padma Nyinje, an emanation of my speech.[127]
> That scion of the victors will uphold the victory banner
>   of accomplishment.
> He will uphold a beacon amid the darkness at time's end.
> If ayusadhana is completed, he will live to eighty-five.
> If interdependence is well arranged, he will uphold the
>   teachings until ninety.

126. The year was 1853 C.E.

127. Palpung, the informal name of Situ Rinpoche's monastery, could be taken to mean Glorious Mountain.

Prince, you will meet him in your twenty-fifth year.
Trust him without reservation; conceal nothing from him.
This will bring about a great deal of spontaneous
   interdependence.

Chokgyur Lingpa followed these prophetic instructions and thereby established the correct fundamental interdependence. He then received profound dharma, including the generation of bodhichitta, from the great abbot and bodhisattva Dabzang Rinpoche. From me he received *Mahakarunika the Embodiment of All Sugatas*, then the empowerments and explanations of the *Mayajala Peaceful and Wrathful Deities*, and most of the kama Nyingma dharma and many terma dharmas as well. Especially, from the *Summary of Interdependence*:

Prince, your final birth will be as
A person with the aspiration to reveal
The profound termas hidden in the treasury of space.
At that time most of the pandits, translators, and disciples
   will be reunited.
Especially, the king and the prince will meet.
Supporting one another, your karma will be awakened.
You will encounter my ultimate instructions.
In pure visions you will actually meet me.
I will teach you how to practice guhyamantra.
Practicing, you will effortlessly gain siddhi.
Many disciples will gain siddhi as well.

Many such clear predictions are found within the outer, inner, and secret prophecies among Chokgyur Lingpa's termas. As prophesied, in the month Ashvini of that same year Chokgyur Lingpa went to meet our lord guru, the crown ornament of the ocean of scholars and siddhas of Tibet, the lord of all the Buddha's teachings, Jamyang Khyentse Wangpo. Our lord guru, in consideration of their connection throughout many lives since their birth as father and son monarchs, first dispelled all outer, inner, and secret obstacles by bestowing upon Chokgyur Lingpa the *Very Secret Razor Kilaya* and then the great empowerment of the Sakya tradition's *Vajrakilaya*.

When our lord guru subsequently gave Chokgyur Lingpa the empowerments of the *Wish-Fulfilling Jewel: The Quintessence of Guru Vimalamitra*, Chokgyur Lingpa saw him as the mahapandita Vimalamitra in person. Chokgyur Lingpa had other extraordinary pure visions and recognized naked awareness. When our lord guru gave the *Entrustment of the Essence of Ekajati*, both our lord guru and Chokgyur Lingpa saw Ekajati and experienced an awesome glory as intense as an earthquake. She told them that three years later she would provide them both with great siddhi. This was a prophecy of their discovery of the *Three Classes of the Great Perfection*.

In the month Ashvini of his twenty-seventh year, the Year of the Wood Hare, Chokgyur Lingpa received the great empowerment of the *Nine Deities of Perfect Heruka* from our lord guru.[128] He experienced our guru, in the form of Heruka, dissolving into him through the top of his head. As a result, the channel knots of his heart were loosened. From then on vajra songs burst forth spontaneously from within him. Although he had previously been unable to decipher the symbol script of his *Sadhana of the Guru's Heart: Removing All Obstacles*, he immediately understood it easily. He also found that it was mostly identical in both words and meaning with our lord guru's profound terma the *Sugatas' Assembly Sadhana of the Guru's Heart*. They therefore combined the two termas and transcribed them without impediment. They also performed the terma accomplishment together. During it they were embraced by the compassion of Guru Rinpoche and Yeshe Tsogyal, and had numerous other pure visions. They received lists of many other termas and established many gates of auspicious interdependence.

Their mutual trust was so great that our lord guru received the nectar of the empowerments and instructions of Chokgyur

---

128. The year was 1855 C.E.

Lingpa's new termas. He acclaimed Chokgyur Lingpa as a great tertön, causing him to be accepted beyond dispute and to become as famous as the sun and the moon.

Chokgyur Lingpa wrote:

> From the beginning, four teachers have been very
> kind to me.

In writing this he was referring to the abbot from whom he received the outer pratimoksha, Taklung Ngawang Tenpe Nyima; the kalyanamitra from whom he received the inner vow of bodhichitta, Dabzang Rinpoche Karma Ngetön Tenpa Rapgye; his vajracharya of guhyamantra, me, Padma Garwang Lodrö Taye; and his ultimate root guru of the definitive meaning, Padma Ösal Dongak Lingpa.[129] There appear to have been valid reasons for these designations of the four of us.

Chokgyur Lingpa then went to the Yarkhyil hermitage, where he performed the approach and accomplishment of the *Very Profound Embodiment of the Three Jewels*. He then went on to Akanishtha Karma Monastery, where he remained in retreat for three years, as instructed by Guru Rinpoche. He was diligent throughout his life in all stages of meditation and perfected the practice of generation, completion, and the Great Perfection, manifesting countless signs of siddhi. He became, as I can attest on the basis of direct experience, a great lord and master of the four activities. Especially, from the prophecy from the *Three Classes of the Great Perfection*:

> Kama unbrokenly passed,
> Actual profound terma and that of mind,
> Terma rediscovered and recollected,
> Profound visions and whispered lineages:
> The rivers of these seven dispensations will flow
> To the monarchs, father and son, bringing
> A great harvest of dharma in a time of degeneracy.
> The sunlight of the profound and the vast will shine widely.

129. Padma Garwang Drodül Trinley Tsal was Jamgon Kongtrül's vajrayana name; Lodrö Taye was his bodhisattva name; Ngawang Yönten Gyamtso was his vinaya name; and Chime Tenyi Yungdrung Lingpa was his name as a tertön.

As described in that and many similar prophecies, the two great tertöns—our lord guru Jamyang Khyentse Wangpo, the emanation of King Trisong; and Chokgyur Lingpa, the emanation of Prince Murub—each received the seven dispensations that are subdivisions of the three categories of profound dharma: kama, terma, and pure visions.

Chokgyur Lingpa received most of the long lineages of kama—the first dispensation—that exist nowadays. He widely taught the *Mayajala*, the anuyogasutras, and the mind-class Great Perfection. In addition, because his profound termas contain dharma terminology identical to that found in those original texts, these termas constitute a wondrous and unprecedented renewal of the ancient kama tradition and are therefore in essence a dispensation of kama.

The second dispensation of Chokgyur Lingpa was the earth terma he revealed. In his thirteenth year he revealed the *Twenty-Four Sadhanas Practiced by Prince Murub* and scepters symbolic of the *Guru's Wisdom Assembly*—a vajra, a kapala, and a mirror—at White Rock Little Fortress. This was the first of his thirty-seven earth termas. He revealed the last of them in his thirty-ninth year: After receiving a terma guide and encouragement from our lord guru, Chokgyur Lingpa revealed the *Holy Dharma: The Seven Jewel Cycles*, an image of Guru Rinpoche, and the jewelry of Guru Lion's Roar from Tsike Three Brother Jewels. In addition to his thirty-seven earth termas, Chokgyur Lingpa also revealed the *Seven Cycles of Pacification* from Drakyangdzong.

Among these thirty-seven termas were many terma guides, prophetic instructions, quintessential instructions, heart instructions, and physical termas. The foremost among them were these: *The Sadhana of the Guru's Heart: Removing All Obstacles*, which Chokgyur Lingpa revealed at Danyin Kala Rongo; *Mahakarunika Padmoshnisha*, which he revealed at Nabun Dzong; the *Seven Profound Yidam Cycles*, which he revealed behind Akanishtha Karma Monastery; the *Tantra and Agama Supplements to the Seven Profound Yidam*

Cycles, the *Root Sadhana of the Guru's Heart: The Gathering of All Wisdom*, and two images of Guru Rinpoche, all of which he revealed at Yegyal Namkha Dzö; the *Holy Dharma: The Three Great Classes of the Great Perfection*, which he revealed at the Lotus Crystal Cave of Meshö Dzamnang; the *Holy Dharma of Six Folios*, which he revealed from the lower part of Great Lion Sky Rock; *Mahakarunika Padma Mayajala* and *Mahakarunika Who Empties Samsara to its Depths*, which he revealed at the Fortress of a Hundred Thousand Dakinis; the *Embodiment of All Matrikas*, which he revealed at Glorious Stone near Karma Monastery; the *Sadhana of the Guru's Mind: The Wish-Fulfilling Jewel*, which he revealed at Tsike Three Brother Jewels at the instruction of our lord guru; the *Eight Dispensations: The Assembly of All Sugatas* and the *Profound Great Perfection Like Refined Gold*, which he revealed at Yubal Rock in southern Yegyal; the *Sadhana of the Guru's Heart: Vajra Wrathful Might* and the *Five Essence Cycles*, which he revealed at the Tiger's Lair of Rongme Karmo; and *Chakrasamvara the Union of All Buddhas*, which he revealed at the Snowy Wilds of Rudam.

These are just examples, however; at each terma site Chokgyur Lingpa revealed dharma and many samaya substances, images, and scepters. Most of his revelations occurred in public, which caused him to be undisputed because of his many witnesses. It was prophesied that Chokgyur Lingpa would reveal a hundred sacred places of body, speech, mind, qualities and activity; a hundred cycles of the *Heart Essence*; and many substances that bestow liberation through taste. At Vira Hayagriva Rock he revealed the *Guide to the Twenty-Five Great Sacred Places*, and subsequently clarified the location of each of these along with their branch sites. He revealed three great images of Guru Rinpoche as terma; he had the second of these reproduced and widely distributed. His earth termas are inconceivably amazing.

The third dispensation of Chokgyur Lingpa was his rediscovery of reconcealed terma. This includes his revelation of the *Wrathful Guru: The Heart Essence of Red H̤UM*, which was originally a terma of the great tertön Sangye Lingpa, one of Chokgyur Lingpa's past lives. Chokgyur Lingpa received its dispensation through the power of blessing. He also received a short lineage of the dakini Kunga Bum's *Mother Tantra: Bringing the Secret onto the Path*. He bestowed its empowerments and instructions upon me.

Chokgyur Lingpa's fourth dispensation was his profound mind terma. Based on Arya Tara's triple pronouncement of "Excellent!" he revealed the *Profound Essence of Tara*.

His fifth dispensation was recollection, which is an extension of mind terma. Based on his recollection of his past life as Nup Khulungpa Yönten Gyamtso, Chokgyur Lingpa wrote down in concise form the *Anuyoga Vajra Array*, which had been the final instruction given by Nupchen Sangye Yeshe before his passing, and the *Boast of Nup*. He also recollected from that life the melody for chanting the RULU mantra and countless dance movements. Based on his recollection of his past life as Sangye Lingpa he wrote down *Detailed Instruction on the Nine Yogic Exercises of the Guru's Wisdom Assembly*.

Chokgyur Lingpa's sixth dispensation was pure vision. While he was revealing the sacred place Wangshu Mountain he saw the mahapandita Vimalamitra in Vimala's cave of accomplishment there. He wrote down the instructions he received from him as the *Profound Essence of Vimalamitra*.

His seventh dispensation was the whispered lineage, which is similar to pure vision teachings. In a vision he went to the Glorious Copper-Colored Mountain and received the *Profound Heart Essence of Ati* from Guru Rinpoche, which he subsequently wrote down.

This is just a summary of Chokgyur Lingpa's seven dispensations. Throughout his life he repeatedly saw the faces of deities of the three roots and received their prophecies. Dharmapalas and the protectors of terma constantly served him through their activity. In visions he visited the Glorious Copper-Colored Mountain on Chamaradvipa several times, and gave several descriptions of it based on these visits. However, this short summary is sufficient to indicate his greatness.

Including the Great Assembly Accomplishments he convened himself and those he presided over as vajra master at the invitation of others, Chokgyur Lingpa performed thirty-three Great Accomplishments with the complete four branches of approach, close approach, accomplishment, and great accomplishment.

He strongly compelled the obedience of spirits at critical sites throughout both central and eastern Tibet such as Samye and Mount Hepo. He performed many consecrations of sacred places and thereby prevented invasion and other disturbances. He actively and greatly increased the wellbeing of this entire land, as was prophesied.

Chokgyur Lingpa directly and indirectly bestowed the empowerments and instructions of his profound dharma on the lineage holders of many traditions. These included the Gyalwang Karmapa, the Drukchen Rinpoche, the heads of the Drikung and Talung schools, and their heart sons, among the Kagyu; the throne holders of Mindröling, Kathok, Palyül, Shechen, and Dzogchen Monasteries among the Nyingma; and lineage holders of the glorious Sakya tradition.

Chokgyur Lingpa's generosity with substances that liberate through taste pervaded every region of Tibet.

Because he established the necessary interdependence with most of his ten prophesied main dharma heirs, the activity of his terma dharma and especially that of the *Sadhana of the Guru's Heart: Removing All Obstacles* has been vast. As indicated by his establishment of the medium-length dance of the *Great Accomplishment of Perfect Heruka and Vajrakilaya* at Akanishtha Tsurphu Monastery, it appears that the celebration of the longer and shorter practices of his new termas is steadily growing in many monasteries.

Chokgyur Lingpa wrote out the *Dharma Cycle of Interdependence*, one of his *Ten Dharmas for the Wellbeing of*

All Tibet. He presided over the ritual celebration of the holy days of the abbot, master, and king taught in that cycle—a wondrous ceremony that causes the study, practice, and activity of the twofold dharma of sutra and tantra to increase—at the monasteries of Palpung, Kathok, and Dzogchen. At his main seats—Karma Mountain, Elder Ridge, and Tsike Junction—Chokgyur Lingpa built temples and furnished them with images. He established monastic communities and colleges for the study and practice of sutra and tantra at the latter two seats.

Having achieved so much, he considered the great needs of beings elsewhere, and appeared to become ill in his forty-second year, the Year of the Male Iron Horse.[130] He experienced pure visions foretelling his departure for an utterly pure Buddha realm. On the first day of the fifth month he displayed wondrous miracles, such as the earth shaking and rainbow light, and entered the peace of the dharmadhatu.

His main lineage holder, his son Gyurme Tsewang Drakpa, who was a prophesied emanation of Nup Namkhay Nyingpo, performed extensive funerary observances and offering ceremonies. He interred Chokgyur Lingpa's entire remains within a stupa of copper and gold that was one story in height. He completed the construction of one of his father's seats, Tsike Norbu Ling, which was uncompleted at the time of Chokgyur Lingpa's passing.

As I have mentioned above many holy beings, led by our precious lord guru, have spread the activity of Chokgyur Lingpa's profound dharma and of the substances that liberate through taste that he discovered. Since Chokgyur Lingpa also kindly bestowed his profound dharma on inferior persons such as me, I have done my best to serve his tradition through the performance of approach, accomplishment, and great accomplishment; through teaching; and through the composition of empowerment liturgies and so forth. When I visited central Tibet I first offered Chokgyur Lingpa's new termas to the fathers and sons of the Karma Kagyu and Drukpa Kagyu.

130. The year was 1870 C.E.

I performed accomplishment ceremonies at Crystal Cave, where I convened an amrita accomplishment assembly of the *Peaceful and Wrathful Mayajala*, and at every one of Guru Rinpoche's places of accomplishment, using one or another of Chokgyur Lingpa's *Seven Profound Yidam Cycles*. In each place I performed a thousand ganapujas. I have served his tradition a little, such as by being the first to make his name and termas known in Ngari, central Tibet, and Tsang.

On the fifteenth day of the month Mrigashira in the year of Chokgyur Lingpa's passing our lord guru, the great chakravartin among all the tertöns and siddhas of Tibet Padma Ösal Dongak Lingpa, had a pure vision. He saw Chokgyur Lingpa, who had taken the form of the bodhisattva Lotus Shoot in the western pure realm Covered by Lotuses. Our lord guru received from him his sadhana, his empowerment, and the nectar of his oral instructions. He kept these under the samaya-seal of secrecy for one month. Then, on the tenth day of the month Paushya he revealed them in conjunction with a ganapuja; I served as his scribe. The earth suddenly became warm, causing ice to melt and form streams. As I witnessed these good signs with my own eyes, I have seen real evidence of this sadhana's blessing.

This cycle of instructions, the *Trikaya Embodying All Families*, was given especially for the benefit of Chokgyur Lingpa's followers. It includes his final, posthumous instructions condensed into their essence. It is therefore very important for disciples of Chokgyur Lingpa's tradition to make it the essence of their practice. I mention this as a digression.

Chögyal Dorje

The vidyadhara Chögyal Dorje was an emanation of Prince Mutri Tsenpo. He was born in the nomad community of Gegyal in Dotö. He entered the dharma gate of the glorious Drukpa Kagyu, and received many teachings from the

Drukchen Rinpoche and other masters. In particular, Chögyal Dorje received profound instructions on the uncommon path of means from the realized lord among yogins Lhundrup Rapten, and perfected their practice.

For many years Chögyal Dorje one-pointedly practiced Yongey Mingyur Dorje's *Padmavajra*, living austerely at Nyen Fortress Vajra Garuda Cave. He recited the *Padmavajra* essence mantra seven hundred million times, and manifested signs of siddhi. It is said that even after he left that cave the clear sound of the mantra continued to be heard there by everyone for some time.

Chögyal Dorje received many prophecies of his discovery of profound terma. He once had a vision in which the Queen of Great Bliss extracted a vase containing terma parchment from the Vajra Garuda Cave's rock, showed him the parchment, and deciphered it for him. Once he had memorized the terma's contents, she replaced the vase in its prior place of concealment.

Chögyal Dorje later received a further terma scroll urging him to reveal the contents of the prior terma, as it was the right time to do so. He wrote down the terma as instructed; it is the especially profound cycle of the *Five Deity Mandala of the Blue Wrathful Guru*. He also revealed the root of this cycle as earth terma from the Black Stupa of Samye.

He received the *Prosperity Sadhana of the Five Deity Mandala of White Jambhala* as mind terma, and relics of Langdro the Translator and samaya substances called Sealed by AH as earth terma. His benefit of beings was so vast that the great tertön Chokgyur Lingpa, the great abbot Dabzang Rinpoche, and other eminent masters venerated him as one of their gurus.

Chögyal Dorje principally entrusted his terma dharma and other teachings to the king of siddhas Tsoknyi Rinpoche, who practiced them. I also received Chögyal Dorje's termas from Chögyal Dorje himself. His lineage is flourishing.

Padma Ösal Dongak Lingpa

Now I shall write of our lord guru Padma Ösal Dongak Lingpa, the great chakravartin among all the learned, all the attained, and all tertöns. His life has been greater in many ways, in this end-time of disputation, than any of those described above. I will base my brief account on his autobiography.

In essence, this lord is the compassionate embodiment of both Acharya Manjushrimitra and Mahapandita Vimalamitra. In the experience of various disciples he appeared in India as the mahasiddha Vajraghanta, the pandita Boundless Gates of Intelligence, and the mahapandita Forest Jewel. In Tibet he appeared as the dharma king Trisong Detsen, Guru Chökyi Wangchuk, Rechungpa Dorje Drakpa, the mahasiddha Thangtong Gyalpo, Lhatsün Namkha Jikme, and many other holy beings who upheld the Sarma and Nyingma dharma.

Based on this lord's recollections of his previous lives and on Prince Chokdrup Gyalpo's prophecy that he would take thirteen successive births as tertöns, the first of these was Sangye Lama and the twelfth Chöje Lingpa. Padma Ösal Dongak Lingpa is the thirteenth, as clearly indicated in vajra prophecies. It was predicted:

There will be five kings among tertöns;
They will be surrounded by a hundred subjects.

The fifth of the five prophesied kings was to be called Dongak Lingpa. Although it was said that this referred to Chokden Gönpo, he mistook interdependence and never acquired any terma; his deeds ended suddenly. It is therefore certain that the prophesied Dongak Lingpa, the fifth king among tertöns, is Padma Ösal Dongak Lingpa. There are valid proofs of this. In particular, it is evident that all of the recent authentic tertöns are or have been his subjects.

The place in which Padma Ösal Dongak Lingpa began the display of magical emanation in this life was predicted in the terma prophecies of Lord Nyang:

> In front of a mountain called Tsegang,
> On a boulder shaped like a coiled naga-king,
> Your majesty will appear with the name Manjughosha.[131]
> This thirteenth rebirth will reveal profound terma.

131. Manjughosha is Jamyang in Tibetan.

This was also clearly predicted in the terma prophecies of Rinchen Lingpa, Dorje Lingpa, the mahapandita of Ngari, Düdül Dorje, and other tertöns. In accordance with those prophecies, our lord guru was born in the town of Dilgo, which rests on a hill of rock shaped like a coiled snake, and is in front of a mountain called Tsegang in the kingdom of Derge in eastern Tibet.

Padma Ösal Dongak Lingpa's father was named Rinchen Wangyal. He was a high-ranking civil servant in the administration of the dharma king of Derge. His wisdom in both wordly and dharmic matters was exemplary. Our lord guru's mother was of the Gerap Nyerchen family of Mongolian origin; her name was Sönam Tso.

Padma Ösal Dongak Lingpa was born on the fourth day of the month Ashadha, the holy day of the Buddha's first turning of the dharmachakra, in the Male Metal Dragon year, while his family was staying in a white cotton tent at their summer pastures near Great Garuda Rock.[132] He was born with a full head of black hair, and several wondrous signs accompanied his birth. From the terma prophecy of Guru Tseten Gyaltsen:

132. The year was 1820 C.E.

> A tall boy born with a full head of hair
> Will appear at the foot of Great Garuda Mountain.

Padma Ösal Dongak Lingpa's birth fulfills this prophecy extremely well.

From the earliest age he can remember, our lord guru was lovingly cared for by the Six-Armed Wisdom Protector and by Ekajati, the protectress of mantra. He also had partial recollections of previous lives. From an early age his mahayana disposition was awakened. In particular, he was only interested in a lifestyle of renunciation. His intelligence and capacity for clear thinking were peerless, and he learned to read and write without difficulty. Just by reading a book once he retained both its words and its meaning.

In his twenty-first year he undertook completion in the presence of the abbot Rikdzin Zangpo of Mindröling Monastery. He generated bodhichitta by receiving the two traditions of the bodhisattva vow from the Sakya throne holder Dorje Rinchen and the Mindröling throne holder Gyurme Sangye Kunga. From the abbot of Tartse and that master's brother he received *Chakrasamvara* and *Hevajra*. From the throne holder of Mindröling he received the *Perfect Heruka of the So Tradition* and the *Heart Essence of the Vidyadharas*. From the omniscient Shechenpa Gyurme Tutop Namgyal he received the empowerment of the *Guhyagarbha Mayajala*. In that way he planted the roots of the vows of mantra.

Although Padma Ösal Dongak Lingpa is a recognized tulku and was born in a noble and powerful family, he has cast aside all privilege and pride of position and undertaken a life of great austerity. Through great effort he has managed to study with about one hundred and fifty teachers in both central and eastern Tibet. These include vajra holders, kalyanamitras, and those learned in the sciences. He has achieved a perfect mastery of the ten sciences, including the arts, medicine, linguistics, and logic; and of the treatises of the causal vehicle, including the *Vinaya*, the *Abhidharmakosha*, Madhyamika, and the *Abhisamayalankara* on the Prajnaparamita. He has received all of the ripening empowerments and liberating instructions of all of the Vajrayana traditions that still exist, including those of the Nyingma lineages of kama and of terma; of the Kadampa and Gelukpa traditions;

of the Sakya tradition, and of its Ngorpa and Tsarpa branches; of the Karma, Drikung, Taklung, and Drukpa Kagyu; and of the Jonang, Shalpa, and Bodong traditions.

Padma Ösal Dongak Lingpa has studied all of the existing exegetic traditions of the *Mayajala Guhyagarbhatantra*, the *Kalachakratantra*, the *Chakrasamvaratantra*, the *Hevajratantra*, the *Guhyasamajatantra*, and the shastras based on those tantras. He has received the reading transmissions for about seven hundred volumes, including the precious *Translated Words of the Buddha*, the *Collected Nyingma Tantras*, the parts of the *Translated Shastras* for which the transmission exists, and the Tibetan shastras of all traditions. For thirteen years he devoted himself exclusively to study, and learned most of the traditions of those renowned as the *Ten Great Columns Who Have Supported the Lineage of Explanation*.[133]

Although our lord guru understands and retains the meaning of every book he reads just by reading it, he has never limited his study of anything to just receiving it. In order to demonstrate the great importance he places on dharma, he has cultivated a perfect understanding of and familiarity with every tradition. He knows, with the flawless eye of dharma and in precise detail, the view, conduct, assertions, and customs of each tradition, as well as whether or not each is true to its origin. It seems that there is no one presently living, high or lowly, who has equaled him in even this.

Padma Ösal Dongak Lingpa has repeatedly taught most of the sutras, tantras, and shastras he has received; and has also conferred the corresponding empowerments, transmissions, and practical instructions. There is nothing that he has received that he has not taught at least once. Through his generosity of dharma free from any hope for acquisition, he has fulfilled the hopes of seekers including both holy beings and lowly beggars.

From childhood he has never engaged in the perverted practice of performing ceremonies in villages for gain and call-

133. The Ten Great Columns Who Have Supported the Lineage of Explanation are Tönmi Sambhota, Vairochana, Kawa Paltsek, Chokro Lu'i Gyaltsen, Shang Yeshe De, Rinchen Zangpo, Dromtön Gyalway Jungne, Ngok Loden Sherap, Sakya Pandita, and Gö Khukpa Lhetse.

ing it "the benefit of disciples." Nevertheless, his inner qualities have manifested externally as the three blazes and the three gatherings, and he has always acquired whatever he needs without effort. He has never wasted any of his acquisitions on inappropriate expenditures. He has used them to sponsor about two thousand supports of body cast from copper and gold; almost forty printed volumes, and about two thousand volumes if we include both printed and handwritten books, as supports of speech; and supports of mind such as the great Lhundrupteng Stupa as well as more than a hundred others, all cast of copper and gold. He has built thirteen finely decorated temples to house these supports of body, speech, and mind; and supports both the continuous and periodic presentation of offerings within them.

Given the times in which we live, it is difficult to found new sangha communities. He has therefore not troubled to do so. Nevertheless, when most monasteries were damaged during the recent fighting between eastern and western kingdoms, our lord guru made contributions to their restoration appropriate to the size of each monastery, and has sponsored three thousand tea services. He has engaged in diplomacy, creating harmony among the rulers of Tibet and China, as well as the dharma king of Derge and his cabinet. This significant action has brought about both restoration and new foundations. He has contributed to offerings and kindly given useful and timely advice to many. He has offered the funds for four thousand tea services in connection with his sponsorship of yearly dharani, mantra, and aspiration festivals at each of our large and small sangha communities.

Because of the stability of his twofold precious bodhichitta; and because he has only a pure attitude toward and devotion for every tradition, without a single negative thought, his disciples from every tradition are countless. They include the great and famous lineage holders of the Sakya, Kagyu, Nyingma, and Geluk schools; kalyanamitras, retreatants, and modest practitioners from those schools; and adherents of the

Bön tradition. Every single day he bestows dharma, according to their individual wishes, upon innumerable disciples who gather before him, including both Chinese and Tibetan leaders. It seems there is no one who has not formed a connection with him either through his removal of their adversity or bestowal of empowerment or blessing.

As Padma Ösal Dongak Lingpa is free from the bondage of the eight worldly concerns, he has eradicated all human frailties such as trying to ingratiate himself with others, high or low; and hope and fear about others' opinions. His life has therefore been that of a king among renunciates. He has spent about thirteen years of his life engaged in the approach and accomplishment of many yidams of the Sarma and Nyingma tantras. He has practiced each of the profound instructions he has received, such as the *Hundred Instructions* of Jetsün Kunga Drölchok. He is therefore also peerless in his fulfillment of samaya and commitments.

All of the above has been a brief summary of Padma Ösal Dongak Lingpa's outer life, concerning his engagement in the three wheels of study, meditation, and work.

The renowned Eight Chariots of the Practice Lineage of Tibet are: the Nyingma tradition of the early translations, which arose through the kindness of the abbot Shantarakshita, the master Padmasambhava, and the king Trisong Detsen; the Kadampa tradition endowed with seven deities and dharmas, which is the tradition of the glorious lord Atisha; the *Path and Result*, the quintessential teaching of the mahasiddha Virupa, instructions passed down through the fathers and sons of the glorious Sakya tradition; the instructions of the Four Dispensations of Tilopa, passed down by Marpa, Mila, Gampopa, and the four great and eight lesser divisions of the Dakpo Kagyu; the glorious Shangpa Kagyu, which holds the Golden Dharmas of the learned and accomplished Khyungpo the Yogin; the Six-Branch Yoga, the vajrayoga of the completion stage of *Shrikalachakra*, the king among all tantras; the *Holy Dharma of the Pacification of Suffering,* the teachings of the mahasiddha Padmapa Sangye, along with its offshoot, *Severance*; and the *Approach and Accomplishment of the Three Vajras*, which was directly bestowed by Vajrayogini upon the mahasiddha Ugyenpa.

Padma Ösal Dongak Lingpa, with boundless devotion, intense diligence, and a complete lack of concern for his own exhaustion, has received the complete and correct empowerments and instructions of each of these traditions from masters who held their unbroken and original lineages. He has clarified his understanding of them through analytical thinking and put them into practice through meditation. While doing so he has in reality, experience, and dreams received the blessings of the bodies, speech, and minds of learned masters and siddhas of India and Tibet, of peaceful and wrathful yidams, and of the dakinis of the three places. They have bestowed upon him their instructions as short lineages. To write that at every instant he experiences boundless pure visions is an understatement. Although he never speaks of his pure visions, supercognitions, and superhuman qualities, we can infer them from the above.

In particular, because of his full understanding of the two stages as practiced by each of the Eight Chariots, his abilities in teaching, debate, and composition are unlimited. Being free from even a trace of delusion, he cares for fortunate disciples. That is an account, as tiny as a seed, of his inner life.

Especially, from the *Vajra Prophecies* of the mahasiddha Thangtong Gyalpo:

> A yogin not other than me
> With five attributes
> Will appear seven hundred years from now
> In a Dragon year in eastern Tibet.
> A vidyadhara of the Nyö clan, a child of Ga,
> His element will be metal; he will bear the marks of a vira.

Blessed by Padmaraja,
He will be called Dongak Lingpa of the Seven Dispensations.
Blessed by Vimalamitra,
He will be called Ösal Trülpe Dorje.
Blessed by Manjushri's emanation, the dharma king,
He will be called Dharmamitra.
This magical man will appear.

As predicted in the prophecy from the *Three Classes of the Great Perfection* that I quoted in my account of Chokgyur Lingpa's life, and as repeatedly proclaimed in many vajra prophecies, Padma Ösal Dongak Lingpa gained full possession of the seven dispensations and has greatly helped beings and the teachings.

In his eighth year Padma Ösal Dongak Lingpa became extremely ill and was tormented by a great deal of pain. Guru Rinpoche and Yeshe Tsogyal appeared to him, blessed him, empowered him in the mandala of Vajrakilaya, and instructed him. He overcame the obstacle to his health.

In his fifteenth year, in a pure vision, Padma Ösal Dongak Lingpa went to Vajrasana in India. Coming to a cave with nine levels, he entered the bottom level and gradually climbed up through the others. On the eighth level he encountered the master Manjushrimitra, who was dressed as a pandita. Many books were piled up on Manjushrimitra's left and right. Padma Ösal Dongak Lingpa prostrated with great devotion and supplicated. In response Manjushrimitra took up a book that had been to his left and showed it to Padma Ösal Dongak Lingpa, who saw that it was the *Collection of the Prajnaparamita* in Sanskrit. Manjushrimitra, placing the book on Padma Ösal Dongak Lingpa's head and directing his attention to him, said, "By this you have received the complete transmission of all dharma of the causal vehicle."

Manjushrimitra then picked up a book that had been to his right and showed it to Padma Ösal Dongak Lingpa, who saw that it was the Great Perfection Tantra called the *Mirror of Vajrasattva's Heart*. Manjushrimitra, placing this book on Padma Ösal Dongak Lingpa's head and directing his attention to him, said, "By this you have received the complete blessing of both the words and meaning of all the vajrayana, and especially of the three classes of the Great Perfection."

He bestowed a few prophecies on Padma Ösal Dongak Lingpa and then, with a joyous demeanor, melted into light and dissolved into our lord guru, who became absorbed for a time in samadhi free of thought. When Padma Ösal Dongak Lingpa arose from that samadhi and was leaving the cave he discovered that a great fire was burning immediately outside the cave's doorway. Having no choice but to pass through the fire, he entered it. His coarse body was incinerated, leaving him with a resplendent body of light that he felt was that of Vimalamitra.

Around the same time Padma Ösal Dongak Lingpa saw the face of the lord of siddhas Thangtong Gyalpo in a dream and received his blessing. The mahasiddha gave our lord guru both instructions and advice, of which he only wrote out a *Gurusadhana* at that time. Later, once the command seal of secrecy expired, Padma Ösal Dongak Lingpa gradually wrote out the rest of Thangtong Gyalpo's instructions. They include the *Root Verses of the Six Completion Stages*, the *Five Sadhana Cycles*, and the *Heruka Assembly of All Sugatas*. All together, they comprise the *Heart Essence of the Siddha*.

Padma Ösal Dongak Lingpa also saw the face of the Buddha Amitayus and his consort and received their blessing. Special sadhanas arose from this, although he only committed the *Sadhana of Chandali the Mother of Life* to writing.

In these ways he has had innumerable pure visions of all of the deities of the three roots, but is so careful to keep them secret that others have known nothing about them. In particular, while it seems that he has received many prophecies throughout the years, he described his attitude toward them when he said, "The saying 'tertöns are ruined by prophecies' is true. Once you write something down and call it a prophecy you have to follow its instructions. No one does that, and therefore the prophecies are never fulfilled. Talking too much is how Mara enters your speech!" He therefore doesn't give out prophecies, and does not take pleasure in the prophecies of others. There appears to be great significance to this.

In a pure vision that occurred in the early morning of the tenth day of the month Vaishakha in his sixteenth year Padma Ösal Dongak Lingpa visited Lotus Light in Chamaradvipa. He saw a massive mountain of rock with extremely beautiful clouds on its peak. Within the clouds was Guru Rinpoche, the Lake-Born Vajra, surrounded by a gathering of dakinis. Guru Rinpoche blessed Padma Ösal Dongak Lingpa by directing his attention to him and bestowed empowerment through symbols. After assuring Padma Ösal Dongak Lingpa, in great detail, of his future possession of the seven dispensations Guru Rinpoche engaged in the gaze of meditation and said this:

Unstained by apprehended objects,
Unsullied by thoughts of an apprehender,
Sustaining naked awareness-emptiness
Is the wisdom of all Buddhas.

After saying that, Guru Rinpoche and his entourage dissolved into Padma Ösal Dongak Lingpa. He experienced the mixing of Guru Rinpoche's mind and his own. Since then his realization of the primordially pure nature of things has been stable.

Delighted by this experience, Padma Ösal Dongak Lingpa supplicated Guru Rinpoche one-pointedly. His prayer enabled him to effortlessly obtain not only the well-known lineages, but even extremely rare ones, of the dharma of sutra and tantra, Sarma and Nyingma, kama and terma. He received their empowerments, instructions, and transmissions. He has practiced them and taught them. By doing so, he has revived the dying fire of the teachings. That is his first dispensation.

Padma Ösal Dongak Lingpa's second dispensation is earth terma. In his twentieth year, while he was visiting Red Rock

Fine Throat, a wisdom dakini directly gave him the terma coffer containing the *Mahakarunika the Mind Itself at Rest* cycle and the relics of twenty-one brahmins. At Damshö Heart the great nyen Thanglha extracted the *Sadhanas of the Four Kayas of the Guru* and shariram produced from one of Guru Rinpoche's teeth, and offered these to Padma Ösal Dongak Lingpa. At Siduk Turquoise Lake Padma Ösal Dongak Lingpa revealed the *Mayajala of the Three Roots*. At Terma Valley Lotus Crystal Rock dakinis miraculously extracted the *Embodiment of the Three Roots* and offered it to him. He has revealed many other earth termas, but has transcribed few of them aside from the fundamental texts of some. At the encouragement of Chokgyur Lingpa, Padma Ösal Dongak Lingpa revealed the *Sadhana of the Guru's Heart: The Wish-Fulfilling Jewel* and the image of Guru Rinpoche called Glorious Blaze of Siddhi at Tsike Three Brother Jewels, and completely transcribed that cycle. The *Four Gurusadhana Cycles*, the *Heart Essence of Vairochana*, the *Three Classes of the Great Perfection*, and other termas appear to have been revealed by Padma Ösal Dongak Lingpa and Chokgyur Lingpa in common.

Padma Ösal Dongak Lingpa's third dispensation is rediscovered terma, which is an extension of earth terma. In the Earth Sheep year, Guru Rinpoche appeared to him in the form of the great tertön Sangye Lingpa, gave him a book, and blessed him.[134] This extraordinary vision opened the door to Padma Ösal Dongak Lingpa's receiving the dispensation of all previous terma. He became clearly aware of the lives of all past tertöns and of the extent and contents of their termas. In most cases wisdom dakinis have extracted and offered him the parchments reconcealed by each tertön in the past. He has then deciphered and transcribed them. In some cases the symbol script has appeared to his eyes. In some cases the past terma has effortlessly appeared within his mind. In these cases too, he has transcribed them.

Guru Rinpoche has appeared to Padma Ösal Dongak

134. The year was 1859 C.E.

Lingpa on the occasion of each rediscovery, either as Guru Padma himself or as the particular tertön whose terma has been rediscovered, and bestowed the ripening empowerments and liberating instructions together. This is amazing! Even though the time and place in which we live are extremely degenerate, we have the very good fortune to receive and practice this profound dharma! Knowing that the rediscovery of even a single lost terma of the past is more wondrous than anything else, I have repeatedly supplicated Padma Ösal Dongak Lingpa with great enthusiasm. In response, he has revealed Sangye Lama's *Combined Sadhana of the Three Roots*, Gya the Translator's *Gurusadhanas of the Two Doctrines and Three Cycles*, Nyima Senge's *Mahakarunika the Peaceful and Wrathful Lotus*, Rongzom the Translator's *Dakini Who Dispels Ignorance*, Ugyen Lingpa's *Ocean of Dharma: The Assembly of Dispensations*, Jomo Menmo's *Secrets of All Dakinis*, Ramo Shelmen's *Vajramrita*, Drime Kunga's *Gurusadhana* and *Mahakarunika Jinasagara*, Gyatön Padma Wangchuk's *Guru Chakrasamvara*, Lhatsün Ngönmo's *Seven Cycles of Pacification*, Ah Hum the Nepali's *Yaksha Jambhala: Piled Jewels*, mantradharin Letro Lingpa's *Red Padma Shavari*, Prince Mekhyil's *Hayagriva the Wheel of Meteoric Iron*, Yakchar Ngönmo's *Green Tara Who Protects from All Dangers*, Shakya Ö's *Vajra Fire the Lord of Secrets*, Bönpo Draktsal's *Amitayus and Guru Rinpoche Combined*, Samten Dechen Lingpa's *Eight Dispensations: Conquering the Aggressive*, Chokden Gönpo's *Five Fierce Deities*, Mingyur Letro Lingpa's *Fierce Padma*, Garwang Letro Lingpa's *White Varahi the Illuminator of Wisdom*, and other cycles. He has kindly bestowed their combined ripening empowerments and liberating instructions upon me.

In response to my supplications, Padma Ösal Dongak Lingpa has also kindly and happily bestowed upon me the empowerments and instructions of other lost past termas including Nyangral's *Guru Lake-Born Vajra* and the long empowerment of his *Mahakarunika the Tamer of*

Beings; the empowerment of Rashak's *Mamo Gangshar*; Jangchup Lingpa's *Terma of Samantabhadra's Heart*; Drugu Yangwang's *Hayagriva: Liberating All the Aggressive*; Dorje Lingpa's *Gurusadhana, Great Perfection*, and *Mahakarunika*; Rinchen Lingpa's *Great Perfection: Instant Liberation of All*; Drodül Letro Lingpa's *Mahakarunika: Torch Illuminating the Truth* and its dharmapala cycle; Wönse Khyungtok's *Wisdom Life-Essence Ayusadhana*; Rokje Lingpa's *Wondrous Secret Ayusadhana*, and others.

It appears that Padma Ösal Dongak Lingpa has received many other rediscovered termas and short lineages that remain to be transcribed.

His fourth dispensation is profound mind terma. In his twenty-ninth year, the Year of the Earth Monkey, he traveled through the nomad plateau on his way to central Tibet.[135] At Gegyal he performed a tenth-day ganachakra, during which he saw Guru Rinpoche's face and received his blessing. Padma Ösal Dongak Lingpa continued his journey and eventually reached Samye. While he was presenting offerings before the image of Guru Lake-Born Vajra there (a terma of Nyangral Nyima Özer), the image was transformed into the actual Guru Lake-Born Vajra, who blessed him and bestowed instructions upon him. Based on those instructions Padma Ösal Dongak Lingpa revealed the *Heart Essence of the Lake-Born Guru*, which is the secret sadhana among his three gurusadhana cycles.

In the month Paushya of his thirty-fifth year, the Year of the Wood Tiger, while Padma Ösal Dongak Lingpa was performing the approach and accomplishment of White Tara, the Immortal Wish-Fulfilling Wheel, he saw Arya Tara's face and heard the sound of her ten-syllable mantra.[136] She blessed him, and he was subsequently also blessed by three masters who had accomplished immortality.[137] Based on this he revealed the *Heart Essence of Immortal Arya Tara*.

I have already related the origin of the *Heart Essence of the Siddha*.

---

135. The year was 1848 C.E.

136. The year was 1854 C.E.

137. These were Guru Rinpoche, Vimalamitra, and Shilamanju.

All of Padma Ösal Dongak Lingpa's mind termas fully deserve their classification as such. Their vajra words are indistinguishable from those of the tantras. They surpass the conceptual mind of any ordinary person.

Padma Ösal Dongak Lingpa's fifth dispensation is recollection, which is an extension of mind terma. While he was traveling through central Tibet and visiting the lower valley of Uyuk in Tsang, he clearly recollected the location and events surrounding Chetsün Senge Wangchuk's departure in a body of light. He revealed, on the basis of that recollection, the *Heart Essence of Chetsün*.

Through the recollection of his past life as Langdro Könchok Jungne, Padma Ösal Dongak Lingpa revealed the *Heart Essence of Vairochana Ayusadhana*, the *Rasayana of White Singhamukha*, and other cycles.

His sixth dispensation is pure vision. This includes the *Sadhana of Chandali the Mother of Life* that I mentioned earlier; it is part of his *Immortal Heart Essence*. Also in this category are his writings concerning the *Bindu-Sealed Gurusadhana* from the *Heart Essence of the Vast Expanse* and his *Trikaya Embodying All Families* gurusadhana of Chokgyur Lingpa. There is undoubtedly much more, but this seems to be about all that he has disseminated.

Padma Ösal Dongak Lingpa's seventh dispensation is whispered lineages, which are similar to visionary teachings. While he was residing at the sacred place Dzongshö Sugatas' Assembly, he traveled in a pure vision to the Delightful Edifice Stupa. In the four directions and four corners surrounding the stupa were the Eight Names of Guru Rinpoche, with the Guru Rinpoche embodying all of them in the center. These nine forms of Guru Rinpoche bestowed upon him the whispered lineages' quintessential empowerments and instructions of the Eight Dispensations and the Peaceful and Wrathful Mayajala. Of these he has disseminated the *Whispered Lineage Yamantaka*, *Perfect Heruka*, and *Vajrakilaya*; I have received them through his kindness.

That is a brief account of his secret life. More extensive accounts can be found in his termas, each of which contains prophecies, exhortations, guides, and other indications of the source of its dispensation; and detailed accounts by him of how he revealed the terma, what visions he had while practicing it, how he received its empowerments and instructions, and how long he kept it secret until the time of its dissemination to the fortunate had certainly come. As I am in the midst of supplicating him to write an extensive autobiography describing all his revelations, I will write only this much here.

I pray that his life remain stable and lasting in these degenerate times, and that he continue to protect beings and the teachings for more than a hundred years!

Padma Ösal Dongak Lingpa has told me that while engaged in the *Gurusadhana of Vimalamitra* he received a prophecy that at the end of his life he will dissolve into the heart of Vimalamitra on Five Peak Mountain, that five emanations of him will appear, and that they will accomplish great good for the teachings of many traditions.[138]

138. Of the five predicted, the best known are Dilgo Khyentse Rinpoche and Dzongsar Khyentse Rinpoche.

Other Revealers of Earth Terma

That completes my account of those revealers of earth terma, starting from the past and continuing up to the present day, whose order of appearance is certain. There are, however, others mentioned in older accounts of terma, although the order of their appearance is uncertain. I will now summarize their deeds.

The tertön Daben Ziji Bar revealed the *Heart Mirror of Forceful Mantra*, a fragmentary tantra of eleven chapters extracted from the *Black Guhyachandra Gathering of Life Tantra*; and the *Jewel Torch: A Key to Forceful Mantra*, written by the master Tsuklak Palge, from White Rock Vajra Peak. I do not know what other termas he revealed. His lineage seems not to exist.

Rokben Sherap Ö is said to have revealed a *Sadhana of the Fifty-Eight Deity Mandala of Perfect Heruka*, a *Sadhana of the Nine Lamps of Perfect Heruka*, and many other termas.

Drom Chökyi Nyingpo was born in Tsangrong. He revealed teachings on the mind class of the Great Perfection as well as the intermediate *Heart Essence of Vimalamitra* of the instruction class and the *Turquoise Tree: The Various Profound Vehicles and Systems* from a place called Purna Heart Mountain. He revealed the *Great Collection of Forceful Mantra* from Yerpa.

Özer Tönpa revealed *Averting Warfare by Means of the Protector Trakshe* and other termas.

Menyak Drakjung revealed *Profound Protection from Lightning* from the Menyak Temple.

Padma Wangyal revealed the *Sadhana of Vajrasadhu with a Spear*, an extraordinarily profound way of bringing miraculous manifestations upon enemies, from the same site. Its lineage survived until fairly recently.

It is said that the tertön Dawa Dorje revealed a few profound termas.

Nyangtön Sherap Drakpa of Tsang revealed the *Profound Means of Entrustment to Rahula* from the Narrow Rakshasa Cave at Kujuk Bumthang.

Tsangtön Chöbar revealed especially profound means of protection from hail in reliance upon a blue stupa.

Khampa Mezor revealed instructions on the protection of livestock from illness from Gyawo Rock in Tsang.

The mantradharin Wangchen Zangpo revealed the *Black Puri Entrustment to Rahula* cycle from the capital of a pillar in the northern Traduntse Temple.

Sarpo Jaugön revealed the *Black Razor of Life* cycle from the genitals of an image of wrathful Hayagriva in the Place of Virtue Temple in Bumthang. He gave it to Lhatsün Jamyang Rinchen.

Kyebu Zangling Wangchuk revealed the *Manjushri Yamantaka Activity of Entrustment and Ruination* cycle that has become so widespread.

Senge the Hermit of Yangbön revealed the *Victor's Words: Prajnaparamita* of exceptional magical power from the Khothing Temple of Lhodrak. It seems that writings on it by Jangdak Tashi Topgyal and Padma Trinley still exist.

Changmön Döndrup Dargye revealed the *Tarima* cycle on protection from poison from Arrow Feather Black Rock in lower Nyal. Several physicians have written about it.

Gö Padma revealed a *Devi Budzima Cycle*, a divination cycle, and others. I've wondered if his Budzima cycle might not have been identical to the terma revealed by Dorje Lingpa, the lineage of which still exists.

Rangjung Yeshe revealed the *Rasayana of Ever-Crying Bodhisattva* and many other applications of the sutras from Lhodrak Kharchu.

Seben Nyimai Nyingpo revealed the *Planetary Instruction Sealed by Command* and a few other writings on the planets and protection.

Kunga Zangpo of Lhodrak revealed the *Five Heart-Essence Cycles* from Shang Zabulung.

Khampa Drukgom Shikpo revealed a *Black Hayagriva Cycle* as terma. It is said that his descendants are still living in the Nangchen region.

Lhasumza Jangchup Palmo, who appears in the lineage of the Drikung *Yamantaka of Molten Metal*, was born in the Sokrong area and benefited beings among the Mongolians. It is said that she revealed a *Sadhana of the Goddess Who Rides a Wolf* and a few other termas. However, because of circumstances beyond her control she was unable to benefit others much by means of her termas. According to the writings of Taksham Nüden Dorje she went to Kongpo in her later life, and also to Powo, where she lived in a cave that he identified. She was skilled in direct action and especially in the *Yamantaka of Molten Metal*. There are many stories of the clear signs of her mastery of forceful mantra.

A tertön called Mahavajra appeared in Nakshö. It appears

that he revealed a *Guide to the Sacred Sites at Rakshasi Fortress* and an actual vajra made of meteoric iron as terma. It is said that he also revealed a few other dharma termas and substance termas, but that he passed away prematurely because he let the time for the revelation of a terma pass by. The vidyadhara Jatsön Nyingpo identified him as one of his previous lives.

Section Two
Mind Terma

I will now briefly recount the emergence of profound teachings revealed through pure visions and as mind terma. One of the aspirations made by bodhisattvas is:

> May beings unceasingly hear
> The sound of dharma
> From birds, trees, rays of light,
> And from the sky.

It is taught that because of such powerful aspirations and because the bodhisattvas who make them possess the causes of hearing dharma, they unceasingly hear the sound of dharma within the sounds of the elements and the sounds made by birds and animals. Buddhas and other bodhisattvas reveal their faces to them and teach them dharma. From the *Sutra on the Samadhi that Gathers All Merit*:

> Stainless Magnificence, bodhisattva mahasattvas with an excellent motivation and great devotion who desire dharma will see the faces of Bhagavan Buddhas and hear their dharma even if they are living in a different world.

Especially, in the perception of great bodhisattvas all appearances are pure; there are no impure appearances. They are therefore continuously engaged in a wondrous dharmic dialogue with countless deities of the three roots, and innumerable profound instructions arise from this. They then disseminate these instructions to fortunate disciples in ways appropriate to the interests of each. This is how all of the dharma that has arisen from pure visions and that has been brought into the realm of common experience has appeared. This is described in the biographies of the panditas and siddhas of India and the great kalyanamitras and tertöns of the Sarma and Nyingma traditions in Tibet. Similarly, the dharma called Mind Terma is spoken of in the sutras:

> Manjushri, the four elements arise as treasures of space.
> In the same way, all dharma arises as the treasure of the Buddhas' minds. Learn how to find this treasure!

Accordingly, it is taught that the treasure of dharma bursts forth from within the expanse of aryas' minds. From the *Sutra of the Perfect Gathering of All Dharma*:

> All instructions arise from the wish for them that
> is present within the minds of bodhisattvas with
> pure intentions.

From another sutra:

> If the meaning is confidently ascertained,
> Hundreds of thousands of dharma treasures will burst
> forth from the mind.

Accordingly, in India, Nepal, and Tibet great learned siddhas have given us countless profound instructions that have arisen within their minds. This continues in our present day. Here I will write of those well-known revealers of such teachings who have appeared in Tibet and have been connected to the Nyingma tradition of vajrayana. I will order my account of them sequentially, the first of them being the bodhisattva

Dawa Gyaltsen, who was a contemporary of Bari the Translator and Jetsün Milarepa.

Dawa Gyaltsen

The bodhisattva Dawa Gyaltsen was Avalokita in person, and is very well-known. He received the Dawa Gyaltsen tradition of Hayagriva, known as the *Fire of Time*, from Guru Rinpoche directly. Its sadhana, blessing ceremony, and applications all bear great blessing. Their lineage still exists; I have received it and placed it in the *Treasury of Precious Terma*.

Rechungpa

Rechung Dorje Drakpa was the moonlike heart-son of Jetsün Milarepa. While he was visiting India he received from the Mother Queen of Siddhas, who was in nature identical to Guru Rinpoche's consort Mandarava, what are now known as the *Three Dharmas of Rechungpa*. They are the accomplishment of longevity in reliance upon Amitayus, the accomplishment of the supreme siddhi in reliance upon Mahakarunika, and the removal of obstacles in reliance upon Shrihayagriva.

Of the three, the *Five Deity Mandala of Mahakarunika Jinasagara* was received by the Queen of Siddhas from Guru Rinpoche. She gave it to Rechungpa, who gave it to the guru Zangri Repa, who gave it to Drogön Rechen, who gave it to the bodhisattva Pomdrakpa, from whom its dispensation was received by the mahasiddha Karma Pakshi. It has passed down through the Karma Kagyu without impairment to the present day, and is greatly treasured as especially profound dharma. It must be considered visionary dharma, because although Jetsün Rechungpa met the Queen of Siddhas she was not seen by most people.

Shakyashri

The Kashmiri mahapandita Shakyashri, who is famous throughout the world, was an emanation of the future Buddha Utterly Brilliant. He had four special dharmas that he particularly treasured. One of these was the *Sadhana of Perfect Heruka Using a Single Flame and a Single Skull*, which gave one the ability to wear only a cotton robe in the coldest weather. Shakyashri had received this from Guru Rinpoche directly.

Shakyashri wrote down its instructions as a wonderful, concise text that was translated by the translator Rapchokpal and Shakyashri together. The original lineage of its ripening empowerments and liberating instructions did not survive down to the present day, but our lord guru received them from Chal the Translator in a dream. I have received this short lineage of blessing.

Yutok Yönten Gönpo

Yutok Yönten Gönpo was a second Bhaishajyaguru. He was blessed by the leader of dakinis Shrimala Mandarava. Based on that, Yutok Yönten Gönpo revealed the *Heart Essence of Yutok* as profound mind terma. This great tradition is famous throughout Tibet.

The lotuslike marks and signs of the nirmanakaya Yutok Yönten Gönpo bloomed amidst wondrous miracles at Goshi Rethang in the upper valley of Nyangtong Gyaltse. His father was Khyungpo Dorje, a son of Dreje Vajra. Yutok Yönten Gönpo's mother was Padma Öden.

Immediately after his birth Yutok Yönten Gönpo began to recite the Bhaishajyaguru dharani and gazed with open eyes upon his mother. In his third year his propensity for medicine was awakened. In his eighth year knowledge of the five sciences and medicine burst forth from within him. Especially, in his fourteenth year he received empowerment from the goddess of medicine in a dream. She prophesied the appearance of the *Four Medicinal Tantras*, which later appeared as she predicted.

In his eighteenth year Yutok went to India and met the dakini Shrimala, who bestowed upon him both common and special instructions. In all he visited India six times and imbibed the amrita of the teachings of many learned siddhas. He overcame an attack by tirthikas and displayed a boundless array of magical appearances, causing a king and others to venerate him with faith.

Yutok's main Tibetan heart-son was Sumtön Jnanadhara, who supplicated Yutok with great austerity and effort. In response, Yutok bestowed upon Sumtön the complete ripening empowerments and liberating instructions of his *Heart Essence* at Kyirong in Mangyül. Sumtön achieved both common and supreme siddhi, and this tradition with its magnificent blessings has passed down from him to the present day. I have through great effort managed to receive it twice, and have served it through the composition of a clear and concise practice liturgy, empowerment liturgy, and approach manual.

The supreme siddha Yutok did immeasurable good for beings and the teachings through his amazing deeds. Finally, in his seventy-sixth year, he departed for the realm of Akshobhya Bhaishajyaguru without leaving his body behind, amidst an array of pure appearances beyond imagination.

Kyergangpa

Wöntön Kyergang Chökyi Senge is well-known as the fifth of the Seven Jewels of the glorious Shangpa Kagyu. He was an emanation of Mahakarunika. In a lucid dream he traveled to the Glorious Copper-Colored Mountain and asked Guru Rinpoche for instructions on how to conquer the demon kings and succubi who cause so much harm to Tibet.

In response Guru Rinpoche arose in the form of Shrihayagriva and bestowed upon Kyergangpa the complete empowerment and instructions of the *Secret Sadhana of Hayagriva*. He also told Kyergangpa, "A mantrin with karma in Nyemo has revealed this as terma. Receive it from him as well."

Accordingly Kyergangpa went to Gya Gangri and received this sadhana from Sangye Wangchen based on his terma text. This lineage therefore combines kama and terma. As Kyergangpa used this practice to cure about eighty people of insanity caused by the demon king Karchung and others, it is famous for its great blessing and has spread throughout all the Sarma and Nyingma lineages. The magnificence of its blessing has remained unbroken down to the present day.

Rangjung Dorje

Rangjung Dorje, Lokeshvara in person, was the Third Karmapa and an emanation of Simha, the sixth Buddha of this fortunate kalpa. The story of his life is well-known. In particular, the way in which he received the dispensation of pure vision is this:

While Rangjung Dorje was meditating in a hermitage at Akanishtha Karma Monastery, the terrestrial wheel of speech, nowadays often called Karma Mountain, the pandita Vimalamitra appeared in the eastern sky and dissolved into Rangjung Dorje's forehead. This caused all of the words and meaning of the great *Heart Essence of Vimalamitra* to arise within his mind. He wrote down the vajra words of its root instructions and also composed complete texts for its ripening empowerments and liberating instructions. Its lineage still exists, and I have received it.

Through the blessing of Guru Rinpoche, Rangjung Dorje revealed the profound cycle of the *Combined Sadhana of the Three Roots* as mind terma. Later, the Eighth Gyalwang

Karmapa Mikyö Dorje practiced it and received its short lineage through pure vision. He composed both an account of this and a versified root text. The Ninth Gyalwang Karmapa Wangchuk Dorje composed an activity liturgy and long empowerment liturgy for this cycle, and it was on the basis of these that I received it through the kindness of the glorious Fourteenth Gyalwang Karmapa Tekchok Dorje. I have also served this cycle through composition.

As the deities and mantra in this cycle are identical to those in the vidyadhara Chöje Lingpa's later terma, the *Combined Sadhana of the Immortal Three Roots*, their two lineages are one in essence.

Longchenpa

The omniscient king of dharma Longchenpa Drime Özer revealed vast and profound mind terma presented as shastras. This is exemplified by the two unsurpassable secret *Heart Essences* of the Great Perfection, but his revelations were countless. Their activity has continuously increased down to the present day. They are supreme among all profound mind terma. Extensive accounts of them may be found in the histories of the two *Heart Essences* and in Longchenpa's *Web of Light: My Visions*.

Lekyi Dorje

Namkha Gyaltsen the siddha from Lhodrak, also called Lekyi Dorje, was the son of Shubu Namkha Gyalpo, who was the twenty-fifth lineal descendant of Shubu Palgyi Senge. All twenty-five were siddhas. Lekyi Dorje's mother was Semo Rinchen Gyen. He was born to his parents, as prophesied by Guru Rinpoche, having passed out of his preceding life in the southwestern land of rakshasas.

In his third year Lekyi Dorje received a *Vajrakilaya* empowerment. During it he saw many dakinis dancing. In his fifth year he received an empowerment of the Great Perfection, during which he had a vision in which he met the gurus upon whom he had relied in the past and received teaching from them. He recollected his previous life, such as when he heard the sound of the conch announcing meals and took it to be the musical summons of rakshasas to dharma assemblies.

Lekyi Dorje received the upasaka vow from his uncle, the great abbot Gyalsay, and undertook complete renunciation in the presence of the great abbot Rinchen Tashi. He received much dharma and meditated undistractedly day and night. An Indian yogin came to him, instructed him, blessed him, gave him a kapala filled with amrita, and told him, "Do not engage your mind in ordinary thought. Do not fetter yourself with the bonds of hope and fear. Go to attend ganachakras in Uddiyana."

Escorted by viras and dakinis, Lekyi Dorje went to Uddiyana. He encountered Guru Rinpoche, who was seated on a lotus in a palace of rainbow light on the peak of a mountain, surrounded by many dakinis presenting a vast array of offerings, many male and female siddhas engaged in yogic conduct, many panditas discussing dharma, and many gods and goddesses listening to dharma and presenting offerings. Guru Rinpoche was simultaneously celebrating a great ganachakra, bestowing empowerment, explaining a tantra, giving practical instructions, and enjoying the feast. The teachings Lekyi Dorje received from Guru Rinpoche on that occasion include the *Ocean of Secret Amrita: Instructions on the Four Tantras*, the *Four Empowerments: The Precious Vase*, and the *Completion Stage: Natural Primordial Liberation*. Although these certainly comprised an extraordinary treatise on the *Great Perfection Heart Essence*, nowadays they are not to be found in the *Book of Vajrapani*, the extant collection of Lekyi Dorje's visionary teachings.

Although it is unclear whether Lekyi Dorje composed any

other writings on the whispered lineage, he was a great kalyanamitra of the Kadampa tradition. Lord Tsongkhapa therefore touched his feet and received most of the Kadampa teachings from him, including the *Stages of the Path*. He was Tsongkhapa's foremost root guru.

Lekyi Dorje's early ancestors were Nyingma, but his family had come to emphasize the Kadampa tradition at the time of the great abbot Namkha Senge. He was therefore a holder of the united Kadampa and Nyingma traditions. Accordingly Lekyi Dorje made the Nyingma *Matrika* and *Yamantaka* the essence of his practice. Through them he gained signs of siddhi; he is therefore among the ranks of great Nyingma vidyadharas. In addition, all of the teachings he received from Vajrapani and that are found in the collection of his profound visionary dharmas known as the *Book of Vajrapani*, other than his rearrangements of pre-existing teachings, employ the dharma terminology of the Great Perfection. In particular, the dialogue known as the *Supreme Medicinal Amrita* is mostly identical to the dialogue in the *Heart Essence of the Dakinis* known as the *Golden Garland*.

In any case, the empowerments and transmissions for the *Book of Vajrapani* eventually became rare. At the encouragement of the omniscient Fifth Dalai Lama, the vidyadhara Terdak Lingpa went to great effort in order to receive them and disseminate their lineage. Nowadays they are widespread within the Gelukpa tradition.

Lekyi Dorje's profound and extensive outer and inner autobiographies are to be found in his *Book of the Whispered Lineage of Vajrapani* and in the *History of the Stages of the Path*.

Palden Dorje

Palden Dorje of Penyül was one of the Three Dorjes, three holders of Lord Tsongkhapa's lineage named Dorje who achieved siddhi. Palden Dorje transformed his impure body into a rainbowlike wisdom body. While living at Jomo Lhari he had a pure vision in which he received the *Ayusadhana of the Immortal Vajra Life-Tree* from Guru Rinpoche. He bestowed it upon the Third Dalai Lama Sönam Gyamtso in the latter's residence at Drepung Monastery. Its lineage continues unbroken; I have received it.

Shrivanaratna

Shrivanaratna was a wondrously great pandita and siddha. He was born as the son of an inexhaustibly wealthy great dharmaraja of the Chandra dynasty in a town called Sat in Senagar to the east of Vajrasana. He mastered the Vedas and their branches, and casting his throne aside as if it were spittle, undertook renunciation and completion in the presence of the mahapandita Ratnakirti. He studied countless profound dharmas of sutra and tantra. One-pointedly immersed in vajrayoga, living as an actionless yogic renunciate, he visited most of the sacred places in Jambudvipa. He was blessed by many yidams, and manifested the qualities of the vajrayana paths of accumulation and juncture. Especially, after he was accepted as a disciple by the wisdom body of Shavaripa, Shrivanaratna achieved the wisdom of that-alone and passed into the exalted state of an arya.

Shrivanaratna saw the faces of and received instruction from many lords among siddhas, including the mahasiddha Virupa, the master Vakishvarakirti, and Padmasambhava. Encouraged by a prophecy he received from Shavaripa, Shrivanaratna visited Tibet twice and helped beings and the teachings there immeasurably. The first time he visited Tibet he went to Guru Rinpoche's place of accomplishment at Paro in the south and stayed there for a long time. He later said, "Paro is just like the sacred places in India. My meditation progressed there."

In particular, Shrivanaratna was accepted by Guru Rinpoche in the following way: As he later described it, "I was led by a woman into what at first seemed to be a cave. Once inside it, however, I found myself within a magnificent mansion. There, I encountered Padmasambhava and his large entourage. I remained there for a long time and took part in the ganachakra in which Padmasambhava was engaged. Since then I have encountered him many times."

Shrivanaratna received the profound instructions called *Padma's Guidance on Ayusadhana* from Guru Rinpoche on that occasion. He practiced them in complete secrecy, and later gave them to the Drukpa Lord of Dharma Gyalwang Kunga Paljor. The lineage of these instructions was once widespread but seems to have disappeared. However, our lord guru Padma Ösal Dongak Lingpa, who is definitely an emanation of Shrivanaratna, has said that he clearly recollects that life. It therefore appears that he possesses a short lineage of blessing for these instructions.

The second time Shrivanaratna visited Tibet he accepted the qualified consort of the vidyadhara Vulture Feathers as a mudra, aided by the use of substances that cause invisibility. She was called Emanated Great Mother and was a queen among siddhas.

Finally, Shrivanaratna displayed the appearance of death in Nepal. When his remains were cremated one night at the Ramadoli charnel ground, the entire area became filled with bright light, and his remains disappeared. He has reappeared several times, and there is an account of his appearance to the mahapandita of Ngari in the latter's biography. It is therefore certain that Shrivanaratna accomplished a wisdom body.

Among all of the Indian panditas who visited Tibet in later times, none were greater than Shrivanaratna and Buddhaguptanatha, a guru of Jetsün Taranatha.

Kunga Paljor

The lord of dharma Gyalwang Kunga Paljor was an unmistakenly recognized emanation of the protector of beings Tsangpa Gyare, and was born to the latter's family. His life is well known. He was the principal dharma heir of the vidyadhara Ratna Lingpa, and received all of the *Former* and *Latter Termas* as well as the *Wisdom Assembly of the Guru*. In addition, while Gyalwang Kunga Paljor was residing at Salje Gangra he was directly accepted by Guru Rinpoche and received from him instructions on the Great Perfection. Based on the unbroken lineage of these instructions the omniscient Padma Karpo composed a profound and extensive guidance text; its lineage still exists.

Samten Lingpa

The history of the cycle called the *Ati of Samten Lingpa* is as follows: Samten Lingpa was born at Tsethang Samten Ling into the nephew lineage of peerless holders of the glorious Sakya tradition that began with Chökyi Wangchuk the Learned One of Gyaltsa and continued down to Samten Lingpa's uncle Sönam Gyalchok. Samten Lingpa was known during his life as the peerless Namkha Sönam. He received from his uncle Sönam Gyalchok the ripening empowerments and liberating instructions of an ocean of tantras. This awakened Samten Lingpa's good habit from many previous lives in which he had mastered the Great Perfection, and he encountered Guru Rinpoche, other gurus, and many yidams directly, in meditation experience, and in dreams; and received the amrita of holy dharma from them. Based on this, the quintessence of the generation and completion stages of Perfect Heruka and Vajrakilaya arose spontaneously within the expanse of his mind. He disseminated it, and its lineage was widespread for a time, but it is uncertain whether or not it still exists.

In the collected works of Sherap Özer, the tertön of Trengso, there is a brief summary of the stages of the path based on the *Ati of Samten Lingpa*. I have received it and have placed it, along with a guidance text, together with my liturgical arrangement for the *Vajrakilaya of the Sakyas*.

Tongwa Dönden

While the Sixth Gyalwang Karmapa Tongwa Dönden was meditating in the sacred region of Tsaritra, Guru Rinpoche sent the mahasiddha Chandra to him from Chamaradvipa as a messenger. The mahasiddha gave Tongwa Dönden instruction on a profound ayusadhana. Later, the Ninth Gyalwang Karmapa Wangchuk Dorje placed this ayusadhana within the "Garland of the Peaceful" section of *Liberating All by Knowing One*.

Rechen Paljor Zangpo

Rechen Paljor Zangpo was the famous foremost heart-son of the mahapandita Bodong Chokle Namgyal. Through his mastery of the channels and energy Rechen Paljor Zangpo became peerless in his display of miracles and supercognition. While he was residing in the Secret Cave of Great Splendor in Tsaritra, he received a sadhana of the seventeen deity mandala of Amitayus directly from Guru Rinpoche. It is called the *Growing Arrow* after the display of miraculous signs that it is known to produce.[139] The lineage of its empowerment still exists, and I have received it. Its instructions are mostly identical in both words and meaning to Loro Rinchen Lingpa's *Ayusadhana*. In addition, Rechen Paljor Zangpo received the lineage of Rinchen Lingpa's *Ayusadhana*, so it seems that their

139. When ayusadhana is performed successfully, the arrow used as its support increases in length, indicating that the life of the beneficiary has been prolonged.

lineages may be regarded as two streams united into one.

The *Growing Arrow Ayusadhana, the Chandali in Seven Days*, and the *Khechari Ejection* are collectively known as the *Three Dharmas of Rechen*. It appears that they are still widespread within the Bodong tradition.

Bodong Sangye Gönpo

The great lord among siddhas Sangye Gönpo, the realized one of Bodong, received and practiced the long lineage of *Singhamukha* which stemmed from the guru Vajrasanapada and Bari the Translator. At Tana in Shang he was accepted as a direct disciple by the wisdom dakini Singhamukha, and Guru Rinpoche bestowed the complete ripening empowerments and liberating instructions upon him. Based on this, he composed a book which contains her ten authorizations, her generation and completion stages, and their applications. Its lineage has remained unbroken, and I have received the authorizations and placed them within the *Treasury of Terma*. The siddha Karma Chakme principally relied upon this cycle in his practice of Singhamukha.

The Drukpa Kagyu Wrathful Kilaya

The omniscient Padma Karpo, the nirmanakaya of Ja Jamyang Chökyi Drakpa, the emanation of the Lord of Victors, the Drukchen, is as famous as the sun and moon. Once, when he was faced with an obstacle to his life, he experienced a pure vision in which Guru Rinpoche and his emanations came to him from Chamaradvipa and instructed him. He committed these highly regarded instructions to writing, and they are widespread even now. I have received them completely.

Padma Karpo's nirmanakaya was Gyalwa Paksam Wangpo. Starting with him and down to the present day, his successive incarnations have been great illuminators of the teachings of both the Drukpa Kagyu and Nyingma traditions.

Jatsön Mebar

Gyalsay Tenpe Jungne, also known as the lord of dakinis Jatsön Mebar, was an emanation of Nupchen Sangye Yeshe. He was born as the son of the vidyadhara Chokden Gönpo. His deeds were wondrous and many. In later life he resided at Glorious Mountain in Chongye. The *Profound Embodiment of All the Three Roots*, which had been concealed in front of the door of Mara's Spirit Castle, was destined to be his terma. Because of circumstances he did not reveal the terma parchment, but protective dakinis gave him the complete terma in a series of pure visions. It consists of one volume, and is accepted as authentic by everyone. Although it appears that this terma was once widespread, its lineage does not seem to exist nowadays.

Tashi Gyamtso

Tashi Gyamtso, the vidyadhara of Nangsal, was an emanation of Acharya Sale and Rechungpa. He encountered Guru Rinpoche in a pure vision and received from him the *Single HRIH Sadhana of Amitayus*. It was passed down as a sealed whispered lineage to Zur Chöying Rangdröl and Drikungpa Chökyi Drakpa. It was widespread for a time, but its lineage no longer exists.

Drikung Shapdrung Könchok Rinchen

The glorious Drikung Shapdrung Könchok Rinchen is said to have been the rebirth of Gyalwang Sönam Gyamtso. There is an entire volume of teachings arisen from Drikung Shapdrung

Könchok Rinchen's pure visions of Mahakarunika and other deities of the three roots. Although the lineage of the empowerments and transmissions of this volume survived for a time, it seems to no longer exist.

Drikungpa Chökyi Drakpa

Drikungpa Chökyi Drakpa was an emanation of Lord Rinchen Puntsok. He was both a pandita learned in the five sciences and a great threefold vajra holder. Although he had the dispensation to reveal profound earth treasure, he did not do so. However, because he was accepted as a direct disciple by many gurus and deities including Shrichakrasamvara, Manjushri Yamantaka Ayupati, and Nagaraksha, he revealed a profound and vast mind treasure, his *Yamantaka Reversal* cycle, as a shastra. Its lineage is widespread.

While Drikungpa Chökyi Drakpa was residing at Tashi Dowoche near Sky Lake, he received the especially profound *Uttarakuru Ayusadhana* and related prophecies in pure visions. It is widespread and I have received it completely.

Lhatsün Namkha Jikme

Lhatsün Namkha Jikme was the embodiment of the compassion of both the mahapandita Vimalamitra and the omniscient Longchenpa Drime Özer. He was born in a Female Fire Bird year in the southern Jar region to a family descended from the ancient dharma kings.[140] He was marked by extremely clear AH syllables between his eyebrows, on his tongue, and on the tip of his nose, and had other wondrous marks as well. He undertook renunciation at Sungnyen Hermitage in the presence of the nirmanakaya Ugyen Paljor, and received the name Kunzang Namgyal. He studied extensively at Thangdrok College. Especially, from the Great Perfection mas-

140. The year was 1597 C.E.

ter Sönam Wangpo he received the complete *Heart Essence* instructions. Practicing them, he gained full realization.

Lhatsün Namkha Jikme visited all the sacred sites of Tibet while engaged in the conduct of awareness-discipline, and achieved the exalted state of a siddha. As the channel-knots in his throat loosened, everything he said came to be excellent in both words and meaning.

He subdued a tirthika king in India and converted him to Buddhism. He enlisted the aid of spirits in Tibet and restored Samye. He reversed a massive landslide in Tsari by means of his gaze and a threatening gesture. His miraculous powers were unimaginable.

Encouraged by the vidyadhara Jatsön Nyingpo and others, Lhatsün Namkha Jikme went to Luminous Essence Divine Mountain in Sikkim and, for the benefit of all Tibet, opened the door to its sacred valleys. As prophesied, he built a temple and retreat facility there.

As instructed by dakinis, he took up residence in the Dakinis' Heart Cave at White Rock Auspicious Plateau. While there, he received the *Sadhana of the Vidyadharas' Essence* cycle, uncommon instructions on the unsurpassable *Heart Essence* of atiyoga, in pure visions. He then visited Jakmalung, a branch of the same sacred area, and encountered the wisdom body of his guru Jetsün Sönam Wangpo riding a tiger. Sönam Wangpo bestowed the empowerment of awareness-display upon him. Based on this pure vision, Lhatsün Namkha Jikme revealed his *Spontaneous Song of the Clouds of Vajra Essence*, which is regarded as the quintessence of all terma, the very point of all whispered lineage instructions, a cycle that liberates through sight, sound, touch, and memory.

He wrote down both of his terma cycles and bestowed the amrita of their empowerments and instructions upon fortunate disciples. He also engaged in extensive activity, teaching and disseminating the Great Perfection. His tradition came to be known as the *Great Perfection of Sikkim*, and its lineage holders have spread it everywhere. Its lineage of instructions continues unbroken, and I have received the complete *Sadhana of the Vidyadharas' Essence* cycle. It is well known that no siddha and master of yogic conduct has appeared in latter days greater than Lhatsün Namkha Jikme.

Sangdak Trinley Lhundrup

The great vidyadhara Nyötön Sangdak Trinley Lhundrup was an emanation of both Nupchen Sangye Yeshe and Drenpa Namkha. Sangdak Trinley Lhundrup was born as a fifth-generation descendant of Padma Lingpa, and became the life-tree of the Nyingma teachings. In a pure vision the dakini Queen of Great Bliss bestowed upon him a prophecy called *Clear Instructions on What to Do and What Not to Do*; instructions on the use of a corpse in the achievement of the body of appearance-emptiness called *Revealing the Channels*; an instruction called *How to Gain Guru Rinpoche's Blessing*; and other wondrous teachings. He committed them all to writing.

The Fifth Dalai Lama

The Fifth Dalai Lama, whose secret name was Dorje Tokme Tsal, was an activity emanation of the dharma king Trisong Detsen. He was prophesied in many earlier and later termas, and was the embodiment of the compassion of Avalokita, the protector of Tibet. He was born to a family in Chongye Taktse that was descended from the royal family of Zahor. His father was Lord Düdül Rapten; his mother was Tricham Kunga Lhadze. Dorje Tokme Tsal was born in a Female Fire Snake year amid wondrous signs.[141] The vidyadhara Ngaki Wangpo gave him the empowerments of *Amitayus* and *Guru Rinpoche* in order to dispel obstacles; this brought about

141 The year was 1617 C.E.

an auspicious start to Dorje Tokme Tsal's life.

Panchen Lozang Chökyi Gyaltsen recognized Dorje Tokme Tsal as the rebirth of the Fourth Dalai Lama Gyalwa Yönten Gyamtso and brought him to the great Drepung Monastery. Panchen Rinpoche accepted the fruits of Dorje Tokme Tsal's crown, named him Ngawang Lozang Gyamtso, and placed him on his lion throne.

Dorje Tokme Tsal mastered the ten sciences. Relying on many extraordinarily learned and attained tutors he received and studied thoroughly most of the empowerments, transmissions, and instructions of sutra and tantra that existed in Tibet at that time, especially those of the Geluk, Sakya, and Nyingma traditions. His *Record of Teachings I Have Received* fills four volumes and is viewed by everyone as the standard for such records. Through his practice of meditation he perfected relinquishment and realization.

Especially, the manner in which Dorje Tokme Tsal received the dispensation of profound pure visions was this: From the *Terma Prophecies* of the glorious Tashi Topgyal:

You who are now the king of Tibetans
Will reveal, in your fifth birth through pure aspiration,
Twenty-five termas and especially five of the heart.

As prophesied in those inerrant vajra words, while Dorje Tokme Tsal was visiting the glorious Samye Monastery he perceived the interdependence for the revelation of earth terma. Although, because of the circumstances of time and place he did not extract it from its place of concealment, the countless deities of the three roots subsequently revealed their faces to him and bestowed both prophecy and empowerment. He committed these teachings to writing; they are his renowned *Twenty-Five Sealed Dharmas*. Together with his supplemental writings, they fill two volumes. Dorje Tokme Tsal bestowed their complete empowerments and instructions on his great disciples, and especially those who upheld the

Nyingma tradition, such as the king of dharma Terdak Lingpa and the vidyadhara Padma Trinley. The *Twenty-Five Sealed Dharmas* became extremely widespread. Their lineage remains unbroken, and I have received them all.

In the realm of government, in Dorje Tokme Tsal's twenty-fifth year Gushri Tendzin Chögyal conquered all of western and central Tibet and offered all of these areas, including their devas and people, to him as his realm and subjects. Dorje Tokme Tsal was then invited to Beijing by the Emperor of China, who accorded him the title of Tishri and presented him with an imperial edict to this effect in writing. From that time on, down to the present, Dorje Tokme Tsal and his successive rebirths have been the great protectors who have preserved the spiritual and secular well-being of all Tibet.

In the realm of dharma, Dorje Tokme Tsal turned countless dharmachakras of sutra and tantra, Sarma and Nyingma, kama and terma. The father and sons of the glorious Sakyas; the supreme nirmanakaya Panchen Rinpoche and those of the Drikung, Talung, and Drukpa Kagyu; the throne holder and other senior masters of Ganden; and most of the lineage holders in Tibet became his disciples. In particular, the great chariots of the Nyingma tradition, including the king of dharma Terdak Lingpa, the vidyadhara Padma Trinley, Lhodrak Tukse Tendzin Gyurme Dorje, and many others capable of reviving this tradition gathered around him. He was peerlessly kind, both directly and indirectly, to the Nyingma teachings.

Having completed such deeds, Dorje Tokme Tsal passed into peace in his sixty-fourth year, on the twenty-fifth day of the month Chaitra at his great palace, the Potala. His immediate rebirth, Rinchen Tsangyang Gyamtso, was born in the south to the descendants of Padma Lingpa. Since then his rebirths have continued to appear in succession down to the present day, as is well known throughout the world.

Bhuprana

The instructions on *Bhuprana* are a means of accomplishing a body of light in a single lifetime. They are a special teaching of Guru Rinpoche, the second Buddha.

Guru Rinpoche emanated in India as the mahasiddha Mahanatha and bestowed these instructions on a fortunate disciple, who became the lord among yogins Jatavira and accomplished a body of wisdom light. Jatavira had countless disciples who achieved undefiled rainbow bodies. The most famous among them were eight disciples who were all named Natha. It is said that they are still encountered by fortunate people in our own day, who also receive the amrita of their teachings.

Among those eight, as prophesied by their guru Jatavira, it was Manikanatha who first came to Tibet. He gave Nesarwa Jamyang Khyentse Wangchuk the root instructions of Jatavira. That was the first dispensation of *Bhuprana* in Tibet. Then Vajranatha came to Tibet and gave Drikung Chögyal Rinchen Puntsok the outer, inner, and secret teachings of Jatavira on prana. That was the second dispensation. Later, the mahasiddha Nyida Longsal, an emanation of Prince Mune Tsenpo, received the complete short lineage of these teachings. That was the third dispensation.

According to the long lineage, these instructions were received from Drikung Rinchen Puntsok by Dzogchen Tsultrim Sangye, who practiced them in Zabulung for seven years, relying only on prana for sustenance. He mastered prana-mind and displayed many miraculous physical appearances. He was able to travel to the twenty-four sacred places and Buddha realms. These instructions were received from him by Ösal Chokden of Ngari.

Ösal Chokden relied upon many great beings and became a treasury of Sarma and Nyingma dharma and instructions. Especially, he perfected the practice of *Bhuprana*. He saw the face of the mahasiddha Jatavira three times and received his blessing. He also saw the faces of four other siddhas and received many extraordinary instructions from them in pure visions. He lived into his one hundred and fifty-seventh year.

In the *Command Seal Prophecy* from the *Guru's Wisdom Assembly* it was predicted that an emanation of King Trisong's speech named Dharma would appear. This was Jamyang Chögyal Dorje, the great guru from Sikkim. He received the Bhuprana teachings from Ösal Chokden. Jamyang Chögyal Dorje possessed all the attributes of a great and holy being. He was greatly learned in all of the Sarma and Nyingma traditions of kama and terma. He had relied upon many masters such as the Great Translator of Gongra and resolved all doubts. He practiced with fierce austerity and fortitude, saw the nature of things, and gained siddhi. His qualities, such as clearly knowing the past, present, and future, were inconceivable.

The mahasiddha Nyida Longsal received the *Bhuprana* instructions from Jamyang Chögyal Dorje. Nyida Longsal was attended by many dakinis even in childhood. He was repeatedly blessed by the wisdom dakini Sukhasiddhi, who gave him her *Six Dharmas*, their exercises, and a direct introduction to the channels and chakras. In Nyida Longsal's tenth year a scroll containing Jatavira's instructions fell into his hands from the sky. Relinquishing all attachment to his parents, family, and wealth, he went to receive dharma from the vidyadhara Jamyang Chögyal Dorje. Nyida Longsal received many empowerments, transmissions, and instructions of kama and terma from Jamyang Chögyal Dorje, particularly those concerning the Great Perfection, and most especially the complete instructions of Jatavira. His guru Jamyang Chögyal Dorje praised him as a fortunate disciple and proclaimed him his regent in benefiting beings.

For six or seven years Nyida Longsal practiced in an isolated hermitage, forsaking all coarse food, relying upon rasayana, and meditating solely on the instructions of prana-sustenance. Wisdom dakinis came to him and assisted him by bestowing bliss, removing hindrances, and bringing progress to his practice. Especially, he saw the face of the mahasiddha Jatavira. They remained together for thirteen days, during which Jatavira bestowed upon Nyida Longsal the short lineage of his instructions. Every day Jatavira bestowed the *Fire Empowerment*, brought down blessings, and invoked auspiciousness. From then on Nyida Longsal had control over prana-mind; he had reached the exalted state of a siddha. He composed the *Self-Liberated Rainbow Body of Appearance-Emptiness: Jatavira's Instructions on Prana*, which has twenty sections. He was also accepted by Guru Rinpoche and countless other deities of the three roots and therefore committed to writing a number of dharma cycles that he received in pure visions. These include the *Guru of Self-Illuminating Wisdom*, a *Longevity Empowerment*, *Mewatsekpa*, a *Dakini Empowerment*, *Guidance on Channels and Prana*, *Twenty-Three Teachings on Prana*, and his *Very Profound Sealed Protection from Lightning*. I have received the complete empowerments and instructions of his *Self-Liberated Rainbow Body of Appearance-Emptiness* through the kindness of our lord guru.

Nyida Longsal's seat was Yangchö Padma Lhunding on the north side of the Tsangpo River. His main lineage holder was Garwang Dorje, whose rebirth was the vajra holder Tukse Kunzang Chöwang. From his time down to ours, the lineages of disciples and sons have been unbroken. Nyida Longsal's seat was protected from harm during the war with China by dharmapalas, who concealed it from the invading forces. Most of the lineages of the empowerments, transmissions, and practical instructions for Garwang Dorje's termas still exist, including his *Instructions of Vajrasattva*.

Namchö Mingyur Dorje

The vidyadhara Namchö Mingyur Dorje was the immediate rebirth of Trülshik Wangdrak Gyamtso, an emanation of both the great translator Vairochana and Shubu Palgyi Senge.[142] He was born in Ngom, in the South, to a family descended from the ancient dharma kings. At the age at which he became able to communicate verbally he began to clearly describe his previous lives. Discovered by the learned and accomplished Karma Chakme, Mingyur Dorje was brought to Palritse Monastery in his fifth year. He learned to read and write there.

In childhood Mingyur Dorje became affected by contamination because of poor hygiene. Karma Chakme Rinpoche repeatedly performed cleansing and purification ceremonies for him. This enabled Mingyur Dorje to once again clearly recollect past lives. His first pure visions were those in which he saw the faces of Amitabha and Guru Rinpoche. He also clearly remembered about two hundred previous lives, and began to demonstrate the supercognition of knowing others' thoughts.

Starting in his twelfth year, countless deities of the three roots revealed their faces to Mingyur Dorje in succession and bestowed instruction. Chakme Rinpoche wrote down these instructions, and they comprise the collection of twelve little volumes called *Sky Dharma*, or *Namchö*. Beginning in his sixteenth year profound mind terma began to burst forth from Mingyur Dorje's heart. Chakme Rinpoche wrote this down as well; it comprises two volumes.

Chakme Rinpoche practiced each of the sadhanas revealed by Mingyur Dorje in sequence until signs of attainment arose. He composed many concise and clear writings concerning them, such as the necessary liturgical arrangements and guidance texts. The empowerments, instructions, and applications of these practices bear greater blessing than other teachings.

142. Namchö Mingyur Dorje lived from 1645 to 1667.

Even the simplest ransom ritual from this tradition can be proven through direct experience to be extremely beneficial.

During this period Mingyur Dorje remained in meditation retreat for three years, during which time wondrous signs were witnessed by everyone living in the area. Whenever he experienced any difficulty in the acquisition of food or other necessities he dispelled his temporary poverty through the slightest rectification of interdependence. He did this many times.

Introduced to one another by Karma Chakme, Mingyur Dorje and the vidyadhara Düdül Dorje met and received teachings from one another. Düdül Dorje held Mingyur Dorje in high esteem; their two minds became as one.

Mingyur Dorje went to Nangchen and opened the doors to about nine previously unknown sacred places, including Dzatö Kyodrak, Khandro Bumdzong, and Nabundzong.

In his nineteenth year Mingyur Dorje was invited to Kathok Monastery. Considering this invitation to be timely, he traveled there and visited both the royal palace of the king of Derge and Kathok Monastery. He continued along the Drichu River, visiting Sangen and Markham. During his travels he turned countless dharmachakras and benefited everyone who formed a connection with him through sight, sound, thought, and touch.

He settled in Muksang and twice bestowed the complete empowerments, transmissions, and experiential instructions of his *Sky Dharma* upon his principal lineage holder, Kunzang Sherap the vidyadhara of Palyül, and gatherings of about two thousand disciples in all.

Having achieved the perfect benefit of beings and the teachings, in his twenty-fourth year he announced that he needed to go to the realm called Array of Flowers in order to serve as the regent of the Buddha Pushpa, who was about to pass into parinirvana. On the sixteenth day of the month Chaitra he withdrew the array of his rupakaya, promising that twenty-five emanations of him would appear.

Although there was a prophecy that Mingyur Dorje would reveal a hundred earth termas, he did not do so because of certain circumstances. It is said that the minds of both Taksham Nüden Dorje and Yongey Mingyur Dorje were blessed by Namchö Mingyur Dorje's great wisdom so that they could reveal them in his stead.

His lineage has been transmitted by both the Nemdo Kagyu and Palyül Nyingma traditions. They have filled all of eastern Tibet with the activity of his teachings. I have received his complete *Sky Dharma* from both traditions.

The immediate rebirth of the vidyadhara Mingyur Dorje was Mokdrup Namkha Chöwang, who is well known to have been a chakravartin mong siddhas. He revealed a great deal of earth terma, including dharma, supports, and riches. However, due to certain circumstances he did not transcribe his earth terma dharma. There exists a short mind treasure of his, a sadhana called the *Dakinis' Eight Dispensations*, which is essentially a concise daily practice of the *Sugatas' Assembly*. Some of the wondrous supports he revealed can still be seen. He discovered a vase filled with gold at Adö on the Dzachu River, and used its contents to restore the Kumbum Ringmo Stupa at Kathok; this is proven by the fact of its restoration.

His nirmanakaya was Jikdral Chöying Dorje. He and all his successive rebirths have done beings and the Nyingma teachings immeasurable good, as is well known.

Karma Chakme

143. Karma Chakme lived from 1613 to 1678.

The learned and attained Karma Chakme was an emanation of both Chokro Lu'i Gyaltsen and Prince Senalek.[143] He was born in the Ngom region as the son of the mantradharin Padma Wangdrak, who was of the nephew lineage of Dong Khachöpa. In his childhood he mastered reading, writing, and both the Indian and Chinese systems of divination. He gained stability in the generation stage and recognized the nature of the mind. He received all the Nyingma dharma that his father possessed.

Karma Chakme offered both the fruits of his crown and an account of his realization to the great Fourth Trungpa Kunga Namgyal of Surmang, who gave him a thorough introduction to the nature of the mind. He then went to Zadam College in Penyül, where he perfectly studied the treatises of sutra and tantra. He undertook complete renunciation in the presence of the Sixth Shamarpa Garwang Chökyi Wangchuk, from whom he also received many teachings such as *Mahamudra* and the *Six Dharmas*, and whom he regarded as his root guru.

As prophesied by the Eighth Gyalwang Karmapa Mikyö Dorje, it is certain that Karma Chakme was an emanation of the Karmapa. It was in consideration of necessity that he adopted the name Karma Chakme.[144]

From many teachers he received many empowerments, transmissions, and instructions, especially those of the Karma Kagyu and Nyingma traditions. He took Nemdo Palritse as his seat, and except when he travelled for others' benefit, he remained there in retreat. He completed more than a hundred sadhanas of deities of the three roots and the dharmapalas, practicing each one until signs of siddhi became evident. He achieved the level of realization called "one taste."

Karma Chakme experienced numerous signs of the blessing of his gurus and yidams. Once he had a vision of Guru Rinpoche riding a revenant, after which four lines of verse appeared before his eyes. Based on this he wrote the *Direct Instructions of Mahakarunika: An Ocean of Benefit for Beings* in eighteen chapters, along with its supporting commentaries. After completing this he received the prophecy, "This dharma will cause one million eight hundred thousand beings to go to Sukhavati."

His writings, from *Mountain Dharma: Instructions for Retreat* to his essays on ransom rituals and divination, fill more than fifty volumes. As everything he wrote was composed after he received the authorization to do so from a

144. *Chakme* means "Free from Attachment."

deity, his writings bear blessing and have been of vast benefit to beings. They are therefore even more wondrous than most terma.

Having completed such deeds, Karma Chakme departed for Sukhavati in his sixty-fourth year. There is a detailed account of his journey to Sukhavati, recorded by his nephew Lama Chöwang Kunzang, the latter's mother, and Chakme Rinpoche's attendants. Starting with his emanation Trinley Wangjung his emanations have appeared successively.

The lineages of his disciples include the eastern Nemdo Kagyu of Sangphu Padma Kunga and his successors; and the Golden Garland of the western Nemdo Kagyu, which began with Tsöndrü Gyamtso and has remained unbroken down to the present day. Chakme Rinpoche's foremost disciples included both Dzogchen Padma Rikdzin, an emanation of Vimalamitra; and Palyül Kunzang Sherap. They spread his teachings among the holders of the Nyingma tradition throughout most of eastern Tibet.

I have received the *Direct Instructions of Mahakarunika* from the Fourth Chakme Rinpoche; and most of Karma Chakme's other works, including his *Mountain Dharma*, from many different gurus.

Dorje Drakpo

The vidyadhara Tukyi Dorje or Dorje Drakpo Trinley Düpa Tsal was an emanation of the dharma king Trisong Detsen. He was born in a place called Takzik in southeastern Tibet. He was recognized as the fourth rebirth of the lord of siddhas Sönam Gyamtso and enthroned at his seat, Dzigar Tashi Chöling Monastery. He offered the fruits of his crown to the omniscient Eighth Situpa Chökyi Jungne and received the name Kagyu Trinley Nampar Gyalwe De. He received countless profound dharma teachings from the Eighth Situpa, the omniscient Drukchen, the master Jampal Pawo, and Khampa Rinpoche Tendzin Chökyi Nyima. Especially, from the vidyadhara Tamdrin Gönpo he received many termas, including Ratna Lingpa's *Vajrakilaya*.

Dorje Drakpo perfected the practice of the generation and completion stages; saw the faces of many deities of the three roots, especially the peaceful and wrathful forms of Guru Rinpoche; and received their blessings. Through his peerless magical power he bound newly appeared demons to samaya and could bring pacification and protection simply by writing a letter. When he visited Tsaritra the spirit Chikchar Marpo offered him a wonderful stone statue of Arya Simhanada. There is an entire volume of profound dharma that arose spontaneously from Dorje Drakpo's mind, including his *Wrathful Kilaya* and his *Red Tara*. I have received the empowerments and instructions for these. His mind termas have especially great blessing in the protection of crops from frost damage and of persons from injury caused by demon kings, as well as in the pacification of earth spirits. It appears that their activity has benefited many.

The principal heirs to Droje Drakpo's mind termas were the Thirteenth Gyalwang Karmapa Düdül Dorje, Drukchen Chökyi Nangwa, Tai Situpa Padma Nyinje Wangpo, and other truly great beings; they included many of the lineage holders of all traditions, especially the Karma and Drukpa Kagyu.

After enacting such vast activity, Dorje Drakpo displayed the manner of departure for other realms. Padma Nyinje Wangpo reminded him to enter samadhi and performed all the other duties related to his passing, including elaborate observances.

Dorje Drakpo's nirmanakaya Trinley Lhundrup and his successive rebirths including his current one have spread the teachings of both the Drukpa Kagyu and Nyingma traditions.

Padma Nyinje Wangpo

The main heart-son of Dorje Drakpo was our glorious protector Lord Maitreya, the Ninth Tai Situpa Vajradhara Padma Nyinje Wangpo.[145] He was born the son of Ngawang Gönpo to a noble family at Yilhung in Markham. When the marks and signs of his lotuslike form bloomed, wondrous omens appeared. Lord Pawo Tsuklak Gawa recognized him as the unmistaken rebirth of the Eighth Situpa Tenpe Nyinje. With the concurrence of the fathers and sons of the Karma and Drukpa Kagyu, he was brought to his seat, Palpung monastery, in his fifth year. From the *Command Seal Prophecy from the Wisdom Assembly of the Guru*:

> In the future there will be six with eyes of dharma
> And six with lotus tongues.

Padma Nyinje Wangpo was definitely the first of the prophesied lotus-tongued ones. In accordance with Lord Pawo's pure vision and this prophecy, he was crowned with the name Padma Nyinje Wangpo. He was also known as the glorious Padma Wangchen. When he undertook renunciation in the presence of the Thirteenth Gyalwang Karmapa he received the name Palden Tendzin Nyinje Trinley Rapgye Chokle Nampar Gyalwe De.

Padma Nyinje Wangpo formed a dharmic connection with Shamarpa Chödrup Gyamtso, Drikungpa Döndrup Chögyal, the all-seeing Drukchen Chökyi Nangwa, Garwang Chökyong Gyurme, Dzigar Kagyu Trinley Namgyal, and Tsewang Paldar, the son of the great vidyadhara Tsewang Norbu. He mainly relied upon the Thirteenth Gyalwang Karmapa Düdül Dorje as his guru. From his teachers Padma Nyinje Wangpo received all of the existing Karma Kagyu empowerments and instructions as well as a vast number of Drikung, Drukpa, and Nyingma empowerments and instructions. He became supreme among all monastics in his con-

---

145. Padma Nyinje Wangpo lived from 1774 to 1853.

stant adherence to the three vows. Gaining great knowledge of the common sciences and especially of the treatises of sutra and tantra, he became the greatest of scholars. With vast bodhichitta he was solely focused on helping beings and the teachings. His excellent activity spread throughout all space.

Padma Nyinje Wangpo primarily devoted himself, both constantly and during periods of intensive practice, to profound yoga. It is certain that he achieved the exalted state of a siddha. Nevertheless, like the great kalyanamitras of the Kadampa tradition, he hid his qualities like a butter lamp in a vase. His discretion was so great that no one knows the profundity of his attainment. However, he was unable to conceal the fact that grain cast by him in blessing would appear a great distance away, or the footprints he left in solid rock, or that his feet sometimes did not touch the ground. These things were witnessed by everyone. As his supercognitive knowledge of others' thoughts and his recognitions of nirmanakayas were always of benefit to the teachings, it is evident that he was free from even the slightest trace of delusion.

He visited central Tibet three times and ceaselessly turned the dharmachakra at his seat and throughout the nomad communities of eastern and western Kham. His principal heart sons included the Fourteenth Gyalwang Karmapa Khyapdak Tekchok Dorje, Drukchen Chökyi Nangwa and his rebirth, Pawo Tsuklak Chögyal, and all the great beings of the Karma and Drukpa Kagyu. His inner heart sons also included Datrül Rinpoche Karma Ngedön Tenpa Rapgye, Wöntrül Rinpoche and his rebirth from Palpung Monastery, and Karma Gyurme of Palyül Monastery. Most of the great holders of the Karma Kagyu and Nyingma lineages were his disciples. Those minor disciples like me who are dedicated to praying to him with devotion are innumerable.

Our holy guru Jamyang Khyentse Wangpo received the empowerments and instructions for *Mahamudra* and the *Six Dharmas* from Padma Nyinje Wangpo, who felt such great trust for Jamyang Khyentse Wangpo that, as Padma Nyinje

Wangpo declared himself, he blessed Jamyang Khyentse with the transmission of the ultimate lineage. Padma Nyinje Wangpo also advised him, "It would be good if the earlier termas were collected so that they can continue to be taught and disseminated."

In essence, this was his command to create the *Treasury of Precious Terma*. Jamyang Khyentse Wangpo is therefore a great heart son of Padma Nyinje Wangpo's in that he has enacted the latter's vision for the teaching of dharma. Beyond that, both the Gyalwang Karmapa and the supreme nirmanakaya of Padma Nyinje Wangpo have received profound dharma from Jamyang Khyentse Wangpo. He and I, master and disciple, have completed the compilation of the *Treasury of Precious Terma*, and have therefore fulfilled Padma Nyinje Wangpo's prophetic instruction.

Padma Nyinje Wangpo displayed no great enthusiasm for the composition of new treatises or liturgies; he was more devoted to the use and preservation of those that already existed. However, at the insistence of the Gyalwang Karmapa and many disciples from all ranks of life, he wrote three volumes of sadhanas, mandala rituals, empowerment liturgies, guidance essays, and instructions. I had the good fortune to receive most of these transmissions, instructions, and profound blessings from him, as well as his authorization to teach and disseminate them to others.

As Padma Nyinje Wangpo was utterly immersed in the bodhisattva conduct of the four attractions and generosity, he donated silver three times to all of the larger and smaller Karma and Drukpa Kagyu monasteries throughout Tibet, from Ngari in the west to Jang at the Chinese border. He sponsored the building of three stupas at a total cost of thirty thousand large measures of silver. He also funded countless perpetual offering observances. He built the peerless golden reliquary stupa at his seat, Palpung Monastery. He provided monastics with their robes and other necessities, so that they could become an ornament to the eyes of future adherents of

Buddhism. His wheel of activity was inconceivably vast.

From his sixty-first year until his passing Padma Nyinje Wangpo never left the enclosure of the Great Retreat of Palpung. During those eighteen years he remained one-pointedly immersed in the wheel of renunciate meditation.

After perfecting such deeds of the three wheels and thereby upholding, preserving, and disseminating the Buddhadharma, Padma Nyinje Wangpo passed away in the middle of the night on the seventh day of the month Jyeshtha in the Year of the Iron Ox, his eightieth year.[146] At the time of his passing he displayed no particular illness, and passed away with full knowledge of the realms to which he was, for the time being, departing. As a sign that he had fulfilled his intention, the sky became cloudless and utterly free from any precipitation. Everyone felt the earth shake, and there were many other wondrous omens as well. When his precious remains were cremated many amazing relics appeared from them. Fragments of his bones reached the hands of some of those who had faith in him; these relics produced shariram, which seem to have increased.

The observances connected with Padma Nyinje Wangpo's passing included means of fulfilling his wishes as well as great offering ceremonies. We convened large assemblies that continually practice the *Nine-Deity Hevajra Sadhana of the Marpa Tradition*, the *Guhyasamaja Akshobhyavajra Sadhana*, and the *Five-Deity Mahamaya Sadhana*. The performance of these sadhanas and offering ceremonies is ongoing.

Padma Nyinje Wangpo's supreme nirmanakaya was recognized by the Gyalwang Karmapa and named by him Padma Kunzang Chökyi Gyalpo. He is the second of the prophesied Tai Situpas called "lotus-tongued."

Not only did our guru Padma Nyinje Wangpo never speak about his visions or give prophecies based on them; he never even mentioned his dreams. It is therefore unknown whether he received teachings in pure visions or as mind terma. However, in response to the insistent supplication of the

---

146. Although our text says that he passed away in the Iron Ox year, 1853 was the Water Ox year, and was Padma Nyinje Wangpo's eightieth year.

accomplished Lama Kamtsang Norbu, Padma Nyinje Wangpo bestowed upon us the profound *Gurusadhana of Guru Rinpoche Accompanied by his Twenty-Five Disciples*. It is mind terma presented as a shastra. I received its lineage from him in connection with the four empowerments from the *Very Profound Embodiment of the Three Jewels*, and have included it in the *Treasury of Precious Revelations* as the quintessence of that collection.

The Eighth Pawo Rinpoche

The glorious Eighth Pawo Rinpoche Tsuklak Chökyi Gyalpo was the nephew of Lord Padma Nyinje Wangpo. He was an emanation of both the Indian scholar Prajnakara and the great translator Vairochana, and became a great treasury of Sarma and Nyingma dharma. He benefited beings and the teachings greatly and also received the dispensation of profound terma, revealing both terma parchment and a sword that is a dharmapala support from the sacred Chijam Rock. It is said that the parchment contained a Yamantaka cycle, but it seems to be unavailable. As the sword holds great blessing and miraculous power it appears to be kept among his supports.

Tsuklak Chökyi Gyalpo clearly remembered past events such as hearing profound dharma from Guru Rinpoche in the middle temple of Samye and receiving the name Padma Garwang Drodül Gyalpo Tsal. Based on these recollections he revealed the *Good Vase of Amrita Ayusadhana*, which I received from him.

The Fourth Chakme Rinpoche

The Fourth Chakme Rinpoche Karma Tendzin Trinley was a heart son of Padma Nyinje Wangpo and among the greatest of scholars, renunciates, and siddhas. He was accepted by the

Fourteenth Gyalwang Karmapa as one of his main teachers.

While Karma Tendzin Trinley was engaged in the approach and accomplishment of Ratna Lingpa's *Quintessential Heart Sadhana* in the Palritse Hermitage, the *Sadhana of the Three Stick-Brother Gods of Wealth*, a concise and complete terma that had been reconcealed by the First Karma Chakme, fell into his hands. He transcribed it, and I have received its empowerments and instructions. I have also received the transmission for the litrugy composed by Dechen Nyingpo, the siddha of Nemdo, for Karma Tendzin Trinley's mind terma *Padmaraja*.

Padma Gyepa

Padma Gyepa, the teacher of Ngapö, was the subsequent birth of the renunciate Losal Gyamtso, whose mind was of the same stream as that of the vidyadhara Terdak Lingpa. Padma Gyepa was a heart son of Lord Rinchen Namgyal and others. He was vastly learned in sutra, tantra, and the sciences, and gained siddhi through the vajrayana path. There exists a guru-sadhana cycle that he received in pure visions; I have received its root empowerment.

Tsewang Mingyur Dorje

The learned Tsewang Mingyur Dorje lived at around the same time as Padma Gyepa. He was a heart son of the great tertön Terdak Lingpa and his children as well as of the vidyadhara Padma Trinley. Tsewang Mingyur Dorje was a great scholar and siddha. There exists a *Chakrasamvara Cycle*, wondrous in words and meaning, that he received in pure visions. He gave it to Tendzin Yeshe Lhundrup and others; its lineage appears to have survived.

The Omniscient Jikme Lingpa

The omniscient Jikme Lingpa was an emanation of the mahapandita Vimalamitra, the dharma king Trisong Detsen, and Prince Lharjey. He was the immediate rebirth of the vidyadhara Chöje Lingpa. Jikme Lingpa was a chariot of the teachings of the *Luminous Heart Essence* and received the great dispensation of profound mind terma.

As prophesied in Guru Chökyi Wangchuk's *Khari Dialogue* and in the terma prophecies of Sangye Lingpa, Chöje Lingpa, and Ratön and his son, Jikme Lingpa was born near Palri Monastery, south of the Red Tomb of Songtsen Gampo in Chongye, on the morning of the day of commemorative offerings to the omniscient Longchenpa in the month Paushya of the Female Earth Bird year to the family of the nephew of Gyadrakpa, one of the six great heart-sons of the Dharma Lord of the Drukpa Kagyu.[147]

In childhood his disposition toward holiness was awakened, and he remembered his previous births as the great tertöns Sangye Lama and Chöje Lingpa. In his sixth year he entered the dharma college at Palri Monastery, a place that bore the undiminished imprint of the noble lord Prajnarasmi's deeds of the three wheels.[148] He offered the fruits of his crown to Tsogyal Tulku Ngawang Lozang Padma and received the name Padma Khyentse Özer. He later received the shramanera vow from Nesarwa Ngawang Kunga Lekpe Jungne. He received the empowerments and transmissions of the *Essence of Liberation* and the *Guru's Wisdom Assembly* from Neten Kunzang Özer.

Especially, in his thirteenth year Jikme Lingpa met the vidyadhara Tukchok Dorje and received *Mahamudra: Wisdom that Liberates Upon Sight* and other dharma from him. As this ripened him, Jikme Lingpa considered Tukchok Dorje to be his supreme root guru, and later encountered his wisdom body. He also received all of the Nyingma kama teachings; the main termas, such as those of Nyangral and Guru Chöwang; and some Sarma empowerments and instructions from teachers including the great tertön Drime Lingpa, Jikme Lingpa's own maternal uncle Dharmakirti the Meditator, Shrinatha the Lord of Siddhas from Mindröling, Tendzin Yeshe Lhundrup, Tangdrok Pön Padma Chokdrup, and Lama Dargye from Mön Dzakar.

Jikme Lingpa learned a little about astrology and other sciences at Palri Monastery, but he never studied much; his heart was utterly focused on the practice of the essence. His magnificently beautiful writings, with their perfect exposition of the secret meaning of all the great treatises of sutra and tantra, burst forth spontaneously from the expanse of the wisdom with which he was born.

147. The year was 1729 C.E.

148. "Prajnarasmi" is a Sanskrit translation of *Sherap Özer*.

On the Day of Miracles in his twenty-eighth year, the Year of the Fire Ox, he began a three-year retreat in the meditation hall called the Single Tilaka at his own Palri Monastery.[149] With firm resolve he practiced the generation and completion stages of the great tertön and king of dharma Drodül Lingpa Sherap Özer's wonderful profound terma, the *Essence of Liberation: Self-Liberated Wisdom*. Jikme Lingpa held its dispensation through both long and short lineages. Through its practice he gained extraordinary indications of approaching realization. He also completed the approach and accomplishment of many deities from authentic profound termas such as those of Nyangral and Guru Chöwang, and achieved the state of a fully ripened vidyadhara. Through his mastery of channels, energy, and essence, the channels and essences of the sambhogachakra in his throat dissolved into a cloud of syllables, and appearances arose as texts for him. A vast treasure of dharma such as vajra dohas, perfect in words and meaning, began to burst forth from within him.

While Jikme Lingpa was performing the approach and accomplishment of the *Guru's Wisdom Assembly* the sound of a horse neighing came from the top of his head, and Guru Rinpoche crowned him with the name Pal Padma Wangchen. He was directly blessed by the master Manjushrimitra, and thereby experienced the authentic wisdom of example. He thereafter began the conduct of great discipline, wearing the costume of a heruka. Especially, as an appearance of the clear light, he was given expanse-script bearing the symbols of the dakinis by the dharmakaya wisdom dakini at the Great Stupa of Unintended Permission at Bodha in Nepal. He thus gained possession of the world-famous great treasury of dharma called the *Collected Dispensations: The Heart Essence of the Vast Expanse of the Great Perfection*.

Although he had now achieved the exalted state of a wise siddha, Jikme Lingpa was not content with just that. Vowing intently to achieve the wisdom of the arya paths, he went to Samye Chimpu as soon as his first three-year retreat was over.

---

149. The year was 1757 C.E.

For another three years he immersed himself one-pointedly in practice of the essence in the Great Secret Flower Cave there, living with an austerity that vied with that of Jetsün Mila Shepa Dorje. During those years he had countless pure visions. In particular, he met the wisdom body of the omniscient dharma king Drime Özer Longchen Rapjam Zangpo three times. The blessings of Longchenpa's body, speech, and mind were transferred to Jikme Lingpa, and he also received the great authorization of Longchenpa's speech. Through these blessings Jikme Lingpa achieved the ultimate wisdom of the arya paths, and saw the truth of the Great Perfection.

He revealed his great mind terma and named it the *Heart Essence of the Vast Expanse*. He first opened the door to its ripening empowerments and liberating instructions at Samye Chimpu to fifteen fortunate disciples. Starting then, he gradually disseminated the profound meaning widely; he became the single chariot of the *Heart Essence of the Great Perfection*.

From the *Khari Dialogue*, a profound terma of Guru Chöwang:

At Chongye my beneficial emanation will appear.
People will say, "We don't know who he is."
At Chingbardo, south of the Red Tomb,
He may build a Descent Stupa and a monastery.

After completing the three years of practice he had undertaken at Samye Chimpu, Jikme Lingpa fulfilled the vajra prophecy cited above. The wisdom body of Tsele Natsok Rangdröl entrusted him with his intentions, and Jikme Lingpa returned to his birthplace, relying on many aspects of interdependence, including symbols. In the upper valley of Dönkhar, hidden among the mountains south of Songtsen Gampo's tomb at Chongye, he built and furnished the hermitage of Padma Ösal Tekchok Ling at glorious Tsering Jong. He lived there as a hidden yogin free from action for the rest of his life.

Jikme Lingpa's countless karmic disciples came from all over Tibet, Bhutan, and even the border regions of India. He taught them all of the authentic kama and terma Nyingma dharma and especially the old and new *Heart Essences*; his activity of speech was wonderful.[150] He also made ten-thousandfold offerings to the three dharmachakras and saved the lives of countless beings whose death was otherwise certain. Jikme Lingpa's vast generosity of dharma was free from any ambition for repayment or even karmic maturation. He offered a dharmachakra of pure gold to Samye Monastery, sponsored the creation of a silver image of the victor Maitreya, and reconsecrated Samye itself. When a large Gurkha army, having adopted the behavior of asuras, was marching on Tibet Jikme Lingpa successfully repelled it magically. In such ways his wheel of activity was so helpful to the spiritual and secular wellbeing of Tibet that the Tibetan government treated him with the utmost respect.

The nine volumes of Jikme Lingpa's writings have been printed from woodblocks carved at the King of Derge's capital. They include the two volumes of the root texts of his great mind terma, the *Heart Essence of the Vast Expanse*, together with his clarifications; the single volume of his *Tantra-Tradition Vajrakilaya*, which he arranged based on the instructions he received from Langchen Palgyi Senge when the latter empowered him in an emanated mandala; and the six volumes of his own compositions. Foremost among those six volumes are the two volumes of his *Treasury of Precious Qualities* with its autocommentary. It presents the stages of the path of all the Buddha's teachings and is a mind treasure presented as a shastra, written by Jikme Lingpa through the blessing of the great omniscient Longchenpa.

The disciples born from Jikme Lingpa's speech included great masters such as the throne-holder of the glorious Sakyas Ngawang Palden Chökyong and his brother; the two nirmanakayas of the victor Drikungpa; the nirmanakaya of the supreme vidyadhara of Dorje Drak Monastery; Lhodrak

---

150. The old Heart Essences are the *Nyingtik Yashi*; the new Heart Essence is the *Longchen Nyingtik*.

Sungtrül and Lhodrak Tukse; Jora Rinpoche, the great holder of the Bodong lineage; Ganden Shartse and Jangtse, great holders of the Geluk lineage; and Tsona Göntse Tulku of Bhutan. Jikme Lingpa's disciples also included other great and powerful people as well as actionless practitioners and renunciates. His disciples were countless; most of the Nyingma lamas and tulkus of eastern Tibet touched his feet.

Jikme Lingpa's foremost inner heart-son was the lord of siddhas Jikme Trinley Özer, an emanation of Prince Murup Tsenpo. Other heart sons were Jikme Gyalwe Nyugu, whose deeds for the benefit of others were as inconceivable as those of Arya Avalokita; and Jikme Kundröl of Bhutan. Such disciples spread the light of his teachings all the way to India in the south and China and Mongolia in the east. No one in recent times has equaled Jikme Lingpa's activity. He said of himself, "My teachings have spread because I spent seven years in solitude meditating one-pointedly on bodhichitta."

There is hardly any place to which the ripening empowerments and liberating instructions of Jikme Lingpa's *Heart Essence* have not spread, and it seems that they continue to spread even more widely as time passes. This is the fulfillment of prophecy.

I received the complete empowerments and instructions of this mind terma as well as the reading transmission of Jikme Lingpa's collected writings through the kindness of the compassionate great tertön Gyurme Tendzin Pelgye and the second omniscient one Jamyang Khyentse Wangpo.[151]

Having perfected such deeds of the three wheels, Jikme Lingpa departed for the great pure realm of Lotus Light, without significant illness, amid many signs and miracles on the third day of the month Ashvini in his seventieth year at his Namdröl Yangtse hermitage above Tsering Jong. His posthumous observances were performed extensively and exactly according to his wishes, as recorded in the verse and prose testaments he had composed not long before, by his nephew Özer Trinley and others.

151. Jamyang Khyentse Wangpo is called the second omniscient one here in recognition that he was an emanation of Jikme Lingpa.

Jikme Lingpa had only one son; he was enthroned at the seat of the Drikung Kagyu and named Gyalsay Nyinje Özer and Chökyi Gyaltsen. His life was that of a wondrous holy being, but it seems that he did not achieve much benefit for beings or the teachings.

Padma Chöjor Gyamtso

Padma Chöjor Gyamtso, a nirmanakaya of Palri Monastery, was a disciple of Jikme Lingpa. His life was one of wondrous learning, discipline, and benevolence. The goddess Chandali directly gave Padma Chöjor Gyamtso a cycle of instructions called the *Mother of Life* and the protectress *Umadevi*. These instructions comprise one small volume, from which I have received the root empowerment and instructions.

Jikme Trinley Özer

Jikme Trinley Özer, the first Dodrupchen Rinpoche, was the principal heart-son of the vidyadhara Jikme Lingpa and a great lord among siddhas. As clearly predicted in the *Command-Seal Prophecy* from the great tertön Sangye Lingpa's *Wisdom Assembly*, Jikme Trinley Özer was born in a Female Wood Ox year to a family of the Mukpo Dong clan in the western part of a region called Do in eastern Tibet.[152] At an early age his propensity for holiness was awakened and he began to have pure visions. In the region of his birth there were seats of both the Kagyu and Palyül traditions; he received complete instruction in both Mahamudra and the Great Perfection from kalyanamitras of those schools. He offered the fruits of his crown to Gyurme Kunzang Namgyal, the Second Shechen Rapjam Rinpoche, and received the name Kunzang Shenpen. He lived as a brahmacharya upasaka. Jikme Trinley Özer achieved the exalted state of a siddha by practicing one-pointedly, as he did for seven years at the

152. The year was 1745 C.E.

hermitage called Snowy Fastness of Great Bliss.

He visited central Tibet four times. The first two times he diligently entered the gate of dharma. He visited Daklha Gampo and received much profound dharma from the mahasiddha Damchö Wangchuk and refined his experience and realization. Then, and at various times, he received countless teachings, especially those of the Nyingma tradition, at the lotus feet of twenty masters such as Palyül Karma Tashi and his students, Shechen Gyurme Kunzang Namgyal, Katok Drime Shingkyong, Jewön Padma Kundröl Namgyal, and Ngedön Tendzin Zangpo.

Especially, in his forty-first year Jikme Trinley Özer traveled to central Tibet a third time and went to Dönkhar Tsering Jong to meet the vidyadhara Jikme Lingpa, who recognized Jikme Trinley Özer as an emanation of Prince Damdzin. Jikme Lingpa came to care for him with the love of a father for his only son, and empowered him as his principal dharma heir, placing upon his head the crown of the name Jikme Trinley Özer. He bestowed a vast amount of dharma on him, especially the old and new *Heart Essence* cycles, and Jikme Trinley Özer spread their activity throughout space.

He traveled to central Tibet a fourth time and again entered the presence of the omniscient Jikme Lingpa, presented offerings, and received all the dharma that he had not previously. At that time conflict between Tibet and Nepal was escalating, and people of all ranks in central Tibet were boiling with fear. Jikme Trinley Özer performed ritual service in order to avert warfare and prophesied that central Tibet was in no danger. As his prediction came true he was accorded immeasurable honor and respect by the Tibetan government. It was at that time that he came to be known as Dodrupchen, the Mahasiddha from Do.

Jikme Trinley Özer traveled on pilgrimage to Tsari and then returned to eastern Tibet. He became the guru of the queen of Derge and her son the crown prince. With their sponsorship he turned the dharmachakra for the lamas and tulkus of

Shechen, Dzogchen, and Kathok, transmitting to them all the dharma he had received from the omniscient Jikme Lingpa, including the Nyingma Tantras, the old and new *Heart Essence* cycles, and Longchenpa's *Seven Treasuries*. He founded two dharma communities upholding the omniscient Jikme Lingpa's tradition to the west and east of the Dzachu River. In particular, in the prophecy of Rongtön Dechen Lingpa it is written:

> A courageous bodhisattva, an emanation of the prince,
> Will lead a flock of meditators on ati, the Great Perfection.
> He will establish three monasteries in western and eastern Ser.

As clearly predicted in the above-cited prophecy, Jikme Trinley Özer built the Shukchen Tagor Temple with its three supports, but it did not last. He then established his seat at Padmakö in a place called Yarlung in western Ser, and lived there for the rest of his life. Disciples, high officials, and sponsors gathered like clouds around him, coming from Derge, China, Mongolia, Gyarong, and other places. His spiritual and secular activity flourished. He ceaselessly turned the dharmachakra. As a result his disciples included all of the great lamas of Kathok, Dzogchen, Shechen, and Gyarong. In particular he engendered the supreme scholar Jikme Kalzang; the lord of siddhas Damtsik Dorje; Do Khyentse Yeshe Dorje, the supreme nirmanakaya of the omniscient Jikme Lingpa; the chariot of the Nyingma teachings, the bodhisattva Shenpen Taye; and many other great beings able to uphold the teachings.

Having completed such inconceivably great deeds, Jikme Trinley Özer passed into the great peace of the dharmadhatu amid signs and miracles and without apparent illness, after describing the dissolution of the energies and bestowing an extensive final testament, at around midnight on the thirteenth day of the first month in his seventy-seventh year, the Year of the Snake.[153] His nephew and disciples preserved his body in gold and performed all the other posthumous observances.

153. 1821 C.E.

Jikme Trinley Özer's emanations of body, speech, and mind have continued to appear down to the present; they have all been great illuminators of dharma, both learned and accomplished.

In particular, the way in which Jikme Trinley Özer received the dispensation of profound terma was this: Based upon the prophecies that he had received at various times he was certain that he was entitled to reveal earth terma, but did not implement these prophecies. However, he repeatedly saw the face of the protector Amitabha and was also blessed by Guru Rinpoche and the omniscient father and son.[154] Based on that he revealed the holy dharma called the *Supreme Path of Great Bliss* as mind treasure and disseminated it. It includes complete empowerments and instructions for outer, inner, and secret sadhanas of Amitabha; a very secret sadhana of Hayagriva; and the emanated protector Mahadeva.

154 Longchenpa and Jikme Lingpa.

Based on pure visions, Jikme Trinley Özer also revealed the *Sadhana of the Twelve Teachers of the Great Perfection*; the *Gurusadhana of Jetsün Milarepa*; the *Sadhana of Machik Lapdrön* and its empowerment; and the *Two United Streams of Severance*. These and his other visionary teachings have survived unimpaired down to the present. I have received some of his Amitabha cycle.

Ngawang Dorje

The learned and accomplished Ngawang Dorje was born in Eyül, the source of knowledge. He became the lama of E Nering West Monastery, where the Nyingma dharma lineage was upheld. Ngawang Dorje mainly followed the Mindröling tradition. He was learned in both spiritual and secular matters; his activity was great. In particular he eventually came to receive the dispensation of profound terma, and his revelations were received by both the Omniscient One of Jora and the Nirmanakaya of Dakpo. I have received his concise and especially profound *Sadhana of Mewatsekpa*, which is an accessory to his *Very Profound Embodiment of the Three Roots*.

Kunzang Ngedön Wangpo

Kunzang Ngedön Wangpo of Kathok is said to have been an emanation of Nupchen Sangye Yeshe. He is renowned as a great scholar and siddha. As prophecied by the omniscient Jikme Lingpa, Kunzang Ngedön Wangpo was definitely a destined tertön. However, because of his great attachment to celibacy he did not engage in tantric conduct and therefore did not acquire any earth treasure. Nevertheless, through the blessing of the three masters Kathok Dampa Deshek, Tsangpa, and Jampa he revealed the *Pure Vision of Dampa* and the *Empowerment of Vajra Speech*. He also revealed a short sadhana of White Tara as a mind terma; I have received it.

Mingyur Namkhay Dorje

The First Dzogchen Rinpoche, Padma Rikdzin from eastern Tibet, was an emanation of both the mahapandita Vimalamitra and Lang Palgyi Senge. He was one of the foremost heart-sons of the mahasiddha Karma Chakme Rinpoche and, as the accomplishment of his powerful aspirations, vastly increased the activity of the Nyingma vajrayana teachings throughout all Tibet.

His rebirths have appeared in succession. The Fourth Dzogchen Rinpoche was known as Mingyur Namkhay Dorje Tsewang Drupa Tsal or Jikme Khyentse Wangchuk Trinley

Namgyal Dorje. Mingyur Namkhay Dorje had continuous visions of countless deities of the three roots and dharmapalas. He possessed unobscured supercognition of the three times, as was clear to everyone who knew him.

Especially, there are several dharma cycles that he revealed through profound pure visions. The first of these was the *Vajra Knot Ayusadhana*, which is both concise and complete. He bestowed it many times upon his disciples. The great tertön Chokgyur Lingpa went to receive it from Mingyur Namkhay Dorje, and I received it as well. As Mingyur Namkhay Dorje completed his full lifespan and activity, it was very auspicious for us to receive it.

Conclusion

I have based these brief accounts of the great and minor tertöns on the list given to me by the fearless great master Padma Ösal Dongak Lingpa, who is an authentically holy being, a lord among siddhas and scholars no different than Padmakara the second Buddha. I have included all of the tertöns whose terma are included in the *Great Precious Treasury of Terma* as well as some authentic tertöns of the past whose lineages are unavailable.

It appears that there are authentic tertöns whom I have not included here. As adherents of the Sarma traditions and Nyingma tertöns view one another with great suspicion, exaggerating one another's faults and underestimating one another's virtues, the stupid who lack the eye of dharma, do not grasp the secret wisdom of tertöns, and are stubbornly sectarian appear to be casting themselves into the abyss of wrong thinking. It therefore seems important to me that knowledgeable people compile separate accounts of those tertöns I have omitted.

Emanated tertöns have appeared sequentially, one after another; and also simultaneously, with many appearing at one time. Some have appeared during the later life of the one who preceded them. The prophecy in the *Great Testament of Padma* is not sequential, as it bears concealed meaning. It is therefore difficult to definitively state the sequence of their appearance.

However, if I may attempt a rough sequential ordering of them, King Langtarma destroyed Buddhism in Tibet in the Iron Bird year.[155] Fifty-two years later, the Water Ox year, marked the beginning of the later dissemination of the teachings.[156] Five years after that, in the Horse year, the great translator Rinchen Zangpo was born.[157]

It appears that it was during the time of both Rinchen Zangpo and Lha Lama Yeshe Ö that great emanated tertöns began to appear. The first of them was Sangye Lama. He was followed by Gyaben Dorje Ö, Tsuklak Palge, Gya the Translator, and Guru Humbar. Slightly after them, during the time of Lhatsün Jangchup Ö and Lord Atisha, Khyungpo Palge, Shami Dogyal, Wönse Khyungtok, and others appeared.

During the time of Lord Marpa Drapa Ngönshe, Shangtsün Tarma Rinchen, Dorbum Nanam Thugyal, Sangye Bar, Gya Shangtrom, Setön Ringmo, Gya Purbu, Geshe Drang Kundrak, Bönpo Lhabum, Lharje Nupchung, Gyatön Tsöndrü Senge, and others appeared.

Then, in the Female Fire Rabbit year, the *Kalachakratantra* and its commentaries arrived in Tibet.[158] The first of the sixty-year cycles began. During that cycle, the time of Jetsün Milarepa and the great translator Ngok, lived Jangsem Dagyal, the tertön Dangma Lhungyal, Chetsün Senge Wangchuk, Lhatsün Ngönmo, Nyima Senge, Sarben Chokme, Rashak Chöbar, Nyenlo Tarma Drak, Uru Tönshak, Bönpo Draktsal, and others.

During the second sixty-year cycle, at the same time as Lord Phamodrupa and the First Gyalwang Karmapa Dusum Khyenpa, lived Nyalpa Josay, Zangri Repa, Nyamo Gyagong Riwa, Ngödrup the Siddha, Lord Nyang, Ramo Shelmen, Nyemo Shuyay, Drugu Yangwang, Chupo Tokden, Bakhal Mukpo, Sumpa Jangchup Lodrö, Prince Mekhyil, Kusa the Physician, Chebom Nakpo, Shangtön Tashi Dorje, and others.

During the third cycle, the time of Jetsün Drakpa Gyaltsen and Sakya Pandita, lived Drekyang Sumpa Sumtsok, Yutok

155. 961 C.E.
156. 1013 C.E.
157. 1018 C.E.
158. 1027 C.E.

Yönten Gönpo, Talung Sangye Wön, Nyi Ösal the Physician, Nyalpa Nyima Sherap, Trophu the Translator, Yeben Yabön, Yakchar Ngönmo, Balpo Ahum, Ajo Pawo, Darchar the Siddha, Dugu Rinchen Senge, Tsangring Sherap, Tulku Marpo, Shangpa Repa, and others.

During the fourth cycle, at the same time as Chögyal Pakpa, lived Guru Chökyi Wangchuk, Jomo Menmo, Melong Dorje, Drumdang Kharnak, the Fortunate Child, Rakshi the Teacher, Khampa Nyima Drak, Gyatön Padma Wangchuk, Drangti Kharbu, Gomchen Drukpa, Nyentön Jambhala, Padma Drakpa, Döndrup Senge, Guru Jotse, Tseten Gyaltsen, the First Dungtso Repa, and others.

During the fifth cycle, at the same time as the omniscient Third Gyalwang Karmapa Rangjung Dorje, Butön, and Dolpopa, lived Kunga Bum, the Indian tertön Vajramati, Doben Gyamtso, the Second Dungtso Repa, Ledrel Tsal, Gyalsay Lekpa, Longchen Rapjam, Rinchen Lingpa, Dragom Chödor, Nyida Sangye, Ugyen Lingpa, Dorje Lingpa, Ugyen Zangpo, Sherap Mebar, Dol Letro Lingpa, Zangpo Drakpa, and others.

During the sixth cycle, at about the same time as the Fourth Gyalwang Karmapa Rölpe Dorje, Ngorchen Kunga Zangpo, and Lord Tsongkhapa, lived Sangye Lingpa, Drime Lhunpo, Drime Kunga, the Vidyadhara Vulture Feathers, Jangchup Lingpa Palgyi Gyaltsen, Karma Lingpa, Jamyang Lama, Thangtong Gyalpo, and others.

During the seventh cycle, at the same time as the Sixth Gyalwang Karmapa Tongwa Dönden, the First Dalai Lama Gendun Drupa, and Gö Shönnu Pal the Translator, lived Longpo Samten Dechen Lingpa, Gönpo Rinchen, Ratna Lingpa, Lekden Dorje, Nyangpo Chokden Dorje, Padma Lingpa, Chak Jangchup Lingpa, Yölmo Shakya Zangpo, Kunkyong Lingpa, Dongak Lingpa, Tenyi Lingpa, Droshül Drodül Letro Lingpa, and others.

During the eighth cycle, the time of the Eighth Gyalwang Karmapa Mikyö Dorje, Drukchen Padma Karpo, and the

Ninth Gyalwang Karmapa Wangchuk Dorje, lived the Mahapandita of Ngari, Gyama Mingyur Letro Lingpa, Rinchen Puntsok, Shikpo Lingpa, Sherap Özer, Lekden Je, Matiratna, Paro Tsering Dorje, Jamyang Khyentse Wangchuk, Gyalsay Tenpe Jungne, Nangsal Tashi Gyamtso, and others.

During the ninth cycle, at the same time as the Dalai Lama Sönam Gyamtso and Jetsün Taranatha, appeared Droshül Dechen Lingpa, Jangdak Tashi Topgyal, the vidyadhara Ngaki Wangpo, Garwang Letro Lingpa, Yongdzin Ngawang Drakpa, Drikung Könchok Rinchen, and others.

During the tenth cycle, the time of the Tenth Gyalwang Karmapa Chöying Dorje and the omniscient Fifth Dalai Lama, appeared Raṣhi Padma Rikdzin, Jatsön Nyingpo, Longpo Tashi Tseten, Düdül Nüden Dorje, Lhatsün Namkha Jikme, Namchö Mingyur Dorje, Garwang Dawa Gyaltsen, Terdak Lingpa, Longsal Nyingpo, Dakpo Zangpo Dorje, Yölmo Tendzin Norbu, Yongey Mingyur Dorje, and others.

During the eleventh cycle, at the same time as the Twelfth Gyalwang Karmapa Jangchup Dorje, the Dalai Lama Kalzang Gyamtso, and Situ Chökyi Jungne, appeared Taksham Nüden Dorje, Ngaki Dorje, Takmo Wönse Khyungtok, Chöje Lingpa, Ratön Topden Dorje, Khampa Ngawang Kunga Tendzin, Surmang Rölpe Dorje, Rongtön Padma Dechen Lingpa, Tukchok Dorje, the vidyadhara Tsewang Norbu, Tau Rokje Lingpa, and others.

During the twelfth cycle, the time of the Thirteenth Gyalwang Karmapa Düdül Dorje and the Dalai Lama Jampal Gyamtso, appeared Tekchen Drime Lingpa, Traktung Dechen Gyalpo, the omniscient Jikme Lingpa, Dorje Drakpo, Mokdrup Namkha Chöwang, and others.

During the thirteenth cycle appeared Kunzang Özer or Chime Dorje, Draksum Dorje Tokme, Padma Chöjor Gyamtso, Lhading Shapdrung Daway Özer, the lord of siddhas Kunzang Shenpen, E Nering Chöje, and others.

During the fourteenth cycle, the time of the Fourteenth Gyalwang Karmapa Tekchok Dorje, appeared Pawo Tsuklak

Chögyal, the Fourth Karma Chakme Rinpoche, Chögyal Dorje, the Fourth Dzogchen Rinpoche, Padma Ösal Dongak Lingpa, Chokgyur Dechen Lingpa, and others.

The greatness of all of them is combined in our lord guru Padma Ösal Dongak Lingpa, the possessor of the seven dispensations. He is inconceivably wonderful. He has been praised in the vajra prophecies of Guru Rinpoche as the single protector of Tibet amid these terrible dregs of time when the asuras are active. He is living and turning the dharmachakra in our present fifteenth cycle. I pray from the depths of my heart that he remain alive for more than a hundred further years in the permanent, stable vajra nature.

I have given a rough approximation of the sequence of these tertöns' appearance; I am unable to tell you their precise order. Some, such as Ngödrup the Siddha and Nyida Sangye, had very long lives. Thangtong Gyalpo, for example, lived through two cycles and an additional five years. Some of them were born and died and reborn once or even twice within the same cycle. It also appears that many authentic tertöns have appeared at the same time.

Because of the residue of their past karma tertöns have had varying degrees of control over their revelation of terma. Because of other circumstances such as their varying degrees of training in that life, better or worse temperament, and coarser or more refined behavior, they have had varied success in establishing the interdependence taught in their prophecies. This has led to varying degrees of benefit for others.

However, any authentic tertön free from deceit is definitely a holy being with powerful aspirations and training from previous lives, all contact with whom will be beneficial. In Guru Rinpoche's vajra words:

Tertöns and their disciples who hold Padma's lineage,
Even if they behave like dogs or pigs, are karmically destined.
They are unlike ordinary people, superior to them.

> There are hidden Buddhas everywhere.
> Deceptive charlatans are great hypocrites.
> Gold and clods of earth are not the same.

Generally, a tertön who reveals gurusadhana, Great Perfection teachings, and Mahakarunikasadhana is called a great tertön; one who reveals less than all three is called a minor tertön. However, Ugyen Terdak Lingpa wrote:

> A great tertön is one whose dharma includes everything a single person needs to traverse the path to Buddhahood. A minor tertön is one whose terma is limited to a few sadhanas or magical applications.

All of the tertöns who have appeared among us have engaged in a variety of means of taming beings through their activity, principally through the dharma and samaya substances that they have revealed as terma. They have helped countless beings of all classes, even dispelling immediate adversity and increasing the wellbeing of animals. They have all protected beings from lower states and samsara, and led them toward supreme liberation. Some of them, because of the times in which they have lived, have saved Tibet from invasion. They have all achieved great activity, and have all been wonderfully kind. All of them have arisen from the compassion of Guru Rinpoche, Tibet's only protector. He wrote:

> To give inexhaustible dharma to future beings
> Padma has filled existence with terma.
> All who reveal it will be my emanations.
> Their costume and conduct may vary.
> The perception of those with faith will change upon a
>   single encounter,
> But they will be difficult for others to judge.

The above is definitely true. It is therefore fitting to recollect in your heart the unimaginably great kindness of Guru

Rinpoche and Yeshe Tsogyal; present them your life, body, possessions, and virtues as clouds of offering; and diligently and constantly pray to them, fulfilling their intentions.

I have collected the complete teachings of the authentic tertöns who have appeared in Ngari in the west, in central Tibet and Bhutan, and in all of eastern Tibet, and are known to holy beings. Here, I have briefly related their lives. I dare to boast that, due to the kindness of our lord guru the omniscient, great, wondrous, emanated tertön Padma Ösal Dongak Lingpa, what I have compiled and written is authentic.

I have also heard that there have appeared many other people called tertöns in remote places who have benefited beings with various dharma teachings. Guru Rinpoche's Buddha activity is beyond near and far; it always arises in accordance with the needs of disciples, and is beyond our apprehension. I therefore have respect for and faith in them, although I have been unable to include them here. Indeed, there is little need to do so. While the deep and vast ocean of the pure amrita of the Sarma and Nyingma dharma of kama and terma remains available to us, it seems best not to quench our thirst in little pools.

Some, not only devoid of undefiled supercognition, even lack the slightest pure generosity of dharma. Based on some vague visions that are really obstacles on the path, and with the intention of promoting themselves and denigrating their opponents, they seek to gain advantage by calling all who fail to bow to them "emanations of Mara" and "purveyors of perverted dharma." Such persons are continually adding to their great burden of wrong views and the rejection of dharma.

Worst of all, they subtly criticize and turn their backs on holy beings whose powerful activity benefiting others is evident. Those who follow such people are going against the four reliances and are therefore not followers of our teacher, Buddha Shakyamuni. The omniscient Buddha said:

> Only I or someone like me can judge another. Anyone else who does so will be diminished.

As people like the Buddha are rare in this world, do not become attached to sourceless gossip. If you open wide the eyes of pure perception you will avoid planting the seed of birth in Avicci and will enter the good path of liberation.

Even if a terma prophecy is revealed without any selfish intent, its context and intention must be verified without contradiction. Without distinguishing between the indicative and the definitive, one should not one-sidedly cling to the literal meaning of the words of prophecy. One reason for this is that sometimes prophecies such as "this good or bad period will occur" may not be fulfilled because circumstances have changed.

As for the future, it is certain that emanated tertöns will continue to appear. This is established both by vajra prophecy and by manifest evidence. However, among the tertöns of the past, only the three supreme nirmanakayas and some of the great Lingpas have completely fulfilled their prophecies. As the future will become progressively more and more degenerate, and as beings' merit will continue to diminish, it appears that perfect interdependence will be difficult to create. Nevertheless, Guru Rinpoche's compassion and blessing will become progressively speedier. Therefore, those who encounter profound terma: Do not immediately lose yourselves to the maras of pride, conceit, social compliance, and the eight worldly things. Follow the instructions about what to do and what not to do that have been given with great kindness to his followers by Padmakara, our wish-fulfilling jewel. Do not fall under the power of human failings such as editing his advice, nonsensical thinking, thinking, "This is enough," or laziness. If you obey Guru Rinpoche's commands, vast benefit for yourself and others will occur spontaneously.

My sources in writing this have included the biographies and terma histories of the most famous tertöns, such as Nyang and Guru Chöwang; old histories; many of the historical accounts within the Nyingma kama; earlier and later indexes to the *Nyingma Tantras*; especially, on the subject of terma, *Dispelling the Mind's Darkness*, the biography of Guru Rinpoche by Sokdokpa Lodrö Gyaltsen; the *Wish-Fulfilling Tree in Full Bloom*, a history of terma by Shazukpa Tashi Namgyal; a *History of the Hundred Tertöns* by Zaplung Densapa Wangi Gyalpo; a *Treasury of Jewels*, the dharma history by Yakde Düldzin Khyenrap Gyamtso; *Delight for the Wise*, a history of Nyingma dharma by the supreme scholar Ngawang Lodrö; the sections on the Nyingmapa in the dharma histories by Gö Shönnu Pal the Translator and Pawo Tsuklak Trengwa; the *Supplication of the Hundred Tertöns* by Jangdak Tashi Topgyal; the great *Record of Dharma I Have Received* by the omniscient Fifth Dalai Lama; and the *Record of Dharma I Have Received* by the great tertön of Mindröling.

I read all of the above carefully, and consulted our lord guru, the omniscient holder of the seven dispensations Padma Ösal Dongak Lingpa, whenever there appeared to be omissions or the meaning was unclear. With his stainless eyes of dharma and his wondrous wisdom beyond delusion he clarified all such instances. Therefore, although this book is brief, it is ultimately superior to all previous histories of terma.

Om Svasti Siddhi!
Your vajra body fills all space. Your form appears before
  each being you tame.
Your inexpressible speech, profound and secret, is heard in
  every tongue there is.
Your unimaginably luminous mind pervades the still, the
  moving, existence, and peace.
Mahasukha, splendor of the hundred families, bless us
  with goodness
In the beginning, middle, and end.

This coffer of jewels, the *Treasury of Terma* which frees
  in all four ways,
With its vajra seals well-broken,
Will dispel poverty now and forever

In all parts of this snowy land.

Wondrous, passed from one to another,
The wondrous liberation of these protectors of decadent
  beings
Is like a mala of jewels, a source of all one wants.

Fortunate, intelligent followers of Padma:
Enjoy this brief yet deep account of the greatest siddhas,
The tertöns who've come among us over time.
Wear at your throats this beautiful
String of stainless beryls.

Just as a pleasant, colorful lotus garden
Blooms in summer's glory,
These clouds of emanated vidyadharas
Have arisen in the wisdom sky of All-Good Padma.

In ultimate space there is neither one nor many. JEWELS
In accord with disciples' needs they appear.
The wise who understand this secret
Are freed from thoughts of better and worse.

From this seed may a million branches of good teaching
Bloom as a new wish-fulfilling tree.
May all beings rest in its shade with trusting faith.
May the painful heat of existence be cooled forever.

May the teaching of profound terma cover the earth.
May this profound, secret amrita, with splendid,
  unmistaken blessing
Unsullied by the water of sophists
Remain forever, and never dwindle.

May the wishes of past vidyadharas be fulfilled.
May those now here live long and achieve their aims.
May those in the future, unhindered, perfectly accomplish
  the two goals.

May Padma's teaching, their source, flourish.

May I be accepted by Guru Rinpoche in every life.
With peerless wisdom, love, and power
May I bring all beings throughout space together
To the city of supreme, secret liberation.

Finally, may we achieve the same three secrets
As Padma the Holder of All.
May we emanate boundless clouds of bodies and realms,
Accomplishing the inconceivable deeds of a Buddha.

May all the perfect virtue in existence or peace be gathered as one
As a right-turning conch of dharma, the emblem of virtue.
May its sound be heard by all the ears in the universe.
May its melody fill all worlds forever.

I have written this brief history to explain the origin of the *Great Treasury of Precious Terma*, which contains the most important profound, secret, vajra speech of the lord among victors Padmakara, the single, glorious protector of all Tibet. It was written by one who was accepted by Vajradhara bearing the name Padma, by the all-seeing Gyurme Tendzin Pelgye, and by many other holy masters of the Sarma and Nyingma traditions; one who, especially relying upon the kindness of the great tertön, our omniscient guru Dorje Ziji Tsal, has heard many sutras, tantras, and scientific treatises; one whose pure perception of all traditions is expansive; one with only the appearance of a renunciate named Karma Ngawang Yönten Gyamtso Lodrö Taye, also called the vidyadhara Padma Garwang Trinley Drodül Tsal. It was written with great faith, devotion, and effort. May it cause me and all beings to become fit to receive Guru Rinpoche's blessing. May it cause the terma teachings to spread throughout the world and last forever. May virtue and goodness increase!

Alphabetical list of the Hundred Tertöns

Acharya Yeshe Yang, The 52
Ajo Palpo 191
Atisha 174
Bakhal Mukpo 185
Balpo Ah Hum Bar 190
Bay Gyalway Lodrö 56
Bhikshu Namkhay Nyingpo, The 40
Bhuprana 351
Bodong Sangye Gönpo 344
Bönpo Draktsal 80
Chak Jangchup Lingpa 225
Chetsün Senge Wangchuk 179
Chögyal Dorje 311
Chokden Dorje 224
Chokden Gönpo 144
Chokgyur Lingpa 300
Chupa Tokden 184
Conclusion 378
Dangma Lhungyal 89
Dawa Gyaltsen 333
Dechen Lingpa 169
Denma Tsemang 54
Dhatishvari Mandarava 62
Doben Gyamtso 108
Dorbum Chökyi Drakpa 176

Dorje Drakpo 358
Dorje Lingpa 149
Dorje Tokme 296
Dragom Chödor 111
Drangti Gyalnye Kharbu 200
Drapa Ngönshe 91
Drenpa Namkha 57
Drikung Shapdrung Könchok Rinchen 345
Drikungpa Chökyi Drakpa 346
Drime Kunga 212
Drime Lhunpo 210
Drime Lingpa 291
Drodül Letro Lingpa 227
Drokmi Palgyi Yeshe 46
Drugu Yangwang 186
Drukpa Kagyu Wrathful Kilaya, The 344
Drum and Karnak 113
Düdül Dorje 250
Düdül Lingpa 249
Dugu Rinchen Senge 192
Earlier Dungtso Repa, The Earlier 201
Eighth Pawo Rinpoche, The 364
Fifth Dalai Lama, The 347
Fortunate Child, The 199
Four Assistants, The 200
Fourth Chakme Rinpoche, The 364
Garwang Chime Dorje 295
Garwang Dawa Gyaltsen 261
Garwang Letro Lingpa 246
Geshe Dranga Dorje Kundrak 178
Gönpo Rinchen 221
Great Tertön of Mindröling, The 136
Great Translator Kawa Paltsek, The 54
Great Translator Vairochana, The 48
Great Vidyadhara of Ngari, The 238
Guru Chökyi Wangchuk 101

Guru Humbar 173
Guru Jotsay 106
Gya Purbu 178
Gya Shangtrom Dorje Öbar 77
Gya the Translator 75
Gyaben Dorje Ö 173
Gyalmo Yudra Nyingpo 51
Gyalsay Lekpa 204
Gyalwa Chokyang 38
Gyatön Tsöndru Senge 179
Jampal Dorje 229
Jatsön Mebar 345
Jatsön Nyingpo 162
Jikme Trinley Özer 372
Jomo Menmo 194
Kalden Dorje 224
Karma Chakme 356
Karma Guru 243
Karma Lingpa 217
Khampa Rinpoche 274
Kharchen Palgyi Wangchuk 53
Khyentse Wangchuk Dongak Lingpa 241
Khyungdrak Dorje 284
Khyungpo Palge 87
King Trisong Detsen 31
Kuchok the Actionless 267
Kunga Bum 202
Kunga Paljor 342
Kunzang Dechen Gyalpo 292
Kunzang Ngedön Wangpo 376
Kusa the Physician 84
Kyergangpa 335
Lang Palgyi Senge 47
Langdro Könchok Jungne 59
Lasum Gyalwa Jangchub 60
Later Dungtso Repa, The 203

Latö Marpo 194
Lekyi Dorje 337
Lhabum the Bönpo 86
Lhalung Palgyi Dorje 59
Lharjey Nupchung 179
Lhatsün Jangchup Ö 174
Lhatsün Namkha Jikme 346
Lhatsün Ngönmo 114
Longchenpa 337
Longsal Nyingpo 254
Ma Rinchen Chok 58
Mahasiddha Kyeuchung Lots, The 56
Mahasiddha Sokpo Lhapa, The 153
Mamaki Shakyadevi of Nepal 64
Mantradharin Letro Lingpa, The 209
Mantradharin Shakya Zangpo, The 225
Matiratna 240
Meben Rinchen Lingpa 120
Melong Dorje 198
Mingyur Letro Lingpa 232
Mingyur Namkhay Dorje 376
Namchak Mebar 233
Namchö Mingyur Dorje 354
Nanam Dorje Düdjom 51
Nanam Yeshe De 53
Nanampa 76
Ngaki Wangpo 244
Ngawang Dorje 375
Ngödrup Gyaltsen, the Vidyadhara Vulture Feathers 214
Ngödrup the Siddha 82
Nirmanakaya Ugyen Lingpa, The 122
Nupchen Sangye Yeshe 36
Nyalpa Nyima Sherap 189
Nyalpo Josay 183
Nyangral Nyima Özer 93
Nyemo Shuyay 81

Nyen the Translator 182
Nyida Sangye 208
Nyima Drakpa 115
Nyima Senge 78
Odren Palgyi Wangchuk 57
Omniscient Jikme Lingpa, The 366
Omniscient Longchenpa, The 127
Other Tertöns of Earth Terma 327
Padma Chögyal 283
Padma Chöjor Gyamtso 372
Padma Dechen Lingpa 280
Padma Gyepa 365
Padma Kunkyong Lingpa 140
Padma Ledrel Tsal 116
Padma Lingpa 158
Padma Nyinje Wangpo 360
Padma Ösal Dongak Lingpa 313
Padma Rikdzin 248
Padma Wangchuk 107
Padma Wangchuk 283
Padma Wangyal Dorje 229
Palden Dorje 339
Palden Jamyang Lama 218
Palgyi Gyaltsen of Langlo 216
Pandaravasini Kalasiddhi 64
Physician from E in Jarong, The 110
Pönsey Khyungtok 268
Prince Mekhyil 185
Rakshi the Teacher 109
Ramo Shelmen 99
Rangdröl Tingdzin Gyalpo 297
Rangjung Dorje 336
Rashak the Great 92
Ratna Lingpa 222
Ratön Topden Dorje 273
Rechen Paljor Zangpo 343

Rechungpa 333
Rokje Lingpa 132
Rokje Lingpa 294
Rölpe Dorje 276
Rongzom Chökyi Zangpo 176
Samayatara Tashi Khyidren of Bhutan 65
Samten Dechen Lingpa 166
Samten Lingpa 269
Samten Lingpa 342
Sangdak Trinley Lhundrup 348
Sangye Bar 177
Sangye Lama 73
Sangye Lingpa 153
Sangye Wangchen 184
Sarben Chokme 181
Setön Ringmo 177
Shakya Ö the Teacher from Uru 79
Shakya Zangpo 182
Shakyashri 334
Shami Dorgyal 88
Shangtsün Tarma Rinchen 175
Sherab Mebar 207
Sherap Özer 235
Shikpo Lingpa 167
Shrivanaratna 340
Shubu Palgyi Senge 55
Sumpa Jangchup Lodrö 187
Taklungpa Sangye Wönpo 188
Tashi Gyamtso 345
Tashi Tseten 248
Tendzin Norbu 258
Thangtong Gyalpo 219
Three Tertöns 191
Tongwa Dönden 343
Translator Nyak Jnanakumara, The 42
Trophu the Translator 189

Tsangring Sherap 193
Tsasum Terdak Lingpa 287
Tsering Dorje 240
Tseten Gyaltsen 118
Tsewang Mingyur Dorje 365
Tsewang Norbu 285
Tsuklak Palge 83
Tukchok Dorje 290
Ugyen Tenyi Lingpa 147
Ugyen Zangpo 206
Vajramati 204
Wönsay Khyungtok 98
Yakchar Ngönmo 112
Yeben Yabön 190
Yeshe Tsogyal, the Emanation of Sarasvati 44
Yongdzin Ngawang Drakpa 247
Yongey Mingyur Dorje 263
Yutok Yönten Gönpo 334
Zangpo Dorje 259
Zangpo Drakpa 209
Zangri Repa 183

Illustrations

Jamgön Kongtrül Lodrö Taye 2

Guru Rinpoche 20

King Trisong Detsen 31

Nupchen Sangye Yeshe 36

Gyalwa Chokyang 38

The Bhikshu Namkhay Nyingpo 40

Yeshe Tsogyal, the Emanation of Sarasvati 44

The Great Translator Vairochana 48

The Omniscient Longchenpa 127

The Great Tertön of Mindröling 136

Chokgyur Lingpa 300

The Omniscient Jikme Lingpa 366

KTD Publications

Gathering the garlands of the gurus' precious teachings

KTD Publications, a part of Karma Triyana Dharmachakra, is a not-for-profit publisher established with the purpose of facilitating the projects and activities manifesting from His Holiness Karmapa's inspiration and blessings. We are dedicated to gathering the garlands of precious teachings and producing fine-quality books.

KTD Publications
Woodstock, New York, USA
www.KTDPublications.org

Published translations by Lama Yeshe Gyamtso

Amrita of Eloquence: A Biography of Khenpo Karthar Rinpoche, by Lama Karma Drodül, 2009

A Garland of Jewels: The Eight Great Bodhisattvas, by Jamgön Mipham Rinpoche, 2008

Treasury of Eloquence: The Songs of Barway Dorje, 2007

Nyima Tashi: The Songs and Instructions of the First Traleg Kyabgön Rinpoche, 2006

Chariot of the Fortunate: The Life of the First Yongey Mingyur Dorje, by Je Tukyi Dorje and Surmang Tendzin Rinpoche, 2006

The Vajra Garland, The Lotus Garden: Treasure Biographies of Padmakara and Vairochana, by Jamgön Lodrö Taye, 2005

Precious Essence: The Inner Autobiography of Terchen Barway Dorje, 2005